1 MONTH OF
FREE
READING

at
www.ForgottenBooks.com

By purchasing this book you are eligible for one month membership to ForgottenBooks.com, giving you unlimited access to our entire collection of over 1,000,000 titles via our web site and mobile apps.

To claim your free month visit:

www.forgottenbooks.com/free259545

ISBN 978-0-267-50187-8
PIBN 10259545

This book is a reproduction of an important historical work. Forgotten Books uses
state-of-the-art technology to digitally reconstruct the work, preserving the original format
whilst repairing imperfections present in the aged copy. In rare cases, an imperfection in
the original, such as a blemish or missing page, may be replicated in our edition. We do,
however, repair the vast majority of imperfections successfully; any imperfections that
remain are intentionally left to preserve the state of such historical works.

Vol. XII   No. 1

APRIL, 1918

The Playground

OVER two million dollars more spent last year in America for playgrounds, recreation centers and athletic fields than during the year before the war. The world war makes the need for community centers greater than ever before.   ::   ::   ::   ::

The Playground

Published monthly at Cooperstown, New York

for the

Playground and Recreation Association of America

1 Madison Avenue, New York City

Membership

Any person contributing five dollars or more shall be a
member of the Association for the
ensuing year

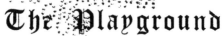

Table of Contents

Entered as second-class matter August 8, 1916, at the Post Office at
Cooperstown, New York, under the act of March 3, 1879

The Victrola in Open Air Calisthenics, Benton School, Kansas City, Mo.

Sailor Drill with the Victrola, Field Day, Evansville, Indiana.

The Efficiency of a Nation

requires that its citizens must be physically fit.

In the Golden Age of Greece, the city of Athens was supplied with ample playgrounds and gymnasia for the training of its youth.

The schools are the laboratories for future citizenship. Every American boy and girl is entitled to correct and carefully supervised bodily development as a part of his school course.

The Victrola and Victor Records

furnish music which makes Physical Education more attractive, and which makes pupils more responsive in rhythmic feeling.

Have you tried these selections in your school?

Marches and Rhythms

18209 { Boy Scouts of America—March
10 in.   (Sousa)   Victor Military Band
75c   { Blue-White March
                Victor Military Band

18253 { Motives for Skipping (Kindergarten
10 in.   Rhythm)   Victor Band
75c   { High Stepping Horses and Rein-
      deer Running   Victor Band

35228 { Eros—Scherzo Valse (Martin) (Butterfly Dance)
12 in.$1.25   Victor Orchestra
    { Golden Trumpets—Schottische (Rollinson)   Sousa's Band

35532 { Cupid and the Butterfly—Intermezzo (Claude d'Albert)
12 in.$1.25   Victor Military Band
    { Dorothy Three-Step—Mazurka (J. B. Lampe)
                      Victor Military Band

Folk Dances by Victor Band

18331 { Arkansaw Traveler—American Country Dance (Burchenal)
10 in. 75c { Soldiers' Joy—American Country Dance

18004 { Black Nag (2) Grimstock (From "Country Dance Tunes,"
10 in. 75c   Sets III and IV) (Cecil J. Sharp)
    { Newcastle (2) Sweet Kate (From "Country Dance Tunes,"
      Sets III and VI) (Cecil J. Sharp)

17158 { Dance of Greeting—Danish Folk Dance (From "Folk Dance
10 in. 75c   Music,") (Burchenal and Crampton)
    { I See You—Swedish Singing Game (From "Folk Dance Book")

Ask any Victor dealer to play the above selections for you. For further information, write to the

Educational Department
Victor Talking Machine Co.
Camden, N. J.

Victrola XXV, $75
specially manufactured
for School use

When the Victrola is not in use, the horn can be placed under the instrument safe and secure from danger, and the cabinet can be locked to protect it from dust and promiscuous use by irresponsible people.

Victor

HIS MASTER'S VOICE

To insure Victor quality, always look for the famous trademark, "His Master's Voice." It is on all genuine products of the Victor Talking Machine Company.

Put the Liberty Loan across the Line

A Message to American Children
BY
JOSEPH LEE

If you have ever read Shakespeare's play of "As You Like It," you may remember the wrestling match in the first act and Celia saying: "I would I were invisible, that I might catch the big fellow by the leg." I suppose we have all felt that way in a football game when we have been on the side lines, wishing we could give just one push to help the ball down the field for our side. Of course that would not be fair even if we could do it in a football game, but it is fair in war. War is a contest between nations and everybody is in the game from start to finish. The Liberty Loan in fact is a way of getting other people to play the game, to put the push their money represents behind the runner. The money they put into the loan is like an arm with which they reach out across the sea and give that push just at the point where it is wanted. It makes their day's work on the farm or in the office or the factory take effect upon the firing line so that every sod they dig, every blow they strike, every figure they write down, has its part in holding or advancing the line of those who are fighting for the world's liberty.

Here, in working for the Liberty Loan, is a chance where you can help the runner with the ball and perhaps give just that little extra push that will enable him to cross the line. In this greatest game that ever was played on this earth you can not only root for the home team but be a member of it, and when at last, after another year or two years, or whenever that final touchdown is scored—the biggest score ever made in history—you may be able to feel that you had your little part in it.

Not that you are then or ever to think that you have done enough. When our friends are dying for us the only limit to what we are called upon to give is all we have. We do not need to kill ourselves—indeed that would be of little use to anybody—but we should live so as to put the last ounce there is in us in the fight—and then some.

You are on the team and this is the game of your life that we are playing. It is the time to win your star, whether you get one that can be seen or not.

Playground and Recreation Association
of America

Playground Facts

The compilation of facts for the 1917 Year Book has in-volved correspondence with approximately 1,800 cities, 1,260 of which have sent information regarding conditions relating to play-ground and recreation center work. Many interesting facts have been received about recreational developments in hundreds of cities but it has been possible to include in the Year Book table only those communities whose reports indicate that play leaders were employed at the playgrounds and play centers.

The War and Recreation The effect of the war on the recreation move-ment in the United States is a matter of great concern to all who have known the unfortunate results in the allied countries of the letting down of the bars safe-guarding the physical well-being of the children and the leisure time activities of the working girl and boy. The reports re-ceived of recreational activities conducted during 1917, the first year of America's participation in the world war, are very en-couraging in their indication of increased development rather than retrenchment. Of the cities discontinuing their playground work during the past summer only seven, two of which were Canadian cities, indicate that the work was abandoned because of the stress of war. In one of these cities the playground was turned over to the soldiers in the near-by training camp for recreational purposes and in still another the ground was used for drill by the men in training. In three other communities gardening was substituted for normal playground activities. The official in charge in one of these cities reports, however, that this plan was not successful and that every effort will be made to resume playground activities in 1918. The fact that 52 new cities started playground work last summer—an increase of 21.1 per cent over 1916's newly organized centers—and that at least 13 cities have since Novem-ber, 1916, placed their recreation work on a permanent year-round basis with a superintendent employed the entire year, are encouraging indications of America's determination to make and keep her young people physically fit.

**Play Centers
in 504 Cities**
During the year ending November 1, 1917, the 481 cities sending reports complete enough for publication maintained 3,944 playgrounds and neighborhood recreation centers under paid leadership. At least 23 other cities sent in partial information indicating work conducted with paid leaders in charge, making a total of 504 known to have conducted work in 1917. These reports indicate an increase over 1916 of 17.8 per cent in the number of cities and 15.8 per cent in the number of centers conducted.

MANAGEMENT

Municipal

The reports received on administration and management indicate that in 291 of the 481 cities sending complete information, playground and recreation center work was administered wholly or in part by some department of the municipality; that is, 60.4 per cent of the total number of cities reporting have some form of municipal control.

In 48 cities playground and neighborhood recreation centers were maintained by Playground or Recreation Commissions; in 22, by Playground and Recreation Departments and Divisions or Boards or Bureaus of Recreation. In 108 cities School Boards conducted playground and recreation center work; in 59, Park Boards: in 9 cities, City Councils or Boards of Selectmen were in charge of the work. Other municipal departments managing recreation work were: Departments of Public Works operating in 5 cities; Department of Public Safety in one; county authorities in 7, and municipal playground committees in 8.

A number of cities reported a combination of municipal departments in the administration of the work. In 5 cities Boards of Education and Park Departments were associated; in 6, Boards of Education and Recreation Commissions and Boards; in 2, Boards of Education and the city; in one, Department of Public Welfare and the city. In 4 cities the Department of Parks and Public Property, the Boards of Education, the County Park Commission and the Recreation Commission work together in various combinations.

4

PLAYGROUND FACTS

Private

In 48 cities playground and recreation center work was conducted by Playground and Recreation Associations and Leagues; in 17, by Civic Clubs and Associations; in 4, by Improvement Clubs; in 9, by Parent-Teachers' Associations and Home and School Leagues; in 6, by Y. M. C. A.'s; in one by the Y. W. C. A.; in 6, by Playground Committees; in 12, by Social Service Leagues, Welfare and Relief Associations and Settlements. In 10 cities industrial plants maintained the work; in 2, Chambers of Commerce or Rotary Clubs; in 5, private individuals. In 6 cities such organizations as Political Equality Leagues, Chautauqua Associations, community Bible classes and Sunday School athletic associations carried on the work while in 5 cities a combination of private organizations was responsible for the maintaining of activities.

Municipal and Private

A combination of municipal departments and private organizations was reported in a number of cities. In one community the Board of Education combined with the Recreation Committee; in 2, the Park Department and Charity Organization Society worked together; in 2 others the Park Department united with the Y. M. C. A., and with industrial and charitable institutions. In 5 cities, the Park and Playground Commissions combined with Playground Associations; in 2, municipal playground committees joined with Playground Associations and Social Service Federations. In 4 others the City Councils and other municipal departments combined with private organizations in assuming responsibility for recreation work.

ORGANIZATION

Reports which were received regarding forms of organization show a number of communities where existing Playground and Recreation Commissions are not as yet conducting work or are acting in a purely advisory capacity to sub-committees or organizations which are actively engaged in carrying on recreational activities. A study of these facts with the data on administration furnished by cities actively conducting work shows the following forms of administration:

PLAYGROUND FACTS

Municipal—Playground or Recreational Commissions
   or Departments . . . . 84 cities
Private—Playground Associations or Leagues . . 113 cities
Both . . . . 5 cities

Sources of Support

In 253 cities the playgrounds and neighborhood recreation centers were supported by municipal funds; in 109, by private funds; in 103, by both municipal and private; in 6, by county; in 5, by municipal and county. In 5 instances the sources of support were not stated.

Expenditures

A total expenditure of $6,659,600.80 was reported, representing an increase over 1916's reported expenditures of $2,424,882.35. Of the total amount $3,848,084.38 was expended in 390 cities for salaries alone.

Employed Workers

In the 481 cities sending complete reports on playground and neighborhood center work conducted under paid leadership, 8,748 workers were employed, an increase over 1916 of 1,626 workers. Of these, 2,758 were men, 4,940 were women. In 1,050 instances the sex was not given. In addition to these workers 2,126 caretakers were employed. One hundred forty cities reported 1,454 workers employed the year-round. The reports sent by 7 of these cities, however, indicate that 29 workers were physical directors or teachers in charge of organized play in connection with the school program.

During 1917, 75 cities maintained training classes for playground workers. Of these, 50 reported 2,070 students in attendance. In addition, 11 cities reported weekly conferences of workers.

Thirty-four cities reported that their recreation positions were filled by Civil Service examinations.

Playgrounds and Neighborhood Recreation Centers Established in 1917

Fifty-two cities stated that playgrounds and neighborhood recreation centers were opened for the first time in 1917 under paid leadership.

6

PLAYGROUND FACTS

BOND ISSUES

Eleven cities reported bond issues authorized in 1917. The total amount represented by these issues is $473,800.

DONATED PLAYGROUNDS

Forty-three cities reporting on donated playgrounds placed the valuation of these grounds at $420,600.

LENGTH OF PLAYGROUND TERM

One hundred thirteen cities reported 757 playgrounds and neighborhood recreation centers open the year round. In 7 of these, however, the centers reported open referred to school centers at which organized play was conducted in connection with the school program. Two thousand five hundred ninety centers were open only during the summer season.

One hundred eighty cities had their centers open on holidays; 79, on Sundays.

ATTENDANCE

Of 481 cities, 422 reported a total average attendance of 737,519 during the summer months. One hundred fourteen cities reported an attendance at winter centers of 230,897.

SEPARATE SPACES FOR BOYS AND GIRLS

One hundred thirty-eight cities reported 847 playgrounds with separate spaces for boys and girls.

EVENING PLAYGROUNDS

One hundred forty-three cities reported 629 playgrounds opened and lighted evenings under leadership; 116 reported an average attendance of 550,371 on these playgrounds.

EVENING RECREATION CENTERS

In 148 cities evening recreation center work was carried on in the schools. One hundred forty-six of these cities reported 643 school buildings open evenings. The total attendance in 100 cities was 55,434.

BUILDINGS FOR RECREATION PURPOSES

Eighty-nine cities reported buildings used solely for recreation purposes. Six cities reported 285 such buildings with a total average attendance in 66 cities of $360,264. The value of the recreation buildings in 45 cities was $4,670,674.

STREETS FOR PLAY

In 23 cities streets were closed for play. Eighteen of these cities reported that play leaders were in charge of the street playgrounds. One city reported block dances held in the streets. In 106 cities coasting was permitted.

PUBLIC SWIMMING POOLS, BATHS AND BATHING BEACHES

One hundred fifty-one cities reported on public swimming pools, 149 of this number having 328 pools.

Ninety-eight cities reported 381 public baths.

One hundred nine cities reported 192 public bathing beaches.

SPECIAL PLAY ACTIVITIES

Special play activities in connection with their recreation work were reported by cities as follows:

Badge Tests	108	Libraries	107
Bands	53	Moving Pictures	81
Boy Scouts	193	Orchestras	58
Camp Fire Girls	132	Pageants	93
Debating Clubs	40	Self-Government	50
Dramatics	98	Singing	176
Folk Dancing	281	Skating	102
Gardening	176	Social Dancing	106
Girl Scouts	52	Storytelling	275
Industrial Work	167	Summer Camps	56
Junior Police	24	Swimming	200
Lectures	111	Tramping	158
	Wading	120	

SPECIAL WAR ACTIVITIES

During the past summer many playground officials introduced into the play program a number of activities specifically related to the war and tending towards the fostering of a spirit of patriotic service among the children. The following activities were developed:

8

Americanization Classes	.	30	Junior Red Cross . . .	60
Canning		87	Knitting	.184
Domestic Science . .	.	67	Military Drills . .	.100
First Aid Classes . .	.	101	Sewing for War Relief	. 106
Hiking	.	102	War Gardens . . .	.119

OUTLOOK FOR 1918

The passage in a number of cities of compulsory physical training laws requiring a certain amount of time for games and recreational activities, the effecting of organization, securing of funds and completion of plans for work in a number of cities which have never before had an organized program of recreation work, make the outlook for the recreation movement in 1918 an encouraging one.

SUMMARY

Playgrounds and Recreation Centers	NUMBER OF CITIES	
Under paid leadership	.504	
Under volunteer leadership	.33	
Under no leadership	70	
School Playgrounds	70	
Work Started:		
Organization effected	6	
Definite plans made	4	
Land secured	4	
Funds raised	6	
Experimental grounds conducted	2	
Bond issues secured	1	
Campaign being conducted	1	28
		628

The splendid response which hundreds of busy playground workers and officials have made to the requests for information regarding the recreation work in their cities, and the interest they have taken in this cooperative undertaking to further the recreation movement throughout the country augurs well for the future of the work. The year which is coming, however, with its uncertainties and readjustments will make severe demands upon the strength and devotion of the many individuals who as leaders in the movement to safeguard the birth-right of America's children must take their stand together for the continuation and enlargement of recreational facilities.

OFFICERS OF RECREATION COMMISSIONS AND ASSOCIATIONS

State and City	Name	President or Chairman	Secretary
ALABAMA			
Bessemer City	Bessemer Playground Association	Mrs. J. M. Martin	Mrs. J. A. Snider
CALIFORNIA			
Berkeley	Berkeley Playground Commission	Mrs. A. F. Pillsbury	Mrs. A. E. Chandler
Fresno	Playground and Recreation Commission	Ben Epstein	Mrs. S. S. Hockett
Los Angeles	Los Angeles Playground Commission	J. E. Cowles, M. D	Charles S. Lamb
Oakland	Board of Playground Directors	Ethel Moore	George E. Dickie
San Bernardino	San Bernardino Playground Association	Mrs. W. S. Ingram	Mrs. J. W. Bishop
	Commission Parks and Playgrounds	R. R. Davis	
San Diego	Board of Playground Commissioners	Melville Klauber	Sherwood Wheaton
San Francisco	Playground Commission of San Francisco	Rev. D. O. Crowley	F. A. Lawler
	Recreation League	Jesse W. Lilienthal	Mrs. E. L. Baldwin
Stockton	Playground Commission	Mrs. C. M. Jackson	Mrs. Richard Lauxen
COLORADO			
Colorado Springs	Colorado Springs Playgrounds Commission	Asa T. Jones	Anna Louise Johnson
Denver	Denver Playground Association	Frederic S. Titsworth	F. W. Huling, Supt.
Pueblo	Playground Department	F. E. Olin, Park Com'm'r	
CONNECTICUT			
Ansonia	Ansonia Playground Association	George C. Bryant	O. E. Bath
Bridgeport	Recreation Board	Rev. John R. Brown	Mrs. Sanford Stoddard
Derby	Derby Playground Association	Terrance S. Allis	Ada S. Shelton
Hartford	Park and Recreation Department	Mrs. A. R. Hillyer	F. G. Whitmore
New London	Playground and Recreation Association	Louis B. Doane	Cora A. Marsh
Norwich	Norwich Playground Association		Arthur L. Peale
Putnam	Putnam Playground Association	Mrs. C. D. Arnold	Mrs. H. L. Pease
Stamford	Playground Commission	Dorothy Heroy	Mrs. Clement A. Fuller
Torrington	Torrington Playground Association	Marjorie S. Turner	James Doughty

Wallingford...............	Wallingford Playground and Recreation Ass'n....	Mrs. J. C. Wrinn
DELAWARE		
Wilmington...............	Wilmington Playground Association...............	Edna Thomas
DISTRICT OF COLUMBIA		
Washington...............	Municipal Playground Department..............	Mrs. Susie Root Rhodes, Sup'r.
FLORIDA		
Daytona...................	Daytona Playground Commission...............	Mrs. Gte Hinks.............	Lew Smith
Jacksonville...............	Playground Commission...............	F. P. Conroy...............	Mrs. T. P. Denham
Tampa...................	Tampa Playground Association..............	J. E. Paterson.............	
GEORGIA		
Atlanta...................	Playground Association of Atlanta.............	Mrs. F. M Tibbets.............	Loudie Holland
Macon...................	Recreation and Playground Association............	Nelson Mallary.............	Florence Bernd
Savannah...............	Recreation Commission...............	H. L. Kayton.............	C. R. Goette
ILLINOIS		
Aurora...................	Playground Commission...............	Jane K. Snook.............	George Dieterich
Chicago...................	Bureau of Parks, Playgrounds and Bathing Beaches............		Walter Wright
East St. Louis.............	East St. Louis Playground Association.............	William J. Veach.............	E. P. Griffin
Evanston...............	Small Parks and Playground Association............	D. H. Burnham, Jr..............	Mrs. U. S. Grant
Moline...................	Moline Municipal Playground Commission............	E. E. Parsonage.............	Mollie McEnery
Peoria...................	Peoria Recreation Commission...............	S. Eckley............. –	R. M. Field
Quincy...................	Quincy Playground Association.............	Rev. Lyman 1 fan............	Mrs. Ella Gilmer
Springfield...............	General Committee on Supervised Play............	Mrs. sBn H. Caldwell.............	Abram G. Bergen
Urbana-Champaign............	Twin City Recreation Association...............	Paul Busy.............	Mrs. Morgan Brooks
Winnetka...............	Recreation Committee.............		
INDIANA		
Evansville.............	Evansville Playground Association.............	R. R. Williams.............	Rev. J. U. Schneider
Indianapolis.............	Recreation Department...............	Charles C. 3h, Commissioner	Giles ary
South Bend.............	Municipal Recreation Committee.............	L. M. Hammerschmidt.............	Mrs. Homer J. Miller

11

State and City	Name	President or Chairman	Secretary
IOWA			
Ames	Playground Association of Ames	F. W. Hicks	Mrs. Galen Tieden
Cedar Falls	Cedar Falls Playground Association	Mrs. W. C. Nuhn	W. H. Wing
Clinton	Playground and Recreation Association	Mrs. M. J. Gates	
Ottumwa	Ottumwa Playground League	Mrs. D. C. Brockman	Mrs. H. L. Sedgwick
KANSAS			
Hays	Playground Commission	C. A. Shively	Mrs. W. W. Paul
Junction City	Junction City Playground Association	Y. Y. Young	Charles A. Wagner
LOUISIANA			
New Orleans	Board of Com'n. of Public Playgrounds	Mrs. A. J. Stallings	Mrs. J. H. Douglas
MAINE			
Portland	Recreation Commission City of Portland	Hon. W. G. Chapman	Granville R. Lee
MARYLAND			
Baltimore	Children's Playground Association of Baltimore	Mrs. Charles E. Ellicott	Mary Claire O'Brien, Exec. Sec'y
	Public Athletic League	Robert Garrett	William Burdick
MASSACHUSETTS			
Boston	Park and Recreation Department	Daniel J. Byrne	S. K. Nason
Brookline	Brookline Playground Commission	George S. Baldwin	Mrs. N. P. A. Carter
Chicopee	Chicopee Playground Commission	James E. Hafey	E. V. Ambler
Dalton	Committee on Community Recreation	Thomas H. Mooney	Alice M. Wiggin
Franklin	Franklin Playground and Garden Association	Orestes T. Doe	Mary E. Hussey
Holyoke	Holyoke Playground Commission	A. A. Brooks	William V. Crawford
Lawrence	Playgrounds Department	John A. Flanagan	Charles F. Johnson
Newton	Playground Commission	William C. Brewer	

Northampton	Northampton Playground Association	Dr. S. Chase Tucker	Gordon Campbell
Peabody	Peabody Playground Commission	Rev. William H. Beers	L. G. Davies
Pepperell	Playground Commission	William C. Stevenson	Rev. Dudley R. Child
Pittsfield	Park and Playground		Joseph E. Pierson
Reading	Playground Commission	Hon. Albion A. Perry	Mrs. J. R. Aldrich
Somerville	Somerville Playground Association. Recreation and Commission.	Charles S. Clark	George L. Dudley; F. A. Wald
Southbridge	Playground Committee	J. G. E. Page	
Taunton	Playground Commission	Rev. E. J. Moriarty	
Waltham	Board of Recreation	Gleason Wood	W. W. Norcross
Watertown	Playground Department	O. H. O'Halloran	Mrs. Gladys Bogren
Wayland	Wayland Park and Playground Association	H. B. Putnam	D. M. Cole
Westfield	M. B. Whitney Public Playground Commission	R. B. Pillsbury	H. A. Goodman
West Springfield	West Springfield Playground Commission	Frederick E. Moore	A. G. Treadway
Williamstown	Williamstown Association	George F. Booth	George S. Barton
Worcester	Parks and Recreation Commission		
MICHIGAN			
Detroit	Recreation Commission	William T. Dust	I. A. Jayne
Grand Rapids	Grand Rapids Recreation Association	J. Arthur Whitworth	Frances Van Buren
Harbor Beach	Harbor Beach Recreation Association	E. J. Engle	B. F. Huestis
Jackson	Recreation Commission	W. H. Poole	
Sault Ste. Marie	Playground Association of Sault Ste. Marie	W. J. Graves	F. A. DuBridge
Wyandotte	Wyandotte Recreation Board	E. C. Bryan	A. W. Seldon
Ypsilanti	City Committee on Public Recreation	W. P. Bowen	Carl Switzer
MINNESOTA			
Rochester	Rochester Playground Association	Mrs. Witherstone	Mrs. Bratoger
St. Paul	Department of Parks, Playgrounds and Public Buildings	J. D. Hyland, Commissioner	E. A. Giantvalley
Winona	Winona Playgrounds Association	Rev. T. S. Devitt	C. D. Tearse
MISSOURI			
St. Louis	Parks and Recreation Department	Nelson Cunliff, Park Com'r	R. H. Abeken, Supt.
NEBRASKA			
Omaha	Board of Public Recreation	J. B. Hummel	C. J. Carlson

13

OFFICERS OF RECREATION COMMISSIONS AND ASSOCIATIONS—*Continued*

State and City	Name	President or Chairman	Secretary
Stella	Stella Playground Association	R. A. Clark	Mrs. I. E. Martin
NEW HAMPSHIRE			
Keene	Municipal Playground Committee	Adolf W. Pressler	Mrs. W. H. Goodnow
Lebanon	Lebanon Playground Association	Marion J. Carter	Mrs. C. L. Flanders
NEW JERSEY			
Bridgeton	Johnson Reeves Playground Association	Archer Platt	Alice Service
Camden	Board Recreation Commissioners	Frederick A. Finkeldey	B. W.
East Orange	Board Recreation Commissioners		I. E. owl Ry
Elizabeth	Board Recreation Commissioners	Walter H. Baldwin	Dean P. Otis
Haddonfield	Haddonfield Playground Association	Mrs. William Allen, Jr.	Mrs. E. H. Barnes
Kearny	Kearny Playground Committee	P. Stevenson	A. J. Iber
Morristown	Morristown Playground Society	Grinnell Willis	F. W. Ford
Mt. Tabor	Mt. Tabor Playground Association	William C. Cudlipp	J. Harvey Swenarton
Newark	Recreation Department—Department Public Affairs	Mayor Charles P. Gillen	
Paterson	Board of Recreation Commissioners		Albert H. Kreamer
Perth Amboy	Board of Commissioners	C. L. Riley	W. W. Pierce
Plainfield	Public Recreation Committee	John Zerega	W. H. P. Vesey
	Public Recreation Commission	Jesse Mt.	George
Red Bank	Red Bank Recreation Association	afles E. Colley Mr.	J. S. Applegate, Jr.
South Orange	Board Recreation s	Mrs. William Mr.	E. E.
South River	Playground 1 e	Loris H. Phelps	Sarah T. M. Brown
Westfield	nd Commission	e Goldner	E. W. Wittke
West Hoboken	Board of Playground Commissioners	R. J. Miller	Arthur F. Norton
West New York	Recreation Commission	R. M. Colgate	Suel Schoor
West Orange	Playground Commission	Mrs. Horace Nixon	J. M. Maghee, M. D.
Woodbury	Woodbury Playground Association		Mrs. W. B. Wey

14

NEW YORK

City	Organization		
Beacon	Public Recreation Commission.	Dillon Wallace.	Mrs. Elizabeth Tiele
Buffalo	Bureau of Playgrounds.	Hon. C. M. Heald, Commissioner Public Affairs.	Charles W. Dilcher
Canajoharie	Canajoharie Public Playground Committee.	F. E. Barbour.	
Elmira	Municipal Playground Committee.	Harry N. Hoffman.	Benjamin Levy
Glens Falls	Recreation Commission.	Willis Dodge.	Helen W. Streeter
Gloversville	Playground Committee.	S. E. Burton.	
Hornell	Municipal Playground Committee.	W. H. Prangen.	Katherine Frawley
Hudson	Department of Recreation of Board of Education.	S. Mitchell Rainey.	C. S. Williams
Huntington	Recreation and Playground Association, Inc.	R. K. Toaz.	Charles E. Sammis, Jr.
Little Falls	Little Falls Playground Association.	Frank Simon.	Mrs. R. D. Spears
Mt. Vernon	Public Recreation Com'n. of Mt. Vernon, N. Y.	William S. S. Graham.	Gertrude L. Fiske
Newburgh	Newburgh Recreation Com'n.	T. W. Stewart.	Mrs. Pierre Northrip
New York	Bureau of Recreation, Department of Parks.	George Gordon Battle.	William J. Lee, Supervisor
	Parks and Playgrounds Ass'n. of the City of New York.	Martha L. Draper.	Lulu Morton
	Public Schools' Athletic League (Girls' Branch).		Mrs. Gustavus Towne Kirby
	(Boys' Branch).		C. Ward Crampton, M. D.
Portchester	Recreation Commission.	George W. Wingate.	Elmer S. Redman
Rochester	Bureau of Playgrounds and Recreation-Department of Parks.	William Ward.	
Scarsdale	Recreation Committee.	Robert A. Bernhard, Supt.	Catherine M. Kreckel
Suffern	Suffern Playground Association.	Rev. Arthur Pritchard.	
Tarrytown	Municipal Recreation Commission.	A. P. Burroughs.	Mrs. Charles A. Pace
Tuxedo	Tuxedo Playground Association.	F. R. Pierson.	T. W. Garey
Utica	Playground and Recreation Association.	Mrs. Henry Ludin.	Ida J. Butcher
Yonkers	Playground and Recreation Commission.	Walter F. Haskett.	Florence J. Parsons

NORTH CAROLINA

City	Organization		
Raleigh	Raleigh Recreation Commission.	Charles Lee Smith, M. D.	R. Russell Miller

OHIO

City	Organization		
Akron	Children's Playground Committee.	F. W. Work.	Maude Herndon
Athens	Athens Playground Association.	H. D. Zenner.	Mrs. C. L. Jones

15

OFFICERS OF RECREATION COMMISSIONS AND ASSOCIATIONS—*Continued*

State and City	Name	President or Chairman	Secretary
Bellaire	Bellaire Playground Association	Charles Dickens, Jr.	James Wagner, Jr.
Canton	Canton Park and Playground Association	C. B. Sala	Mrs. A. E. Sprentall
Cleveland	Division of Recreation	J. F. Potts	
Columbus	Division of Public Recreation		
Dayton	Division of Recreation		
	...nd and Garden Association	Rabbi David Lefkowitz	
Kenton	Kenton Playground Association	Mrs. W. W. Bowers	Mrs. W. S. Robinson
Martins Ferry	Martins Ferry Playgrounds Association	George G. Ralston	Royer Lupton
Oberlin	Recreation League of Oberlin Federation	H. A. Mer.	M. A. Houghton
Springfield	...nd Association	Donald Kirkpatrick	Charles E. Ashburner
Toledo	Playground Association of ...to	Reverend S. C. Black	
Youngstown	...n Playground Association	Leo Guthman	A. L. Button
PENNSYLVANIA			
Allentown	...n Playground ...ation	Percy B. Ruhe	Mary E. Leiley
Bristol	Bristol Playground Association	Mary W. Swain	Mrs. Luis C. Spring
Catasauqua	Catasauqua Park and Playground Ass...ation		S. S. Stillman
Chester	...er Playgrounds Association	Mrs. H. C. ...ne	Katherine Barker
Conshohocken	Conshohocken Playground Association	C. F. Teglmeier M. D.	Dorothea B. Jones
Danville	Danville ...nd Committee	Mrs. Edward S. Gearhart	Cadwalader Phillips
Farrell	Farrell Playground Association	a...es Phillipps	John D. Davis
Gettysburg	Kurtz ...al ...ciation	T. J. ...ller	William c ...id Mc-...an
Greensburg	Greensburg Playgrounds and Civic Association	Mrs. L. B. Huff	Mrs. F. W. Frazier
Hazleton	Hazleton Playground Association	S. Sager	S. K. Barber
Johnstown	Recreation Commission	Charles Stroup	
Lancaster	Playground Association of Lancaster		W. F. Carey
Lebanon	Lebanon Athletic and Playground Association	Alfred C. Hersh	H. C. Uhler
	Southeastern Playground Association	L. W. Richards	Irwin B. Homan
Lock Haven	Wilson Kistlee Playground Association	Mrs. Charles Dunn	

Meadville	Meadville Playground Association	Mrs. Charles Johnson	B. Lyons
Middleburg	Middleburg Playground Association	J. G. Thompson	George W. Wagenseller
Northampton	Northampton Playground Association	George W. Conrad	H. T. Bilheimer
Philadelphia	{ Board of Recreation of Philadelphia	Ernest L. Tustin	Sophia L. Ross
	Playgrounds Association of Philadelphia	Montgomery Harris	Joseph Wood Draper
Phoenixville	Phoenixville Playground Association	Rev. F. C. Hartshorne	Mrs. G. A. Lambert
Pittsburgh	Bureau of Recreation	John Swan	Fred L. Roberts, Acting Supt.
Pittsburgh, N. S.	Playground and Vacation School Ass'n. of Allegheny	Mrs. John Cowley	Mame M. Stoner
Reading	Reading Playground Association	Wellington M. Bertolet	J. J. Strickland
St. Clair	St. Clair Playground Association	Rev. S. F. Faust	W. J. Evans
Scranton	Bureau of Recreation	Rev. Robert P. Kreitler	Mrs. Edwin W. Gearhart
Shillington	Playground Committee	F. A. Gehret	F. Mae Smith
Steelton	Parks and Playgrounds Commission	Charles S. Davis	Charles P. Feidt
Uniontown	Uniontown Public Playground Association	Mrs. William McClelland	Mrs. Alonzo C. Hagan
Washington	Playground Association of Washington	Rev. Matthew Rutherford	Mrs. Edwin Linton
West Chester	West Chester Playground Association	Plummer Jeffries	Jane R. Baker, M. D.
West Reading	West Reading Park and Playground Association	Mr. John Walker	Mr. W. D. Heinly
Wilkinsburg	Wilkinsburg Playground Association	E. R. Spencer	W. D. McCoy
Windber	Windber Playground Association	Mrs. C. A. Davis	Mrs. Eva Hill
Wyomissing	Wyomissing Playground Association	H. M. Fry	H. A. Garner

RHODE ISLAND

Cumberland	Valley Falls Playground Association	Andrew J. Currier	J. V. Broderick
Lonsdale	Lonsdale Garden and Playground Association	Robert Stewart	Mrs. E. C. Mowry
Newport	Board of Recreation Commissioners	Colonel Joseph H. Willard	Ruth B. Franklin
Pawtucket	Playground Committee of City Council	Fred F. Halliday, Jr.	
Providence	Board of Recreation	Hon. J. H. Gainer	J. J. McCaffrey

SOUTH CAROLINA

Columbia	Playground Department	C. N. Asbill	

OFFICERS OF RECREATION COMMISSIONS AND ASSOCIATIONS—*Continued*

STATE AND CITY	NAME	PRESIDENT OR CHAIRMAN	SECRETARY
TENNESSEE			
Memphis............	Memphis Recreation Commission....	R. B. Maury, M. D....	Charles D. Johnston
TEXAS			
Fort Worth........	Recreation Committee................	Harry Adams............	Ella Forbess
Galveston..........	Galveston Playground Association....	George Waverly Briggs....	W. A Eicher
Snyder............	Snyder Playground Association.......	Mrs. E. J. Anderson....	
UTAH			
Salt Lake City	Playground and Recreation Association of Salt Lake City................	Kate Williams..........	W. C. Ebaugh, M. D.
VERMONT			
St. Albans........	Stranahan Club Playground...........	Mrs. William B. Fonda....	William P. Jackson
VIRGINIA			
Lynchburg..........	Lynchburg Playground and Recreation Ass'n....	Mrs. Max Guggenheimer....	C. R. Warthen
Norfolk............	Playground Committee of City Council....	Philip Roskam.........	R. E. Steed
Portsmouth........	Park and Playground Commission.......	C. N. Markham, Commissioner	
Richmond..........	Citizens' Committee on Recreation and Playgrounds............	L. McK. Judkins........	Julien H. Hill
WEST VIRGINIA			
Bluefield..........	Bluefield Playground and Recreation Ass'n......	Harry S. Mabie....	J. E. McMullin

McMechen	McMechen Playground Association	Mrs. J. A. Jennings	Mrs. J. D. Marple
Parkersburg	Parkersburg Playground Association	H. E. Odgers	Ada B. Weyer
Wheeling	Wheeling Playground Association	Mrs. C. R. Hubbard	John Wallace

WISCONSIN

Manitowac	Manitowac Playground Association	Bajemil Nespor	Mrs. Margaret Primm

CANADA

Winnipeg, Man.	Winnipeg Playground Commission	Robert Fletcher	A. K. Morrison
Fort William, Ont.	Playground Commission		F. Stephenson Sup'r.
Ottawa, Ont.	Ottawa Playgrounds Association	Gerald H. Brown	J. C. Spence
Peterborough, Ont.	Peterborough Playground Association	W. G. Morrow	E. J. H. Vanstone
Montreal, Que.	Parks and Playgrounds Department	J. P. Gadbois	

TERRITORY OF HAWAII

Honolulu	Committee on Parks, Playgrounds, School Grounds, and Public Buildings	Ben Hollinger	

Foot notes indicated by signs after the names

STATE AND CITY	Population*	Number of Centers Maintained under Paid Leadership				Number of Paid Workers Exclusive of Caretakers			Caretakers	Hours During Which Centers Are Open under Leadership			Average Daily Attendance	
		Year-round	Summer Only	Other Seasons	Total	Men	Women	Year-round		Summer	Spring and Fall	Winter	Summer Months	Winter Centers
ARIZONA														
1 Tucson †	16,750				6	6			1	8:30-5			2,700	
ARKANSAS														
1 Crossett	2,038		1		1	1				7-10			300	
CALIFORNIA														
1 Alhambra	5,021		1		1	1				6			100	
2 Berkeley	57,653	5	4		9	6	9	15	4	8½	4	....	2,500	1,100
3 Fresno	34,958	7	1	3	11	8	10	16	3	'9-11:3-6 7-9	3-till dark	3-till dark	134	....
4 Los Angeles	503,812	10	‡22	1	33	27	24	23	10	7	6½	6½	6,497	3,450
5 Modesto	4,034		1		1	1	2		1	9-5			....	
6 Oakland	198,604	44	20		44	20	44	....	18	8	5	4	5,907	3,154
7 Oroville		1			1	1	2	1		1	1	1	30	30
8 San Bernardino	16,945		2		2	1	1		1	5			....	
9 San Diego	53,330	4			4	7	7	14	6	6½	6½	6½	663	500
10 San Francisco	463,516	27			27	14	31	45	12	9-7	12-7	12-5	8,100	5,400
11 San Jose †	28,902	2		9	11	3	2	5	1	9-5	ᴿ9-5	9-5	125	1,500
12 Stockton	35,358	5		3	8	5	5	10		9-6	3:30-6	3:30-5	483	483
COLORADO														
1 Boulder City	11,669		1		1	1	1		3	8-6			200	
2 Colorado Springs	32,971		3		3		6			6			650	
3 Denver	260,800	{ 1	15	54	54	12	50	4	15	9-9	1½	9-10	3,920	....
		14		1	1		1							500
4 Pueblo	54,462	{		1	1		1		1	6	2½		755	75
													60	
CONNECTICUT														
1 Ansonia	16,704		3		3	3	2		1	9-6			500	
2 Bridgeport	121,579		4		4	5	4			8 1(9-5)			....	
3 Derby	9,655		2		2	1	2			1(9-12) 10-6			150	
4 Hartford	110,900	{ 2	13	2	17	8	30	3	13	9-10	9-10	2-10	5,000	500
			9			7	112						2,702	
5 Meriden †	34,183	12	7		14	8	7	3	3	8-5	9-5:30	9-5:30	2,000	1,000
6 Middletown	22,799		1	1	2	2	1			7	24 per wk.		45	25
7 Naugatuck	14,093		1		1		2			9-5			....	
8 New Haven	149,685		12	40	42	15	120	1		9-4	3:30-5:15		3,500	
9 New London	20,985		5		5	6	5			9-12:1-5			....	
10 Norwich	29,419		4		4	1			3	7			99	
11 Rockville	7,977		1		1	1	2			5			90	
12 So. Manchester	9,000	1	2		3	3	3	3	2	9-9	....	8-10:30	900	
13 Stamford	35,119	{ 1	5		5	4	5		1	9-5			....	
		1			1	1	1	1		....	....	12-10		
14 Thompsonville	6,000		1		1		1			 1-6			100	
15 Torrington	19,597		1		1	1	2			1-6			300	
16 Wallingford	12,508		2		2	2	4	3	1	8:30-8			725	
17 Waterbury	86,973	{ 1	1		1	1	4		5	9 3	2	....	150	
		1	8		9	8	5	1	3	10	....	6	1,700	150
18 Windham	14,154			1	1	1			1	10-10	....		....	
19 Windsor Locks	3,500		1		1	1	1		1	10-9			125	
DELAWARE														
1 Henry Clay	1,000	1			1	2	3	2	1	4	5	5	40	175
2 Wilmington	94,265	{ 7			7	3	9	2	2	7			1,414	
		1			1	1	2	1	1	8	2		350	

of cities follow the "small community" table

Authorities Managing Playgrounds and Neighborhood Recreation Centers	Expenditures Last Fiscal Year				Sources of Financial Support of Playgrounds and Neighborhood Recreation Centers	Year First Center Was Established under Leadership	Sources of Information
	Land Buildings Permanent Equipment	Upkeep Supplies and Incidentals	Salaries	Total			
1 Board of Education.........	$ 1,700.00	$	$ 2,000.00	$ 3,700.00	Municipal...........	1917	Harold Steele
1 Y. M. C. A...............	....	....	....	....	Private.............	......	C. H. Winston
1 City..............			200.00	200.00	Municipal.........	1915	C. E. Barber
2 Playground Commission.....	2,678.45	2,274.65	8,274.90	13,228.00	Municipal...........	1911	Gustavus Schneider
3 Playground and Recreation Commission...............	3,172.66	2,246.58	10,698.6u	16,114 03	Municipal...........	1914	R. L. Quigley
4 Playground Commission......	17,223.63	17,485.69	58,239.37	92,948.68	Municipal...........	1905	Charles S. Lamb
5 Woman's Improvement Club					Private.............		Mrs. William Folger
6 Board of Playground Directors..................	15,000.00	17,500.00	67,500.00	100,000.00	Municipal...........	1908	J. B. Nash
7 Y. M. C. A..............	3,000 00	200.00	1,800.00	4,000 00	Private.............	1916	F. M. Duckles
8 Com'n. Parks & Playgrounds Playground Association	400.00	100 00	180.00	780.00	Municipal and Private	1917	Mrs. W. S. Ingram
9 Board Playground Com'n't's..		6,000.00	16,933.00	22,933 00	Municipal...........	1910	F. S. Marsh
10 Playground Commission......	25,000 00	35,000.00	35,000.00	95,000 00	Municipal...........	1910	E. B. De Groot
11 Board of Education.........	2,380 00	200.00	3,590.00	6,170.00	Municipal...........	1915	Alexander Sheriffs
12 Playground Commission.....		1,529 55	4,240.56	5,770.11	Municipal...........	1914	E. J. Richards
1 Colorado Chautauqua Ass'n.	85.42	325.00	243.40	653.82	Municipal and Private	......	William V. Casey
2 City.....................		1,090.00	910.00	2,000.00	Municipal...........	1912	Celia Gormley
3 Park Department...........	13,742.84	3,601 03	9,961.87	27,305.74	} Municipal.........	1905	Anna Johnson
3 Board of Education..........	500.00	500.00	4,693.59	5,693.59	}		
4 Playground Department......		608.00	2,217.00	2,825.00	} Municipal.........	1913	F. W. Huling
4 School District No. 20.......	....	....	....	....			
1 Playground Association......		90.00	500.00	590.00	Private.............	1910	H. E. Green
2 Recreation Board..........		2,000.00	2,000.00	4,000.00	Municipal...........	1912	B. F. Cooney
3 Com. of Woman's Club......		101.90	335.00	436 90	Municipal and Private.	1913	Ada S. Shelton
4 Board of Education.........		262.16	4,694.50	4,956.66	} Municipal and	1896	T. S. Weaver
Park Department..........		7,000.00	9,330.00	16,330 00	Private		S. W. Dixon
5 School Committee.........	2,400 00	1,400.00	1,800.00	4,600 00	Municipal and Private	1909	David Gibbs
6 Social Service League.......		430.00	427.00	857.00	Municipal and Private	1909	Mrs. C. A. Howland
7 Board of Education.........			240.00	240 00	Private.............	1917	F. W. Eaton.
8 Recreation Com. of Civic Federation..................	600.00	2,400.00	5,000.00	8,000 00	Municipal...........	1909	H. J. Schnelle
9 Playground and Recreation Association..............		143.84	865.71	1,009.55	Municipal...........	1909	Cora A. Marsh
10 Playground Association.....		153.74	411.05	564.79	Municipal and Private	1909	Mary F. McKay
11 School Committee		90.00	100.00	190.00	Municipal...........	1916	Tracy Noble
12 Town Recreation Com......						......	J. H. Mueller
13 Playground Commission.....	....	422.73	1,576.35	1,999.08	{ Municipal and Private	1913	Dorothy Heroy
Recreation Committee......	....						
14 So. End Playground Com....			120.00	120.00	Private.............	1914	Norma Allen
15 Torrington Playground Ass'n.		112.00	220.00	332.00	Private.............	1909	Marjorie Turner
16 Wallingford Playground and Recreation Association......		272.45	453.00	725.45	Municipal and Private	1912	Mrs. J. C. Wrinn
17 Associated Charities.......				600.00	} Municipal and Private.....	1908	Eugene Kerner
Waterbury Industrial School	30.00		200.00	230.00			
Waterbury Park Department	200.00	300.00	3,000.00	3,500.00			
18 American Thread Company ..	....	....	....	....	Private.............		
19 Playground Committee......		252.65	100.00	352.65	Municipal and Private	1914	Mrs. J. DeF. Phelps
1 Hagley Community House ...		2,836.71	3,484.50	6,321.21	Private.............	1913	Clara B. Bubb
2 Park Commission...........	4,381.03	578.31	1,297.40	6,256.74	} Municipal and Private......	1906	E. R. Mack
People's Settlement.........			300 00	300.00			

Foot notes indicated by signs after the names

STATE AND CITY	Population*	Number of Centers Maintained under Paid Leadership				Number of Paid Workers Exclusive of Caretakers			Caretakers	Hours During Which Centers Are Open under Leadership			Average Daily Attendance	
		Year-round	Summer Months	Other Seasons	Total	Men	Women	Employed year-round		Summer	Spring and Fall	Winter	Summer Months	Winter Centers
DISTRICT OF COLUMBIA														
1 Washington	363,980		35		35	10	50		30	....			4,200	
		15	2		17	5	23	15	14	9-dark	11:45-dark	11:45-dark	6,816	6,220
FLORIDA														
1 Daytona	3,082		1		1		1			3½			30	
2 Jacksonville	76,101	3	2		5	2	2	2		5	3½	3	160	136
3 Tampa	53,886	1			1	1	1	2		8	7		380	240
GEORGIA														
1 Atlanta	193,558		11		11	5	38			9-12:3-6			700	
2 La Grange	5,587	2			2	1	1			3-6	8-5	8-5;8-4	450	340
3 Macon	45,757	5			5	5	6	11	1	4:30-9:36; 7-10	2:36-dark	2:30-dark	1,014	654
4 Rome	15,120		1		1	1	1			6			100	
5 Savannah	68,805		6		6	7	9	16		4½	4½	3½	1,200	2,000
ILLINOIS														
1 Aurora	34,204		1		1	1	3		1	12			350	
2 Belvidere	7,253		2		2		3		2	3-5			50	
3 Cairo	15,794		5		5		2		2	10			100	
4 Champaign-Urbana	23,897		3		3	1	2			8;4			30	
		68		1	69	70	70	86	70	8:30-9	8:30-9	8:30-9	580	580
5 Chicago	2,497,722	15	6		21	53	48	52	346	8-11	12-11	12-11	....	....
		11	4		15	38	40	31		9-10	3-10	3-10	4,000	335
		4	1		5	21	3	24	5	9-9	9-9	1-10	650	300
		5			5	10	10	....	..70	9-10	9-10	9-10	40,000	25,000
6 Chicago Heights	21,693		2		2		2			6			60	
7 East St. Louis	74,708	1	1		4	3	2	2	1	8	8	8	550	50
		1		1	2	2	2	9	1	3	10	4	600	200
8 Evanston†	28,591	2		6	8	2	9	1	9	8		2	200	200
		1		3	4	1	1	1	4	8		4	150	800
9 Freeport	19,568	3			3		1		3	....			200	
10 Granite City	15,142	4			4		4			....			3,000	
11 Kewanee	13,561	1			1		1						85	
													300	
12 Lake Forest	3,349	3	2		5	3	2		1	10-12:2-5: 6-9;2-6:7-10				
13 La Salle, Peru-Oglesby	12,221	1			1	2	2	5	2					
14 Lincoln	11,838		1		1		1			9-6			150	
15 Moline	26,403		4	1	5	5	8			9-5:30	Evngs and Sat. P. M.		675	176
16 Oak Park	26,654		1	5	6	4	2		6	1-6	3-5:30	7-9:30		
17 Peoria	71,458		4	4	4	8	7	1		9-12:1-6		7-10	438	40
18 Pontiac	6,090		1		1	1	2		10	4			100	
19 Quincy	36,798		3		3		3			9-5			200	
20 Rochelle	2,732		1		1		2			9-12:2-5			50	
21 Rockford	55,185		6		6	7	5		6	8			150	
22 Rock Island	28,926		5		5	3	4			6			250	
23 Springfield	61,120		8		8	1	9			....			120	
24 Winnetka	3,168	2	3		5	3	3	3	7	....				
INDIANA														
1 Bedford	10,349		1		1	1				9-11:30:2-5	....		75	
2 Bloomington	11,383		1		1	2	1			9-5			350	

of cities follow the " small community" table

Authorities Managing Playgrounds and Neighborhood Recreation Centers	Expenditures Last Fiscal Year				Sources of Financial Support of Playgrounds and Neighborhood Recreation Centers	Year First Center Was Established under Leadership	Sources of Information
	Land Buildings Permanent Equipment	Upkeep Supplies and Incidentals	Salaries	Total			
1 Department Special Activities of Board of Education...... $		$ 3,818.22	$11,088.77	$14,906.99	} Municipal and.....	1906	W. B. Patterson
Municipal Playground Department....................	11,887.46	18,316.19	30,635.00	60,838.65	} Private..........		Ella Gardner
1 Parent-Teachers' Association .			125.00	....	Private............	1916	Edythe Bainter
2 Playground Commission......		1,225.00	1,775.00	3,000.00	Municipal and Private	1912	L. G. Haskell
3 Tampa Playground Ass'n....		900.00	1,500.00	2,400.00	Municipal and Private	1911	J. P. Rovira
1 Park Department..........	1,300.00			7,000.00	Municipal and Private	1906	Loudie Holland, Mrs. F. M. Tibbets
2 Dunson Cotton Mill Co...:..	2,300 00	350 00	720.00	3,370.00	Private............	1914	Julia Corless
3 Joint Com. of City Council and Recreation and Playground Association.............		2,141.96	5,438.23	7,580.19	Municipal..........	1911	E. J. Garmhausen
4 Women's Club..............				276.50	Municipal and Private		Mrs. A.W.VanHoosen
5 Recreation Commission.....		2,635.00	11,984.70	14,609.70	Municipal..........	1914	C. R. Goette
1 Playground Commission.....				2,800.00	Municipal..........	1912	Jane K. Snook
2 Parent-Teachers' Ass'n......		450.00	150.00	600.00	Private............	1914	Mrs. FrancesBurstatte
3 Park Commission.....					Municipal..........		C. R. Dunlop
4 Twin City Recreation Ass'n.		50.00	350 00	400.00	Municipal and Private	1911	L. C. Griggs.
5 { Bureau Parks, Playgrounds and Beaches..............	183,470.34	21,803.69	121,087.91	326,361.94		1901	T. A. Gross
South Parks..............	400,000.00	240,000.00	160,000 00	800,000.00			J. R. Richards
West Chicago Park Com'n....		100,000.00	115,684.81	215,684.81	Municipal......	1908	T. J. Smergalski
Park Com'n. Northwest Park District....................	57,047.24	226,682.86	30,541.77	110,271.87		1916	E. C. Nitsche
Com'n. of Lincoln Park.....						1908	R. W. Black
6 Woman's Club		100 00	270.00	370 00	Municipal and Private	1911	Mrs. J Gravelot
7 East St. Louis Park District..		400.00	1,800.00	2,200.00	Municipal..........	1913	E. P. Griffen
8 City....................		1,500.00	2,000.00	3,500.00			
School Board, District 75....		1,000.00	1,600.00	2,600.00	} Municipal........	1909	Edith M. Ennis
School Board, District 76....		500.00	800.00	1,300.00			E. H. Selle
9 Freeport Park District.......	6,000.00				Municipal..........		L. P. Frohardt
10 Board of Education.........				3,000.00	Municipal..........		
11 School Board..............		30.00	115.00	145.00	Municipal..........	1916	
12 Park Board................	4,269.86	139.91	1,243.90	5,653.67	Municipal..........	1915	L. W. Thompson
13 LaSalle-Peru High School..... Social center	919.98	347.71	4,307.26	5,574.95	Municipal..........	1913	T. J. McCormack
14 Board of Education.........		25 00	150.00	175.00	Municipal and Private	1917	William Hawkes
15 Playground Commission.....		338.00	1,462.00	1,800.00	Municipal..........	1912	Mollie McEnery
16 Board of Education........				5,000.00	Private............		Arthur F. Baker
17 Recreation Commission......		400.00	2,300.00	2,700.00	Municipal..........	1916	W. B. Martin
18 Y. M. C. A. and City Council		115.00	285.00	400.00	Municipal..........	1912	C. W. Le Messurier
19 Quincy Playground Ass'n.....			200.00	200.00	Private............	1915	Charles M. Gill
20 Women's Club.............		25.00	50.00		Private............	1915	Mrs. W. C. Whitcomb
21 Park Commissioners.........	800.00	250.00	1,700.00	2,750.00	Municipal..........	1910	F. J. Winters
22 Civics Dept. Womans' Club .		150.00	700.00	850.00	Municipal and Private	1913	Mrs.F.O.VanGolder
23 Board of Education.........		35.00	331.00	366.00	Municipal..........	1916	A. G. Berger
24 Recreation Committee.......		13,308.64	9,525.00	22,833.64	Municipal and Private	1910	H. P. Clarke
1 Board of Education.........				90 00	Municipal..........		J. B. Fagan
2 Individual..................	600.00	20.00	1,500.00	2,120.00	Municipal..........	1916	G. E. Schlafer

Foot notes indicated by signs after the names

STATE AND CITY	Population*	Number of Centers Maintained under Paid Leadership				Number of Paid Workers Exclusive of Caretakers			Caretakers	Hours During Which Centers Are Open under Leadership			Average Daily Attendance	
		Year-round	Summer Months	Other Seasons	Total	Men	Women	Employed year-round		Summer	Spring and Fall	Winter	Summer Months	Winter Centers
INDIANA *Continued*														
3 Connersville....	7,738	1		1	1	1	1		1	10	2		250	
4 Danville.......	1,640	1			1					2:30-6			18	
5 East Chicago† ..	28,743	3		5	5	4	4	8		1-6	8-5	8-9	500	3,000
6 Elwood........	11,028		3		3	1				8-12:2-6			50	
7 Evansville......	76,078		6		6	5	3	1		8			908	
8 Fort Wayne....	76,183		6		6	1	5		6	8:30-5			300	
9 Indianapolis....	271,708		28		28	20	70		15	12			....	
10 Richmond......	24,697		5	1	6	5			3	8:15-5:30	after school		....	
11 Seymour.......	6,305	1			1	1			1	1			80	
12 Shelbyville.....	10,965	1			1		2		1	9-5			75	
13 South Bend.....	68,946	6	8	13	17	8	14	2	7	12	8	3	1,918	551
IOWA														
1 Cedar Falls.....	6,284		1		1		1			9-8			75	
2 Charles City....	6,374		1		1		1			9-9			150	
3 Clinton........	27,386		4		4	4	4			1:30-dark			1177	
			1		1		1			1:30-dark			....	
4 Des Moines.....	101,598		8		8	3	9	1	8	9-9;9-5			52	
5 Fort Dodge.....	20,648	1	4	3	8	5	6	2		9:30-11:30 2-5:6:30-8	....	7-9	529	30
6 Grinnell........	5,061		2		2	1	1	2	2	2-5			51	
7 Rock Rapids....	2,031		1		1		1		1	1-5			30	
8 Sioux City......	57,078	20	4	7	31	12	10	2		9-9	4-9	4-9	60	40
9 Webster City...	5,834		1		1	1			1	8-9			200	
KANSAS														
1 Ashland........			1		1	1			1	9-4			100	
2 Chanute........	12,455		2		2	1	1			....				
3 Fredonia.......	3,473			2	2		2				8	8	....	600
4 Hays...........	2,339		1		1	1	1			7-9	7-9		150	
5 Independence...	14,506		5		5	2	1		5	8-6			....	
6 Junction City...	5,798		2		2	1	1			1-8			100	
7 Kansas City....	99,437		2		2	1	2			9-9			300	
8 Manhattan.....	6,816	1			1	2	1	1	1	1:30-5			100	
9 Newton†.......	7,620			5	5	1	4		5	8:30-4:30			70	
10 Pittsburg......	17,832		7		7		2			8-5				
11 Topeka........	48,726		8		8	10	10			9-12			1,200	
12 Yates Center †..	2,199	1			1	1			1	2:30-5:30	School hrs.	School hrs.	125	
KENTUCKY														
1 Covington......	57,144		1		1	1	4		2	....		7	1,000	
2 Lexington......	41,097		5		5	6	6		7	7			400	
3 Louisville......	238,910		7	8	15	2	16			9-6;9-9	3-6;3-9		10,000	
4 Paducah.......	24,842		2		2	2				9-12:2-5			75	
LOUISIANA														
1 Lake Charles ...	14,447	4			4	1	2			....				
2 New Orleans....	371,747	11			11	1	11	12	1	4	3½	2½	1,800	1,000
MAINE														
1 Auburn........	16,393		2		2		2			....			150	
2 Lewiston.......	27,809	1			1	1	2			....			1,000	
3 Portland.......	63,867		10		10	1	18	1	1	5½			2,500	
4 Saco...........	6,583	1			1	1	2		2	9-12:2-4			75	
5 Westbrook......	8,908	1	1		2	2	2	2	2	8-5	....	9-10	225	60

of cities follow the " small community " table

Authorities Managing Playgrounds and Neighborhood Recreation Centers	Land Buildings Permanent Equipment	Upkeep Supplies and Incidentals	Salaries	Total	Sources of Financial Support of Playgrounds and Neighborhood Recreation Centers	Year First Center Was Established under Leadership	Sources of Information
3 Board of School Trustees.....	$100.00	$222.00	$300.00	$662.00	Municipal and Private	1914	E. L. Rickert
4 Parent-Teachers' Ass'n.......				75.00	Private............	1917	Ethel Peyton
5 Board of Education..........				10,500.00	Municipal..........	1913	E. N. Canine
6 Elwood School City........	525 00		225.00	750.00	Municipal..........	1917	A. W. Konold
7 Board of Education........		350.00	1,100 00	1,450.00	Municipal..........	1909	Julius Doerter
8 Board of Education..........	463 08	100 81	1,694.14	2,386.37	Municipal..........	1907	C. A. Snively
9 Department of Recreation....	23,000.00	1,500.00	14,000.00	38,500 00	Municipal..........	1914	W. A. Ocker, M. D.
10 Board of Education..........		150.00	900.00	1,050 00	Municipal..........		Robert Nohr, Jr.
11 City Park Board...........		75.00	475.00	550.00	Municipal..........	1914	T. A. Mott
12 City and Clubs..............	300.00	60.00	150.00	510.00	Municipal and Private	1917	J. W. Holton
13 Municipal Recreation Com....	20,500.00	3,230.00	6,707.00	30,437.00	Municipal..........	1914	L. M. Hammer-schmidt
1 Playground Association......		50 00	150.00	200.00	Private............	1915	A. H. Speer
2 City Improvement Ass'n......	200.00	10.00	90.00	300.00	Municipal..........	1914	F. T. Vasey
3 Playground and Recreation Association............				} 1,417.07	Private............	1914	W. H. Wing
Iten Biscuit Co.............							
4 City Council and School Board		304.07	2,842.26	3,146.33	Municipal..........	1904	Margaret McKee
5 Board of Education..........		260.50	2,484.50	2,745.00	Municipal..........	1917	Strong Hinman
6 Board of Education..........		300 00	191.00	573.00	Municipal..........	1915	Eugene Henely
7 City Park Commission.......	600.00	285.00		670.00	Municipal and Private	1917	A. G. Miller
8 Board of Education..........		3,200.00	8,000.00	11,200.00	Municipal..........	1913	M. G. Clark
9 Park Commission............			300.00	1,600.00	Municipal..........		Louis Follett
1 Parent-Teachers' Ass'n......				125 00	Municipal and Private	1916	L. E. Fitts
2 Child Welfare Association....				200.00	Municipal and Private	1914	Mrs. F. A. Parsons
3 Board of Education..........	1,000.00	100 00	1,200.00	2,300.00	Municipal..........	1911	A. I. Decker
4 Playground Commission......	75.00	25.00	100.00	200.00	Municipal..........	1915	C. A. Shively
5 Board of Education..........		300.00	1,780.00	2,080.00	Municipal..........	1913	C. S. Risdon
6 Board of Education..........	600.00	100.00	500.00	1,200.00	Municipal..........		C. A. Wagner
7 City Commissioners.........				1,300.00	Municipal..........	1915	Mrs. J. S. Detwiler
8 Board of Education..........		100.00	1,000.00	1,100.00	Municipal..........	1912	F. L. Gooch
9 Board of Education..........		2,520.00		2,520.00	....		B. F. Martin
10 Board of Education..........	320 00	70.00	360.00	750.00	Municipal..........	1916	J. F. Bender
11 Board of Education..........	565.60	3,424.45	2,299.13	6,289.18	Municipal..........	1912	M. C. Holman
12 Board of Education..........		380.00	720.00	1,100.00	Municipal..........	1914	A. D. Catlin
1 Civic Department of Art Club			660.00	660.00	Municipal and Private	1901	Kate Scudder
2 Civic League..............		200.00	1,200.00	1,400.00	Municipal and Private	1907	G. H. Mummert
3 Board Park Commissioners...	83.88	1,073.98	1,913.03	3,073.89	Municipal and Private		Frederick Lee
4 Woman's Club.............				750.00	Municipal and Private	1914	Mrs. Gus Edwards
1 Rotary Club..............			675.00	675.00	Private............	1917	J. M. Yeager
2 Board of Commissioners of Public Playgrounds.......		2,235.00	4,606.90	6,842.10	Municipal and Private	1907	L. di Benedetto
1 Woman's Literary Union of Androscoggin County......					Municipal..........	1905	Mrs. Chas. McGraw
2 Woman's Literary Union of Androscoggin County.....					Municipal..........	1905	Mrs. Chas. McGraw
3 Recreation Commission.....				8,000.00	Municipal..........	1900	G. R. Lee
4 Women's Educational and Industrial Union..........		30.46	178.80	209.26	Private............	1910	Mrs. C. F. Cortland
5 Individual................					Private............	1904	Cornelia Warren

Foot notes indicated by signs after the names

STATE AND CITY	Population	Number of Centers Maintained under Paid Leadership				Number of Paid Workers Exclusive of Caretakers			Caretakers	Hours During Which Centers Are Open under Leadership			Average Daily Attendance	
		Year-round	Summer Months	Other Seasons	Total	Men	Women	Employed year-round		Summer	Spring and Fall	Winter	Summer Months	Winter Centers
MARYLAND		1	11	51	63	30	15	18	9	11 9-12:2-6;	2½	3 3-5;9-12:	2,204	1,008
1 Baltimore	589,621	5	58	31	94	2	79	18	17	3-6;5-9;8-11	3-6:7-9;8-11	8-10;8-11; 7-9	3,888	813
2 Cumberland	26,074		2		2	1			2	2 9-5			125	
3 Frederick	11,112		1		1		1		1				50	
MASSACHUSETTS														
1 Attleboro	19,282		2		2	2	2			....			....	350
2 Belmont	8,081		3	1	4	1	3		2	9-9	3-6	3-6 Sat. and Sun.	85	30
3 Beverly	21,645		6		6		5			9-5			350	
				10	10	10	1		11	....		....		273
4 Boston	756,476		70	60	130	60	200		70	9:45-5	3:30-5:30		15,000	
		‖1	6		7	34	39	73	14	2-5:7-10	2-5:7-10			3,079
5 Brockton	67,449		10		10	2	10			10			150	
6 Brookline	32,730	7	7		14	15	28	15	18	9-5:7-9:30 9-11:30:	6:30-10;9 -10:30	9-10	2,500	600
7 Cambridge	112,981		10		10	11	27			1:45-4:30			3,500	
8 Chicopee	29,319		4		4	4	5			9-12:2-5			....	
9 Clinton	13,075		3		3	1			3	9-5				
10 Concord	6,681		.2		2	2	2		2	9-5			100	
11 Dalton	3,858		1		1	2	1			9-5				
12 Easthampton	10,360		1		1	1	2			9-5 9-11:30			125	
13 Fall River	128,366		12		12	6	39			2:30-5			3,456	
14 Fitchburg	41,781		6		6	7	7		3	7			939	
15 Framingham	13,982		6		6	6	8		1	6½			....	
16 Franklin	6,440		1		1		2		1	1:30-5:30			75	
17 Gardner	17,140		1		1	1	1			9:30-5:30			360	
18 Gloucester	24,398		1		1		1			6			125	
19 Greenfield	11,998		2		2		6			2-5			60	
20 Haverhill	48,477		2		2		3		2	8			450	
21 Holyoke	65,286		13		13	10	36	3	7	7			3,712	
22 Lawrence	100,560		8		8	9	10		7	5½			2,035	
23 Lowell	113,245		9		9	5	25		3	4½			3,000	
24 Lynn	102,425		6		6	9	12			9-6				
25 Malden	51,155		4		4	5	4			9-5			1,000	
26 Manchester	2,945		1		1	1	1		1	9-5			175	
27 Milton	8,600	2 / 1	1		2	1	1	2	3	10 9-11:30:	3 8	4 16	150 50	80 125
28 New Bedford	118,158		7	1	8	9	16		8	1:30-4:30			1,007	
29 Newburyport	15,243		2		2		4		1	5 Tues. Thurs. 1:30-5 all day Sat.	Tues. Thurs. 1:30-5 all day Sat.	Tues. Thurs. 1:30-5 all day Sat.	500	
30 Newton	43,715	3		17	17	11	16	4	8	Sat. 3	Sat.	Sat.	3,500	500
31 North Adams	22,019		3		3		3			3			....	
32 Northampton	19,926		2		2	2	3		2	9-12:1-5			200	
33 Norwood	9,605		3		3	3	3		5	6 9:30-11:30			....	
34 Peabody	18,360		7		7	7	7		1	2-5			145	
35 Pittsfield	38,629		6		6	8	14		2	9-5			1,912	
36 Quincy	38,136		5		5	6	6			4	2 afternoon a week		613	
37 Reading	6,805		1		1		1			.			....	
38 Salem	48,562		10		10	10	10		5	9-5			3,500	
39 Somerville	87,039		8		8	2	12			5			3,000	
40 Southbridge	14,205		6		6	2	20		2	9-5			1,000	

of cities follow the " small community" table

Authorities Managing Playgrounds and Neighborhood Recreation Centers	Expenditures Last Fiscal Year				Sources of Financial Support of Playgrounds and Neighborhood Recreation Centers	Year First Center Was Established under Leadership	Sources of Information
	Land Buildings Permanent Equipment	Upkeep Supplies and Incidentals	Salaries	Total			
1 Public Athletic League......	$269.30	$8,307.08	$27,292.62	$236,869.00	} Municipal.........	1897	William Burdick
Children's Playground......		4,637.00	24,073.00	28,700.00			Mary C. O'Brien
Association of Baltimore							
2 Civic Club..............	30.00	25.00	170.00	225.00	Municipal and Private	......	Mrs. D. P. Hartzell
3 Civic Club..............		50.00	100.00	150.00	Private............	1916	Edith M. Osborn
1 Park Department.........	....	....	....	700.00	Municipal..........	1915	C. A. Mooers
2 School Committee.........		400.00	500.00	900 00	Municipal..........	1912	C. L. Shrader
3 Public Works Department....	....	....	....	3,800 00	Municipal..........	......	J. G. Macdonald
4 Park and Recreation Department.................		68,496.93	....	....	} Municipal........		
School Committee.........		10,000.00	30,000.00	....			
Department of Extended Use of Public Schools.........		7,782.81	14,235.50	....			
5 School Department.........			1,410.00	1,410 00	Municipal..........	......	John F. Scully
6 Playground Commission......	17,600.00	60,700.00	24,000.00	92,300 00	Municipal..........	1908	S. K. Nason
7 Board Park Commissioners...		610.00	3,100.00	3,710.00	Municipal..........	1911	T. F. Downey
8 Playground Commission......			1,150.00	2,000.00	Municipal..........	1910	Mrs.N.P.A.Carter
9 Board of Education.........	....	....	....	700.00	Municipal..........	......	E. G. Osgood
10 Board of Selectmen.......		100.00	575.00	675.00	Municipal..........	1913	W. A. Hall
11 Com. on Community Recreation.................	1,374.99	180.45	714.81	2,270.15	Municipal and Private	1916	E. V. Ambler
12 Public Schools............		10.00	142.00	152.00	Municipal and Private	1911	
13 Board Park Commissioners...		306.31	2,678.98	2,995.29	Municipal..........	1912	Howard Lothrop
14 Park Commission..........	231.65	953.09	1,383.25	2,567.99	Municipal	1909	D. S. Woodworth
15 Parks and Playground Com'n..		585.00	1,215.00	1,800.00	Municipal..........	1910	Florence Hilton
16 Franklin Playground and Garden Association...........		25.00	95.00	120 00	Municipal and Private	1912	L. O. Cummings
17 Park Commission.........	....	....	....	700.00	Municipal..........	......	A. W. Bancroft
18 Ward 2 Parent-Teachers' Association.................		39.00	105.00	144.61	Municipal and Private	1914	Mrs. H. F. Smith
19 Mothers' Club............				180.00	Municipal..........	......	W. P. Abbott
20 Board Park Commissioners...			877.92	986.28	Municipal..........	1909	Henry Frost
21 Holyoke Playground Com'n...	4,000.00	5,000.00	6,000.00	15,000.00	Municipal..........	1910	P. H. Kelly
22 Playground Department.....	679.40	1,364.35	2,956.25	5,000.00	Municipal..........	1912	W. V. Crawford
23 Board Park Commissioners...		1,500.00	2,500.00	4,000.00	Municipal..........	1906	J. W. Kernan
24 Park Commission.........				20,000.00	Municipal..........	1909	Florence M. Brown
25 Park Board.............			700.00		Municipal..........	......	J. G. Tilden
26 School Department.........	200.00	260.00	640.00	1,100.00	Municipal..........	1909	J. C. Mackin
27 Park Commission.........	2,000.00	500.00	2,960.00	5,460.00	Municipal and	1912	M. W. Souders
Cunningham Fund..........	500.00	1,200.00	3,500.00	5,200.00	Private............		
28 School Board..............		318.87	2,558.25	2,877.12	Municipal..........	1910	A. P. Keith
29 Park Commissioners.........	200.00	100.00	250.00	550.00	Municipal..........	1900	Madeline Hewett
30 Playground Commission......	7,900.00	10,000.00	8,300 00	26,200.00	Municipal and Private	1889	Ernst Hermann
31 School Department and Recreation Committee..........					Private............	1914	B. J. Merriam
32 City Schools.............	600.00	50.00	450 00	1,100.00	Municipal and Private	1910	Irving Maurer
33 Norwood Civic Association...						1914	J. H. Smith
34 Playground Commission......	1,675.65	371.00	1,310.00	3,356.65	Municipal..........	1912	L. G. Davies
35 Park Commission..........		965.12	2,524.88	3,500.00	Municipal..........	1913	J. M. Flynn
36 Park Commission..........			1,320.00	1,320.00	Municipal..........	1910	J. H. Slade
37 Individual.............	....	....	....		Private............	1916	Genevieve Kingman
38 Park Department..........		3,000.00	3,500.00	6,500.00	Municipal..........	1914	Christian Lants
39 Recreation and Playground Commission.............		130.39	477.47	607.86	Municipal and Private	1909	Mrs. J. R. Aldrich
40 Playground Committee......		798.00	1,142.00	2,000 00	Municipal..........	1911	Margaret Butler

Foot notes indicated by signs after the names

STATE AND CITY	Population*	Number of Centers Maintained under Paid Leadership				Number of Paid Workers Exclusive of Caretakers			Caretakers	Hours During Which Centers Are Open under Leadership			Average Daily Attendance	
		Year-round	Summer Months	Other Seasons	Total	Men	Women	Employed year-round		Summer	Spring and Fall	Winter	Summer Months	Winter Centers
MASSACHUSETTS *Continued.*														
41 Springfield......	105,942	3	15	6	24	47	51	5	22	9-5 9-12	9-5	9-9:30	....	....
42 Taunton.......	36,283		2		2	1	3			1:30-5			440	
43 Waltham.......	30,570		7		7	4	12			9-12:2-5			634	
44 Watertown.....	14,867		2		2	3	3			7			....	
45 Webster........	13,210		3		3	3	3		3	5			300	
46 Wellesley.......	6,439		2		2		4			9-5			125	
47 Westfield.......	18,391		1		1	2				1	1	1	175	
48 West Springfield	10,555		3		3	3	3			9-12:2-5			75	
49 Williamstown...	3,981	1			1	1			1	....	..	....	....	....
50 Winchester.....	10,603		1		1	1	1		2	9-5			90	
51 Woburn........	15,969		1		1	1				12			57	
52 Worcester......	163,314	1	15	1	16	11	33	1	15	9:30-11:30 2-5	7 p. m.- 11:30	7 p. m.- 11:30	6,709	35
MICHIGAN														
1 Ann Arbor.....	15,010		4		4	4	4			6			482	
2 Benton Harbor .	10,833		1		1	1	1			12			100	
3 Detroit........	571,784	31	28	37	96	46	120	70	18	12:30-8:30	3-9:30	3-9:30	12,200	5,300
4 Flint...........	54,772		3		3	3	3		3	8-5:7-9			355	
5 Grand Rapids ..	128,291	{	10		10	17	19		7	8			....	
6 Harbor Beach**	1,556			10	10	20	50					2		67
7 Jackson........	35,363		1		1	1	1						1,182	
			4		4	5	4			8-9:8-5 8:30-11:30 3-8	8:30-11:30 1-3:30	8:30-11:30 1-3:30 7:30-9		
8 Kalamazoo:....	48,886	3	3	10	10	7	14	3	3				389	100
9 Ludington......	10,367		2	1	2	1	‡	1		5	2		82	
10 Marquette......	12,409		1		1	1				9-5			208	
11 Muskegon......	26,100		4		4	1	1	2		7			638	
12 Negaunee......	9,416		1		1	1			1	1-8			200	
13 Pontiac........	17,524	1	6		7	1	2		2	3	....	4	250	75
14 Sault Ste. Marie	13,919		4		4	1	1			8-8			250	
15 Ypsilanti......	6,230		2		2	1	1		2	1-5			100	
MINNESOTA														
1 Albert Lea.....	6,192		1		1	1				9-5			....	
2 Cloquet........	7,031		2		2	2			2	9-6			356	
3 Duluth........	94,495	{ 3	5	12	5	5	5	1	12	9-30-9:30	3-10	10-10	1,500	2,400
			8		11	8	8	1	3	9:30-9:30	3-10	10-10	1,500	900
4 Eveleth........	7,036		4		4	2	3	2	5	9-9	9-5		150	
5 Minneapolis....	363,454	{ 2		15	17	20	20	3	16	1-9 9-12	3-9	all day and evening	15,000	8,000
			16		16	11	23		16	1:30-5			1,529	
6 Rochester†.....	7,844	1		6	7	1	6	1	7	5	5	5	200	....
7 St. Paul.......	247,232	2	11	3	16	11	11	4	10	10-10	3:30-10	3:30-10	....	....
8 Virginia........	15,193		4		4	3	4		2	8			200	
9 Wheaton........	1,300	1			1	1	1		1	9-8	9-8		60	75
10 Winona........	18,583		3		3	4	3			....			....	
MISSOURI														
1 Joplin..........	33,216		5		5	3	1			9-12:2-9	3:30-9		200	125
2 Kansas City....	297,847	2	10		12	4	12	4	25	8-6		8-11	1,460	150
3 Lexington......	5,242		1		1	2	1		1	8			....	
4 Nevada........	7,176		1		1		1			9:30-5			50	
5 St. Charles.....	10,350		1		1		1		1	8-2			250	
										8-9:12-1; 3:30-8:30	8-9:12-1; 3:30-5:30;			
6 St. Louis.......	757,309	14	11	2	27	26	75	10	21	9-9	7:30-10:30		6,160	1,400
7 Springfield......	40,341		1		1		1			9-9			950	

of cities follow the " small community" table

Authorities Managing Playgrounds and Neighborhood Recreation Centers	Expenditures Last Fiscal Year				Sources of Financial Support of Playgrounds and Neighborhood Recreation Centers	Year First Center Was Established under Leadership	Sources of Information
	Land Buildings Permanent Equipment	Upkeep Supplies and Incidentals	Salaries	Total			
41 Park Department..........	$.........	$.........	$........	$25,069.13	Municipal..........	1901	A. E. Metzdorf
42 Playground Commission.....	1,055.00		245 00	1,300.00	Municipal..........	1911	E. J. Moriarty
43 Board of Recreation.........	110 00	709.23	2,081.50	2,900.73	Municipal..........	1903	H. H. Reinhardt
44 Playground Department......		595 48	641 00	1,236.48	Municipal..........	1912	W. W. Norcross
45 School Committee..........		400 00	600 00	1,000.00	Municipal..........	1913	Winifred Potter
46 Friendly Aid Society Village Improvement Society		100.00	400.00	500.00	Private............		
47 Playground Commission.....	200.00	300.00	300.00	800.00	Municipal..........	1908	D. M. Cole
48 West Springfield Playground Commission.............	243.25	177.74	638.76	1,059.75	Municipal..........	1912	H. A. Goodman
49 Williamstown Playground Association................	500.00		2,200 00	2,700.00	Private............	1916	Mrs. S. F. Clarke
50 Park Commission..........	2,500.00	1,335.00	425.00	4,260.00	Municipal..........	1904	G. T. Davidson
51 Department Public Works ...		92.66	268 91	361.57	Municipal..........		
52 Parks and Recreation Commission................	3,366.37	18,755.19	1,683.20	23,804.76	Municipal..........	1910	T. E. Holland
1 Board of Education.........		257.37	940.00	1,200.00	Municipal..........	1914	H. M. Slauson
2 Individuals................	500.00	100 00	660 00	1,260.00	Private............	1914	H. S. Gray
3 Recreation Commission.....	32,289.52	60,078.26	115,499.68	207,867.46	Municipal..........	1912	G. F. Ashe
4 Board of Education.........	1,142.44	2,442.35		3,584.79	Municipal..........	1915	A. N. Cody
5 Department Public Welfare...	25,000.00		9,242.93	34,242.93	} Municipal.........	1910	Eva H. Reynier
Board of Education.......		1,000.00	9,000.00	10,000.00			
6 Board of Education.........	....			225.00	Municipal and Private	1917	E. J. Engle
7 Board of Education and City		353.50	1,646.50	2,000.00	Municipal..........	1911	F. J. Steinhilber
8 Board of Education.........	200.00	325.06	15,293.64	15,818.70	Municipal..........	1907	Ethel Rockwell
9 Board of Education.........		50.00	1,800.00	1,850.00	Municipal..........	1917	W. L. Kunkel
10 Board of Education.........		25.00	2,585.54	283.54	Municipal..........		E. D. Cushman A. R. Watson
11 Board of Education.........	583.56	210.75	1,285.25	2,079.56	Municipal..........	1916	S. O. Hartwell
12 Board of Education.........	41.65	84 01	1,586.00	1,711.66	Municipal..........	1915	Orr Schurts
13 Board of Education.........			2,000.00	2,000.00	Municipal..........	1917	G. H. Rogers
14 Playground Association......		50 00	225.00	275.00	Municipal and Private	1914	F. A. DuBridge
15 Board Park Commissioners...	1,000.00	100.00	200 00	1,300 00	Municipal..........	1913	W. P. Bowen
1 Park Committee...........	....	....	150.00	....	Municipal..........	......	C. C. Baker
2 Park Board and Y. M. C. A.			600.00		Municipal..........		Peter Oleson
3 City.....................		2,300 00	4,500 00	6,800 00	} Municipal.............		
Board of Education.......		2,300 00	2,000.00	4,300.00	and Private	1916	J. R. Batchelor
4 Independent School Dist. 39..		300.00	1,883 00	2,183.00	Municipal..........	1917	A. W. Lewis
5 Board Park Commissioners..	164,120.00	59,715.00	12,503.50	226,338.50	} Municipal.........	1906	F. C. Berry
Board of Education.......	....		....	5,000.00		1910	C. H. Keene
6 Board of Education.........		500 00	5,000.00	5,500.00	Municipal..........	1916	E. B. Anderson
7 Bureau of Playgrounds.......	12,997.29	3,500.27	13,113.73	29,611.29	Municipal..........	1904	J. L. MacBean
8 Board of Education.........				1,100.00	Municipal..........	1915	P. P. Colgrove
9 Community School..........	1,000.00	700.00	1,500.00	3,200.00	Municipal..........	1916	V. E. Anderson
10 Playgrounds Association.....		95.72	775.00	870.72	Private............	1913	C. D. Tearse
1 City Park Board..........				2,300.00	Municipal..........	1913	M. H. Black
2 Park Commissioners...	3,944.82	1,336.47	17,280.00	22,561.29	Municipal..........	1909	R. R. Benedict
3 Board of Education.........	....	....	....		Municipal..........	1915	B. M. Little
4 Parent-Teachers' Association	....	....	....	125.00	Private............	1917	T. H. Barbee
5 Chamber of Commerce.......	100.00	50.00	100.00	250.00	Private............	1917	Hugh H. Mace
6 Parks and Recreation Dept.	....	....	....	30,000.00	Municipal..........	1907	R. H. Abeken
7 Park Department...........	....	....	....	18,000.00	Municipal..........	1915	Mrs. E. E. Dodd

29

Foot notes indicated by signs after the names

STATE AND CITY	Population*	Number of Centers Maintained under Paid Leadership				Number of Paid Workers Exclusive of Caretakers			Caretakers	Hours During Which Centers Are Open under Leadership'			Average Daily Attendance	
		Year-round	Summer Months	Other Seasons	Total	Men	Women	Employed year-round		Summer	Spring and Fall	Winter	Summer Months	Winter Centers
MONTANA														
1 Missoula†	18,214			9	9	7	9		9	2	2	2	....	1600
NEBRASKA														
1 Beatrice	10,287	1			1	1				3-6			40	
2 Columbus	5,014		2		2		2			9-6			50	
3 Hastings	11,021		3	1	4	1		1	1	1:30-6			35	
4 Lincoln†	46,515	4		17	17	10	13	4	10	9-11:5-8	4-5:30	7-9:15	250	75
5 Omaha	165,470		13	9	22	10	18	1		13	6	3½	4,000	
NEW HAMPSHIRE														
1 Concord	22,669	1			1	1	1		1	2-5 3 days week			75	
2 Keene	10,633	2			2	1	1			9-12:1-5			80	
3 Laconia	11,528	2			2	1	2			8½			331	
4 Lebanon	4,500	1			1	1				9-11:1-4		9-12	25	
5 Somersworth	6,704	1			1	1	1			1:30-5:30			....	
NEW JERSEY														
1 Atlantic City	57,660		9			11	16			1-5:9-7:15			1,000	
2 Bayonne	69,893	1			1	1				9-5	9-5		5,834	
			4		4	3	6			9-5			607	
		1		3	4	3	2	1	4	9-5	9-5:7-11	7-11	....	
3 Belleville	12,393	1			1	1			1	1			150	
4 Bernardsville		1			1		1			10-5			75	
5 Bloomfield	18,466	1			1	1	2		4	10-12:1-6			15	40
				1	1	1			1	2½				
6 Bridgeton	14,395	1			1	1	1		1	9-12:1-6			105	
7 Burlington	8,928	1			1		1			9-12:2-4			35	
8 Camden	106,233	1	14		15	21	23	2	1	9-5			3,509	
9 Carney's Point		2			2	2	4			9-5			295	
10 Chatham	2,207	1			1	1	1		1	9-12:2-6			140	
11 Dover	8,971	1			1	1	1			9-4:30			100	
12 East Orange	42,458			1	1	3	3		5	8-6	3-6		1,558	
			5		5	1	8		5	9-12:2-5			225	
13 Edgewater	3,150		3		3		3		3	10-12:1-5			....	
14 Elizabeth	86,690		3	7	10	15	16	1	10	10-12:2-9	2-5	7:30-10:30	2,746	274
15 Englewood	12,231	1			1	1	1			10-5			100	
16 Hoboken	77,214	4			4	6	1	5	1	....	....	9-6	....	....
17 Harrison	14,520	1			1	1				9-5	9-5		8,350	
18 Irvington	16,039	1			1	1	1	2		10-12:1-6			7,350	
19 Jersey City	306,345	9		17	17	21	20			9-5:1-5			24	....
			3		12	7	6	13	10	8-6	9-5 after school		2,493	
				1	1	1	1			9-5			5,834	
20 Kearney	23,539		2		2	1			1	10			100	
21 Madison	5,628		2		2	1	1		1	9-12:2-5			100	
22 Montclair	26,318	1			1	2	2			10-12:1-6			....	
23 Morristown	13,284	1			1	2	1	1	1	1	1		599	
24 Mt. Tabor		1			1	1				6			35	
25 Newark	408,894	11	2		13	15	15	30	12	8-6	8-6	9-5	....	200
		20		24	46	84	160	23		3½	2	3	350	
			5		5	7	11			10-12:1-6			7,156	
26 North Bergen		1			1	1				9-5			645	
27 New Brunswick	25,512	2			2	3	1			9-6			212	
28 Nutley	7,987	1			1	1	1			10-12:1-6				

of cities follow the " small community" table

Authorities Managing Playgrounds and Neighborhood Recreation Centers	Expenditures Last Fiscal Year				Sources of Financial Support of Playgrounds and Neighborhood Recreation Centers	Year First Center Was Established under Leadership	Sources of Information
	Land Buildings Permanent Equipment	Upkeep Supplies and Incidentals	Salaries	Total			
1 Board of Education..........	$.........	$1,000.00	$16,000.00	$17,000.00	Municipal............	......	J. U. Williams
1 Woman's Club.............	....	....	....	60.00	Private..............	......	Grace Liddicott
2 Board of Education.........	....	....	....	225.00	Municipal...........	1916	R. M. Campbell
3 Board of Education.........	....	....	200.00	200.00	Municipal...........	......	P. J. Stephens
4 Physical Education Ass'n....	....	450.00	8,400.00	8,450.00	Municipal...........	1912	R. E. Cowan
5 Board of Education..........	817.65	1,971.16	17,220.88	20,009.69	Municipal...........	1913	J. J. Isaacson
1 City Government...........	96.08	192.72	169.65	458.45	Municipal...........	1910	W. J. Jones
2 Municipal Committee........	....	....	....	500.00	Municipal...........	1914	N. J. Miller
3 Park Commission...........	....	200.00	375.00	575.00	Municipal and Private	1913	Mrs. A. H. Hamnian
4 Playground Association.....	....	110.79	32.00	142.79	Private.............	1917	Mary A. Poke
5 Board of Trustees..........	....	....	300 00	2,000.00	Municipal and Private	1917	Judge C. H. Wells
1 Department Parks and Public Property................		345.11	2,928.65	3,273.76	Municipal...........	1914	S. M. Bennett
2 Hudson Co. Park Com'n.....	....	....	....	....		1917	W. G. Muirheid
Board of Education........	....	829 00	1,119.00	1,048.95	} Municipal and....	1916	P. H. Smith
Department of Parks.......	....	....	....	1,000.00	} County..........	1916	D. P. Otis
3 Board of Education.........	11,000.00	....	800.00	11,800.00	Municipal...........	1915	G. R. Gerard
4 Association for Social Work..	....	....	....	....		......	Margaret Watkins
in St. Bernard's Parish....	....	....	....	††	County	1914	L. C. Wilsey
5 Essex Co. Park Commission	....	....	450.00	450.00	Municipal and Private	1912	F. E. Mohrman
Town Improvement Ass'n...							
6 Johnson Reeves Playground Association.............	....	25.00	300.00	325 00	Private.............	1911	D. C. Porter
7 Woman's Civic League.......	....	....	....	24.00	Private.............	......	Margaret Haines
8 Board Recreation Commissioners...................	2,000.00	2,500.00	4,500.00	9,000.00	Municipal...........	1908	F. A. Finkeldey
9 Y. M. C. A..............	....	1,423.64	905.20	2,328.84	Private.............	1916	J. H. Greenwood
10 Board of Education..........	....	50.00	280.00	330 00	Municipal...........	1915	Mrs. F. I. Krauss
11 South Side Home and School Association..............	125.00	25.00	100.00	250.00	Private.............	1917	W. V. Singer
12 Board Recreation Com'n'rs...	....	242.46	875.00	1,117.46	} Municipal.........	1908	L. E. Rowley
Board of Education.........	....	1,678.25	6,058.80	7,737.05	}		
13 Board of Education.........	....	....	360.00	360.00	Municipal...........	1915	W. F. Conway
14 Board Recreation Com'n'rs...	....	1,165.00	4,900.00	6,065.00	Municipal...........	1910	D. P. Otis
15 Board of Education..........	....	....	....	500.00	Municipal...........	1907	E. C. Sherman
16 Department Parks and Public Property................	800.00	2,000.00	4,000.00	6,800	} Municipal and.....	1910	Julius Durstewitz
Hudson Co. Park Commission	....	814.32	766.00	1,580.00	} County...........	1911	W. G. Muirheid
17 Hudson Co. Park Commission	93.26	883.86	519.50	1,496.88	County.............	1910	W. G. Muirheid
18 Essex Co. Park Commission	....	....	....	††	County.............	1911	L. C. Wilsey
19 Board of Education.........	....	....	....	6,000.00		......	Dr. Henry Synder
Department Parks and Public Property................	1,200.00	2,560 00	7,344.50	11,104.50	Municipal and......	1909	A. H. Moore
Hudson Co. Park Com'n.....	....	469.37	687.25	1,156.62	County.............	1906	W. G. Muirheid
20 Playground Committee.......	....	....	....	....		1910	A. J. Oliver
21 Thursday Morning Club.....	50.00	50.00	320.00	420.00	Municipal...........	......	Annabelle Miller
22 Essex Co. Park Commission.	....	....	....	††	County.............	1912	L. C. Wilsey
23 Playground Society.........	....	660.00	2,340.00	3,000.00	Private.............	1910	A. C. Fairlamb
24 Playground Association.....	....	100.00	125.00	225.00	Private.............	1911	W. C. Cudlipp
25 Recreation Commission.....	....	10,296.73	45,062.35	55,359.08	} Municipal.........	1907	V. K. Brown
Board of Education.........	....	5,000.00	14,000.00	19,000.00	} and.............	1898	R. H. Warden
Essex County Park Com'n....	....	....	....	††	} County..........	1906	L. C. Wilsey
26 Hudson County Park Commission..................	....	....	....	....	County.............	1917	W. G. Muirheid
27 City Improvement Society. ..	288.75	94.86	604.15	987.76	Municipal...........	......	Mrs. W. T. Marvin
28 Essex Co. Park Commission	....	....	....	††	County.............	1917	L. C. Wilsey

Foot notes indicated by signs after the names

STATE AND CITY	Population*	Number of Centers Maintained under Paid Leadership				Number of Paid Workers Exclusive of Caretakers			Caretakers	Hours During Which Centers Are Open under Leadership			Average Daily Attendance	
		Year-round	Summer Months	Other Seasons	Total	Men	Women	Employed year-round		Summer	Spring and Fall	Winter	Summer Months	Winter Centers
NEW JERSEY *Continued*														
29 Orange........	33,080	{1	1 4		1 5	1 4	2 6	2	2	10-12:1-6 1-7;4-9	8-sunset	8-sunset	76 1,332	231
30 Passaic........	71,744		3		3	8	5		2	9-5			1,700	
31 Paterson........	138,443			10	10	10	14	2	2	10-6 2-5	3-6	3-9:30 7-11	175 80	90 200
32 Plainfield......	23,805	{	5 5	5	5 5	1	9 8	1		9-12:2-5 4	8-15-8:45: 1	8-15-8:45:	100 450	
33 Princeton†.....	5,678		2		2	1	1		1	8-12:3-5	3:30-5:30	3:30-5:30	50	750
34 Rahway........	10,219		1		1		1			8½			175	
35 Red Bank......	8,631	2	2	2	6	3	4	1	5	9-12:3-7	3:30-5:30	3:30-5	187	50
36 Salem.........	6,953		2		2		2			5½			250	100
37 South Orange...	5,866	1			1				1	11½	10		90	
38 South River....	6,691		1		1		1		1	5			500	
39 Summit........	9,136		3		3	3	2		3	9-5:30				
40 Trenton........	111,593		13		13	13	10		8	4			3,750	
41 Westfield.......	8,147		1		1		1			9:30-4:30			727	
42 West Hoboken..	43,139		6		6		1		6	8-9			1000	
43 West New York	18,773	1			1	2	1		2	9	8 after school and Sat.	8 after school and Sat.	700	
44 West Orange....	13,550		3	1	3	4	4		2	8-6			860	
45 Woodbury......	5,288		1		1		1			9-5			35	
NEW MEXICO														
1 Albuquerque†...	14,025	1			1		1			9-5	9-5	....	400	....
NEW YORK														
1 Albany.........	104,199		5		5	5	8			1-6			1,000	
2 Amsterdam.....	37,103		7		7	8	7			4			1,400	
3 Batavia........	13,350		1		1		1			1-6			50	
4 Binghamton....	53,973		10		10	11	14			9-12:2-5			751	
5 Buffalo........	468,558	15			15	18	15	15	15	9-10	8	6	6,077	750
6 Canajoharie....	2,474		1		1		1			2-6:7-9			80	
7 Canandaigua...	7,501		1		1	1	1			....			500	
8 Cohoes.........	25,211		3		3	3	4			4			250	
9 Corning........	15,406		1		1	1		2		8-8			300	
10 East Chester....			1		1		2			9-5			65	
11 Elmira.........	38,120	1	{ 4		4	1	8 1	1	4	9-5:30			600 40	50
12 Forest Hills.....		1			1		1	1		9:30-12: 2-5:30	2:30-5:30	3-5 3 after noons	68	15
13 Fredonia........	5,328		1		1		1			1-8			....	
14 Geneva........	13,711		1		1	1				8			95	
15 Glen Cove......	5,000	1			1		2	1		9-5	....	3-5	50	25
16 Glens Falls.....	16,894		3		3	4	3			6½			90	
17 Highland Falls..	2,518		1		1		1			9-12:2-5 9-12:2-5:			82	
18 Hornell........	14,685		5	4	5	2				7-8:30			....	
19 Hudson........	12,705		1		1		3			6			125	
20 Hudson Falls...	5,585		1		1	1	1			6			136	
21 Huntington.....	5,000		1		1	1				8-6			100	
22 Ilion..........	8,900		2		2	1	3			9-11:45: 1:30-4			280	
23 Irvington-on-Hudson......	2,370		1		1		1			6			18	
24 Ithaca.........	15,848		2	1	3	2	2		1	10-12:2-5 8½	2		184	

32

of cities follow the " small community " table

Authorities Managing Playgrounds and Neighborhood Recreation Centers	Expenditures Last Fiscal Year				Sources of Financial Support of Playgrounds and Neighborhood Recreation Centers	Year First Center Was Established under Leadership	Sources of Information
	Land Buildings Permanent Equipment	Upkeep Supplies and Incidentals	Salaries	Total			
29 Essex Co. Park Commission Department Parks and Public	$.........	$.........	$.........	$......††	} Municipal and.... County.........	......	L. C. Wilsey
Property.................		2,684 59	3,644.28	6,328 87		1906	S. Fred Wright
30 Board Playground Com'n'rs...		949.25	1,479 61	2,428 86	Municipal...........	1909	Katherine Dyt
31 Board Recreation Com'n'rs...	6,000.00	2,500.00	6,500 00	15,000.00	Municipal...........	1914	J. K. Alverson
32 Public Recreation Com......	1,250.00	1,250.00	2,000.00	4,500.00	} Municipal and....	1910	Lillian Lamson
Public Recreation Com'n.....	300.00	1,700.00	1,000.00	3,000.00	} Private	......	J. F. Zerega
Playground Commission.....	....	....		1,600.00			
33 Board of Education.........		181.14	1,400.00	1,581.14	Municipal and Private	1913	Mabel Vanderbilt
34 Board of Education.........	198.92	158.70	100.00	457.62	Municipal...........	1915	G. M. Howard
35 Red Bank Recreation Association, Board of Education ..	350.00	300.00	1,800.00	2,450.00	Municipal and Private	1913	Mary E. Hannah
36 Woman's Club.............	....		180 00	184.40	Municipal and Private	1914	Ellen B. Smith, M.D.
37 Board Recreation Com'n'rs...	1,186	652.00	1,168 00	3,006.00	Municipal and Private	1913	A. E. Clough
38 Playground Committee	46.35		75.00	121.35	Municipal and Private	1917	Supt. of Schools
39 Town Improvement Ass'n....		800.00	350 00	800 00	Private.............	1909	Gertrude Gross
40 Department Parks and Public Property.................	195.00	2,853.38	4,804.48	7,852.86	Municipal...........	1911	W. F. Burk
41 Westfield Playground Com'n..	....	....	....	500 00	Municipal...........	1912	E. W. Wittke
42 Board Playground Com'n'rs.	....	....		2,925.00	Municipal...........	1917	George Goldner
43 Recreation Commission......	31,360.00	500.00	2,500 00	34,360.00	Municipal and Private	1914	R. J. Miller
44 Playground Com'n..........		1,223.38	2,594.00	3,817.38	Municipal and Private	1910	S. F. Wright
45 Woodbury Playground Ass'n..		110.00	320 00	430 00	Private.............	1916	M. G. Thomas
1 Board of Education.........		200 00	1,000 00	1,200 00	Municipal...........	1913	John Milne
1 Mothers' Club.............				1,000.00	Municipal and Private	1899	Mrs. J. D. Whish
2 Board of Education				1,800 00	Municipal.............	......	H. T. Morrow
3 Political Equality League				100.00	Private.............		Mrs. Frances Wilson
							Helen Schoenfeld
4 Board of Education.........		206.14	1,805.75	2,011.89	Municipal...........	1915	D. J. Kelly
5 Bureau of Playgrounds......		6,575.00	31,590.00	38,165 00	Municipal...........	1901	C. W. Dilcher
6 Playground Committee.......		60.00	100 00	160 00	Private.............	1916	F. E. Barbour
7 Individual	....	....		....	Private.............	[1900	L. N. Steele
8 Woman's Municipal Welfare League...................	218.00	250.00	405 00	873.00	Private and Municipal	1915	Grace Reavy
9 Board of Public Works..	1,120 00	32.00	780 00	1,932 00	Municipal...........	1917	W. O. Drake
10 Woman's Guild of the Pelhams	125.00		250.00	375.00	Private...........	1917	Mrs. A. V. Roe
11 Municipal Committee.......	60.00	320.00	620 00	1,000 00	} Municipal and..... } Private............	1908	Helen Whitehead
Elmira Federation for Social Service...................	778.36		1,000 00	1,778.36			
12 The Community Council.....			1,500 00	2,500 00	Private.............	1915	Anne R. Smith
13 Y. W. C. A..............		5.00	70 00	75 00	Private.............	1913	
14 Park Commissioners........	200.00	75 00	150.00	425.00	Municipal and Private	1917	C. M. Baldwin
15 Glen Cove Neighborhood Association.................						1914	A. L. Rowe
16 Recreation Commission......	500.00		....	1,500 00	Municipal...........	1912	Laura L. Sweet
17 Civic League..............		5.00	200.00	205.00	Pr.vate.............	1917	Martha Speakman
18 Municipal Playground Com...		53.00	447.00	500.00	Municipal...........	1908	Mrs. F. W Sherwood
29 Board of Education.........		15.00	250.00	265.00	Municipal...........	1915	C. S. Williams
20 Board of Education.........		18.53	250.00	268 53	Municipal...........	1912	Mrs. Preston Paris
Woman's Civic League							
21 Recreation and Playground Association...............	50.00	300.00	300.00	650 00	Private.............	1914	C. E. Sammis, Jr.
22 Board of Education.........				575 00	Municipal...........	1914	H. M. Schwartz
23 Board of Education.........			90.00	90.00	Municipal...........	1914	F. J. Bierce
24 Board of Education.........	8,000.00	40.00	340.50	8,380.50	Municipal...........	1916	Julius Kuhnert

33

STATE AND CITY	Population*	Number of Centers Maintained under Paid Leadership				Number of Paid Workers Exclusive of Caretakers			Caretakers	Hours During Which Centers Are Open under Leadership			Average Daily Attendance	
		Year-round	Summer Months	Other Seasons	Total	Men	Women	Employed year-round		Summer	Spring and Fall	Winter	Summer Months	Winter Centers
NEW YORK *Continued*														
26 Jamestown.....	36,580		7		7	7	10			9-12:1-5			700	
27 Kingston.......	26,771	1	9		9	3	6	1	3	12			525	
28 Lackawanna....	15,987	1			1	1	3	2	2	10-9	4-8	....	145	....
29 Little Falls.....	13,451		3			1	2			10-12:1-5			150	
30 Mamaroneck....	7,290		1		1	1	1			....			100	
31 Medina........	6,079		2		2	1	2		2	9-12:1-5			120	
32 Mount Vernon..	37,009	4		6	4	5	4	5		10-12:2-5	8:30-4	8:30-4 8-10 p. m.	1,313	2,800
					8	2	2	1						175
33 Newburgh......	27,876	4			4		5		6	10-12:2-5			....	
		3			3	3	3		1	5			300	
34 New Rochelle...	37,759	4			4	1	7			8:45-11:30 2-5			640	
										10(10-6)				
		1	10		11	6	11	2		1(9-9:30)	....	....	1,971	....
		10	34		44	30	41	22	70	10	7	6	51,000	15,000
		1			1		1	1		8-5				
			1		1		1			9-5:30			194	
35 New York......	5,602,841	15	37		52	7	32	15		9:30-5:30	3-6	3-5:30	4,000	2,500
		35	70		70					9-10	10-10	10-10		
			9	9	9	4	4		9	8-7	8-5		750	
			209	56	265	1050§§				4½		2½	97,970	24,114
36 Ogdensburg.....	16,718		1		1	1	1		1	9-5			74	
37 Oswego........	24,101		3		3	2	3		1	7			350	
										3:30-6:7-10 Sat. 9-12:1-6:7-10				
38 Philmont.......	2,060	1			1	1				Sun. 2-6			40	40
39 Plattsburg.....	12,837		1		2		1	2	2	9-5			150	
40 Poughkeepsie...	30,390		7		7	3	20			9-5			....	
41 Rensselaer......	11,177		2		2	2				7			100	
											11:45-1:15	11:45-1:15		
											3-6	3-6 Sat. 9-		
42 Rochester......	256,417	14	8	6	28	34	44	40	8	9-9	Sat. 9-6	6:7-11	5,912	3,800
43 Rome..........	23,737		3		3	2	2		1	8 till dark			600	
4 Sag Harbor.....	3,245	1			1	2	1	3	2	9-6	4-6	6:30-9	150	100
										9-12				
45 Salamanca.....	8,370		1		1		1			1:30-5			200	
46 Scarsdale.......	2,717		1		1	1				9-5			55	
47 Schenectady....	99,519	6	4	6	16	9	23	1		9-12:2-5	3-5	3:30-6 eve.	3,000	750
48 Syracuse.......	155,624		7		7	34	48		15	9-8			3,602	
49 Solvay........	5,886		2		2	1	3		2	9-5			81	
50 Suffern........	2,781		1		1		2			10-5	3-5:30		70	
51 Troy..........	77,916		5		5		8		5	1-6			2,500	
52 Tuxedo........	2,000		1		1	1	1			1-6			70	
53 Utica..........	85,692		5		5	6	10			8			400	
54 White Plains...	22,465		1		1	2	2			1:30-5:30			300	
												3:30-5:30:		
55 Yonkers........	99,838	2	4	7	13	6	8	8	3	8-9:30	3-7	7:30-10:30	1,800	825
NORTH CAROLINA														
1 Asheville.......	20,823		3	3	3	4	4		1	10-6:30	10-6:30		1,850	
2 Durham........	25,061		4		4	1	1			5			100	
3 Raleigh........	20,127	1	3		4	4	3	2	1	7	7	4	528	126
NORTH DAKOTA														
1 Fargo.........	17,389		2		2	1				10			35	
2 Grand Forks,...	15,837		1		1		1			9:30-12 1:30-5			30	

of cities follow the " small community" table

Authorities Managing Playgrounds and Neighborhood Recreation Centers	Expenditures Last Fiscal Year				Sources of Financial Support of Playgrounds and Neighborhood Recreation Centers	Year First Center Was Established under Leadership	Sources of Information
	Land Buildings Permanent Equipment	Upkeep Supplies and Incidentals	Salaries	Total			
26 Board of Education..........	$121.23	$84.39	$988.39	$1,194.01	Municipal...........	1911	R. R. Rogers
27 Board Public Works, Park Commission..............	650.00	835.00	1,015.00	2,500.00	Municipal...........	1917	A. W. Buley
28 Lackawanna Social Center....			2,280.00	2,280.00	Private.............	1901	Alice P. Vanston
29 Little Falls Playground Association.................		20.37	177.00	197.37	Private.............	1915	H. A. Mills
30 Village Improvement Ass'n. ..		20.00	125.00	145.00	Private.............	1911	Mrs. F. E. Bellows
31 Board of Education..........				160.00	Municipal...........	1915	P. R. Merriman
32 Board of Education..........		300.00	5,000.00	5,300.00	} Municipal.........	1909	Lillian Lamson
Public Recreation Com'n.....	450.00	1,300.00	1,500.00	3,250.00			
Joint Auspices.............				8,650.00			
33 Recreation Commission......	700.00	236.00	590.00	‡‡1,526.00	Municipal...........	1917	Mrs. Pierre Northrip
34 Board of Education..........				750.32	Municipal...........	1914	Albert Leonard
35 Brooklyn Com. Parks and Playgrounds..............							Lillian W. Betts
Dept. Parks, Brooklyn.......	17,612.00	4,000.00	31,555.00	53,167.00			J. J. Downing
Park Dept. Borough Queens..		139.28	1,165.38	1,304.66			
National Highways Protective Association...........					Municial and Private...........	1908	E. S. Cornell
Parks and Playgrounds Ass'n..	216.24	2,666.83	11,174.50	14,369.95			
Bureau of Recreation of Department of Parks.........			79,841.00				W. J. Lee
Dept. of Parks, Bronx.......	4,158.99	11,151.89	6,066.58	21,377.44		1914	A. J. Waldreaon
Board of Education..........			94,118.66				E. O. Gibney
36 City and Y. M. C. A.........	125.00	10.00	100.00	235.00	Municipal and Private	1917	R. K. Hanson
37 Commissioner of Works......	15.00	647.70	542.00	1,204.76	Municipal...........	1911	C. W. Linsley
38 Crusaders Hall..............		600.00	700.00	1,300.00	Private.............	1911	Clara Harder
39 Woman's Civic League.......					Private.............	1914	Bertha Mendelsohn
40 Board of Education..........				2,500.00	Municipal...........	1909	S. R. Shear
41 Suffrage Club...............				360.00	Private.............	1916	Catherine Smith
42 Bureau of Playgrounds and Recreation.................	6,785.54	23,450.55	52,763.91	,000.00	Municipal...........	1903	Robert Bernhat
43 Board Public Works.........		1,000.00	1,600.00	,600.00	Municipal...........	1910	L. M. Kircher
44 Mashashimuet Park and Social Center................	500.00	3,500.00	4,500.00	8?,500.00	Private.............	1911	R. K. Atkinson
45 Commission of Education. ...	200.00	100.00	150.00	450.00	Municipal...........		A. W. Fortune
46 Village Board...............			200.00	400.00	Municipal and Private	1917	
47 Board of Education..........		2,000.00	5,000.00	7,000.00	Municipal...........	1908	Mary G. Mason
48 Department of Parks.........		633.00	10,459.00	11,093.00	Municipal...........	1908	T. F. Keane
49 Board of Education..........			388.80	388.80	Municipal and Private	1915	Anna Murtagh
50 Playground Association......						1916	Mrs. C. A. Pace
51 Department Public Works....	5,000.00	500.00	2,500.00	8,000.00	Municipal...........	1906	Sara Holbrook
52 Playground Association......	100.00	170.00	330.00	600.00	Private..	1914	Constance Irvine
53 Park Board.................	400.00	300.00	2,400.00	3,300.00	Municipal and Private		E. M. Swiggett
54 Board of Education..........		600.36	527.00	1,127.36	Municipal and Private	1911	Mrs. H. P. Griffin
55 Playground and Recreation Commission...............	3,000.00	1,000.00	23,000.00	27,000.00	Municipal...........	1910	E. G. Kingsbury
1 Department Public Safety....	1,850.06	1,050.53	1,987.67	4,888.26	Municipal...........	1916	D. H. Ramsey
2 Board of Education.........			300.00	300.00	Municipal...........	1917	Chamber Commerce
3 Raleigh Recreation Com'n....	300.00	200.00	3,100.00	3,600.00	Municipal and Private	1914	R. R. Miller
1 Board of Education.........		50.00	150.00	200.00	Municipal...........	1917	Arthur Deamer
2 Civic League...............	75.00	50.00		125.00	Private.............	1917	May Sanders, M.D.

Foot notes indicated by signs after the names

STATE AND CITY	Population*	Number of Centers Maintained under Paid Leadership				Number of Paid Workers Exclusive of Caretakers			Caretakers	Hours During Which Centers Are Open under Leadership			Average Daily Attendance	
		Year-round	Summer Months	Other Seasons	Total	Men	Women	Employed year-round		Summer	Spring and Fall	Winter	Summer Months	Winter Centers
OHIO														
1 Akron.........	85,625		6		6	5	9			8:30-5:30			2,310	
2 Athens.........	5,463		1		1	1			1	9-5	3-5		200	
3 Bellaire.........	14,348		3		3	2	4			1-9			180	
4 Bellefontaine ...	9,237		1		1		1			8-11			35	
5 Cambridge.....	13,483			1	1		1			8:15-11:30	all day	all day		300
6 Canton.......	60,852		9		9	2	7			1:15-5:15			912	
7 Cincinnati.....	410,476	{ 3		7	10	12	14		10	9-8:30			7,500	
		17			17	17	33		17	12	5		4,958	
8 Cleveland.....	674,073	{ 1			1	3	7	10	6	7½	4	all day and evening	758	429
		20			20	20	20		20	8½			2,954	
9 Columbus.....	214,878		20	2	22	24	21	4		9-5		9-10	125	100
		{ 2	15	9	24	20	20	6	1	9-5;9-10	3-5	1-10	207	651
		{ 2	9		9	6	8	4	3	6-10	....	8-9	2,538	200
10 Dayton.......	127,224		12		12	1	11			6			953	
11 Galion........	7,214		1	1	1	1	1		1	5am-7pm			50	
12 Gallipolis†.....	5,560	2			2	2	1	2	3	9-11:2-5	3-5	3-5:7-9	....	....
13 Hamilton.......	40,496		1	1	2	1		1		9-5	2-5	2-9	125	90
14 Kenton........	7,185		1		1		1						25	
15 Lebanon.....	2,698	1	1		2	3		3	1	9-12 / 2-7:30	9-12- / 2:7:30		250	350
16 Lorain........	36,964		1		1		1			8-11:2-5			200	
17 Marion........	23,430		1		1		2			8-6			150	
18 Martins Ferry , .	9,996	1			1	1	1		1	9-7:30: / 9-11:30	9-7:30 / 9-11:30	9-11:30	200	
19 Middletown	15,625	1			1		1	1		2-5	3:30-5	3:30-5	90	45
20 Nelsonville....	6,082		1		1	1				9-6			140	
21 Newark.......	29,635		3		3	3	3		3	8-7 / 9-12			700	
22 Niles..........	8,921		4		4	1	5		4	6-8:30	M		227	
23 Oberlin........	4,365		3		3	1	3			7			60	
24 Portsmouth.....	28,741		4		4	2			4	8			400	
25 Sidney........	6,607		1		1	1	1		1	9-5			300	
26 Springfield.....	51,550		11		11	5	7			1:30-5:30			1,002	
27 Toledo........	191,554		4		4	4	4		8				1,500	
28 Wooster.......	6,136	1			1	1				3	3	3	65	120
29 Warren†........	13,059	9			9			9	12	8-8		8-8	2,250	2,250
				12	14	12	10	1	7	9	8-8	3	1,744	200
30 Youngstown....	108,385	{ 14			14	15	14	1	7	9		3	832	150
		2			2	2	2	1	2	10				
		1			1	1	2	1	1	6				
OKLAHOMA														
1 Lawton........	7,788	1			1	1				9-12:2-5 / 7-10	9-12:2-5 / 7-10	9-12:2-5 / 7-10	....	....
2 Oklahoma City .	92,943		17		17	7	19	1	17	8:30-8:30			2,812	
3 Pawhuska.....	2,776		3		3		1			9-11:4-7			60	
4 Tulsa†........	30,575	16			16	2	3			4-9			500	
OREGON														
1 Ashland........	5,020		1		1		1			1-7			35	
2 Portland.......	295,463	2	14		16	17	17	5	20	10		8	3,000	125
PENNSYLVANIA														
1 Allentown......	63,505	{ 4			4	6	4	3	3	9-12 / 1-5:6-8	....	....	....	}
		{ 3	9		9	9	9	6	2	9-12 / 1-5:6-9	....	7 30-10	....	}
2 Altoona.......	58,659		9		9	9	8	1		8:30-9			2,250	
3 Bath..........	1,057		1	1	1	1				5			150	
4 Beaver Falls....	13,532		1	1	1	1			1	7-8	8-6		100	

of cities follow the "small community" table

Authorities Managing Playgrounds and Neighborhood Recreation Centers	Expenditures Last Fiscal Year				Sources of Financial Support of Playgrounds and Neighborhood Recreation Centers	Year First Center Was Established under Leadership	Sources of Information
	Land Buildings Permanent Equipment	Upkeep Supplies and Incidentals	Salaries	Total			
1 Children's Playground Com...	$	$900.00	$2,100.00	$3,000.00	Municipal and Private	1912	V. L. Stevens
2 Board of Education.........	250.00	100.00	200.00	550.00	Municipal and Private	1915	G. F. Morgan
3 Americus Club.............	650 00		600	1,250.00	Municipal and Private	1912	Blanche Kleber
4 Women's City FederationClubs			50-7 00		Private.............	1916	R. J. Kiefer
5 Park Commission............		800.00	1,280.00	2 080.00	Municipal...............		W. E. Arter
6 Park and Playground Ass'n.		566.88	,851.	2,418.78	Municipal and Private		Mrs. A. E. Sprentall
7 Park Board...............		2,050.00	1,150 00	8,200.00	} Municipal.........	1910	Carl Ziegler
Board of Education..........		2,000.00	18,000.00	20,000.00		1907	
8 Hiram House..............		11,627.32	18,173.	29,800	{ Municipal.........		G. A. Bellamy
Board of Education..........		58.47	7,287.	7,346	{ and Private........	1900	E. A. Peterson M.D.
Division of Recreation.......	40,000.00	4,000.00	11,500.	55,500			J. F. Potts
9 Division of Public recreation..	43,071.63	5,496.70	10,320.	58,888	Municipal and Private	1908	Grace English
10 City Dept. of Welfare........		1,100.00	7,500.	8,600	} Municipal.........	1910	H. N. Sollenberger
Playgrounds and Gardens Ass'n		1,000.00	1,500.	2,500	} and Private........		
11 Board of Education..........		100.00	46.00	565.32	Municipal and Private	1915	J. J. Phillips
12 Board of Education..........		500.00	2,700.00	3 200.00	Municipal and Private	1915	O. B. Clifton
Academy Board of Trustees							
13 Federated Charities	1,500.00	200.00	600.00	2,300.00	Private.............	1917	L. J. Gossard
14 Playground Association........			120.00		Private.............	1916	Mrs. W. S. Robinson
15 Civic Trust of Lebanon......			3,500.00	4,675.00	Private.............	1914	R. P. Williams
16 National Tube Company.....		100.00	400.00	500.00	Private.............	1910	
17 Community Club...........	300.00		300.00	600.00	Private.............		H. A. Hartman
18 Playgrounds Association.....		350.00	300.00	650.00	Private.............	1915	G. G. Ralston
19 American Rolling Mill......					Private.............	1917	Margaret Johnson
20 Y. M. C. A.............		56.00	90.00	146.00	Private.............	1916	W. L. Hudson
21 Board of Education.........		500 00	900.00	1,400.00	Municipal.........	1913	Wilson Hawkins
22 Board of Education.........		15.70	286.50	302.20	Private.............	1915	W. C. Campbell
23 Recreation League of Oberlin Federation...............		25.00	400.00	425.00	Municipal and Private	1916	H. A. Miller
24 Bureau Community Service	300.00	50.00	2,265.00	2,615.00	Private.............	1910	M. H. F. Kinsey
25 Board of Education.	500.00	100.00	150.00	750.00	Municipal.........		H. R. McVay
26 Playground Association......	650.00	200.00	600.00	1,450.00	Munic pal and Private	1909	Donald Kirkpatrick
27 Park Board................				33,000.00	Mun cipal.........		S. C. Black
28 Board of Education.........		150.00	1,100.00	1,250.00	Municipal.........		G. C. Maurer
29 Board of Education.........	1,400.00	200.00			Municipal.........		H. B .Turner
30 Playground Association......	200.00	300.00	3,200 00	3,700.00			
Park Board................		900 00	1,600.00	3,500 00	{ Municipa'		
Carneigie Steel Co...........	350.00	2,000.00	600.00	2,950 00	{ and Private........	1905	J. H. Chase
Christ Mission.............		100.00	375.00	475.00			
1 Local Committee...........			360.00	360.00	Private	1915	H. A. Carroll
2 Board of Education..........	9,000.00	300.00	5,275.00	14,575.00	Municipal.........	1917	I. N. Richer
3 Women's Clubs.............			100.00	100.00	Private.........	1916	W. M. Sinclair
4 Board of Education..........			325.00	325.00	Municipal.........	1917	E. E. Oberholtzer
1 City....................	1,000.00	50.00	150.00	1,250.00	Municipal.........	1916	G. A. Briscoe
2 Bureau of Parks.............	12,000.00	18,000.00	9,000.00	39,000.00	Municipal.........	1909	Stella W. Durham
1 Municipal Committee........	350.00	2,500.00	750.00	2,600.00	} Municipal.........	1911	R. J. Schmoyer
Board of Education.........	150.00	500.00	1,045.00	1,695.00			
2 Ward Playground Ass'n......	1,500.00	600.00	2,850.00	4,950.00	Municipal and Private	1916	S. H. Layton
3 Men's Community Bible Class	10.00	100.00	125.00	235.00	Private.............	1916	W. F. Helfrich
4 School Board..............	500.00	500.00	300.00	1,300.00	Municipal.........	1914	C. C. Green

Foot notes indicated by signs after the names

STATE AND CITY	Population*	Number of Centers Maintained under Paid Leadership				Number of Paid Workers Exclusive of Caretakers			Caretakers	Hours During Which Centers Are Open under Leadership			Average Daily Attendance	
		Year-round	Summer Months	Other Seasons	Total	Men	Women	Employed year-round		Summer	Spring and Fall	Winter	Summer Months	Winter Centers
PENNSYLVANIA *Continued*														
5 Bethlehem......	14,142	3			3		4			9-5			210	
6 Braddock.......	21,685	2			2		11		1	9-12			1,000	
7 Bradford.......	14,544	1			1	1				9-5			100	
8 Bristol........	10,608	2			2		4		2	3			100	
9 Butler.........	27,632	2			2	2	2			10-12:2-5			30	
10 Carlisle.......	10,726	2			2		4		1	5			220	
11 Catasauqua.....	5,250	1			1	1	1			10			....	
12 Chester.......	41,396	9			9		21		10	6			1,034	
13 Clairton........	3,326	2			2		1		2	7½			325	
14 Clearfield......	6,851	1			1		1			1-5			50	
15 Coatesville....	14,455	4	4		4	4	6	2	1	9-9	5		300	150
16 Conshohocken ..	7,480	1			1	1	1		1	9-5			140	
17 Danville........	7,517	1			1		1			8-5			65	
18 Duquesne.......	19,964	3			3	4	3			9-9			4,399	
19 Easton.........	30,530	3			3	6	6		2	14	14		800	
20 East Pittsburgh	5,615	2			2		3		2				300	
21 Ellwood........	3,902	1			1	1	2		1	12			711	
22 Erie..........	75,195	6	6		12		6	1	5	9-5		7:30-9:30	182	550
23 Farrell........										9-12				
24 Greensburg....	15,483	2			2	1	5			1:15-5			606	
		4			4	1	6			....			250	
25 Hamburg.......	2,301	1			1		2		1	8			150	
26 Harrisburg.....	72,015	13			13	12	21		12	8			3,343	
27 Hazleton.......	28,491	1			1	1	1			9-6			500	
28 Hollidaysburg ..	3,734	1			1	1	1		1	9-12 4-9:30			....	
29 Johnstown......	68,529	14			14	2	16			9-12:3-8			1,902	
30 Lancaster......	50,853	3			3	4	3			6½			600	
31 Lebanon.......	20,779	1			1	1	1		1	10	8		800	
		1			1		3			9-8			500	
32 Lock Haven....	7,772	1			1	1	1			9-11:30 1:30-5			93	
33 Mahanoy.......	17,463	1			1	1	2		1	5			150	
34 McKeesport....	47,521	5			5	4	2		1	8-9			....	
35 McKees Rock ..	19,949	1			1		1			9-5			80	
36 Meadville......	13,802	2			2	2	2			1-8			400	
37 Millersburg.....	2,394	1			1		1			9-12:1-5			60	
38 Milton.........	7,460			1	1	1			1			Friday 7:30-10		65
39 Monessen.......	21,630	3			3	3				8:30-11:30 2-5			500	
40 Munhall and Homestead...	22,466	1	1		2	6	2	5	2	10-8	4-10	4-10	1,973	150
41 Nanticoke......	23,126	1			1		1			9-4			125	
42 North Braddock	15,148	3			3		8		3	9-12			975	
43 Northampton...	8,729	1			1		1			10			75	
44 Oil City.......	19,297	2			2		4			6			150	
45 Philadelphia....	1,709,518	{ 21 13	136 17		157 35	92 31	167 33	21 64	156 40	7 13	2 hrs.-5 da's 7 hrs. Sat. 9	1½-5 days 7 Sat. 9	12,300 14,413	1,665 8,669
46 Phoenixville....	11,714	1			1	1	1		1	9-5			350	
47 Pittsburgh.....	579,090	7	29		36	58	135	56	29	8:45-9:30	2:45-9:30	2 :45-9:30	30,000	4,000
48 Pittsburgh North Side		15	28		43	22	122	18	3	....			....	
49 Pittston........	18,599	4			4	1	4	1	1	9-8	4-dark		400	
50 Pottstown......	16,794	3			3	3				4½			193	

of cities follow the " small community " table

Authorities Managing Playgrounds and Neighborhood Recreation Centers	Expenditures Last Fiscal Year				Sources of Financial Support of Playgrounds and Neighborhood Recreation Centers	Year First Center Was Established under Leadership	Sources of Information
	Land Buildings Permanent Equipment	Upkeep Supplies and Incidentals	Salaries	Total			
5 Bethlehem School District....	$........	$........	$320.00	$320 00	Municipal........	1913	H. F. Judd
6 Board of Education..........		98.13	450.00	548.13	Municipal........	1910	F. C. Steltz
7 Board of Education......... and Board of Commerce	300.00	50.00	108 00	458.00	Municipal........	1917	E. S. Weber
8 Bristol Playground Ass'n.....		40.00	280.00	320.00	Private...........	1912	Mary Swain
9 Woman's Club..............			290.00		Municipal & Private	1912	Mrs. W. H. Mac-Naughton
10 Civic Club................		189.67	240.00	429.67	Municipal & Private	1909	Mary Bosler
11 Park and Playground Ass'n.	5,600.00	9,535.00	260.00	5,915.35	Private...........	1916	S. S. Stillman
12 Playgrounds Association.....	250.84	285.58	1,966.25	2,502.67	Municipal & Private	....	Mrs. H. C. Cochrane
13 Carnegie Steel Co..........		453.39	587.75	1,041.14	Private...........	1913	H. J. Davis
14 Woman's Club.............			60.00		Private...........	1915	Anna Gingery
15 Committees on Parks and Recreation....	63,811.00	382.85	2,318.72	66,512.51	Municipal........	1915	F. D. Eichbauer
16 Playground Association.....		20 00	320.00	340.00	Private...........	1914	Miss D. B. Jones
17 Civic Club...............	9.36	6.00	50.00	65.36	Private...........	1915	Mrs. E. S. Gearhart
18 Carnegie Steel Co..........					Private...........	1912	C. W. Nethaway
19 City Commission..........				3,000.00	Municipal........	1917	H. A. Bruce
20 Public Schools.............	340.00	50.00	380.00	770.00	Municipal........	1915	H. L. Koons
21 National Tube Co..........	861.17	1,150.45	612.58	2,624.20	Private...........	1914	Margaret Alexander
22 Board of Education..........		324.00	720.00	1,044.00	Municipal........	....	D. G. Evans
23 Playground Association.....		164.31	715.00	879.31	Municipal & Private	1914	Anne Townsend
24 Greensburg Playgrounds.... and Civic Association		112.25	1,260.50	1,645.08	Municipal & Private	1912	Mrs. F. W. Frazier
25 Town League..............	50.00		160.00	210.00	Private...........	1912	C. F. Freeman
26 Department Parks and Public Property................	2,420.95	2,834.99	5,255.94		Municipal........	1908	V. G. Forrer
27 Playground Association.....	400.00	100.00	250.00	750.00	Private...........	1912	E. R. Smaltz
28 Joint Committee of Y. W. C. A.... and Chamber of Commerce		134.83		210.00	Municipal & Private	1917	Mrs.Isaiah Scheeline
29 Board of Education.........	257.03	605.18	3,065.77	3,927.98	Municipal........	1914	C. H. Meyer
30 Playground Association.....				700.00	Municipal........	1909	W. F. Carey
31 Lebanon Athletic and Playground Association........	125.00	37.00	550.00	712.00	Municipal........	1915	A. C. Hersh
Southeastern Playground Ass'n	2,000.00	350.00	300.00	2,650.00	and Private......	1917	L. W. Richards
32 Civic Club................		60.70	175.63	236.33	Municipal........	1911	Mrs. Charles Dunn
33 Sunday School Athletic Ass'n					Private...........	....	
34 Department Parks and Public Property................				1,285.06	Municipal........	....	Conrad Hohman
35 Board of Education.........	650.00	150.00	30.00	830.00	Municipal........	1917	T. K. Johnston
36 Meadville Playground Ass'n.	120.00	80.00	500.00	700.00	Municipal & Private	1908	Elisabeth Garver
37 Civic Club.'...............	600.00	20.00	105.00	725.00	Private...........	1916	Mrs. J. H. Beachler
38 Civic Club, D. A. R., Guild, School Board...........		26.16	42.00	6,416.00	Private...........	1915	C. L. Millward
39 School Board..............		50.00	450.00		Municipal........	1913	H. E. Gress
40 Welfare Department of Homestead Steel Works of Carnegie Steel Co...........		1,311.00	2,335.00	3,646.00	Private...........	1913	L. C. Gardner
41 Board of Education........			200.00	600.00	Municipal........	....	A. P. Diffendafer
42 Board of Education.........					Municipal........	....	Isabel White
43 Northampton Pl'g'd Ass'n....	1,300.00	75.00	120 00	1,495.00	Private...........	1917	H. T. Bilheimer
44 Parent-Teachers' Ass'n......	115.54	22.25	525.96	663.75	Private...........	1915	Mrs. Anna Mount
45 Board Public Education..... Board of Recreation.........	1,093,291.80	43,952.28	121,187.43	57,017.81 1,258,431 51	} Municipal.......	1894	W. A. Stecher W. D. Champlin
46 Playground Association.....			140.00	140.00	Private...........	1912	Mrs. L. A. Lambert
47 Bureau of Recreation.......	3,938.03	66,781.50	52,360.00	123,079.53		1896	Agnes Ferguson, MD
48 Playground and Vacation.... School Ass'n. of Alleghany				32,553.18	Municipal and... Private........	1898	Mrs. John Cowley
49 Department Parks and Public Property................	600.00	90.00	1,030.00	1,720.00	Municipal........	1915	O. M. Wintermute
50 Century Club..............		121.21	100.00	221.21	Private...........	....	Mrs. Leonard Leaf

Foot notes indicated by signs after the names

STATE AND CITY	Population*	Year-round	Summer Months	Other Seasons	Total	Men	Women	Employed year-round	Caretakers	Summer	Spring and Fall	Winter	Summer Months	Winter Centers
PENNSYLVANIA *Continued*														
51 Pottsville.......	22,372		1		1	1	1			6½			260	
52 Reading........	109,381		12		12	14	21		5	9-9			4,111	
53 Rochester......	5,903		1		1	1			3	8			300	
54 St. Clair........	6,455		2		2		2			1:30-4:30 5:30-8			100	
55 St. Marys......	6,346		1		1	1	1		1	7½ 9:30-6			350	
56 Scranton......	146,811	1	11	3	15	16	23	6	16	10-10	10-10	7:30-9:30; 10-10	2,588	458
57 Shillington......	1,427		1		1				1	9-5			50	
58 Somerset.......	2,612		1		1		1		1	9-4			75	
59 Steelton........	15,548		6		6	2	5		2	9-11:30:2- 5:30:6:30-8			1,538	
60 Tarentum......	7,414		2		2		4		2				....	
61 Tidioute........	1,324		1		1		2			9-11:2-4			30	
62 Uniontown.....	20,780		3		3	3	3			9-12:2-4			365	
63 Washington....	21,618		5		5		9			9-12:2-4			500	
64 West Chester...	13,176		1		1	3				8			425	
65 Wilkinsburg....	23,228		5		5	2	9			9-8			400	
66 Williamsport...	33,809		3		3	2	3		2	9-12			600	
67 Wilmerding....	6,133		2		2	3	2			9-5:30			149	
68 Windber.......	8,013		1		1	1	1		1	8-6			150	
69 Wyomissing....	8,013		2		2	2	1			8:30-7:30			175	
RHODE ISLAND														
1 Cumberland....	10,848		1		1	1			1	8:30-5			75	
2 Lonsdale........	4,000		1		1		2			2-5			125	
3 Newport.......	30,108		11	2	13	6	14	1	3	6	3 weekly	3	1,048	200
4 Pawtucket.....	59,411		5		5	5	3	2		9-5			....	
5 Providence.....	254,960	7	16	4	27	51	83	14	7	12 9-11:30	5	4	10,016	5,106
6 Westerly.......	9,422		1		1	1	1			1-5:30			371	
	{		2	1	3	1	1		1	4½			300	
7 Woonsocket....	44,360 {			1	1		2		1			3:30-6 6:30-8		104
SOUTH CAROLINA														
1 Columbia.......	34,611	6			6	3	7	10	1	6½	4	3	1,000	2,000
SOUTH DAKOTA														
1 Aberdeen†......	15,218	7			7	1	1	1	7	4 a week 9-12:2-5	recess and after school	recess and after school	....	....
2 Brookings......	3,416		1		1	1	1						30	
TENNESSEE														
1 Memphis.......	148,995	5	3	4	12	4	12	10		5	2½ 9-6	2	1,388	58
2 Nashville.......	117,057	2	12		14	3	13		1	9-9		9-6	2,500	150
TEXAS														
1 Dallas........	124,527	2	9		11	5	5	10	4	3-10	3-9	3-9	1,000	275
2 El Paso........	63,705		9	9	2	12						8:30-4	5,000	5,000
3 Fort Worth.....	104,562	10			10	10	10	10		3-6	3-6	3-5:30	1,807	7,607
4 Galveston......	41,863	1	1		1		1	1	1	2-9	2-9	2-9	....	650
UTAH														
1 Provo.........	10,645		1	1	2	1				12-6			300	
2 Salt Lake City..	117,399		7		7	6	14		4	10-9			1,500	

of cities follow the " small community" table

Authorities Managing Playgrounds and Neighborhood Recreation Centers	Expenditures Last Fiscal Year				Sources of Financial Support of Playgrounds and Neighborhood Recreation Centers	Year First Center Was Established under Leadership	Sources of Information
	Land Buildings Permanent Equipment	Upkeep Supplies and Incidentals	Salaries	Total			
51 Y. M. C. A.	$	$ 92.00	$176.00	$268 00	Private	1914	J. F. Murray
52 Reading Playground	2,300.00	1,500.00	4,000.00	7,800.00	Municipal	1903	A. A. Harwick
53 School District		300.00	600.00	900.00	Municipal	1913	W. S. Taft
54 Playground Association		50.00	240.00	290.00	Private	1916	Rev. E. G. Faust
55 Village Improvement Ass'n			375.00		Private	1915	Mrs. A. S. Grosh
56 Bureau of Recreation	1,077.50	3,075.06	9,787.11	13,939.67	Municipal	1907	J. A. Mott
57 Playground Com		10.00	70.00	80.00	Private	1916	H. J. Yeager
58 Board of Education		75.00	175.00	350.00	Municipal	1912	J. H. Fike
59 Parks and Playgrounds Com.	322.98	246.74	975.42	1,545.14	Municipal and Private	1916	C. S. Davis
60 Civic Committee	75.00	20.00	105.00	200.00	Municipal and Private	1910	A. D. Endsley
61 Committee of Children's Outdoor Gymnasium	23.00	17.38	33.12	75.50	Private	1916	Martha Jennings
62 Public Playground Ass'n		133.10	170.45	303.55	Municipal	1914	Mrs. A. C. Hagan
63 Playground Association		200.00	500.00	700.00	Municipal	1909	Nanne Young
64 Westchester Playground Ass'n	30.00	209.47	1,231.03	1,470.50	Municipal		Jane Baker, M.D.
65 Wilkinsburg Playground Ass'n		374.00	1,150.00	1,524.00	Private	1917	W. D. McCoy
66 City Committee					Municipal	1909	
67 Y. M. C. A.		410.00	790.00	1,200.00	Municipal and Private	1914	C.E. Kennedy,M.D.
68 Windber Playground Ass'n	100.00	100.00	400 00	600.00	Private	1915	W. W. Lantz
69 Playground Association	470.43	364.66	615.91	1,451.00	Private	1910	H. M. Fry
1 Valley Falls Playground Ass'n			100	100.00	Municipal	1917	J. V. Broderick
2 Garden and Playground Ass'n		25.00	160.	185.00	Private	1911	Mrs. E. C. Mowry
3 Board Recreation Com'n'rs	400.00	3,110.00	3,800.	7,300.00	Municipal	1911	H. F. Cooke
4 Committee of City Council		200.00	1,500.00	1,700.00	Municipal	1911	C. P. Hall
5 Board of Recreation	22,640.16	2,804.70	11,725.66	37,170.71	Municipal	1906	J. J. McCaffrey
6 City Committee		75.00	300.	375.00	Municipal	1913	W. H. Bacon
7 O. M. S. C. and Manville Co.	58.43	250.00	207 00	316.60	} Municipal and.....	1914	Grace Pond
Playroom			540.00	540.00	} Private		Estella Phetteplace
1 Playground Department				2,000.00	Municipal	1913	Adele J. Minahan
1 Board of Education	200.00		2,084.00	2,284.00	Municipal	1912	Frances Brown
2 Board of Education				200.00	Municipal	1917	Rev. Paul Roberts
1 Recreation Commission		874.50	5,125.50	6,000.00	Municipal	1914	C. D. Johnston
2 Park Commission	3,000.00	800.00	3,135.00	6,935.00	Municipal	1910	L. J. Loventhal
1 Park Board	2,500.00				Municipal	1909	Mrs. M. A. Kesner
2 Board of Education		250.00	11,500.00	11,750.00	Municipal and Private	1916	R. R. Jones
3 Park Department	1,000.00	1,518.75	5,419.55	7,938.30	Municipal	1916	Ella Forbess
4 Playground Association					Private	1917	Mildred Dyer
1 City Commissioners			200.00	200.00	Municipal	1916	L. E. Eggertson
2 Department Parks and Public Property	2,000.00	2,350.00	5,100 00	9,350.00	Municipal	1909	Charlotte Stewart

41

Foot notes indicated by signs after the names

STATE AND CITY	Population *	Number of Centers Maintained under Paid Leadership				Number of Paid Workers Exclusive of Caretakers			Caretakers	Hours During Which Centers Are Open under Leadership			Average Daily Attendance	
		Year-round	Summer Months	Other Seasons	Total	Men	Women	Employed year-round		Summer	Spring and Fall	Winter	Summer Months	Winter Centers
VERMONT														
1 Bellows Falls...	4,883		1		1	1			1	8			100	
2 Bennington.....	9,114	1			1		2	2	1	5	....	6	88	48
3 Brattleboro.....	6,517		4		4	4				9-11:30 2:30-5			30	
4 St. Albans......	6,381	1	1		2	1	3	2	1	8:30-12	day and evening	day and evening	98	125
5 Woodstock.....	1,383		1		1	1				9-12			37	
VIRGINIA														
1 Alexandria......	17,846		1		1	1				2 9-12			100	
2 Lynchburg.....	32.940	1	3	1	5	4	5	3	2	2-7:30	3-6	3-5:30	800	50
3 Norfolk........	89,612		7		7	6	10			3:30-6:30			....	
4 Richmond......	156,687		8		8	8	10		3	8	8		4,000	
WASHINGTON														
1 Everett........	35,486		1	1	1	1	1	1		10-9	3-dark		150	
2 Seattle........	348,639	4	5		9	4	6	8	20	8	....	2-10	4,000	1,200
3 Spokane.......	150,323	2	6		8	10	7	2	8	12	....	6	4,000	....
4 Walla Walla....	25,136		2		2		2			10-6;2-8	1-6		184	
WEST VIRGINIA														
1 Bluefield.......	15,442		1	1	1	1			1	10-6 9-12:5:30-			100	
2 Fairmont.......	15,506		2		2	1	2			8:30			150	
3 Huntington.....	45,629		1		1	1	1			8			130	
4 Martinsburg....	12,666		2		2		2		2	(1)7(1)8			137	
5 McMechen.....			1		1	1				1-8			60	
6 Moundsville....	11,153		3		3	1				....			278	
7 Parkersburg....	20,612		4		4	3	3			7			275	
8 Wheeling.......	43,377		3		3	6	6		1	1:30-dark			1,000	
WISCONSIN														
1 Janesville......	14,339		4		4	2	4			12			762	
2 Kenosha.......	31,476		5	3	8	9	21	1	3	5		3	700	440
3 La Crosse......	31,677		3		3	4	4			1-9			965	
4 Madison.......	30,699		2		2	6	5		5	1-8			900	
5 Milwaukee.....	436,535	1	14	7	22	183	140	5	22	9-9:30	....	4-10;7-10	6,418	3,721
6 Oshkosh.......	36,065	5	8	5	13	13	15	5		9-9	....	7:30-9:30	1,923	395
7 Racine.........	46,486	1	10	3	14	9	36	2	3	9	....	3-6	1,123	217
8 Richland Center	2,652		1		1		2			2hrs a. m. 8:30-12			40	
9 Superior........	46,226	10			10	6	5	11	10	1:30-4:30	9-12; 1-5:30	7-30-:930	1,000	2,000
CANADA														
British Columbia														
1 Vancouver......	100,401		1		1	1			1	3-9			400	
Manitoba														
1 Winnipeg.......	225,000		24	18	42	37	41	3	22	8	3	3	7,603	1,035
Nova Scotia														
1 Truro..........	6,107		2		2		1			9-12:2-5			65	
Ontario														
1 Fort William....	16,499		6		6	6	6			....			1,972	
2 Ottawa........	87,062		8		8	9	9			9			2,400	
3 Peterborough...	18,360		2		2	2	2		2	9-5:30			375	
4 Toronto........	376,538	{ 11		11	11	46	54	14	16	9-10	9-10	9:30-10	3,813	3,196
		{ 17			17				17	9-12:2-5			3,275	
Quebec														
1 Montreal.......	470,480	8	1	1	10	22	10	22	12	12	8	12	5,000	5,000
HAWAIIAN ISLANDS		{ 5			5	9	9			4	4	4	....	....
1 Honolulu.......	52,183	{ 1			1	1	1			7	4	4	....	....
		{ 1			1	2	2			7	4	4	....	....
		{ 1			1	1	1			4	4	4	....	....

of cities follow the " small community". table

Authorities Managing Playgrounds and Neighborhood Recreation Centers	Expenditures Last Fiscal Year				Sources of Financial Support of Playgrounds and Neighborhood Recreation Centers	Year First Center Was Established under Leadership	Sources of Information
	Land Buildings Permanent Equipment	Upkeep Supplies and Incidentals	Salaries	Total			
1 Park Department............	$50.00	$150.00	$150.00	$350.00	Municipal...........	.....	Edward Kirkland
2 Public Welfare Association ...		1,836.00	1,202.00	3,043.00	Municipal and Private	1910	Mathilde J. Vossler
3 Parent-Teacher's Association .	10.92	16.50	336.00	363.42	Municipal and Private	1916	Mrs. N H. Arnold
4 Stranahan Memorial Club and Institute.................	....	....	....	....	Private.............	1912	Mrs. W. P. Jackson
5 Woodstock Improvement Society.....................			48.00	48.00	Private.............	1911	Rachel French
1 Parent-Teachers' Ass'n.......	....	....	....	....	Municipal and Private	1914	Mrs. T. C. Howard
2 Playground and Recreation Association...........		675.00	4,050 00	4,725.00	Municipal and Private	1913	C. R. Warthen
3 Playground Committee......		1,941.61	1,824.35	3,765.96	Municipal...........	1913	Mrs.H.C.Whitehead
4 City of Richmond..........	....	....	....	8,000.00	Municipal...........	1909	L. McK. Judkins
1 Board of Education.........		229.60	590.00	819.60	Municipal...........	1912	C. G. Sheldon
2 Park Department..........	3,544.96	358.00	94.41	39,439.37	Municipal...........	1911	F. L. Fuller
3 Board Park Commissioners...	....	....	....	13,000.00	Municipal...........	1913	Mrs. B. A. Clark
4 Park and Civic Arts Club....		72.00	428.00	500.00	Municipal and Private	1914	Rachel Drum
1 Playground Association......	1,200.00	25.00	175.00	1,400.00	Municipal and Private	1915	H. S. Mabie
2 Woman's Club.............	117.56	123.84	325.70	567.10	Municipal and Private	1913	Mrs. J. C. Meredith
3 Huntington Woman's Club...		58.55	375.00	433.55	Private.............	1916	Mrs. S. H. Bowman
4 Good Neighbors' Society...	125.00	28.94	150.00	313.94	Private.............	1912	W. C. Morton
5 Playground Association......	260.00	10.00	79.00	349.00	Private.............	1916	Mrs. J. D. Nearple
6 Municipal Committee.......	150.00		230.00	380.00	Private.............	1917	Marion Hendershot
7 Playground Association......	500.00	500.00	600.00	1,650.00	Private.............	1917	Ada B. Weyer
8 Playground Association......	300.00	900.00	2,000.00	3,200.00	Private.............	1909	Mrs. C. R. Hubbard
1 Board of Education.........		50.00	800.00	850.00	Municipal...........	1913	
2 Board of Education.........		989.75	2,124.65	3,114.40	Municipal and Private	1914	Mrs. M. D. Bradford
3 Board of Education.........		263.83	890.00	1,158.88	Municipal and Private	1913	B. E. McCormack
4 Board of Education.........		100.00	1,610.00	1,710.00	Municipal...........	1906	G. A. Crispin
5 Board of Education.........		9,084.00	52,261.00	61,345.00	Municipal...........	1912	H. O. Berg
6 Board of Education.........	713.25	1,612.70	3,194.05	5,520.00	Municipal...........	1909	A. S. Hotchkiss
7 Board Park Commissioners...	3,090.00	4,580.00	6,235.00	13,905.00	Municipal...........	1911	C. E. Brewer
8 Women's Federation........	....	....	20.00	40.00	Private.............	1917	J. P. Ballantyne
9 Board of Education.........		500.00	3,000.00	3,500.00	Municipal...........	1912	J. G. Moore
1 Board Park Commissioners...		908.00	150.00	1,008.00	Municipal...........	1912	W. S. Rawlings
1 Playground Commission......	7,118.00	850.00	10,947.00	18,915.00	Municipal...........	1908	A. R. Morrison
1 Woman's Local Council.....		140.00	60.00	200.00	Private.............	1913	Mrs. Bessie Kent
1 Playground Commission......	340.81	712.38	1,946.81	3,000.00	Municipal...........	1914	A. McNaughton
2 Playgrounds Association......	1,900.00	600.00	3,200.00	5,700.00	Municipal...........	1912	J. C. Spence
3 P aygrounds Association......	150.00	150.00	500.00	800.00	Municipal and Private	1915	Mrs. F. C. Neal
4 Parks Department..........		11,444.00	28,530.00	39,974.00 }	Municipal........	1909	S. H. Armstrong
Board of Education..........		637.75	4,887.25	5,525.00 }			
1 Parks and Playgrounds Dept.		1,000.00	18,978.00	19,978.00	Municipal...........	1903	J. P. Gadbois
1 Free Kindergartens and Children's Aid Association.....		250.00	3,529.00	3,779.00	} Municipal...........	1911	Frances Lawrence
Palama Settlement..........	....	....	....	....	} and Private......		
Kauluwela Mission..........			480.00	480.00			
Kalihi Settlement...........	....	....	....	....			

43

Foot notes indicated by signs after the names

STATE AND CITY	Population*	Number of Centers Maintained under Paid Leadership — Year-round	Summer Months	Other Seasons	Total	Number of Paid Workers Exclusive of Caretakers — Men	Women	Employed year-round	Caretakers	Hours During Which Centers Are Open under Leadership — Summer	Spring and Fall	Winter	Average Daily Attendance — Summer Months	Winter Centers
ARKANSAS														
1 Crossett.......	2,038		1		1	1				7-10			300	
CALIFORNIA														
1 Modesto.......	4,034		1		1					9-5				
2 Oroville........		1			1	2	2	1	1	1	1	1	30	30
CONNECTICUT														
1 Windsor Locks..	3,500		1		1		1		1	10-9			125	
DELAWARE														
1 Henry Clay.....	1,000	1			1	2	3	2	1	4	5	5	40	175
FLORIDA														
1 Daytona.......	3,082		1		1		1			3½			30	
ILLINOIS														
1 Lake Forest....	3,349	3	2		5	3	2	1	3	10-12:2-5; 6-9;2-6; 7-10			300	
2 Rochelle........	2,732		1		1		2			9-12;2-5			50	
3 Winnetka......	3,168	2	3		5	3	3	3	7	....	....	....	....	....
INDIANA														
1 Danville.......	1,640		1		1		1			2:30-6			18	
IOWA														
Rock Rapids	2,031		1		1		1		1	1-5			30	
KANSAS														
1 Ashland........			1		1	1			1	9-4			100	
2 Fredonia.......	3,473			2	2		2				8	8		600
3 Hays..........	2,339		1		1	1				7-9	7-9		150	
4 Yates Center†..	2,199	1			1	1		1		2:30-5:30	School hrs.	School hrs.	125	
MASSACHUSETTS														
1 Dalton.........	3,858		1		1	2	1			9-5			....	
2 Manchester.....	2,945		1		1	1	1		1	9-5			175	
3 Williamstown...	3,981	1			1	1			1	....	....	....	....
MICHIGAN														
1 Harbor Beach...	1,556		1		1	1	1			....			....	
MINNESOTA														
1 Wheaton.......	1,300	1			1	1	1		1	9-8	9-8		60	75
NEW HAMP-SHIRE														
1 Lebanon.......	4,500		1		1		1			9-11:1-4			25	
NEW JERSEY														
1 Bernardsville...			1		1		1			10-5			75	
2 Carney's Point..			2		2	2	4			9-5			295	
3 Chatham.......	2,207		1		1	1	1		1	9-12:2-6			140	
4 Edgewater......	3,150		3		3		3		3	10-12:1-5			....	
5 Mt. Tabor......			1		1		1			6			35	
6 North Bergen...			1		1	1				9-5			645	

44

of cities follow the " small community " table

Authorities Managing Playgrounds and Neighborhood Recreation Centers	Expenditures Last Fiscal Year				Sources of Financial Support of Playgrounds and Neighborhood Recreation Centers	Year First Center Was Established under Leadership	Sources of Information
	Land Buildings Permanent Equipment	Upkeep Supplies and Incidentals	Salaries	Total			
1 Y. M. C. A.................	$.........	$.........	$.........	$.........	Private...............	......	C. H. Winston
1 Woman's Improvement Club	....	....	....		Private...............		Mrs. Wm. Folger
2 Y. M. C. A................	3,000.00	200.00	1,800.00	4,000.00	Private.............	1916	F. M. Duckles
1 Playground Commission......		252.65	100.00	352.65	Municipal and Privat	e 1914	Mrs. J. DeF. Phelps
1 Hagley Community House ...		2,836.71	3,484.50	6,321.21	Private..............	1913	Clara B. Bubb
1 Parent-Teachers' Association			125.00	....	Private.............	1916	Edythe Bainter
1 Park Board.................	4,269.86	139.91	1,243.90	5,653.67	Municipal...........	1915	L. W. Thompson
2 Women's Club..............		25.00	50.00	....			
3 Recreation Committee.......		13,308.64	9,525.00	22,833.64	Municipal and Private	1910	H. P. Clarke
1 Parent-Teachers' Association	....	....	....	75.00	Private.............	1917	Ethel Peyton
1 City Park Commission.......	600.00	285.00		670 00	Municipal and Private	1917	A. G. Miller
1 Parent-Teachers' Association	....	....	....	125.00	Municipal and Private	1916	L. E. Fitts
2 Board of Education..........	1,000.00	100.00	1,200.00	2,300.00	Municipal...........	1911	A. I. Decker
3 Playground Commission......	75.00	25.00	100.00	200.00	Municipal...........	1915	C. A. Shively
4 Board of Education..........		380.00	720.00	1,100.00	Municipal...........	1914	A. D. Catlin
1 Com. on Comunity Recreation	1,374.99	180.45	714 81	2,270.25	Municipal and Private	1916	E. V. Ambler
2 School Department	200.00	260.00	640 00	1,100.00	Municipal...........	1909	J. C. Mackin
3 Williamstown Playground Association...............	500.00		2,200.00	2,200.00	Private.............	1916	Mrs. S. F. Clarke
1 Board of Education..........	....	....	....	225.00	Municipal and Private	1917	E. J. Engle
1 Community School..........	1,000.00	700.00	1,500.00	3,200.00	Municipal...........	1916	V. E. Anderson
1 Playground Association......		110.79	32.00	142.79	Private.............	1917	Mary A. Poke
1 Association for Social Work in St. Bernard's Parish.....	....						Margaret Watkins
2 Y. M. C. A.................		1,423.64	905.20	2,328.84	Private.............	1916	J. H. Greenwood
3 Board of Education..........		50.00	280.00	330.00	Municipal...........	1915	Mrs. F. L. Krauss
4 Board of Education..........			360.00	360.00	Municipal...........	1915	W. F. Conway
5 P ayground Association......		100.00	125.00	225.00	Private.............	1911	W. C. Cudlipp
6 Hudson Co. Park Com......	....	....	....	....	County.............	1917	W. J. Muirheid

Foot notes indicated by signs after the names

| STATE AND CITY | Population* | Number of Centers Maintained under Paid Leadership | | | | Number of Paid Workers Exclusive of Caretakers | | | Caretakers | Hours During Which Centers Are Open under Leadership | | | Average Daily Attendance | |
		Year-round	Summer Months	Other Seasons	Total	Men	Women	Employed year-round		Summer	Spring and Fall	Winter	Summer Months	Winter Centers
NEW YORK														
1 Canajoharie....	2,474	1		1			1			2-6:7-9			80	
2 Dolgeville......	3,326													
3 East Chester....			1				2			9-5 9:30-12			65	
4 Forest Hills.....		1			1	1		1		2-5:30	2:30-5:30	3-5 3 afternoons	68	15
5 Highland Falls..	2,518		1		1		1			9-12:2-5			82	
6 Irvington-on-Hudson......	2,370	1			1		1			10-12:2-5 3:30-6			18	
7 Philmont.......	2,060	1			1	1				7-10; all day Sat; 2-6 Sun.			40	40
8 Sag Harbor.....	3,245	1			1	2	1	3	2	9-6	4-6	6:30-9	150	100
9 Scarsdale.......	2,717		1		1	1				9-5			55	
10 Suffern........	2,781		1		1		2			10-5	3-5:30		70	
11 Tuxedo........	2,000		1		1	1	1			1-6			70	
OHIO														
1 Lebanon.......	2,698	1	1		2	3		3	1	9-12 2-7:30	9-12 2-7:30		250	350
2 Oberlin.........	4,365		3		3	1	3			7			60	
OKLAHOMA														
1 Pawhuska......	2,776		3		3		1			9-11;4-7			60	
PENNSYLVANIA														
1 Bath..........	1,057	1	1		1		1			5			150	
2 Clairton........	3,326	2			2		1		2	7½			325	
3 Ellwood........	3,902	1			1	1	2		1	12 9-12			711	
4 Farrell.........	....	2			2	1	5			1:15-5			606	
5 Hamburg.......	2,301	1			1		2		1	8 9-12			150	
6 Hollidaysburg	3,734	1			1	1	1		1	4-9:30			....	
7 Millersburg.....	2,394	1			1		1			9-12;1-5			60	
8 Shillington.....	1,427	1			1				1	9-5			50	
9 Somerset.......	2,612	1			1		1		1	9-4			75	
10 Tidioute........	1,324	1			1		2			9-11;2-4			30	
11 Wyomissing....			2		2	2	1			8:30-7:30			175	
RHODE ISLAND														
1 Lonsdale.......	4,000	1			1		2			2-5			125	
SOUTH DAKOTA														
1 Brookings......	3,416	1			1		1			9-12;2-5			30	
VERMONT														
1 Bellows Falls ...	4,883	1			1		1		1	8			100	
2 Woodstock.....	1,383	1			1		1			9-12			37	
WEST VIRGINIA														
1 McMechen.....	2,921	1			1		1			1-8			60	
WISCONSIN														
1 Richland Center	2,652	1			1		2			2 hr. a. m.			40	

* The statistics on population for cities of 8,000 inhabitants and over have been taken from the estimated population April 1, 1916 of the Census Bureau. For the remaining cities the statistics published in Hammond's Handy Atlas 1917 have been used.

† The report sent by this city indicates that the year-round centers or workers reported upon are under the jurisdiction of the Board of Education. Although in some instances playgrounds were conducted during the summer months under paid leadership, the centers open during the school year refer in the majority of cases to organized playground work in connection with the school program.

‡ In addition to the centers reported a summer camp was maintained at a cost of $10,734.69.

§ In addition to these centers a summer camp was opened in 1917.

‖ School buildings are opened in 70 districts for citizens' meetings.

of cities follow the "small community" table

Authorities Managing Playgrounds and Neighborhood Recreation Centers	Land Buildings Permanent Equipment	Upkeep Supplies and Incidentals	Salaries	Total	Sources of Financial Support of Playgrounds and Neighborhood Recreation Centers	Year First Center Was Established under Leadership	Sources of Information
1 Playground Committee.......	$........	$60.00	$100.00	$160.00	Private............	1916	F. E. Barbour
2							
3 Women's Guild of the Pelhams	$125.00			250.00	375.00 Private............	1917	Mrs. A. V. Roe
4 The Community Council.....	....	....	1,500.00	2,500.00	Private............	1915	Anne R. Smith
5 Civic League...............		5.00	200.00	205.00	Private............	1917	Martha Speakman
6 Board of Education.........			90.00	90.00	Municipal..........	1914	F. J. Bierce
7 Crusaders' Hall............		600.00	700.00	1,300.00	Private............	1911	Clara Harder
8 Mashashimuet Park........	500.00	3,500.00	4,500.00	8,500.00	Private............	1911	R. K. Atkinson
9 Village Board.............	....	....	200.00	400.00	Municipal and Private	1917	
10 Playground Association.....	....	....	....	....		1916	Mrs. C. A. Pace
11 Playground Association......	100.00	170.00	330.00	600.00	Private............	1914	Constance Irvine
1 Civic Trust of Lebanon......	....	....	3,500.00	4,675.00	Private............	1914	R. P. Williams
2 Recreation League of Oberlin Federation................		25 00	400.00	425.00	Municipal and Private	1916	H. A. Miller
1 Women's Clubs.............			100.00	100.00	Private............	1916	W. M. Sinclair
1 Men's Community Bible Class	10 00	100.00	125.00	235.00	Private............	1916	W. F. Helffrich
2 Carnegie Steel Co...........		453.39	587.75	1,041.14	Private............	1913	H. J. Davis
3 National Tube Co...........	861.17	1,150.45	612.58	2,624.20	Private............	1914	Margaret Alexander
4 Playground Association......		164.31	715.00	879.31	Municipal and Private	1914	Anne Townsend
5 Town League...............	50.00		160.00	210 00	Private............	1912	C. F. Freeman
6 Joint Com. of Y. W. C. A. and Chamber of Commerce.....		134.83	....	210.00	Municipal and Private	1917	Mrs. Isaiah Scheeline
7 Civic Club.................	600.00	20.00	105.00	725.00	Private............	1916	Mrs. J. H. Beachler
8 Playground Committee.......		10.00	70.00	80.00	Private............	1916	H. J. Yeager
9 Board of Education.........		75.00	175.00	350.00	Municipal..........	1912	J. H. Fike
10 Com. of Children's Outdoor Gymnasium...............	23.00	17.38	33.12	75.50	Private............	1916	Martha Jennings
11 Playground Association......	470.43	364.66	615.91	1,451.00	Private............	1910	H. M. Fry
1 Garden and Playground Ass'n.		25.00	160.00	185.00	Private............	1911	Mrs. E. C. Mowry
1 Board of Education.........	....	....	....	200.00	Municipal..........	1917	Rev. Paul Roberts
1 Park Department...........	50.00	150.00	150.00	350.00	Municipal..........	......	Edward Kirkland
2 Woodstock Improvement Society....................			48.00	48.00	Private............	1911	Rachel French
1 Playground Association......	260.00	10.00	79.00	349.00	Private............	1916	Mrs. J. D. Marple
1 Women's Federation........	....	....	20.00	40.00	Private............	1917	J. P. Ballantyne

¶ The creation of a Recreation and Playground Commission by vote of the Board of Aldermen has put the recreation work of the city on a permanent basis.
** A $50,000 community house is being erected.
†† The total expenditures of the Essex County Park Commission for the playgrounds maintained by it in this and other communities is approximately $22,015.
‡‡ $35,000 will be made available by the city for a recreation park and year-round work will be inaugurated.
§§ Of this number 34 workers were employed at the 15 summer, and 148 at the 56 winter recreation centers maintained by the Board of Education.

Please mention THE PLAYGROUND when writing to advertisers

Petrus Liljedahl, to whom THE PLAYGROUND is indebted for these pictures of homemade apparatus in use on the Lincoln School playgrounds at St. Cloud, Minn., sends the following description:

"Number one is a giant stride made by placing a hind wheel of a wagon on top of an Idaho cedar pole in the same way in which you would put a wheel on a wagon. Arms on top of the wheel, held in place by two clevises, project two feet beyond the rim. An eye bolt is put through the arm about three inches from the end, from which the ropes are dropped to within three feet of the ground. This way of making a giant stride keeps the children far apart, the ropes seldom get tangled and it gives the children a much better swing.

"Number two is a Japanese walking pole. The four braces and the pole were cut right back of the school in an oak forest. The pole is suspended by eye bolts and chains. No child to my knowledge has yet been able to walk the length of the pole without falling off.

"Number three is a 'flying Dutchman' or merry-go-round. The center post is cased in and a circular track, which is nothing more than the rim of a wheel, is placed so as to be about a quarter of an inch above the floor. Under the board and directly above the track on either side are two rollers which make the board whirl easily. The board is three inches thick and can carry as many as can climb on. The beauty about this 'flying Dutchman' is that the board cannot tip and if properly oiled will spin very easily. It is very popular."

St. Cloud, Minnesota   JAPANESE WALKING POLE
(See description, page 150)

St. Cloud, Minnesota   FLYING DUTCHMAN
(See description, page 150)

Orange, New Jersey

TENNIS COURTS MUCH USED BY BUSINESS MEN

Orange, New Jersey

THE SAME COURTS IN WINTER BECOME A POPULAR
SKATING RINK

Maypole Dance with the Victrola, Community Day,
State Normal School, Florence, Alabama.

Do you know that
The Victrola and Victor Records

furnish the best music for plays, festivals and pageants for May Day, Field Day and all closing exercises, indoor and outdoor?

Are you giving an outdoor fete? Use the Victrola. There are records for 100 Games and Dances.

Are you planning an Eighth Grade or High School Commencement? Teach your songs with the Victrola, saving time and securing correct singing. Let the Victrola furnish your incidental music with orchestra, band, violin, cello, harp, etc.

Are you giving Shakespeare's "A Midsummer-Night's Dream"? If so, use the exquisite music of Mendelssohn. The following selections are not only used in giving the play, but are also freely interpreted by the younger children in mimetic play:

35625
12 in.$1.25 — A Midsummer-Night's Dream
—Overture   Victor Concert Orchestra

55060
12 in.$1.50 — Song (from Act II)—"You Spotted Snakes"
Victor Women's Chorus

74560
12 in.$1.50 — Scherzo (Play of the Elves) (After Act I)
Philadelphia Symphony Orchestra

31159
12 in.$1.00 — Wedding March (After Act IV)
Pryor's Band

35527
12 in.$1.25 — Intermezzo (After Act II) (Hermia Loses Her Way, and the Hard Men Enter)   Victor Concert Orchestra
Nocturne (After Act III) (The four Athenians are put to sleep by the magic flower of Puck)   Victor Concert Orchestra

The following Folk Dances and Singing Games, played by Victor Band, are useful at this season of the year:

17087
10 in.
75c — Maypole Dance (Bluff King Hal)
Minuet ("Don Juan")

18010
10 in.
75c — Sellenger's Round (Old English)   [English]
Gathering Peascods (Old

17761
10 in.
75c — Come, Let Us Be Joyful (2)Kulldansen No. 2
Seven Pretty Girls (2)The First of May

18356
10 in.
75c — Old Zip Coon (American Country Dance)
Lady of the Lake (American Country Dance)

Suggest to your outgoing class that they choose as their memorial to the school a Victrola XXV. No other gift can furnish so much real pleasure and useful service.

Have you received your copy of the New 1918 Edition of the Graded List? If not, see your Victor dealer, or drop a post-card to the

Educational Department
Victor Talking Machine Co.
Camden, N. J.

Victrola XXV, $75
specially manufactured
for School use

When the Victrola is not in use, the horn can be placed under the instrument safe and secure from danger, and the cabinet can be locked to protect it from dust and promiscuous use by irresponsible people.

Victrola

"HIS MASTER'S VOICE"

To insure Victor quality, always look for the famous trademark, "His Master's Voice." It is on all genuine products of the Victor Talking Machine Company.

"Let the home influence follow him wherever he goes" is the slogan under which the War Camp Community Service has been established, and which it is trying to carry out by providing for the comfort, welfare and proper welcome and entertainment of the American soldier and sailor when "on leave" in cities and towns near their training camps and stations

LEAVING CAMP SOMEWHERE IN AMERICA

When the officers and men of the American Army and Navy leave their camps and stations and "go to town," they find good clubs, clean entertainment, wholesome recreation and home hospitality open to them through the work being done by the War Camp Community Service. Prominent Army Officers have commended this work highly, and declare that it will do much to add to the morale and the efficiency of the American fighting men

SOLDIERS DANCING VIRGINIA REEL.

Richmond, Virginia, War Camp Community Service

This scene in the Christian Church of Richmond, Virginia, shows a group of soldiers from Camp Lee enjoying the good old-fashioned Virginia Reel. Dancing under proper supervision and in proper surroundings is being encouraged in every city and town near camp centers, so that the men of the American Army and Navy may have plenty of good places to go instead of being dependent upon questionable attractions. In speaking of the work being done by the War Camp Community Service, Secretary of the Navy Daniels says: "We realize that you cannot place thousands of young men in rough camps on the outskirts of strange cities, you cannot neglect them or treat then as social inferiors without the danger of causing them to yield to the temptations which the hospitality of vice and dissipation invites."

Richmond, Virginia, War Camp Community Service

Secretary Baker has said that whenever a soldier is on leave he will "go to town" even if that town is only a cross-roads. In this picture are shown a group of "the boys" from Camp Lee, near Richmond. In order that they may have plenty of good places to go——clubs, entertainments, rest rooms, churches and homes——the War Camp Community Service is organizing the social forces in all camp cities for the benefit of the men.

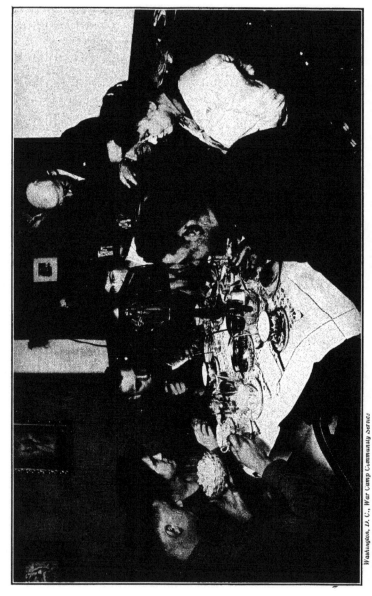

Washington, D. C., War Camp Community Service

"Welcome the Soldiers." In each camp city the War Camp Community Service tries to help keep the American soldiers "fit to fight" by providing for their comfort, welfare and proper recreation when they are on leave in cities and towns near their camp centers. Of this work President Wilson says: "The spirit with which our soldiers leave America, and their efficiency on the battle fronts of Europe, will be vitally affected by the character of the environment surrounding our military camps." This picture shows soldiers from New York, Brooklyn, Boston and Springfield, Mass., as honored guests in a Washington home

Washington, D. C., War Camp Community Service

This group of soldiers, who have just arrived in Washington, are using the balustrade in front of the Union Station as a writing table on which to send messages to their friends and acquaintances. One of the things which the War Camp Community Service has been formed to do is to provide all sorts of comfort and facilities for the men at the training camps when they visit town. It is providing clubs and furnishing many kinds of wholesome recreation as well as home welcome and hospitality for the men

Des Moines, Iowa, War Camp Community Service

Soldiers from Camp Dodge entertaining their friends and relatives in the beautiful parlor for ladies at their Club, under the chaperonage of responsible ladies of Des Moines. Furniture for the parlor was donated by Des Moines firms.

Montgomery, Alabama, War Camp Community Service

This building is used to help visitors, who come to Montgomery, Ala., near which Camp Sheridan is located, to find accomodations and to furnish them with any other information which they may require. This is part of the work being done by the War Camp Community Service in all camp cities in looking out not only for the comfort and welfare of the men when they are "on leave" in town, but also of their visiting relatives and friends.

Washington, D. C., War Camp Community Service

Soldiers, sailors and marines from the camps and stations in and around Washington are frequently entertained at the club quarters provided by the W. C. T. U. This is one phase of the War Camp Community Service which is lining up the good club, fraternal, church and home forces of every city and town near camp centers to provide wholesome recreation and home hospitality for the men of the American Army and Navy when they are "on leave" in town,

Des Moines, Iowa, War Camp Community Service

The War Camp Community Service maintains offices in the Old Federal Building for the convenience of the soldiers and their visitors. An information bureau conducted by the official hostess of the War Board, has listed all available rooms for light housekeeping, rooms for transients, apartments and houses. On an average forty families; and wives of officers and enlisted men are placed in permanent locations every week. The number of soldiers who are sent to good homes in Des Moines when off duty is too numerous to keep track of

San Antonio, Texas, War Camp Community Service

Small section of swimming beach for soldiers at Brackenridge Park at San Antonio. The San Antonio River runs through the park and has been deepened and widened for a half mile to furnish accomodations for 10,000 men at one time.

Washington, D. C., War Camp Community Service

WAR-CAMP COMMUNITY-RECREATION SERVICE

The Church of the Covenant, Washington, D. C., has been among the most active in the National Capital in providing social services for the men of the American Army and Navy stationed at the various camps near Washington. Secretary of State Lansing is a member of this church, which is only a few doors away from his home. The War Camp Community Service has been encouraging and urging churches everywhere to make the men in uniform "at home," and the churches have been responding very cordially to this patriotic duty.

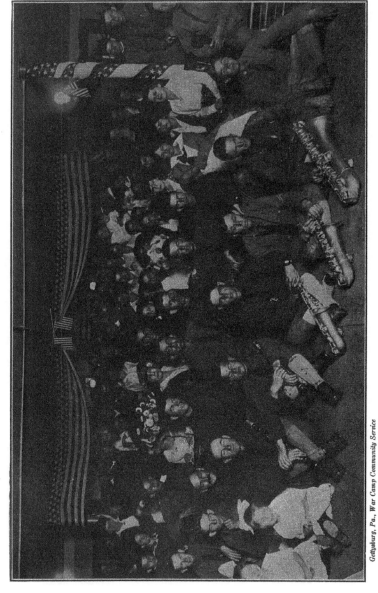

Gettysburg, Pa., War Camp Community Service

One of the ways in which the War Camp Community Service is working to benefit the men of the American Army and Navy is; by getting all the churches in cities and towns near camp centers and naval stations to open their doors to the men in uniform, and make them feel "at home." This picture shows a church entertainment at Gettysburg, Pa.

San Francisco, California, War Camp Community Service

The lunch counter doesn't have to wait until pay day to have a rush on its commodities. All kinds of goodies, sandwiches, soft drinks, ice cream, smokes, picture post cards, and a host of things the men want are sold at minimum prices. The most popular part of the luxuries the lunch counter offers perhaps are the women. The men often enter into conversation with them, telling of their homes, and all they have left behind. This club is always open, from 10 a. m. to 11 p. m.

67

San Francisco, California, War Camp Community Service

This for the quiet studious man. It is a separate reading and writing room, with hundreds of books and magazines. No, NOT *old* magazines, all the latest come in regularly. No matter what the buzz is in the big room, all is serene in here. Couches are being added to this so a man can take a nap any time he feels like it.

Des Moines, Iowa, War Camp Community Service

The Shrine Temple was turned over to the Des Moines War Camp Community Service, completely renovated, shower baths installed, and fully equipped for a soldiers' club, at an expense of $2000.00. It is free to all men in uniform and is maintained at an expense of $10,000 a year by the citizens of Des Moines. The salaries of a paid secretary and employes amount to $315.00 a month. The management of the club is in the hands of a house committee composed of soldiers. Brig. General Getty has interested himself in it and is a frequent caller. On the opening night five hundred soldiers mingled with the best citizens of Des Moines. Some features of this club are a large ball room, reception hall, ladies' parlors, writing room, dining room, kitchen, pool and billiard rooms and shower baths.

POOL ROOM—ARMY CLUB, DES MOINES, IOWA

Des Moines, Iowa, War Camp Community Service.

LEISURE HOURS SPENT IN THEIR OWN CLUB POOL ROOM

San Francisco, California, War Camp Community Service

So said a soldier, speaking of San Francisco's Palace Hotel Club for enlisted men. "Every man in his humor," is exemplified here. Some of the men are dancing, two are playing the piano, some are solving erudite problems in picture puzzles, and all invariably land up at the lemonade table. Attractive ladies, fine company, luxurious accomodations, these are offered every week day, from 6:30 to 11 p. m., Sundays, all day. They never come here without coming back the next day. The dancing room is on the mezzanine floor, and overlooks the beautiful Palm Court of the hotel.

71

TIP TOP SOLDIERS' CLUB, SAN ANTONIO

San Antonio, Texas, War Camp Community Service

TIP TOP SOLDIERS CLUB

Atlanta, Georgia, War Camp Community Service

Hundreds of soldiers enjoy the Valentine Party at the Second Baptist Church. This is one of many churches giving Saturday night socials for the men in uniform.

ONE OF SIX POOL TABLES AT THE JEWISH PROGRESSIVE CLUB

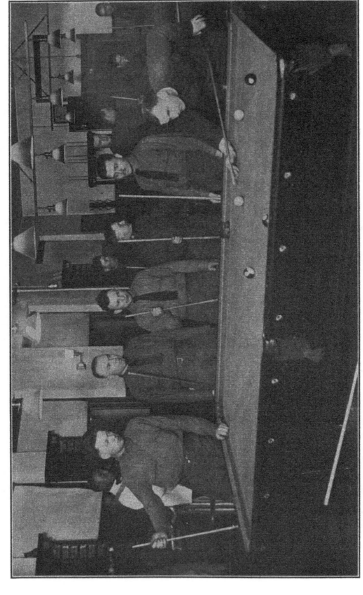

Atlanta, Georgia, War Camp Community Service

Enjoyed by Jewish soldiers free of charge Saturdays and Sundays. Hundreds of soldiers are using this club.

LUNCH AT THE CLUB

Atlanta, Georgia War Camp Community Service

Members of the Community Committee enjoy the lunch as well as the soldiers.

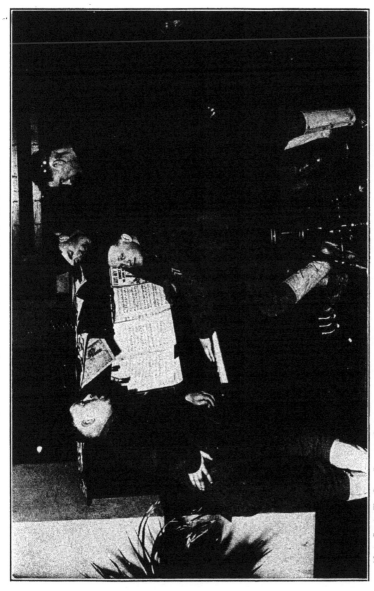

Atlanta, Georgia, War Camp Community Service
Rotary throughout America has done much for the Army. The Rotary Soldiers' Club is the big central club for soldiers. It occupies one-quarter of a block. Thousands of soldiers pass through its doors Saturdays and Sundays.

SATURDAY NIGHT AT THE ITALIAN SOLDIERS' CLUB

Atlanta, Georgia, War Camp Community Service

This Club has been opened by local Italian citizens with the help of the Atlanta War Camp Community Service. A Creek Soldiers' Club is also to be opened.

Montgomery, Alabama, War Camp Community Service

Information Bureau and Rest Room for Women Relatives and Friends visiting Camp Sheridan

Quantico, Virginia, War Camp Community Service

The entertainment provided by the War Camp Community Service is so popular that even the rafters are in use

Charleston, S. C., War Camp Community Service

A POST GYMNASIUM WHERE THE WAR CAMP COMMUNITY SERVICE FURNISHES ENTERTAINMENT WEEKLY

Montgomery, Alabama, War Camp Community Service

MEN ENJOYING ENTERTAINMENT FURNISHED THROUGH THE WAR CAMP COMMUNITY SERVICE IN THEIR OWN TENT CLUB

War-Camp Community Recreation Service

Atlanta, Georgia, War Camp Community Service.
Soldiers and Citizens mingle in Happy, Healthy Contact watching a "Tech-Vandy" Football Game. To men in uniform only half price was charged for admission. Conscious that American Communities are behind them the American soldiers will fight with true American spirit

SOLDIERS SELLING LIBERTY BONDS

Richmond, Virginia, War Camp Community Service.

In return for what the soldiers are doing for their Country, the War Camp Community Service aims to make them as comfortable and happy as possible whenever they are on leave from their camps in cities and towns nearby

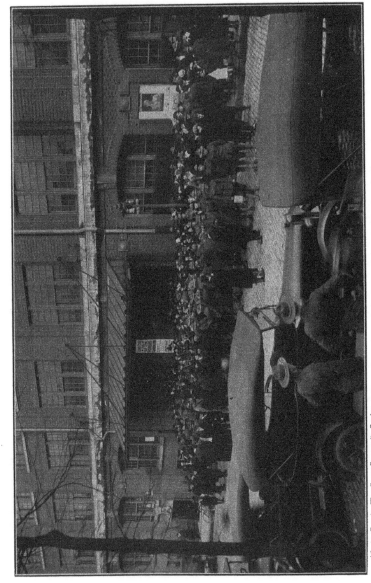

Atlanta, Georgia, War Camp Community Service

PART OF THE CROWD UNABLE TO ENTER CITY AUDITORIUM, WEEKLY SUNDAY AFTERNOON
ENTERTAINMENT

SIGN NEAR MAIN ENTRANCE, CAMP GORDON—FORTY FEET LONG

85

ONE OF MANY   PARTIES IN MILITARY PARK

San Antonio, Texas, War Camp Community Service

San Antonio, Texas, War Camp Community Service

SING SONG AT TRAVIS MILITARY PARK

Des Moines, Iowa, War Camp Community Service
BALL ROOM FOR THE ARMY CLUB. MANY MOTHERS ARE PRESENT

Atlanta, Georgia, War Camp Community Service
TWO HUNDRED BEDS—CLEAN SHEETS, PILLOW SLIPS, SHOWERS—FIFTY CENTS PER NIGHT

War Camp Community Service
EVEN SMALL COMMUNITIES ARE EAGER TO SHOW THEIR LOYALTY
TO OUR ARMY

Please mention THE PLAYGROUND when writing to advertisers

Please mention THE PLAYGROUND when writing to advertisers

What part does the Victrola play in your school?

Now is the time to plan a definite listening course for next year, based upon the

Victrola and Victor Records.

You will find excellent help in formulating a special Victrola course by consulting the new 1918 edition of a

New Graded List of Records for Children in Home and School.

This is a catalogue of 272 pages, beautifully illustrated; it contains a list of over 1000 Victor Records, with descriptive notes classified according to use in various grades and subjects. Have you formed a circulating Record Library for your schools?

Remember that the Victrola has become an indispensable servant of education. It is used to illustrate and vitalize the lesson in Literature, History and Geography. It is used for Physical Education, Nature Study, Penmanship, Typewriting, Voice Culture, Ear Training, Opera Study, Music History, and the study of Orchestral Instruments. From Victor Records, the boys in our Army and Navy are learning Wireless Telegraphy and French.

No school is too remote for the Victrola to bring to its occupants the golden tones of Caruso and Melba, the brilliant violins of Maud Powell and Jascha Heifetz, the piano of Paderewski, and the great instrumental masterpieces played by the world's most famous bands and orchestras.

With this world of opportunity for real culture at your door, can *your school* afford to be without a Victrola and a well-planned course?

Ask your Victor dealer to supply you with copies of "A New Graded List" and "The Victrola in Rural Schools," or send a postcard to the

Educational Department

Victor Talking Machine Co.

Camden, N. J.

Victrola XXV, $75
specially manufactured
for School use

When the Victrola is not in use, the horn can be placed under the instrument safe and secure from danger, and the cabinet can be locked to protect it from dust and promiscuous use by irresponsible people.

Victrola

"HIS MASTER'S VOICE"

To insure Victor quality, always look for the famous trademark, "His Master's Voice." It is on all genuine products of the Victor Talking Machine Company.

Templeton, Mass
A CHALLENGE FROM THE CAMP FIRE GIRLS TO THE BOY
SCOUTS IN A THRIFT STAMP CONTEST. (See Page 111)

Chautauqua, New York.
A BEAUTIFUL WOODED PLAYGROUND

The Playground

Vol. XII No. 3   JUNE 1918

The World At Play

Patriotic Service.—"Never before has recreation been so vitally necessary to the life of the world. A play leader contributes nobly and patriotically to the service of the country when she prepares, by careful training, to do her part in the conservation of the nation. For our children are our future men and women and that they may grow, we must provide the outlet for natural impulses and surround them with an atmosphere of happiness."—Bulletin of the Baltimore Training School for Recreation Workers

Time Both for Work and Play.—Lincoln E. Rowley introduces his annual report of recreation activities in East Orange, New Jersey, as follows:

"Since the declaration of war by the United States the Board of Recreation Commissioners has been without any precedent to guide it in formulating the policies to be pursued. The commissioners believe, however, that nothing within reason should be omitted that would minister to the happiness of small children; that the older children and younger adolescents should be directed in helpful athletics and turned to a thoughtful interest in the country and those defending it in arms; that older boys should have better opportunities for play and physical training during their recreation hours but that they should not be encouraged to spend so much time on play that it interferes with their taking a responsible part in the world's work."

Speeding Up Shipbuilding.—Edward A. Filene, chairman of the Shipping Committee of the United States Chamber of Commerce, in an address before that body at Chicago, pointed out the necessity of community organization to place all of the people of the ship building cities back of the Government in the great program to be carried through. He emphasized particularly the necessity of adequate amusement and leisure-time facilities if labor conditions were to be such as to give maximum efficiency.

War Service in Grade Schools.—The public school

95

children of Rockford, Illinois, have made and turned over to the War Camp Community Service the following articles for the boys at Camp Grant:

Five hundred and fifty-nine field note pads with oil cloth covers and pencils already sharpened for use. Each one cost five cents to make.

Four hundred and thirty letter-cases, with pencils, writing paper and envelopes to match, sure to give much pleasure to the soldiers. The material for each case cost eight cents.

Forty-three checker boards, covered with oil cloth, made to fold so that they can be easily carried into the trenches, or wherever the boys may have a few moments to forget the war. The material for these cost ten cents each.

Thirty-six pin holders made out of scraps. Each holder has a supply of pins.

Over There.—Among the recreation workers of this country who are serving the Y. M. C. A. in France are George Ellsworth Johnson, of Harvard, and E. B. De Groot, of San Francisco. Dr. and Mrs. Luther H. Gulick spent some time abroad as special emissaries of the Y. M. C. A.

The Pageant of Freedom.— The pageant given before 30,000 spectators in San Diego last fall is available under certain conditions for use in other communities. Information may be secured from the author, Arnold Kruckman, San Diego, California.

M i g r a t o r y "Movies."— North Carolina has developed a system of providing moving pictures for rural communities at prices they can pay. The circuit is covered by an automobile with a miniature electric plant. Each "unit" costs $3,000 of which the State pays one-third. Ten communities in Sampson County guaranteed $225.00 each and made money at an admission price of ten cents.

Community Music at Wichitca.—A capacity audience, with hundreds unable to get in, indicated the enthusiasm Wichita feels for its Sunday afternoon musical programs. A band concert, interspersed with a number of vocal solos, and the singing of the Hallelujah Chorus by the Wichita chorus of 200 voices made up the program.

George Sim to Sacramento. —Sacramento, California, has formed a Board of Playground Commissioners to direct the recreation in parks, playgrounds, and in the school yards after school, on holidays and on Saturdays and Sundays.

George Sim, who has served in the South Park Recreation System in Chicago and later in the Playground Department of Los Angeles, has been called to executive leadership for this new position at Sacramento.

More and more, throughout America, there has been a tendency to centralize recreation administration and hundreds of cities will follow this experiment in Sacramento.

Swimming Pool the Slogan. —*American Education,* Albany, quotes from a bulletin of the Massachusetts Institute of Technology:

"A suitable slogan after the war would be—'a clean swimming pool and a large ball field for every boy and girl.' It also adds, for young children, the sand pile and mud pies and ring-around-a-rosey in yard or garden where sunshine is, and the air. There should be some degree of persistent participation in the most intensely active and absorbing kinds of play that makes for strength and, what is more important by far, for the will to use strength to the limit."

Child Welfare in Dallas.— Almost every agency in Dallas, Texas, remotely connected with Child Welfare joined in the Child Welfare Campaign of Education, conducted by the Civic Federation.

"To arouse and educate the public that the child may have his just rights:

To be well born;

To be well nurtured;

To have a happy childhood;

To be physically cared for;

To be well educated."

Child Welfare as war service was the basis of the plea as indicated by the following call in the Dallas Survey:

"The percentage of young men who are physically unfit is revealed with terrifying clearness in examinations for war service. Some form of neglect in birth, childhood and youth has produced most of this disability. The faults lie a generation back of us. These faults not only continue today, but the experience of other nations shocks us into the belief that the demands of war will lay dread hands on the lives of the children.

"We are at the parting of the ways. We have a big decision to make. Shall we give our whole time and thought and energy to the needs of the Nation in War, or shall we give some serious thought and action to the protection of this new generation on whose shoulders will rest the destiny

97

of our country twenty years hence?

"This is not a question to be answered by Government or laws. It must, if democracy means anything, be answered by the people—all of them—the people who are the government.

"Never in the history of nations was the child—well-born, well-nurtured and well-trained —such an invaluable asset as it is today. In a larger measure than ever before the children of this generation are the hope of the nation ten or twenty years hence. In like measure they may be the menace of the nation's life."

Wants the Best.—Edward Kraft, of Red Bluff, California, has not only donated space for a playground for the children of his community, and funds for proper equipment, but has sent the committee of Red Bluff citizens appointed to take charge of the new playground to all the notable playgrounds about San Francisco to get suggestions from experienced workers.

Fulfills Its Purpose.—The Community Building at Washington, Pa., which was opened three years ago by a company formed for the purpose, has been such a success that the Washington Board of Trade

has purchased it for a permanent institution.

Warren R. Jackson writes of it:

"The building is fulfilling its purpose admirably and is now universally recognized as the community center, as was the hope of the promoters in the beginning. It is located on Main Street about one-half square below the Court House, and is readily accessible from all parts of the city. It is two stories in height and contains on the first floor a general reading and assembly room, a dining-room for members of the Board of Trade and their guests, a bakery shop and an insurance office. The revenue from the renting of the rooms used by the insurance office and the bakery shop amounts to approximately $50 per month, which aids very materially in taking care of the maintenance expenses. On the second floor are two offices used by the Board of Trade, the office of the County Agriculturist and a suite of two rooms used as ladies' rest rooms. One of these rooms is equipped as a nursery and has proved quite attractive to women visitors in the city with small children.

"As an indication of the general use which is made of the

structure by the residents of the community, it is interesting to note that last year an average of three hundred and nine persons per day availed themselves of the facilities of the building. On one occasion seven meetings, each one entirely foreign to all the others, were held in the building on the same evening. In the rear of the Community Building a free public hitching yard is maintained for the benefit of the farmers."

Community House in Rutland, Vermont. — Ex-Governor John A. Mead about two years ago presented the Congregational Church in which he was a deacon with a corner lot upon which stood a three-story brick residence. Adjoining the house he built a gymnasium with dressing-rooms and shower baths, and added a tennis court outside. This property is realizing the wish of the donor that it should become a "general center for wholesome recreation and social opportunity."

Take Down the Fences Voluntarily.—A bill has been introduced in the New York Legislature authorizing mayors to appoint a commission to secure the consent of owners of private property to the removal of fences separating yards, so that such yards may be used as playgrounds. No expense to the city is provided for.

The plan has been tried in London, where it has provided hundreds of grounds for play safe from the traffic of the street.

The People Want Them.— Perhaps the biggest boost neighborhood center work has had in Milwaukee came as a result of a movement on the part of some of the members of the School Board to close these centers on Wednesdays and Saturdays. One week after the resolution was adopted the friends of neighborhood center work appeared before the Board to speak against the proposed closing. So urgent were the arguments presented, so eloquently did the neighborhood center's supporters plead its cause and so effectively did the results of six years of the wider use of the school plant for the people speak for themselves, that the matter did not even come to a vote.

Making American Citizens. —An Americanization campaign has been conducted by the Extension Department of the Board of School Directors of Milwaukee in an effort to induce foreigners to enter the night schools and Americanization classes. Under the slogan "Learn more, earn more," foreign-born men and women are being urged through dodgers extending the invitation in six different languages to attend the English classes which are being held in ten of the schools.

"Become a United States citizen" is the invitation proffered by two of the schools through their Americanization classes. The successful completion of eighteen lessons entitles the would-be citizen to a certificate which he may present to the judge upon applying for his citizen's papers.

Window Cards for Gardeners.—Mr. F. E. Wolfe, acting director of the Municipal Recreation Committee of South Bend, Indiana, has sent a letter to Mr. Herbert Hoover, United States Food Administrator, suggesting that some sort of official recognition, possibly a window card, be given to all persons doing gardening during the summer of 1918; also that this recognition possess national significance and indicate that the workers are engaged in national war service.

In South Bend 497 vacant lot gardeners and about 5,000 home gardeners were enrolled last year. Complete figures on the produce of these gardens are not available but many reports have been made and on a conservative estimate based up-

on the average production, the Home and Vacant Lot Gardeners together produced a total of $60,000 worth of produce within the city limits of South Bend.

Liberty Bonds as Garden Prizes.—The National Agricultural Prize Commission, 220 W. 57th St., N.Y., has begun a movement to bring under cultivation all available unoccupied property in cities. After arranging with the municipal administration and committees of private owners for the use of unoccupied land, it will make an educational campaign throughout the city.

The actual work of cultivation will be carried on either by individual housewives or neighborhood committees. The neighborhood committees will raise the food for the consumption of their own members and the families in their respective neighborhoods. Three fifty-dollar Liberty bonds will be awarded during the Summer months to committees reporting the best results in city gardening.

Gardening on the Playgrounds.—At Elmwood Park, East Orange, New Jersey, about three acres were ploughed and marked for planting and 74 different people planted potatoes. The soil was not of the best but all the gardeners worked hard and produced a fair crop. The Board of Recreation Commissioners paid the cost of preparing the ground and furnished seed at cost, each gardener agreeing to contribute one-fifth of his crop to the Red Cross. The cost to the Board was less than the expenses incurred during the previous year for mowing the grass and as there were about five acres left for play no serious interference with the normal activities of this play field resulted. A splendid neighborhood spirit was one of the by-products of this experiment.

At the Oval, the splendidly equipped playground and athletic field of which East Orange is so justly proud, a demonstration garden 20' x 40' was planted in front of the grand stand and the worker in charge gave much helpful advice to many people about soils, planting and the proper care of vegetable gardens. Where flowering plants previously flourished, tomatoes and cabbages were raised, thousands of cabbage plants being sold at a nominal price. The saving on flowering plants and the receipts from cabbage plants and garden vegetables more than met the cost of the gardening.

State Aid for Gardens.—To encourage home g a r d e n i n g throughout the State of New York an arrangement has been effected whereby Cornell University will give $150 and the State $100 to aid in the gardening work of any community in New York State which will raise $100 and engage a full-time worker for the summer.

New York State is bound to do its part valiantly in helping to feed our allies.

Play Ends and Court Begins.*—Judge George W. Wagner, the juvenile court judge for Berks county, spoke at the father and son banquet at the Berkshire Hotel last evening and told some of his experiences as a judge in the juvenile court.

"There are 200 boys and girls in the hands of the juvenile court at this time. They are under probation. Ninety or ninety-five per cent of this number are boys.

"I am not here to-night to speak on a theoretical matter, but on a practical matter. When the playgrounds are closed in the winter time the boys come into court. During July and August, when the playgrounds are open, there are very few hearings held. The reason for this is that the organization we

* Extract from Reading, Pa., Herald

have here, the playgrounds, takes care of the boys at that period of the year.

"Thus we have a practical demonstration of what can be done. I want to add that during the eight or nine years that I have been the juvenile judge I have yet to see the first Boy Scout brought before me.

"We find that boys that come before us have a disposition just exactly like your boy or my boy. Not ten per cent of the 200 under our care at this time are vicious. They are the creatures of circumstance, and the circumstance generally is the want of proper care."

Judge Wagner went on to tell of the work he had done in finding new homes for boys.

"I remember a case of a boy being brought to court. The father was called in, too. I found that the alleged crime took place on a Sunday afternoon. I asked the father whether he went out with his boy and associated with him. He told me he was busy; that he had his dogs on the mountain exercising them. A boy will follow in the footsteps of the father.

"The requisites for a boy are his home and his associates."

A Helpful Suggestion.— Elizabeth O'Neill, Philadelphia, in discussing the subject, The Playground Ball, in *Mind and Body* for February, 1918, says: "The Physical Training Department of the Philadelphia Board of Public Education has decided to use a smaller size ball, the outer-seam soccer Association Football for all games formerly requiring the use of the basket ball and foot ball. It will be more durable, and being used for all purposes we think it will help tremendously to lessen the problem of discipline occasioned by kicking the wrong ball. We feel the children themselves will get a better idea of proper values, through the contrast between the volley ball and soccer so strongly typifying the strong and the weak.

"We shall requisition for the Philadelphia Schools and Playgrounds three balls, the volley ball, baseball (indoor) and the outer-seam soccer, which we shall call the playground ball, and shall await with interest results to be obtained.

"The following is an extract from a letter from a manufacturer in reply to our request for his opinion of the proposed change:

"Replying to your letter would say the change that you contemplate making of using outseam soccer balls instead of basket balls, in our judgment is a wise one—it will not only simplify your problem of ordering goods, but it will also be helpful in enabling you to use one type of ball for the different sports such as dodge ball and captain ball.

" 'There is also another problem that you have not thought of, and that is, the question of price. If you adopt an outseam soccer ball for general use you will be able to save some money, as there is not as much material used in the manufacture of this type of ball as there is in a basket ball, consequently you would be able to save the difference between the cost of the soccer ball and the basket ball.' "

Ring Ball. — Edward A. Werner, Houghton, Michigan, has developed a modification of basket ball for use in play rooms where the ceiling is too low for the regulation game. Further information may be secured from Mr. Werner.

Japanese Neighborhood House Report.—The report of The Yurin En or House of the Friendly Neighbor shows interesting views of recreation activities which are often, as in the case of the English speaking Dramatic Society, linked with international education. Boys' and girls' clubs, a kinder-garten, playground, library, Saturday entertainments are among the activities reported by the House.

First Playground in Lima, Peru.—The last day of the old year witnessed the opening of Lima's first public playground, equipped for games and sports.

Alaskan Gardens.—"Agriculture is being developed through school gardens with very gratifying results. These school gardens may be found in almost every section of Alaska and through this agency not only the interest of the younger generation is being stimulated, but that of the entire village. The energy expended on their gardens will bring especially good returns this year when the prices of food of all kinds are almost prohibitive."—Extract f r o m the Report of the Governor of Alaska to the Secretary of the Interior, 1917

A Visitor from Japan.—Mr. N. Tsukamoto, who has long been connected with the Standard Oil Company, is now on a year's leave of absence spending some time in the United States. He is anxious to study parks and playground systems with a view to preparing recommendations for his own city. He is a member of a Walking Society in Kobe and has been

103

interested in planning out paths through the rolling hills just outside of Kobe which would make possible the most beautiful vistas and views. Before the city spreads too far out on the rolling country they want to plan for playgrounds. At first this work will be undertaken by a private organization and when in this way, they demonstrate the value of playgrounds, they hope that the city will take them over.

Official Organ of Park Superintendents.—The s e c o n d issue of *Parks and Recreation* contains besides many news notes of recreation activities here and there three major articles upon park recreation: Park Recreational Activities by J. R. Richards, giving Chicago's experiences and achievements; Municipal Athletics in St. Louis by Rodowe H. Abeken outlining the development of city-wide football, basket ball, track and field athletics and other sports; and Municipal Golf at Seattle, by Roland Cotterill, describing the beautiful course and the way maximum use of it is being developed.

Street Play and Its Relation to the Neighborhood Center

RUTH R. PEARSON, Director in Charge, Girls' Activites, Bureau of Parks, Playgrounds and Beaches, Chicago, Ill.

Street play presents itself to recreation workers everywhere as the fundamental and universal problem upon which their work is based, for to know the industrial and social conditions of a given neighborhood is not more essential to intelligent recreation service than to understand the life of its streets. Orderly-minded citizens, vaguely aware of the network of small parks and playgrounds covering Chicago, are occasionally surprised to find small boys running about in vacant lots. "Have we not the finest playground systems in the world?" they ask. "Why, then, should any child be found upon the street?" Such is the experience, I suppose, of every town and city which sees before its eyes the practical working out of some attractive theory. Certain facts refuse to fall as rapidly as expected into the pigeon holes prepared for them, and we find that analysis and questioning must still go on. Recognizing these facts, a systematic investigation was made during six months of last year into the spontaneous activities in progress outside the municipal playgrounds of Chicago, as observed and reported by the women assistant directors in each neighborhood. No attempt was made to count the children seen, nor to divide them as to age or sex. The aim was to determine what games were played, what interests occupied the boys and girls under conditions of perfect freedom. The observers, alert to what was going on about them, simply noted, from day to day, each new activity. These reports gathered in monthly and summarized, indicate the range of such activities, their seasonal rotation, and order of popularity in various sections of the city, and show that the street play of children and young people is due not to any one cause, but to many.

What Are They Playing and How   The presence of street games and neighborhood play, although a phenomenon of great interest and importance, is not necessarily so serious an indictment of the child welfare agencies as it would at first seem. The streets *are* dangerous, for certain types of play especially, such as baseball, kite flying, and tag. These must never be forced into the public highway, for lack of space elsewhere. But, under the most ideal conditions, can it be possible that children, full of the play impulse, will ever confine their activity entirely to the area within the fence line of any playground? One of the main functions of directed play is to enrich the whole life of the child, to give to him his birthright of traditional games, together with high standards of sportsmanship, and to supply him with a fund of play knowledge upon which he can draw at any time, wherever he may be. "Doorstep games," so-called, constitute a distinct group, encouraged by play leaders with the hope that they will be played at home, among parents, neighbors, and playmates, substituting purposeful activity for loafing The question, it seems, is not—"Are children playing on the streets?" but—"What are they playing, and how?"

To understand the significance of the following study it is necessary to know something of the recreation centers in connection with which it was carried on. Chicago's system of municipal playgrounds has been greatly expanded within the last two years. Through the cooperation of the Board of Education with the Bureau of Parks, Playgrounds, and Beaches, forty school yards have been graded, equipped with apparatus, small field

105

houses, and opened to the public as supervised, year-round centers. In many neighborhoods, but not yet in all, the school buildings are in use, during the winter, as community centers, under the control of the Board of Education. The playgrounds, however, are operated by the Bureau of Parks and Playgrounds, each ground being in charge of a director, assistant director (woman), and attendant, appointed under the city civil service. In a few cases active neighborhood associations furnish invaluable assistance in the organization of activities expressing common local interests. The beginnings of a new era of community life can be seen, but, needless to say, many problems remain to be adjusted. With the dedication, during 1916 and 1917, of these forty new centers, the municipal system was brought to a total of 69 playgrounds, 55 of which are in school yards throughout the city. The playground is no longer for the congested district only. In residence suburbs and along the boulevard its appeal is before the people, linking them as never before with the problems and the possibilities of the public school. It is in connection with these grounds, that the question of street play is here considered.

Five Types of Street Play A classification, with reference to the playground system, of the "neighborhood survey of play activities" conducted during the summer of 1917, tends to establish five main groups, viz: (1) plays and games of little or no organization, which can be played outside as well as in the playground; (2) those which for various reasons cannot be played within the ground; (3) activities carried on under conditions over which the playground can have no control; (4) those confined to the streets because of playground rules, restrictions, necessary discipline and (5) those which should be included in the playground schedule but are not, because of insufficient space, facilities, or leadership.

First, among activities requiring neither supervision, leadership, nor a large number of players, and which therefore can be played as well, from the child's point of view, outside as in the playground, we find, (a) simple imaginative plays, such as horse, dolls, soldier, house; (b) games of individual skill, hop scotch, jacks, marbles, bouncing ball, and quiet guessing games; and (c) group games of low organization, such as tag, hide-and-seek, New York, and a very few of the traditional singing games. Of the 82 distinct activities reported during June-July, the three most popular were respectively hop scotch, jacks, and "O'Leary," (a bouncing game),—all games of individual skill, requiring a concrete surface. For such play the sidewalks are convenient, while a playground offers no particular advantage except when tournaments are arranged, as has been done in many grounds. A tournament within the ground, moreover, means increased interest in the activity outside, and groups will be found all over the neighborhood, absorbed in practice.

In the second group, i. e., activities which are impossible or impracticable for playground use, we have two types, (a) the individual occupation involving play apparatus excluded from the ground and (b) the group game of low organization for any reason undesirable within. Examples of the former are: bicycle riding; roller skating; use of pushmobiles, wagons, and hoops; kite flying; batting flies, (with hard ball); "junking" (collecting wood, coal, copper); throwing (stones, snow balls); playing in water and mud, and with the bricks, lumber, and sand about new buildings; making bon-fires and other such pursuits. Among the group games impracticable in many small playgrounds, for lack of space, or because of danger to other children, are: *Run, Sheep, Run; Duck-on-a-rock; Shinney; Peg.* Activities under both these heads appeal to strong, fundamental instincts of childhood, and some part of the time of every normal child is sure to be devoted to them. Kite tournaments and roller skating races have been conducted under supervision of the playground directors, in larger open spaces outside the playgrounds, in recognition of the popularity of these sports.

We come next to the third group, which includes activities carried on under conditions over which the playground can have no direct control. Children are often prohibited by their parents from going to the playground, for fear of injury, or because they are wanted within call, or in order that they may care for younger brothers and sisters near home. These may play any of a wide variety of games, including those above mentioned. Other children may be seen playing along the streets going to or coming from the playground, or while loitering on errands. Moreover, the attractions of the street itself cannot be entirely overcome. Advertising displays, carnivals, "the movies," and commercialized amusements of every sort, over-stimulating and often harmful to the child, appeal to his love of adventure and will not be denied. With these

107

the playground competes, and its competition is increasingly suc-successful, as shown by the statistics of attendance.

Among activities of the fourth group, those necessarily confined to the streets, because of necessary discipline within the playground, are included the smoking of cigarettes, gambling, and the unrestricted association of young people, accompanied by "fooling," flirting, and more serious results. The normal desire of boys and girls for social contact, the lure of the theatre, the cheap substitutes it offers in place of the high ideals of life for which they seek, and the tragic outcome of such conditions, have been studied for us by Jane Addams, in her great work, *The Spirit of Youth and the City Streets.* Until we learn to order and control our streets this problem will continue to demand attention. The playground cannot permit gambling and smoking within its bounds, but it can and does overcome, in case after case, the tendency toward these activities, while to provide ample opportunity for wholesome association among people of all ages, should be the one chief aim of every recreation system.

These Ought to Be within the Playground Finally, by the above process of elimination, we find ourselves face to face with the two important groups of activities, at present carried on largely in the commercial establishments, the large parks and the homes; or in streets, back yards, and vacant lots; which *are* desirable, have wide social possibilities, and should be a part of the program of every neighborhood center. These include, (a) the few highly organized games, such as baseball, handball, and tennis, which are played outside the playgrounds; and (b) club and group activities of a general nature—talking, storytelling, listening to music, singing, dancing. There are very definite reasons why these are carried on only in a rudimentary way, within the playgrounds. Lack of space excludes baseball and tennis, which will probably always be confined to the larger parks. Competition along such lines can however be organized through the local center, thus encouraging wider participation and use of the more distant facilities. Most important of all, for the development of neighborhood spirit and the crystallization of community consciousness about the common center, are the club and group interests, which bring together old and young. These are at present hampered by the difficulty of access to the school buildings, a difficulty which awaits only the realization among us

108

of our need. The demand of the future is for the association of citizens, for purposes of civic discussion, participation in music, dancing, dramatics—all the ways of expression which have in them the possibility of development into high forms of community art; and this demand can be met only by perfecting the equipment of the public school, and throwing it open as the people's center.

Street play cannot be considered apart from these all-inclusive problems it opens up. What should our attitude as play leaders be toward the small boy building bon-fires in a vacant lot—toward the small girl absorbed in *Sky-blue* upon the smooth asphalt of the street? We must be alert to distinguish the fundamental character of these activities; to classify them, both in relation to their meaning for the child, and as a commentary on the organized play life of the community. Every street activity is either morally desirable or undesirable. If undesirable we must recognize that here is work to do—a negative expression to be crowded out by the appeal of a positive, constructive one. If morally desirable, the pursuit will fall in one of two groups— either (1) those sports and occupations for some reason not found within the play center, or (2) those which are so popular inside the fence lines that they are carried on spontaneously outside. For some forms of play the streets are very dangerous. To prevent these the only effective method is that of constant public education along "Safety First" lines, combined with ample publicity for all recreation facilities. When this has been achieved, should we not recognize, in group 2 above, proof of the value of directed play; and resolve to bring as many as possible of the activities noted under group 1 within the scheme? A higher type of leadership may be the need. More probably the organization of athletics and games can be improved, to measure up to the standards of child interest, and the active cooperation of neighbors enlisted to make permanent the ideals of sportsmanship attained. Not until all group play about the homes and vacant spaces of a city reflects a spirit of clean, active, joyous self-expression can the play leader ship his oars and sit back against the cushions, and it is the knowledge that this day can never wholly arrive which keeps him, eager, fascinated, at his task.

SURVEY OF STREET PLAY NEAR 101 GROUNDS

ORDER OF POPULARITY:

1st—Run, Sheep, Run	14
2nd—Bicycle riding	12
Playing house	12
3rd—O'Leary	10
Roller skating	9
Ball	8
Jacks	8
Kites	8
Baseball	6
Hop Scotch	6
Minding babies	6
Hide and Seek	5
Tag (It)	5
Crocheting	4
Playing soldier	4
Pushmobiles	4
Baby (Bunny) in the Hole	3
Bounce out (Bounce back, Come back)	3
Clap in—Clap out	3
Peg	3
Fish (Fishing,—Fishing, Fishing, All Night)	3
Playing school	3
Red Light	3
Statue	3
War	3
Bluebird	2
Briar Rosebud	2
Cheese It	2
Dolls	2
Duck-on-a-rock	2
Hand ball	2
Hoops	2
I Spy	2
Jack, Jack, Show Your Light	2
Jumping rope	2
Piggy	2
Playing circus	2
Sand play	2
Scrub	2
Shooting craps	2

Reported *once* each:

Blind (boys with tree branches large enough to hide behind)
Bonfire and potato roasts
Bouncing balls
Buttons
Colors
Colors Steps
Digging trenches
Ditch
Embroidering
Farmer in the Dell
Follow the Leader
Football
Forfeits
Fox Lost His Track
Going to store
Grocery store
Hand tag
Hockey
Indoor ball
"Junking" wood, coal, iron
Kelley
Lagging stones
Last tag
Lead Man
Lemonade-stands
Marbles
New York
Numbers
1-2-3-4-5-6-7-8
Paper dolls

Playing fireman
" policeman
" school
show
store
" Red Cross nurse (in caps)
" robber (goal for jail)
" with mechanical toys
Pies
Prove It
Ring around A-Rosy
Selling lemonade for Red Cross
Shaking dice
Stingo
Stones
Stoop tag
Shuttle Relay
Tip, Tap the Iceman
Taking car numbers
Tapping for white horses
Teacher
Telling stories (original)
Ten Steps
Tennis
Time
Three Dukes
Wheeling go-carts
Tricycles
Washington

39 GROUNDS.   101 ACTIVITIES

Singing games	5	Imaginative plays	15
Games of individual skill	12	Guessing games	3
Games of low organization	35	Activities involving equipment	8
Games of high organization	5	Miscellaneous	19

110

A Thrift Stamp Contest

ARTHUR LELAND, B. P. E., Templeton, Massachusetts

Promoting the sale of thrift and war savings stamps may be made a most valuable adjunct to the war recreation program of any town or city. Recreation directors understand the details attending the organization of competitive contests. That a stamp contest run like a baseball league can be made a wildly hilarious game is shown by the experiment worked out in Templeton, a little village of 400 souls up in the hills of Massachusetts, not far from Camp Devens.

The Camp Fire Girls challenged the Boy Scouts to this contest which resulted in twenty-eight boys and girls selling the equivalent of 3524 thrift stamps in twenty-eight days, bringing in $881 for the government. The contest started in a raging blizzard, was followed shortly by a workless week and workless Mondays which reduced the available funds of the community. The trolley system was buried in snow for two weeks so that the fathers of the children were obliged to walk twelve miles to and from their work in the next village, the children walked to school where formerly they had ridden. None of these obstacles dampened the enthusiasm with which the contest progressed and the children's zeal and achievement suggests the query, if twenty-eight boys and girls can sell 3524 stamps in twenty-eight days under such conditions how many could the twenty million school children of the country sell in seasonable weather?

The challenge was presented with a bit of pageantry which did much to stimulate and maintain interest. The Scouts are at ease by their camp fire; the girls, friendly tribes of Indians, arrive on snow-shoes after a long trip from Washington and their leader sounds the following call to arms:

"Harken, Oh ye Scouts; I Wilnitahnie of the Kenesto Camp Fire Girls bring tidings and a challenge.

"Ye have heard of the great war, of the Huns, devastaters of homes, destroyers of firesides, murderers of women, slayers of children. Our Great White Father at Washington has spoken to us his children. He tells us that peril approaches our beautiful shores, nay is here already, stalking among us. Our enemy is as numerous as the leaves of the forest and as ruthless as the cold north wind. Our own homes and camp fires are threatened. Already our braves, our warriors, our brothers are on the war path.

"That they may have food and clothing and weapons wherewith to fight, our Great White Father has spoken and bids that his people lend to him of their treasure and wampum that he may make his and our warriors invincible. Can our protectors turn back the savage foe with much brave talk? Shall they go forth to fight empty handed? No! Not while the Camp Fire Girls and Boy Scouts can help!

"Our Great Chiefs at Washington have said that two billion dollars must be saved and loaned to the government that our braves and warriors may go prepared to meet the foe and keep him away from our homes. This means that $16.50 must be secured for every man, woman and child in the country.

"You scouts have in times past done noble work selling liberty bonds; we the Kenesto Camp Fire Girls hereby challenge you to a friendly contest in selling Thrift Stamps, and as a token of this challenge—as is the custom among our tribes we hand you this bundle of arrows—see they are peace arrows and blunt signifying that this contest is to be a friendly one.

"I hold here a bundle of war arrows—pointed and sharp, the color of blood, tipped with death. These are for the Huns should they ever land on our shores.

"'Keepers of the Arrows' shall be those who win this stamp contest. The band which sells the most stamps shall be deemed bravest and best fitted to hold this trophy of war to the death against the time when our country may call even us Camp Fire Girls and Boy Scouts to defend with our lives these shores of 'the land of the free and the home of the brave.'

"Accept ye this challenge or look we for others more worthy of conquest.

"If ye accept choose now two chiefs who with your worthy Scoutmaster will meet with two of our chosen ones and our Camp Fire Guardian and arrange for the details of the contest."

SCOUT REPLY

"Listen, oh ye Camp Fire Girls and brother Scouts. Are we chicken-hearted children that we should fail to answer the call

112

of our Great Chief at Washington? When patriotism calls a Scout is loyal.

"Shall we acknowledge ourselves defeated without an effort by refusing to meet the Camp Fire Girls in this contest? Shall we thus brand ourselves as craven?

"Oh no; rather will we be 'Keepers of the Arrows.' Never fear, little girls, look well to your laurels, ye have men and braves and loyal Scouts to meet—not children busy with their toys.

"I move that we accept this challenge and proceed to nominate two captains."

The Guardian and Scoutmaster then purchased stamps at the post office. The postmaster furnished a bulletin board and arranged to keep the score of individuals, teams and organizations in the office. Owing to the blizzard the boys got a "head start," only two of the girls who owned snow-shoes being able to travel through the drifts. Three days before the end of the contest the girls were eight points ahead. The boys were in mortal terror of defeat all the time but finally won out by 68 points, therefore demonstrating themselves to be "Keepers of the Arrows." Honors however were divided as one of the girls' teams was 176 points ahead of the highest Scout team; the girls also claimed the best individual score, Bernice Brooks having sold 501 stamps, 77 more than the highest Scout record. One of the boys said, "the contest is the most excitement that every struck the town." The girls said it was worth all the effort to give the boys such a scare.

Back Yard and Vacant Lot Gardens
A National Necessity

Mr. Charles Lathrop Pack, President of the National Emergency Food Garden Commission, in an article in *The Outlook* entitled *A Munition Plant in Every Back Yard*, points out the seriousness of the problem indicated in the statement that 600,000 men trained in farm work have gone into active service in the army or navy. This must inevitably mean that 1918 will show a more serious shortage of farm labor than did 1917 when the supply failed to meet the demand.

With this handicap in sight, the back yard and vacant lot garden becomes more than ever a war garden and a national necessity. The only solution of the food problem—since no scientist has ever yet discovered a substitute for food—is an increased production. To make this possible, the home gardeners of America face 1918 with a responsibility far greater than that with which they set about their work last season.

There are a number of factors, Mr. Pack points out, which play important parts in the program. The first is the necessity for the conservation of transportation. As far as possible all food should be grown in the immediate neighborhood of the place of its ultimate use. This involves the cultivation of food gardens at every home and on every inch of vacant land in the neighborhood of cities, towns and villages. Last year the National Emergency Food Garden Commission reported the existence of nearly 3,000,000 gardens in yards and vacant lots. This year to meet the increased needs there should be 5,000,000.

A second factor, and this a very favorable one, is the national daylight saving scheme recently adopted. This simple plan of turning the clock forward and starting the day's work an hour earlier during the summer months, will give an extra hour of daylight for the cultivation of the soil. This will give the 1918 war gardeners a great advantage over 1917's experience.

The fact that home gardening has come to be regarded as the gift of a patriotic people to a nation in need, gives added force to the service and provides the needed stimulus. The motive power provided by the impulse of patriotic service is strengthened by the feeling that war gardening is an enterprise of individual benefit. Through gardening activities Americans in hundreds and thousands of households have learned new lessons in the joy of living. Last year's excursion into home gardening was to many a voyage of discovery in the delights of the table when supplied with vegetables freshly gathered from the home garden. It was also a journey of exploration through a land of new helpfulness and strength revealed through the medium of outdoor exercise.

Because of a number of insurmountable difficulties in the way of securing food from other nations, America is the one country upon which the Allies may depend for the feeding of their armies and populations. To enable America to do its share our home gardeners must recognize that they are war gardeners and therefore vital to the success of the armies. They must produce food stuffs on a tremendous scale with the incentive that

114

unending industry on their part will be the price of world-wide freedom.

It will be none too much if two or more war gardens are made to grow where one grew before. By the same logic there must be universal application of the simple principles of home canning and drying of vegetables and fruits. Last year the households of America produced a winter supply of canned goods amounting to more than half a billion jars. This year they must make it more than a billion.

Neutrality in the food question is as impossible as neutrality in the war itself. In the great conflict we shall win or lose according to our solution of the food problem. Let us then plant gardens as never before and grow munitions at home to help win the war.

Garden Song

(Written to the tune *Over There*)

Johnnie get your hoe, get your hoe, get your hoe;
Mary dig your row, dig your row, dig your row;
Down to business girls and boys,
Learn to know the gardener's joys,
Uncle Sam's in need, pull the weed,
    plant the seed,
While the sunbeams lurk do not shirk,
    Get to work,
All the lads must spade the ground,
All the girls must hustle round.

Chorus

Over there, Over there;
Send the word, send the word over there,
That the lads are hoeing, the lads are hoeing,
The girls are showing ev'rywhere,
Each a garden to prepare,
Do your bit so that we can all share,
With the boys, with the boys, the brave boys,
Who will not come back 'till it's over,
    Over There.

115

GARDEN SONG

Do you like it? It is the "Spring Song" of the South which is going solid for the United States School Garden Army.

The enthusiasm started in Kentucky with parades at Lexington, one for white children in the afternoon and another for colored children in the morning. Martha Washington and Thomas Jefferson, both seven years old and colored, were in the morning parade.

The Louisville parade was a marvel of floats and banners and it started things going. The enlistments are coming in so fast that a dozen recruiting sergeants are kept busy all the time.

Texas has grabbed the idea as if it were a new scheme to develop a whole new state full of oil-wells, and on April 8th there were 60,000 actual enlistments with hundreds pouring in.

Alabama is as enthusiastic as Texas, Birmingham having started with an enrollment of 15,000 children in one day. Tennessee is falling in with an enlistment so big that they have not been able to count it, while in Kansas 400,000 children are clamoring for the green ribbon badge of the Garden Army. California is leading the Far West with her magnificent enrollment.

The organizers sent out by the Department of the Interior are going all over the country, millions of children are ready to fight in the Home Garden Army. It is Secretary Lane's idea to have five million boys and girls of the schools in every city, town and village in the country, captained by 40,000 teachers, to produce as nearly as possible all the vegetables and small fruits necessary for their home consumption.

The President approves the design of Secretary Lane to arouse the school children of the United States to "as real and patriotic an effort as the building of ships or the firing of cannon:"

My dear Mr. Secretary:
I sincerely hope that you may be successful through the Bureau of Education in arousing the interest of teachers and children in the schools of the United States in the cultivation of home gardens. Every boy and girl who really sees what the home garden may mean will, I am sure, enter into the purpose with high spirits, because I am sure they would all like to feel that they are in fact fighting in France by joining the home garden army. They know that America has undertaken to send meat and flour and wheat and other foods for the support of the soldiers who are doing the fighting, for the men and women who are making the munitions, and for the boys and girls of Western Europe, and

116

that we must also feed ourselves while we are carrying on this war. The movement to establish gardens, therefore, and to have the children work in them is just as real and patriotic an effort as the building of ships or the firing of cannon. I hope that this spring every school will have a regiment in the Volunteer War Garden Army.

Cordially and sincerely yours,
(Signed) Woodrow Wilson

What Can Be Done in Unpromising Places

A citizen of California offered a small prize to the Congress of Mothers and Parent-Teacher Associations of the State to be awarded for the best report of actual work accomplished in providing recreation during one year.

Reports came from far and near, throughout the length of California's seven hundred miles. What these noble workers whom no one will ever hear of are doing for their communities ought to make a shining page for history. To start or to stimulate such effort is worth the cost of the prize and the labor of deciding the award, in any state.

One school decided to raise $100 for a play leader for the summer months. Most of it was amassed by saving and selling old newspapers. One little girl nine years old brought in 200 pounds. An operetta given to make up the deficit increased the sum to $122.30 instead of the goal of $100.

One school worked on backyard play; another carried on a campaign of newspaper publicity regarding the neighborhood center until the stay-at-homes, fathers and mothers, were so curious they had to come to see what it was all about.

A series of luncheons for the discussion of better recreation conditions and a flower and plant show represented one school's activities. The flowers were sent to hospitals after the exhibit.

A school band was established with fifty-four dollars raised by an entertainment.

A recreation committee raised twenty dollars which was turned into sand-boxes and other playground apparatus by the manual training class. A colonial dance, all of the dancers in costume, giving the dances of the period, was a delight to this same group.

117

Another school gave a dance for its alumni and afterward enlisted them as volunteer assistants to the play leader, so that the play of the district was vastly increased. The mothers' club responsible for this activity also provided chaperons for smaller group dances which grew out of the neighborhood center dances.

And, lastly, the prize winning association seemed almost to combine all these things. The report came in in two parallel columns, "What We Found," and "What We Did." They "found" little—not even enthusiasm—but they brought that. They raised an ungraded school to a graded school. They obtained an extra tax levy, secured $165.00 toward the salary of an additional teacher, remade the library and bought fifty new books. They installed two drinking fountains. They bought a gramaphone and a player-piano. Equipment provided, they began to make good use of it. A recreation afternoon was celebrated each week, with stories, folk dances and games. Fortnightly dances were held for the young people and a musical afternoon for the children. The school became a real neighborhood center— and life became so much the more worth the living.

Fourth of July Program

JOSEPH LEE, President Playground and Recreation Association of America, Boston, Massachusetts

8:30-9 or 9-9:30—Flag raising on local playgrounds for all

9-11—Games on local grounds for young children (Boys—12; Girls—16)
   Games on larger playgrounds for middle-sized boys (12-17)
   Athletic sports, rowing for young men: Watch and participate in games. Watch sports for girls over 16 and grown-ups

11-12:30—Boy Scouts and games on local grounds for young children and middle-sized boys. Games for young men. Exercises might be local as well as central.

2:30-4—Military and other band concerts

118

4-5—Our Allies and Liberty (see special program)

5-6—Folk dancing—Band Concerts

7-10—Singing, Colored Lights, Fireworks (?)

Everybody, so far as possible, should appear, especially at the Allies and Liberty ceremony, in costume or with a special ribbon, cap, or uniform of some sort—not elaborate, but such as can easily be prepared in the home.

The folk dancing should not be spectacular but for the fun of the dancers themselves. Special spaces might be set aside for each nationality.

THE DEFENDERS OF LIBERTY

Special Feature for the Fourth of July

Setting

A Statue of Liberty with a good-sized platform in front and at the sides with broad steps leading up in front. The statue may be only a board but if it is made like the Liberty in New York Harbor everybody will know what it is meant for. A good sculptor could be engaged to make it. There should be a broad open space, for soldiers and others to march in, leading up to the front of the platform. A trained military band and civilian chorus should be seated on each side of the platform and behind the statue.

Ceremony

Unveiling the statue

Soloist and chorus sing *Columbia, Gem of the Ocean.*

Soldiers representing Serbia and carrying the Serbian flag march up in front of the platform. The sergeant with the colors and a small escort march up on the platform and form with the flag in front facing the people.

The bugle plays the salute to the flag.

A soloist and the chorus sing the Serbian national song.

The sergeant with the flag and two of his escort retire to a

119

position abreast of the statue at the side of the platform towards the spectators' right.

The other Serbian soldiers and representatives take up a position prepared for them, preferably where they can be seen by the audience.

The same ceremony is performed by representatives of our other allies, or as many of them as can conveniently be represented, in the order of their entrance into the war, namely: The French, Belgians, English, Japanese, Italians, Roumanians, Chinese. The Poles should be represented even though they are not a nation.

Those taking part in each case should, if possible, include veterans and people in native costume.

The flags should be placed in the order of their entrance, from right to left, making a semi-circle in front of the statue.

An announcer with a megaphone should announce: "Serbia comes to the defense of Liberty." The other Allies are announced in the same way.

Enter America.

The flag should be carried by a Grand Army veteran escorted by a Revolutionary soldier on one side and a Spanish War veteran or one of the present army or navy on the other. The rest of the escort should consist of representatives of the present army and navy.

When the flag is presented, the people should rise and say together with the announcer leading:

"I pledge allegiance to my flag and to the Republic for which it stands; one nation, indivisible, with liberty and justice for all."

Chorus and people sing together *The Star Spangled Banner*.

After all the flags have been presented and lined up in front of the statue there should be some ceremony of holding the flags together in a clump in front of the statue with their staves crossed.

Bugle call salute to the flag.

A soloist sings the verses of the *Battle Hymn of the Republic*, all the people joining in the chorus.

All rise, the flags are placed up against the statue, and the sergeants who held them retire to the back of the platform on each side of the statue.

The bugle sounds the retreat.

120

Community Singing*

How *can* we sing? The autumn leaves are falling on a few little mounds in France, and brave little robins stand sentinel over our boys' last sleep.

How *can* we sing? A little widow walks down the aisle and takes her place in the family pew, two little tots with her looking for the Daddy who will come back no more.

How *can* we sing? Harry Lauder, the prince of comedians, sings to ten thousand soldiers and in the soil of France rests his only son, the bravest of Scotland's bravest.

And yet I want to hear America singing; for can't you hear the tread of many feet, the endless tramp, tramp, tramp, of a myriad heroes who, with laughter in their eyes and a song on their lips, gave their lives in noble and triumphant sacrifice on the Altar of Liberty?

I want to hear America Singing; for there is heard in the land the tramp, tramp, tramp of a hundred thousand men, from the North, the South, the East and the West, journeying as the Crusaders of old to rid the Earth and Mankind of the Arch-Enemy and to establish in glorious victory Truth and Liberty.

I want to hear America Singing; for in palace and tenement, in residence and homestead are the stifled sobs of the mother, the faltering voice of the father, the furtive look in sweetheart's eyes —and we must sing comfort into their hearts and cheer into their lives. America must sing—for we are in the throes of a mighty conflict that is shaking our country to its very foundations; sifting and searching the hearts of men; toppling over mercilessly conventions and castes, bringing humanity to the very primitive— America is being born again; and from the dark valley of the travail of her soul, America must ascend strong, stalwart, noble, and stand on the hill-tops Singing, Singing, Singing.

Community Singing indeed! Do you not remember the Shepherds in the fields of Bethlehem, guarding their sheep by night, when lo! "there was with the angel a multitude of the heavenly host praising God and saying"—you know their song— and oh! only to hear the New America, purged of all that is

---

Extract from address given by J. R. Jones, Director Kansas City Choral Union, published in the *Musical Bulletin*

selfish and vain and filled to the brim with all that is finest and best, singing until the mountains echo back the refrain, "Glory be to God in the Highest and on Earth Peace, good will toward men."

And may I add, that the nation that produced Beethoven, Bach, Wagner and Strauss (to mention a few) is a nation worth saving, though it cost America its last man and last dollar. Long after the Kaiser and his brood have mouldered to dust in their ignoble graves, the mighty soul of Beethoven shall stand a beacon light to the music ensemble of the universe. We are not at war to annihilate Germany; we are shedding our blood to free her from her cruel bondage that is crushing the life-blood out of every soul.

Today we must stand as one people—united solid. And what power on earth can compare with the power of song to stir the souls of men? To bring them together on common footing? What more conducive to our solidarity than the Community Chorus where the trained and untrained, the small voices and the large, the rich and the poor alike can mingle together in one grand cheerful song of hope?

You know of Premier Lloyd George? When that brilliant soul wanted to rest his fragile body awhile, where did he go? To the Welsh Eisteddfod where 10,000 sang his favorite hymns and brought Heaven down to Earth, that he and they might quaff from the holy chalice of the Eternal Trinity, Power, courage and unflinching determination to sacrifice their all, that God and His Righteousness might prevail in the Earth.

Can't you hear America singing?

Joe Simpson, Jr., Takes It Up with the Alderman*

Joe Simpson, Jr., of Chicago, Illinois, believes in taking off his coat and wading in and doing things. He knows that when you want to accomplish a thing you must got to the front and take the matter up with the persons who have the say-so.

---

* Courtesy of Chicago South Side Weekly Times

Joe, in common with nearly every other boy and girl attending school, wants a playground in the school yard. At the present time there is a proposition being put forward to abolish school playgrounds.

This matter will come up in the City Council, and Joe Simpson thinks that Alderman Nance of this ward should be fortified with all the information possible on the subject, that he may resist, if he is so inclined, the taking away of the pupils' playground.

In a manly, well-written letter, Joe, who lives at 6120 Michigan Avenue and is a scholar in Room 300 of Carter Practice School, writes to Alderman Nance as follows:

"Dear Sir: A discussion has recently arisen over our school playground, whether or not it should be retained. For the health and enjoyment of our little children and, yes, our larger boys and girls, it must be retained.

"What is better for a child after being indoors all day than to go to the playground and enjoy himself in the fresh air? Here is where there are so many things that interest him that he never tires of them, and whenever he gets a chance after school (after doing his chores at home), he immediately starts for the playground, where he is welcome. This also takes the worry from his mother, because she knows when her boy is at the school playground, he is under the watchful eyes of the directors, and not in mischief, as he usually is at home.

"Now, if our playground is taken from us, it means the children, large and small, will either be boxed up in the houses or will seek other means of fun and play in the dangerous streets, where automobiles and wagons are liable to injure them at any moment, or in the dirty alleys, or some other place even more dangerous. All this is prevented by the playground—'the joy of the children.'

"Our playground has a reputation all over the city for its wonderful activities in all sports such as swimming, skating and baseball; this adds to the popularity of our school so therefore if we lose the playground we lose one of the most important links in our school system.

"In reference to the sports played on our grounds, 'fairness in play' is one of the most important points taught us by the experienced directors. In being fair while playing on the school

123

playground, when the children grow up they will naturally be the same in their dealings with other people in the business world, thereby being made better citizens. All this is brought about through our playground which we are now fighting for.

"Now, Alderman, if these points are gathered together and thought over as they should be, you will firmly believe in your own heart, as I do, that any person who would do such a thing as take away the children's pleasures and rights is cold-hearted and unfair and never takes into consideration that he was once a child.

"Hoping when this playground question is brought up in the City Council you, as our representative, will use your influence in saving the playground for us, I remain,

"Very truly yours,
Joe Simpson, Jr.,
"Room 300, Carter Practice School"

Not Even the Reporter Could Swear

Last summer, in a city somewhere in Massachusetts, the Superintendent of Schools made up his mind that something must be done for boys. There were playgrounds, to be sure, but they did not help the situation so far as older boys were concerned because there were no men employed as play leaders.

He succeeded in convincing the Mayor that he must have an extra $300 for this particular work and employed two good men whom he put on playfields at opposite ends of the city. These playfields were beautiful areas, but used comparatively little for sports. One of them, in particular, was a sort of loafing place for the gang of the neighborhood.

After the advent of the play leader, a change began to take place, instead of a group of loafers, hanging around the place, there were usually four or five ball teams out on the field. Because the play leader tabooed smoking and swearing among the players, the fellows decided "to quit" rather than to give up the sport. One day something happened that gave every fellow on the ground a new idea. A ball disappeared. The play leader lined the boys up.

"Look here, fellows," he said, "the boy that stole that ball

124

didn't steal it from me, and he didn't steal it from Mr. X. (the Superintendent of Schools). He stole it from you. Why don't you get it back?"

The ball was recovered in short order. One other offense of the kind was committed, but the offender was pursued nearly a half mile by a crowd of angry boys, who not only demanded the purloined property but gave the culprit a good drubbing.

So marked was the change in the neighborhood that people began talking about it, and one morning a young reporter walked into the Superintendent's office and asked for a story. Mr. X told him at length about the work that the young men had done on the playfields and spoke particularly of what had been accomplished in regard to swearing and smoking. The reporter was more than skeptical; he said frankly that he did not believe it. Finally, he agreed to go up to the field, get into a game with the boys—no one would know him—and see for himself.

The next morning he appeared again at the Superintendent's office with this report: He had gone to the playfield, as he had agreed, and had started to play baseball. In the course of the game, a good swift ball struck him fairly and squarely on the ends of his fingers. Before he thought, out slipped a full-sized oath. The next minute, he was electrified by this chorus, "Say, if you're going to swear, you gotta get off the field! There ain't no swearing allowed here!"

"I just came to say, Mr. X, that I take back what I said yesterday," remarked the reporter. "There isn't any more swearing on that playfield!"

Make the Playground both Beautiful and Useful

GEORGE H. MILLER, Town Planner, Boston, Mass.

The means of making a playground attractive are usually the grading and surfacing of the ground, the design and location of architectural features, accessories and apparatus, and the arrangement of trees, shrubs, vines and flowering plants. The latter, the horticultural materials, are especially to be desired because they add the aspect of nature with its attending influences.

125

Being growing things, with life that is easily destroyed, they require care and sympathy and develop consideration that is desirable. No right-minded person ever condemned a love for flowers. The flower bloom creates an ever-changing interest on the part of the children that cannot be other than beneficial. Horticultural material when properly arranged not only provides beauty, but also provides shade, defines travel ways, forms divisions of the grounds and often holds sliding soils. When arranged with nicety it is the most important element in beautifying a playground and often increases the taxable value of adjacent residential property many times its own cost. Certain it is that children are wont to carve the bark of trees, make new paths and break through shrub groups. But children may be taught one thing or another, and the durability of plant growth is often increased by the watchfulness and interest of a competent playground instructor. Children should be taught the names of plants. Wire fencing run through shrub groups in a way to be inconspicuous is a helpful protection, while signs here and there as needed will suggest to children their duty, but an unusually effective protection is to edge the shrub groups with varieties having thorns and prickers that act as reminders in their own peculiar way.

In St. Mary's, Elk County, Pennsylvania, there is a playground consisting of about three acres and having an average attendance of five hundred children three times a day, in the evening under artificial flood light. It is divided into three distinct parts, the athletic field, the children's playground and the little children's portion. These parts are separated and defined by masses of trees and shrubs through which pass connecting paths. The entrances are marked by massive vine-clad stone posts, the paths follow attractive curving lines and shrub groups form naturalistic borders guiding the traffic.

The entrances are at the corners to accommodate diagonal traffic across the park by leading it around the athletic field; this circular path is used also on occasions as a running track. The field was graded to almost level, thus leaving sloping banks at one end where spectators of games may lie in the shade.

Overlooking the field and on its axis is a pavilion providing shelter and storage space. The secluded lawn areas on either side are the little children's portion, where there are sand boxes, and seats in the shade for the mothers.

The children's playground is almost level land and contains the drinking fountain, swings, teeter-totters, glide-for-life, merry-go-round and other apparatus. The space is very shady and tan-bark has made a delightful compact, dustless floor where the grass is worn.

The town has seven thousand inhabitants and this first playground is used to capacity. Its popularity is stimulating a movement for other playgrounds with opportunity for other features. The town inherited the land and the cost of improvements was about five thousand dollars, raised by subscription through the efforts of the Village Improvement Association of which Mrs. Frank A. Kaul was the President. In the design of improvements special stress was put on the matter of planting. St. Mary's has a model playground for a town of its size and has contributed a practical demonstration of the value of a playground that is fully useful because it does not lack being beautiful.

Book Reviews

THE SPIRIT OF THE NEW ARMY

By Joseph H. Odell. Published by Fleming H. Revell Company, New York. Price $1.25

How the Government is keeping America's splendid one hundred per cent manhood at the one-hundred per cent level of efficiency—something no other nation has done—through the Commission on Training Camp Activities of the War Department is graphically told in this first book, the first that has been written of the non-military phase of the soldier's training. It has a preface by Secretary of War Newton D. Baker, in which he says:

"When this war is over and the men and women of America have had an opportunity to obtain a perspective on its conduct and results, there will be an adequate appreciation of Dr. Odell's statement about Camp Hancock: 'I would rather intrust the moral character of my boy to that camp than to any college or university I know. This does not cast any unusually dark shadow upon the educational institutions of the country, but they have never possessed the absolute power that is now held by the War Department.'

"These chapters interested me greatly. . . . In them I found complete understanding of the work of the War Department Commission on Training Camp Activities. The scope of the Commission's activities is even wider than indicated here and its work is growing rapidly. Special library buildings have been built at the camps, and the American Library Association has undertaken the work of conducting them. Camp theatres seating audiences of three thousand have been erected and the men are

BOOK REVIEWS

enjoying the best theatric performances at prices from 10 to 25 cents. Eminent actors and managers are cooperating with us in this field.

"Cooperation indeed has marked the work of the Commission on every turn. Americans acknowledge their debt to the soldier; they believe in him, and in return the soldier believes in his mission. For a succinct statement of the value of this work I cannot improve on what Dr. Odell says:

'If Germany should crumble before these men should get into action, if we have lavished billions of dollars to train men for battles they will never fight, yet the money has been well spent, and I consider it the best investment in citizenship that the country could have made.'"

In his book, Dr. Odell shows an amazing intimacy with army life and traditions which he gained while he was chaplain of a Pennsylvania regiment, a post which he held for ten years. Dr. Odell is now a special writer for *The Outlook*. He was formerly editor of the *Scranton Pennsyvania Times*, and later an editorial writer on the *Philadelphia Public Ledger*. His home is in Troy, N. Y.

PHYSICAL TRAINING METHODS FOR THE SCHOOL ROOM
By Ruth M. Bailey, Physical Director State Normal School, Geneseo, New York

The latter part of this booklet contains suggestions for story plays for younger children which might be the basis for valuable play activities in the hands of a leader with real play spirit.

BUGLE CALLS OF LIBERTY
By Gertrude Van Duyn Southworth and Paul Mayo Paine. Published by Iroquois Publishing Co., Inc., Syracuse, New York. Price, sixty cents

While intended as a school reader, this book will be useful in many ways in the playground and recreation centers, for it gives the great speeches of the present day which are not easily available for group use. Viviani, Lloyd George, Woodrow Wilson and Robert Lansing are represented, besides the more usual patriotic selections.

COMMUNITY DRAMA
By Percy Mackaye. Published by Houghton Mifflin Company, Boston and New York. Price, fifty cents

"What the world is waiting for is a method. * * * for creating the international mind." This method, the author believes may be largely found in the development of Community Drama. "Community Drama is the ritual of democratic religion * * * the social religion of the only commandment of Christ: *Neighborliness.*" Mr. Mackaye has reason for the faith that is in him through long experience in the actual operation and effects of Community Drama. He gives poignant instances of the meaning of such drama in the lives of the participants.

MUNICIPAL PLAYGROUNDS OF NEW YORK STATE CITIES
Report No. 257. Data gathered by the State Bureau of Municipal Information of the New York State Conference of Mayors and other city officials. Published by Public Affairs Information Service, man-

BOOK REVIEWS

aged for cooperating institutions by H. W. Wilson Company, New York City

Information as to the number, cost, administration of playgrounds is given. In answer to the question, "What are results of any effort you have made to determine whether playgrounds reduce juvenile delinquency?" while many answer, "No investigation made," a goodly number indicate the faith that is in them. Binghamton answers "about sixty per cent according to humane officer. In large playground in Johnson City available for Binghamton children, about ninety per cent." Buffalo declares that the judge of the juvenile court states there is a noticeable decrease in juvenile delinquency in sections, where playgrounds have been established." Rochester reports, "General decrease in the pilfering of freight, to such an extent that the New York Central has allowed city to use their grounds for play purposes."

POLITE AND SOCIAL DANCES

A Collection of Historic Dances. Complied and edited by Marie Ruef Hofer. Published by Clayton F. Summy Company, 64 East Van Buren Street, Chicago. Price, $1.00

A really remarkable number of dances little known or incorrectly known are given their traditional form in this volume. The introduction sketches the history of dancing from early Egyptian forms to present-day American. The author looks for the subjective meaning of the dance, the emotional values, the state of mind it interprets. "The close connection between present-day social reform and good form is leading us to search into the recreational interests of the people, only to find therein most vital analogies to the moral life. The history of the dance is a history of social expression of all times and of all classes of men and as such should hold some place in education."

THE SONG PLAY BOOK

Compiled by Mary A. Wollaston. Edited by C. Ward Crampton, M. D. Published by A. S. Barnes Company, New York and Chicago, 1917. Price, $1.80

Fifty song plays, used and tested for years in the New York Training School for Teachers, are presented. They have been selected with the idea of giving as much vigorous exercise as possible in proportion to the singing. They are especially suitable for the first three grades of the public school. Dr. Crampton, in his introduction to the work points out that "One of the most valuable features of the work is Miss Wollaston's unique and definite form of presentation, which, while preserving intact the natural tone of the invaluable traditional spirit, yet brings to bear the latest and best in education." *Looby Loo, The Muffin Man, Jolly Is the Miller* are all present, as well as others not so often used.

CITY PLANNING PROGRESS, 1917

Compiled by the Committee on Town Planning of the American Institute of Architects. Edited by George B. Ford, assisted by Ralph F. Warner. Published by the Journal of the American Institute of Architects. The Octagon, Washington, D. C. Price, $1.50

BOOK REVIEWS

The data covers what has been accomplished, or is projected, in all cities of the United States of over 25,000 inhabitants, and in a few cities and towns where the population is smaller, where the work is of special interest. The status of the park and playground system is indicated in many cases. The material is not copyrighted as the committee desires to make it as widely useful as possible.

THE THEORY AND PRACTICE OF EDUCATIONAL GYMNASTICS FOR BOYS' AND GIRLS' HIGH SCHOOLS

By William A. Stecher. Published by John Jos. McVey, 1229 Arch St., Philadelphia, Pennsylvania. Price, $1.25 net

The material given for use with boys and girls is divided into five parts: I. Tactics. II. Free exercises. III. Rhythmic steps. IV. Games, track and field work and V. Apparatus work. Dodge ball, captain ball, battle ball and volley ball and later baseball, soccer, hand ball, basket ball and tennis are recommended for boys and for girls, with the exception of soccer and hand ball. Emphasis is laid throughout upon the importance of developing a vigorous, natural outdoor life, with skating, canoeing and other sports in season.

FOLK DANCES OF BOHEMIA AND MORAVIA

By Anna Spacek and Neva L. Boyd, of the Recreation Department, Chicago School of Civics and Philanthropy. Published by Saul Brothers, 626 Federal Street, Chicago, Illinois. Price, $1.00

Another of the series of books of national dances compiled by Miss Boyd in collaboration with a native of the country represented gives a large number of dances previously little known. These dances are translations from the work of Miss Nemcova, who secured them from Miss Steyskal, for many years director of an orphanage in Bruo, Moravia. Miss Steyskal went out among the people and collected the dances. All royalties from the sale of the present volume are to be presented to the orphanage in Moravia.

THE PLAY MOVEMENT AND ITS SIGNIFICANCE

By Henry S. Curtis, Ph. D. Published by The Macmillan Company, New York. Price, $1.50

The author recognizes five tendencies in the play movement in America today: that usually thought of as the play movement the effort to provide space for children's play; school play as an organized factor of the curriculum; the effort to provide more adequately for children below school age; public recreation; and the movement "not for the .rbeirth of play but of the spirit of play." Each of these phases is discussed. Especially noteworthy is the description of typical public recreation systems, as those of Los Angeles, Chicago, Philadelphia. Perhaps the author lays more emphasis upon the importance of school play as the solution than all leaders in the play movement would be willing to do, but the description of the successful experiment at Gary gives food for thought.

In his summary, *What Is the Cost,* Dr. Curtis says: "It is often said that education is necessary but play is a luxury. Neither education nor recreation is necessary to existence, as is proved by history, but both education and recreation are necessary to the larger life of the spirit."

130

Please mention THE PLAYGROUND when writing to advertisers

Victrola Appreciation, Primary Grades, Charleston, S. C.   Calisthenics with the Victrola, Erie, Pa.

A Victrola in your school means

increased culture, artistic progress, greater physical fitness, renewed interest in all studies, and the opportunity for every boy and girl to hear and know the world's best music rendered by the world's greatest artists.

The Victrola and Victor Records

are used to illustrate and vitalize the lessons in English Language and Literature, History and Geography. They are indispensable in the teaching of Physical Education, Folk Dancing, Patriotic Songs, Community Singing, Nature Study, Penmanship, Typewriting, Voice Culture, Ear Training, Opera Study, Music History and Orchestral Instruments. From Victor Records the boys in the Army and Navy are learning French, and Wireless Telegraphy.

With all these practical uses, the Victrola has become a real necessity, and should be a regular part of the equipment of your school.

If you would know more about the extensive use of Victor Records in school, see "A New Graded List," which is a catalogue of over one thousand Victor Records, classified according to use in various grades and subjects.

Ask your Victor dealer for a copy of this new list, or send a post card to the

Educational Department
Victor Talking Machine Co.
Camden, N. J.

Victrola XXV, $85
specially manufactured
for School use

When the Victrola is not in use, the horn can be placed under the instrument safe and secure from danger, and the cabinet can be locked to protect it from dust and promiscuous use by irresponsible people.

Victrola

"HIS MASTER'S VOICE"

To insure Victor quality, always look for the famous trademark, "His Master's Voice." It is on all genuine products of the Victor Talking Machine Company.

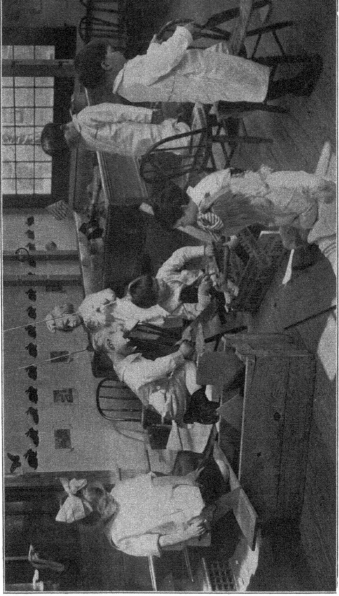

The Kindergarten and First Grade

CONSTRUCTION PLAY THAT EDUCATES

The Playground

Vol. XII No. 4   JULY 1918

The World At Play

Girls of the Hour.—*Wohelo* gives the following patriotic service record of Camp Fire Girls:

70,448 Camp Fire Girls last year planted and cultivated truck gardens; 83,356 contributed money and cooperated with the Red Cross. The Camp Fire Girls throughout the country contributed more than $10,000 to their own War Chest to carry on the war work of the organization. They have sold over $12,000 worth of Liberty Bonds, and thousands of dollars' worth of Thrift Stamps.

Park Fete of New York Girls' Public School Athletic League.—Six thousand children singing and dancing on the green in Central Park, above them, twenty-five Maypoles decked with gay colors —orange and black, yellow and white, pink and white and blue and white! The band of the *S. S. Recruit* occupied a grandstand at the center of the green and furnished the music for the songs and dances. The fete was opened with a roll of drums at which the children massed themselves around the green. At the sound of the bugle they marched to the centre of the field. Then came the raising of the flag and six thousand voices recited the pledge of allegiance. Singing and dancing were then given full sway over the green. Near the end of the hour the Maypoles were wound and the band struck up the *Star Spangled Banner*. All stood at attention and the gaiety of the afternoon was at an end.

The Boy Scouts were on hand wherever any help was needed and they worked like little Trojans, taking down the Maypoles at a slight shower and setting them up again with no delay when the sun came out—and how manly they looked as they stood at attention, never moving a muscle, while the *Star Spangled Banner* was played.

Triangular Discussions.— The Extension Division of the

University of Wisconsin advocates three-sided debates on present day questions and recommends that every such program include an American Song Contest. A special bulletin on this subject is issued by the University.

Twin Ball.—A new game invented by Mrs. G. B. Emerson, of Boston, aims to develop alertness, muscular coordination and accuracy in throwing, especially for children between six and ten. Directions may be secured from Mrs. Emerson or from THE PLAYGROUND.

Jewish Recreation Center.—New York City has a new Jewish center on West Eighty-sixth Street, which aims to unify the religious, social and occupational life of its members. A synagogue, class rooms, auditorium, club rooms, gymnasium and swimming pool give splendid facilities for expression of various interests.

Keeping Fit.—Oneida County Y. M. C. A. in New York State conducted a "Keeping Fit Exhibition" to which only men and boys were admitted, an adult guide to every three boys. Committees in every community were enlisted to secure the attendance of every boy in the district.

Greater Recreation Budget for Detroit.—The City of Detroit has allowed a budget of $437,100.25 for Detroit's recreation program for the coming year. This is twice as large a sum as was allowed last year. Detroit is alive to the fact that directed and equipped leisure-time activities play an important part in maintaining the morale of the people and is setting a standard which will have great influence with other cities throughout the country. It is a significant fact that last year with all the stress of war, the amount of money expended for recreation was greater than ever before.

Looks for Recreation Spurt after the War.—Lieutenant Eustace M. Peixotto, formerly of the Recreation League of San Francisco, writes to his former colleagues:

"Surely the world is moving fast these days along the lines for which we have striven. The Army has adopted the recreation program wholesale and it is being demonstrated on a scale such as few of us ever dreamed we should see in our life time. Every officer I have ever met is in full sympathy with it and ready to do his share toward seeing it go through. After this experience every man who goes back should be a recreation advocate in his own home town, not to mention being a community singer and a few other things. The war will unquestionably halt great expansion in public playgrounds and some other things temporarily, but I do believe that it will be the means of a speedier general adoption of the whole recreation program. The work of the Soldiers' and Sailors' Recreation Committees is bound to have a far-reaching effect, not only on the men who enjoy their benefits but on the communities in which they are organized."

War Gardens in Canada.—It is estimated that Canadian war gardens raised thirty million dollars' worth of food last year. This year the chairman of the vacant lot and home garden section of the Canada Food Board says the record must be doubled.

Recreation Problem in England.—England has a standing committee appointed by the Home Secretary to promote recreation for boys and girls, particularly as a deterrent to juvenile delinquency. In fifty or more large towns committees consisting of representatives of all organizations for child welfare have been working on the problem under the direction of the national committee.

Mass Games for Troops Landing in France.—Since neither space nor time for practice and team play are available for r e c r e a t i o n through baseball, football, track sports, among the soldiers in France in many cases, a method of mass games has been evolved which has proved very successful. One of the great try-outs of this idea was upon the occasion of the landing of the first soldiers in France. The men were eager for a chance to "stretch their legs." Everybody must have a chance in a short time in a comparatively small space. Fourteen hundred forty men were scheduled for the first hour in a great level field a short distance from the dock. Each company followed its band into columns of files, twenty men to a file, eight files to a company. Between company files was a lane six feet wide. First came a company "standing broad jump," in which seventy-one percent of the men cleared the ditch which they were ordered to jump. Followed a company "relay race"—1440 men flying down the field, in a race in which fifty-six percent were ahead of the rope suddenly dropped waist high. "Company soccer" divided the men into eight teams of 175 each.

On four large fields the eight teams played, one side trying to kick over the line or through the posts at one end, the other side at the other end. One point scored for kicking over the line, three points kicking through the goal posts. So lively was the scrimmage that the score-keepers lost count, but one team kicked more than seventy goals in thirty minutes.

Ireland Welcomes Our Sailor Lads.—The Irish ancestry of many of the American sailors in Irish waters, as well as the fact that so many Irish mothers have sons in America has made the Irish welcome to our boys a cordial one. The latch string is out on almost any house. One gathering place which is popular is the United States Naval Men's Club in Dublin, funds for which were supplied by American business men. Baseball follows the flag and the Americans daily playing on the cricket ground are almost convincing the stolid English sailor that "bass ball" may possibly be a real game.

Serving His Country.—A story is told of a young "Tommy" sent to "Blighty," wounded—in football behind the lines! Frequent tales of cricket proceeding earnestly under shot and shell come to

138

us. The indomitable spirit of play is near of kin to "They shall not pass!"

The Old Order Changeth.—Something of what might have been the condition in our own country had it not been for the work of the Commission on Training Camp Activities is indicated by the following from Hawthorne's English notebook, near the end of Volume One under date of April 1st, 1856. Mr. Hawthorne has just been describing a visit to Aldershott Camp, where he and Mr. Bennoch were the guests of Lieutenant Shaw of the North Cork Rifles. The time is that of the Crimean War; Sebastopol has recently fallen into the hands of the British.

"I know not whether I have mentioned that the villages neighboring to the camp have suffered terribly as regards morality from the vicinity of the soldiers. Quiet old English towns, that till within a little time ago had kept their antique simplicity and innocence, have now no such thing as female virtue in them, so far as the lower classes are concerned. This is expressing the matter too strongly, no doubt; but there is too much truth in it nevertheless; and one of the officers remarked that even ladies of respectability had grown much more free in manners and conversation than at first. I have heard observations similar to this from a Nova-Scotian, in reference to the moral influence of soldiers when stationed in the provinces."

The Catholic Soldier.—The National Catholic War Council has published a pamphlet giving the reasons for Catholic support of the work of the Commission on Training Camp Activities, upon which Charles P. Neill, of Washington, is the Catholic member. The work of the Knights of Columbus is outlined and a plan given for diocesan and national organization.

The Camp Workers and Their Work.—One of the first efforts to present in report form the work of the various sections of the Commission on Training Camp Activities is that compiled by Lieutenant Alleyne C. Howell, Senior Chaplain, Division Headquarters and Editor of the *Eighty-third Division News,* at Camp Sherman, Chillicothe, Ohio. The Commission workers at Camp Sherman have always had most helpful support from the commanding officer, Major-General E. F. Glenn, so it is not surprising that the work has attained such scope as to make even a brief report in-spiring and amazing reading.

Liked the Cowboys.—Ladies of Mount Holly, North Carolina, who entertained twenty-five or thirty soldiers from Camp Greene at Sunday dinner, were very enthusiastic about the Wyoming boys. One wrote to the representative of the War Camp Community Service:

"We were all so delighted with the men, every one of whom was a cowboy from Wyoming, that all are clamoring to entertain again next Sunday. If you can send us more Wyoming men, in addition to those who were with us last Sunday, (for we have asked them all to come back next Sunday) we will be glad to receive them. They were such fine fellows. But if it isn't convenient to select Wyoming men, we are assured there are others just as delightful from other states and you must send us at least 25 or 30 for next Sunday dinner.

"I think every woman in Mount Holly, when preparing dinner Sunday, had a soldier guest or two in mind. When the boys who were on horseback rode away, we filled their saddle pockets with fruit and nuts."

One of the dinner guests on Sunday was Lester Kyle, 148th F. A., champion rider

139

from Wyoming, who put his horse through a few stunts, to the huge delight of his audience.

A Soldier's Idea of a Club.— W. A. Wheatley, representing the War Camp Community Service at Camp Greene, Charlotte, North Carolina, invited soldiers to express their idea of what a club should be. Among many letters he received the following:

"Dear Sir—Another building should be built in Charlotte for the soldiers in the nature of a club. Equip the building with a big game room, that is, pool tables, checkers, chess. I would not have a billiard table. All the pool games should be open tables, that is, if one desires to play, all he has to do is to take a cue and join the players at the next game without saying or asking anything.

"I would have a buffet restaurant, something like Thompson's restaurants in Chicago and New York. Soft drinks and plain ice cream only, cigars.

"Shower baths would be a good thing to have, but not any gymnastics, that is, physical exercises or basket ball.

"The reading and writing room should be located somewhere in the building where the patrons will not be both-

140

ered with music, players or diners, or with anybody.

"I would also equip a barber shop in the club.

"Very truly yours,

"PVT................

"Camp Greene, N. C."

What the Soldiers Want.— A private writing of the monotony of camp life declares that entertainment by outsiders gives the greatest relaxation. Music, vaudeville, boxing—"anything that takes a fellow out of himself and takes his thoughts off what he might be doing back home"—that's what he wants.

Athletics after F r e n c h Duty.—One would suppose that sleep, long and undisturbed, would be the sole desire of the soldier just from the trenches. But it has been found that the nervous and mental strain is worse than the physical for the men and sound sleep suddenly is impossible. Lieutenant Herbert of the French navy has devised a scheme by which the soldiers are marched without rest back to the open country, where, stripped to the waist, they set out for a cross-country run, up hill, down dale, climbing trees, crawling through underbrush, until, in a fine glow, they are ready for refreshing slumber.

The same methods of training have been used for soldiers before going to the trenches, especially crawling, lying prostrate, and throwing exercises. Recently in a sham battle the men trained by this method lost four "dead" as against 300 "dead" of their opponents, trained in the old way.

Work for Negroes.—While the Rockefeller Foundation is appropriating $25,000 to enable the War Camp Community Service to demonstrate model recreation conditions for negro soldiers, a company of negro stockholders in New York City is planning to make and keep Harlem negroes physically fit. Thirteen lots have been purchased for a splendid modern recreation plant.

Doing His Bit.—"Was your boy Josh much of a help to you around the farm?"

"Yes," replied Farmer Corntossel. "I didn't realize how much of a help he was. He didn't do much work, but he could play the jewsharp an' tell riddles an' keep the farmhands entertained so that sometimes they would stay for days and days at a time before going."

Pure Democracy in Playground Management

W. C. BATCHELOR, Supervisor of Playgrounds, Utica, N. Y.

The Greenwood Playground is located in the heart of that section of Gardner, Massachusetts, in which the majority of Finns and French Canadians employed in the numerous chair industries of that town, live and raise their large families. A heavy shower, coming suddenly upon the playground one July afternoon, filled the shelter house to its capacity. This was just the opportunity I had been awaiting. Without the necessity of a formal summons, a majority of the representative boys and girls, up to fifteen years of age, were in a position to give me their undivided attention for a brief interval.

I told them that I had a very important matter on which I wanted their opinions. I suggested at once that I felt that they were capable themselves of managing the playground, with its seven acres and accompanying equipment, as well as the large numbers of children in attendance.

"Sure we can," said some.

"I'll lick any kid who don't do as I say," remarked one youngster who appeared to be able to back his statement.

But, in the minds of the more thoughtful ones, serious problems arose.

"My mother wouldn't let me come if there was no one here to take care of us."

"Everybody would get to fighting over the things to play with."

"There's gotta be someone to boss things."

"None of the kids would mind any of the others."

"Well," I suggested, "Suppose we run the playground as the town is run. They have three selectmen who decide between them how things are to be done. The people elect these men themselves. After they have chosen men whom they are willing to trust with the affairs of management, they do as these selectmen say. If the people don't like the way the selectmen run things, they put others in their places at the next election. But, at the time they have to do as the selectmen decide."

"My father is a selectman," said one, "I'd like to be a selectman and then he could tell me what to do."

"But we gotta have more than just selectmen if we're gonna make it like a real town," said a barefooted youngster with a prominent chin, "We gotta have cops and firemen and everything."

"Yes," I continued, "We'd have a police force and a fire department. The cops would see that there was no swearing or vulgar talk; and get after any one who smoked cigarettes, or threw stones, or did anything that was not allowed on the playground."

"But," said he of the square jaw, "if we pinched a feller, what'd we do with him? There oughta' be a judge. Why don't you be the judge?"

I assured him that I should be glad to act in that capacity provided I was appointed.

"What would the firemen do?" asked another, "We never have a fire here."

"No," I replied, "We might never have a fire, but firemen are expected to do anything where dangerous climbing is necessary. They would put up and take down all the swings, rings, giant-strides, teeter-boards and all the other apparatus; and see that everything was always safe to use."

"The one that can climb better than any one else oughta' be

142

chief," proposed he. "I can climb anything here without a ladder or nuthin.' I clumb to the top of the flagpole the other night."

"Then," I went on, "We'd need a board of health. You know their business is to get rid of anything that is dangerous to health. They would keep the ground clear of broken glass; and stop any one from throwing around apple cores, banana skins, watermelon rinds, or anything that would decay or draw flies. Water commissioners would keep the drinking fountain sanitary; see that all drains on the ground were kept clear; and also report to the police any one interfering with these things in any way."

"I saw a kid tryin' to stuff a frog in the drinkin' fountain this mornin' before you come," someone volunteered.

"Park commissioners," I resumed, "would see that no one injured trees or shrubs. They would keep the grounds neat by seeing that no one threw tin cans, papers or anything like that on the grounds.

"Each of these town officers would wear a silver badge with the words 'Greenwood Playground' and his office stamped on it. They would take the same oath of office as the town officers of Gardner now take."

"But what will the girls do?" asked one, in a grieved tone.

"Of course," I replied, "In all up-to-date towns and cities, women vote and hold office just the same as men. If we are going to have a modern government we must have equal suffrage."

"Say, this is going to be great!"

"Ma says she wants to vote; and now I'll get a chance before she does."

"When can we start?" came in a chorus.

"Look what I got!" interrupted a ragged little shaver of eight years, at the same time presenting me with a corn flake box filled with a fine assortment of broken glass, apple cores, candy and gum wrappers, and the like. His aspirations for a place on the board of health were quite evident.

"This is a big change to make," I cautioned, "And we want it to be successful, so we'd better go slowly. You know, this playground, like most other playgrounds, has always been ruled like a kingdom or an empire, by one or two persons; and, if you are now to run things yourselves, it will be a democracy. When a monarchy becomes a democracy through a revolution or abdication

143

of the ruler, a provisional government is generally set up until the people can hold primaries to nominate officers; and then give every one a chance to vote, and elect the officers they want."

"Why don't you say who the ones are to be to run things for awhile," came a suggestion, "Then we can nominate and vote for the regular ones."

"Then we can see how the ones you put in can do it; and we can tell them if we want to elect them for keeps," suggested another.

So in true democratic fashion the will of the people was carried out. The following day the provisional appointments were made; three selectmen, a police chief and three officers, a fire chief and three firemen, three members of the board of health, three water commissioners and three park commissioners. I set myself up as provisional judge with my assistant as a juror. The twenty officers of the town official staff were duly sworn in, their term of office to expire on the day following the regular election. Twenty badges of office were distributed, to be returned at the expiration of the term of office. These proved to be a very important part of the new plan.

Numerous inquiries regarding the duties of office, conduct of primaries and election, and the like flooded the "court"; aside from the cases coming up for trial, which were many and the charges as varied. With the coming of election, the attempts on the part of various candidates to win political favor were characteristic of greater politicians. Generosity was rampant.

It was decided that the minimum age of voters should be ten years. When, finally, the regular officers were elected, and the new democracy firmly established, the development of the various essential qualities of the several officers was phenomenal. Confidential advice from the "bench" now regularly appointed, was often sought. Selectmen were warned against the disastrous effect of an attitude of all-importance toward their townpeople. Tactful aggressiveness, a quality as essential as it is rare in juvenile police officers, was necessarily emphasized. "Safety First," the slogan of the fire department, was applied personally to the ever-reckless members of the department who, to exhibit their rapidly developing skill in putting up and taking down apparatus, insisted upon dispensing altogether with the heretofore necessary ladders. A child eating an apple was shadowed by a member of the board of health, not for "coresy" this time, but to see that

144

the core was properly deposited in the refuse can. The line in waiting at the drinking fountain was no longer given an unappreciated shower bath by some mischievous youngster who had drunk his fill. Those who craved publicity, and, heretofore, carved their initials in playground trees, now satisfied that craving by serving as a park commissioner and protecting the trees from this abuse.

That the effects of this experiment were felt in the homes of the children as well, was soon evident. The police chief, a girl of thirteen, of sturdy physique, showed natural ability in the handling of the three boys under her supervision. However, her duties became particularly trying on Saturday aftenoons when the grounds were used by the town baseball team for a weekly home game. In the presence of the older men, on one of these occasions, members of the force failed to carry out the instructions of their chief, who, as a result, was not on duty the following Saturday. During the next week, however, her mother informed us that she had learned why Nellie was not on the ground. The mother said that she would see that the girl was there Saturday afternoons thereafter, and that if she was not able to do what was expected of her she should resign. She was not absent again nor did she resign.

Another instance of the cooperation of parents came to our attention when the Women's Relief Corps had arranged to present a large flag to the playground. The board of selectmen, two boys and a girl, were called together to decide which should make the speech of acceptance for the town. All refused. The following day, however, the girl said she would do it, her mother having told her that she should show them that women in public office could do things which men had not the courage to attempt.

The crowning feature in this respect came in connection with the town officers' outing. It was reported that on the way home the three police officers and two of the firemen were smoking cigarettes. It was decided that their resignations should be requested, and this fact published in the "Gardner Daily News." Each boy returned his badge upon being notified of the decision. The next day three of these boys came on the ground together, a solemn spectacle. The publicity which they, as town officers, had enjoyed was now their undoing.

One volunteered this bit of information, "My old man give

me an awful beatin', last night. He says to me, 'You'll smoke cigarettes and get thrown out of the playground fire department, will you? I'll show you.'"

Another said more hopefully, "My mother saw it first, and she knew what the old man would do to me, so she didn't let him see it; but just gave me a talking to."

A third produced the condemning item itself, exclaiming triumphantly, "See that! I cut it out as soon as the paper came and told 'em it was just somethin' about the playgrounds that I wanted to keep."

The selectman, a newsboy barely thirteen years of age, who had suggested publishing this, showed a keen perception of the great weight of publicity used as a weapon for punishment.

In general with the passing of the oligarchy, and the dawn of the democracy, the Greenwood Playground became not only a safer place for recreation; but it became a great juvenile educational center.

Extracts from
War-Time Status of Playground Work*

O. W. DOUGLAS

During a time of great national stress the people of a nation turn most naturally to the business of making an inventory, and planning most earnestly and seriously for the future.

Unfortunately the inventory and planning are apt to follow too closely along lines of the purely material. In war time it is only human to think in terms of military expediency, and at the present time there is danger of not looking far enough ahead.

All righteous wars have been fought, not so much for the immediate gain or value to the living adult population, as for the benefit to posterity. It is therefore our children and our children's children that will, we hope, benefit most as a result of this war for the life and perpetuation of democracies. This being true it is especially necessary that we do not neglect those great efforts along child welfare lines so recently and so well begun.

* Courtesy of Pacific Municipalities, June, 1917

146

WAR-TIME STATUS OF PLAYGROUND WORK

"Don't Grind Your Seed Corn" During the waning days of the Southern Confederacy, when it seemed as if the very children would be drawn into the maelstrom, Confederate President Jeff Davis admonished his people, saying, "The children of a nation are its seed corn. Don't grind your seed corn."

This warning by the leader of a lost cause at the time of a great crisis is no less of value at the present time.

A discussion of one result of playground development on civic life will have to suffice in this brief article at this time. This is the result observed and recorded in connection with the juvenile courts. By actual statistics it has been shown that the general average of juvenile delinquency in communities establishing equipped and supervised playgrounds has been reduced fully fifty per cent. In one Ohio city of 35,000 population the Judge of the Juvenile Court reported a decrease of cases coming before him of seven hundred per cent during the first year of playground activity when thirteen units were equipped and supervised. When asked by a newspaper reporter why he had nothing to do he said: "The boys are too busy on the playgrounds to get into meanness." And he said nothing of the reduction of the number of accidents to children when formerly playing in the streets.

Owing, therefore, to the attainment of results enumerated above it may readily be seen that it is not at all necessary to confine playground privileges and activities to the larger cities. Hence towns and villages, and even rural schools, are going into this matter vigorously in many localities with most satisfying results. Even the country boy and girl not only need, but are entitled, to play equipment, supervision and encouragement.

In conclusion, a warning from the experience of England during the present world war is worth most careful consideration in this country at this time.

Owing to conditions soon after the war opened some schools were closed, playgrounds neglected, children were turned loose on the streets, or put at hard work, expenses for schools and playgrounds were reduced, all with appalling results. During the year 1915 juvenile delinquency throughout England showed an average increase of 34 per cent. In the city of Manchester the increase was 56 per cent. England is now struggling to get her children back in school, to restore her playground activities and facilities, and is otherwise endeavoring to attain the necessary normal standards existing before the war.

. ' Nor has England alone suffered. In Berlin juvenile delin-quency doubled during the first year of the war, and in Munich the first three months of 1915 showed a greater total than for the entire year of 1914.

If the above experiences are worth anything as examples they should say to the people of the United States that we must not start retrenchment with the children of our land. Retrench we must, but let it not fall upon the school and recreation work of our children.

"Don't grind your seed corn."

Folk Dancing behind The Lines

One of the very interesting developments in recreational work for the soldiers at the base and convalescent hospitals in France has been the teaching of folk and Morris dancing. The English Folk Dance Society has a representative, Miss D. C. Daking, behind the lines in France teaching the soldiers folk dancing. Extracts from some of her letters to Mr. Cecil Sharp, president of the Society, show the delight with which the men are taking part in these activities and are of special interest in view of the fact that some of the English officers are consider-ing having the English folk and Morris dances introduced into the regular army gymnastics.

DEAR MR. SHARP:

I write you a report of my last four months in France.

I was asked by the Y. M. C. A. to go out to one of the Bases and see if the men would care for folk dancing. It was very difficult at first, because the entertainments and fun con-sisted of comic songs and rag-time and gramaphones, and no one knew anything of folk dancing. I couldn't show it with no one to demonstrate, and people refused to learn till they had seen it.

I used to go round to our huts in the different camps with a set of rappers under my arm, and talk to little bunches of men just where I happened to find interest. They wouldn't learn, because, of course, all classes had to be held in the concert huts, and there were always dozens there watching and that made people shy. Then I got a central class-room from the Y. M.

148

C. A., and picked a man here and a man there, and we began—and then I roped in some of the Y. M. C. A. girls who do clerical work and have their evenings off, and they went crazy over country dances. Then as my few men began to be good, they didn't mind dancing at camp classes, so I could start a class with two men and gradually the watchers would come in.

Since then we have given twelve demonstrations to average audiences of 500. Never less than 300, and often up to 700. I talk a little history and they like that very much. The men are frightfully keen. They cheer the roof off and run with our car all through the camps when we leave afterwards.

I am now the official Folk Dancing Department of the Y. M. C. A. I have been allowed eight military passes for assistants, and am told by the Y. M. C. A. that I may engage whom I choose and place them in other Bases. Of course, I don't want six others all at once, because I think it better to get their Bases ready for them, instead of pitching them into it as I was at first, with no popular opinion for backing and no pupils ready to learn.

I've formed a Y. M. C. A. Branch of the English Folk Dancing Society. I thought it well to make ourselves as official as possible. Members are interested and keen. My idea is that they will join their home branches of the English Folk Dancing Society when they return to England. I have a lot of clergymen on it and all kinds of folk. Martin Harvey joined because it was really good art and genuine; and Gipsy Smith joined because he said it was splendid stuff for keeping the boys out of mischief.

I have a really good class of regular army gym instructors—six of them, mostly sergeant majors. They, of course, are permanent men and in charge of the training camps. I'll be able to make rather fine dancers of them, and they are tremendously keen. They want to put it into the army gyms along with other games. They all mean to come to Stratford after the war.

Yours sincerely,
(Signed) D. C. DAKING

DEAR MR. SHARP:

I've had a thrilling piece of work at Trouville in an enormous convalescent camp. I mustn't of course give you the number of thousands of the men there. All the staff are medical and the whole spirit of the camp is for sports and games and anything to divert the men. I took over a big demonstration (we were hung up there for three days because the weather was too bad for boats to cross, but that's by the way) and we swept every one into real enthusiasm. Since then I have gone over as often as I could and given large classes in two of the camps to the gym instructors and a good many of the N. C. O's. My two colonels are enthusiastic and one or other always drops in to watch the classes. One has said that he would like every man in camp to be able to dance the Kirkby [sword dance]. I am told that last week the gym instructors took fifteen hundred men on the race-course and began to teach steps, with the band in the middle.

Mrs. Kennedy is now looking for some one else, as Abbeville is asking for help. It is most difficult. People have to be so very 'right'. It isn't so much the teaching of advanced work which is needed, but the handling of, very often, rather difficult audiences. And also there's the question of mess invitations and our enertaining. . . .

Then I've had an invitation from a society in Paris called the Academie. It has been started, I think, since the war, for the furtherance of sports and pastimes amongst the women and girls of France. I am invited to go to Paris for a few days to explain and show our dances.

We gave a demonstration on Thursday at a huge French and English Bazaar and the room was packed. And there's our International Concert at the Theatre for which we are doing dances and folk songs. Everything leads to something else.

It is wonderful to be here amongst our own people. Do you know, now they are living such a primitive, simple life, everything seems to have left them but the old wonderful simplicity—and everywhere one goes one sees it most wonderfully —just the very part of us that is shown so clearly in our dances and tunes—and out here it is to be found uppermost in practically every man we come in contact with. I suppose that's one reason why they take so to the dances; it appeals so to them now they've lost their frills and fripperies and city ways.

Yours very sincerely,
(Signed) D. C. Daking

A Word on Recreation

From the Standpoint of the Training Camp

Lieutenant Eustace M. Peixotto writes in the San Francisco *Recreation League Bulletin* for September:

"The first 'recreation instinct' of one who has been kept hard at work at a military camp for a day or days is to get out of it. Change of scene, food, and companions are the prime requisites of a 'good time.' I believe, therefore, that where camps are near cities and not in isolated locations, the work of the committees having to do with soldiers' amusements in those adjacent cities is vastly more important than that of the Y. M. C. A., which is making its field the provision of recreation within the camp boundaries. I do not wish to minimize the work or the possibilities for work of the Y. M. C. A., but I do wish to lay stress on the psychology of change in this connection, for I believe it to be basic.

"Camp life is monotonous. You get up at the same hour every day, work with the same group of men on much the same routine of drills and exercises, eat meals which are prepared and served strictly as replenishers of bodily waste and not as the artistic creations of gastronomic specialists, and your lights go out at exactly the same hour every evening. An excellent life to lead, not unenjoyable in itself, but monotonous.

"Into this regular existence, then, comes at stated intervals, leave. What is your first impulse? To seek something entirely different, to catch the first car for town where lights are bright, streets full of new faces, and everything as different from the camp as day from night. It isn't that you don't like the camp or the army life, not at all. It is just that recreation, variety, and the spice of life are synonymous terms.

"More power then to the Recreation Committee for Soldiers and Sailors. 'Take the boys home to dinner.' Believe me, a home dinner tastes good after a week of camp 'chow'! Provide other amusements, not athletics so much as less strenuous pursuits. Remember the recruits will get a systematic course in physical training for an hour and a half each day besides the military drills, marches and trench digging, so don't think it necessary that the recreation be 'active' and that 'everyone should participate.' Leave that side to the army it-

151

self! With the exception of dancing, which somehow is different, your man on leave will want to be amused, not to give the show himself. To see a play or a movie, to talk to people and get a chance to tell about his new life, to view the sights of the city and surrounding country, preferably in an auto—these are some of the pleasures that would, in my judgment, appeal most to most men.

"From what I know of the plans of the Committee of Recreation for Soldiers and Sailors, it is these things which it is endeavoring to supply. The League as a body and its members as individuals should devote every effort to the furtherance of this work. With San Francisco the daily recreation ground of the thousands at the Presidio and the week-end resort of the tens of thousands at Camp Fremont, it presents a fertile field for work, one that will require all the available labor to produce an adequate crop and to keep it free from weeds and weevils."

Who Is Responsible?

A resident of X while strolling through one of the fields where Pickett made his famous charge in the Civil War, and where some of the men of our National Army are now drilling, came across a tall young soldier lying on the ground crying like a child. She waited until the storm was over, and then asked what the trouble was. He was not afraid to fight, he told her, in a boyish shame-faced manner, but he had just received a letter from his mother who was a cripple, and the thought of her loneliness and grief at his absence was too much for him. He was her only son, and the one member of the family strong enough to carry her in and out of doors.

"Of course," said someone to whom she told the story, "you invited that young man to your home, to meet your daughters and your friends." "Why, no," came the answer, "I never thought of asking a soldier to visit my home."

Here had been a wonderful opportunity which she had failed to grasp—not through lack of heart, but through failure to understand. Her subsequent search for that homesick boy was fruitless: He had been "sent over there."

To help the women of Xville and other cities where our

152

boys are in training realize their responsibilities and opportunities; to help citizens through organized effort to make available for the use of the soldiers all the resources their city has to offer, is the work of the War Camp Community Service maintained by the Playground and Recreation Association of America as it sends to the cities near the camps its community organizers.

Boys in Khaki and Their Clubs

If there is any doubt in your mind about the soldiers' appreciation of the club rooms which War Camp Community Service bureaus are providing in the camp cities, spend an evening at the Soldiers' Club at Ayer, Mass., and talk with the men who are coming there from Camp Devens.

"My mother would like to thank you for this building," said one soldier, "because since I began coming here I have written more letters than in all my three months in camp, all because you have made this place homey and attractive to me."

"My husband telephoned me from here one night," said a young wife. "He said this is the best place yet." And when one of the workers of the club helped her to find a lodging place she said, "You do everything you can for the men, don't you? Isn't there anything I can do for you? Have you sheet music enough?" The worker admitted they had not and she promised to go back and raise some money from her friends to buy popular music.

The men appreciate the homelikeness of scattered tables and chairs, the touch of color in the furnishings of the rooms and other features which make the building attractive and lovable. "Mr. Brown, this reminds me of home," said one lad. "I thank you for such a place to come to. I shall drop in here every time I am down town." "This is the nearest like home I have had since I have been in Ayer," said another. "You fellows certainly try to make us boys enjoy ourselves." A third exclaimed, "My, but I have had a good evening. It is worth a lot to be able to enjoy your club."

From the depths of an easy chair a soldier said, "The first time I came into the club I just sat and rocked all evening. I had not been in a comfortable chair since I came to camp.

You know we always stand or lie in the barracks because there is no good place to sit."

The gratitude of one soldier was of the sort which had to have an outlet. "I have had such an enjoyable time here that I want to contribute $1 towards the up-keep of the place," he said. "I hope I may find just such a place wherever I am sent."

Mothers and Khaki Clubs
It is from the mothers that the most moving expressions of appreciation come. One big-eyed rather pathetic little mother repeated over and over again her appreciation of the fact that such a splendid place had been provided not only for her boy but for all of them. "It keeps them from going to places and doing things that they shouldn't," was the burden of her talk. "My boy was never away from me before," she said, "and I was so afraid he might be led into wrong doing. He had always been such a good boy. I am so glad he has a place like this to come to."

One very charming mother was particularly interested in the way in which the dances were safeguarded by admitting only invited and properly chaperoned girls. Her boy had told her that dancing was practically the only amusement he cared for. "It is the mothers who really appreciate the care in your selection of girls for their sons to dance with", she said. A mother and son and a girl who may have been his sweetheart, though they did not advertise the fact as many young couples do, spent the most of one Sunday at the club house. They were particularly outspoken in their appreciation. "And what do you think, Mother," exclaimed the boy, "you can bowl here for five cents a string." One interesting group who spent most of a day at the club was made up of a soldier, an engineer of the Railroad Engineer group who expected to leave that week for France, and his aunt and cousin who had come to bid him good-bye because he had no family in the East to see him off. It was the first time they had ever seen him in their lives but they were there to represent his family who could not come. They were almost touchingly pleased when the volunteer worker whom they did not know and who normally would have no special interest in them was so anxious to have them comfortable.

154

BOYS IN KHAKI AND THEIR CLUBS

Khaki Clubs Serve All

Perhaps the opportunity for unexpected service that a club can render is as well illustrated by the following instances as in any way. A soldier was found asleep at the Ayer Club with his head on the table. When he woke he was very apologetic, saying that he had a bad headache and that he had just come from a 36-hour stretch of cooking duty with practically no chance to rest, owing to the illness of the man who should have taken his place. The volunteer worker gave him some medicine for his headache and some refreshment. He took a bath and then a bed was made up for him in the balcony where he slept until the middle of the next morning. He was a made-over boy then and so grateful for the rest.

Probably no man has ever been more grateful, however, than the one who brought his charming wife and dainty little five-year-old daughter to the club in desperation after having spent the previous night at an unspeakable lodging house because there was no room anywhere. By rare good chance there was an unused bed—an unusual occurrence—so they were taken in. There is nothing that couple would not do to further the interests of the club.

Then there was the woman who came from Boston on one of the coldest Sundays of all with a three-weeks-old baby in her arms. There were three more at home and the soldier was very much upset because he had to leave his wife alone to look after four children. The baby was put to bed in the janitor's bed and they were given an opportunity for a quiet visit together.

The khaki club is more than a mere recreation place. It is a place to which the men come for help and advice in their difficulties and to which they invariably turn in an emergency.

The greatest surprise of the dozen years in which I have been in the present line of work is the discovery of the important connection between the physical vigor of a community and its output.—ROGER N. BABSON

English Women Play Their Part in the World War

Miss Helen Fraser, an English woman who from the beginning of the war has been associated with work for girls and women in England, painted a vivid picture, at a meeting of the War Workers' Council of the Y. W. C. A., of the work which English women are doing, and of the steps which the government is taking to safeguard them.

Women in Industry
One and one-half million women are taking the place of men in industries. The vast majority of them are in the munition factories, by which is meant not only the plants manufacturing ammunition, but all the factories in which uniforms and all equipment needed in the conduct of the war are made. One hundred of the factories in which women are working belong to the government; five thousand others privately owned are controlled by the government. In Gretna alone, one hundred thousand women away from their own homes have been used by the government, which has built many cottages and a number of large hostels. The Y. W. C. A. has additional hostels here, and many club centers and restaurants.

Welfare Work by the Government
In all government-owned and controlled factories the Welfare Department of the Ministry of Munitions which as a part of its work is training welfare workers, has placed a woman worker in charge. This welfare worker in addition to supervising conditions in the factories relating to the welfare of the women employees, providing rest rooms and recreation for the workers, visits them in their homes, sees to it that the children of the married women are properly cared for and makes their home conditions as much a matter of her concern as factory conditions.

Women Patrols
There are now three thousand women patrols in England patrolling districts near the camps. These women, who are volunteers, give up two or three evenings each week to the work. The

156

government has appropriated four hundred pounds a year for the training of these volunteers.

Policewomen At the beginning of the war there were no policewomen in England. There are now seven hundred women police officers, six hundred of whom are in munition factory districts. They see to it that adequate and good transportation facilities are provided to take the girls to their work, and travel with them to see that conditions are as they should be. They protect girls in every possible way and have the power to remove bad women from the vicinity of the camps. The police have found their services most valuable and they are recognized as one of the big factors in helping to solve England's problem.

England's Army of Women in France At the rate of ten thousand a month English women between the ages of twenty and forty are being recruited to go to the military bases in France for service of various kinds. They are taken first to the bases in England where they are given military training and placed under military discipline under the direction of carefully selected officers. They are paid about thirty-seven cents a day, the pay received by privates in the army and are given uniforms. Girls are recruited to do clerical service, telephoning, telegraphing and light labor. Skilled gardeners and laborers are chosen to care for the cemeteries in France where England's dead are buried. Still another group, comprising the motor corps, performs light transport and ambulance service.

When the women go to France, while they are under military discipline they are to a great degree put on their honor and the fundamental principle which is inculcated in them is that they must do nothing to disgrace their uniform. They live in barracks in the camps and are allowed to talk to and mingle with the soldiers, often entertaining them in their recreation huts which in France are under the direction of the Y. W. C. A.

That the constructive and productive work for girls which has been done in England by the government and private avenues has been effective is evidenced by the fact that for the first two years of the war the birth rate of illegitimate children was lower than it was before the war.

157

"The Wasted Years"*

Preface by Edward T. Hartman, Secretary, Massachusetts Civic
League, Boston, Massachusetts.

PREFACE†

> All through the life of a feeble-bodied man, his path
> is lined with memory's grave-stones which mark the
> spots where noble enterprises perished for lack of
> physical vigor to embody them in deeds.—*Horace Mann*

After the war had been going on for two years the London
Nation published, on September 23, 1916, "The Wasted Years."
The League re-publishes it because of its statesman-like at-
titude toward a fundamental and pressing question.

The article might have been written with reference to any
of the major movements in which the League has been active:
housing, play and recreation, medical inspection in the schools.
Particularly might it have had reference to physical education (man-culture is a better, though unsatisfactory, term)
with which the League is now working. It might have had
reference to the last two years, wasted in this respect by the
Massachusetts legislature.

Massachusetts is under the draft rejecting over 40% of
her young men. The state and its municipalities are spending
over $10,000,000 annually for curative work and care of incur-
ables. Massachusetts has 829 incorporated private charities
which spent $17,339,741 in 1917. A host of unincorporated
charities and trusts spent sundry additional millions.

Thirty million American wage earners lose every year from
sickness an average of nine days each, a wage loss at $2.50 a
day of $675,000,000, with a cost for treatment of $180,000,000.

As *The Nation* points out, we can no longer afford to
ignore the causes. Our patch-work is ruinous both financially
and in demonstrated deterioration of our human staple. And
yet we go on with it, ignoring the economies, the humanity, the
imperative need of a program which will enable us to advance.

Why not adopt a sane, forward-looking policy of constructive prevention? After-care alone, by wholesale public and private charity under various names, means exhausted resources,

*Courtesy of *The Nation* (London) Sept. 23, 1916.
†Courtesy of Massachusetts Civic League

158

human and financial, and an ultimate condition more deplorable than before.

The article appended will warrant your closest scrutiny. After you have read it the League would welcome your suggestions and your active cooperation in forwarding the movement toward a healthier and more capable state and nation.

———

Anyone who watches a number of town recruits at drill and then turns to look at a group of officers will see at once a literal and striking illustration of Disraeli's dictum about the two natures. He understands, at a glance, what a difference it makes whether a man comes from the class that enjoys fresh air, healthy games, and good food from boyhood to manhood, or whether it has been his lot to work during the years of adolescence in exhausted air, with deficient nourishment, and under conditions that arrest development and produce nervous fatigue. Men belonging to the first class who went into the ranks of our New Army were struck by the difficulty which recruits who had come from the mill or the counter found in enduring the strain of a long route march or a hard day's work in the field in the early days of training. It was not merely that muscles which had never been used were being brought into play for the first time, as happens when one learns to ride a bicycle or a horse. There was a general sense of disability which weakened and almost overcame the will: the kind of insufficiency that is to be expected in men or youths who have been living habitually on their nervous energy, when they are confronted with a long and grinding task and cannot find any stimulus to sustain them in their surroundings. In the great story of England's effort, no small part of the credit must go to the pain and struggle with which these men have conquered the terrible legacy of their youth and turned themselves into strong and able soldiers. For to the depressing and accusing spectacle of great numbers of men whose bodies have been cramped and enfeebled by an industrial system which exploited their growing years, there comes a sequel. Probably never in the history of the world has it happened that a great part of a nation has improved its physical standard so rapidly. In whole battalions of Lancashire recruits the uniforms that were issued on enlistment have been exchanged since for larger sizes, and

159

the people of the districts where the new armies have been billeted have remarked the extraordinary change that has come over these soldiers with a few months of open air and good food.

The war has brought home to most of us a sense of guilt and shame in regard to this dreadful waste of the vigor and the happiness of the race. It is therefore to a people awakened as it has never been before, that Sir George Newman appeals in his annual report to the Board of Education published last week; for he speaks to a people agreed that no self-respecting nation can go back after this war to the state of things which makes the proper development of the body and mind the luxury of a small and privileged class. This reparation at least we will make to the thousands to whom their country had given nothing and from whom she has taken their all. It shall never again be said that it is not until they are needed for the terrible uses of war that any care is taken of the mass of the youth of the country. And providence for the future urges the same truth. Some, indeed, are thinking of the soldiers of the future, others of the workmen of the future; others, again, of the citizens of the future; but all who are thinking at all realize that we have to make whatever sacrifices are necessary to secure the conditions of a healthy and vigorous life and growth to all classes. We have had warnings and instructions enough. The Board of Education has reminded us in its excellent literature on physical training that the training of the body is part of the training of the mind, having an important relation to the actual development of the brain. We have had a report on playgrounds which shows how miserably inadequate is the provision made at present for the children in the elementary schools. We have had reports from the Consultative Committee on Continuation Schools which warn us that the tendency to exploit childhood and youth is actually increasing, and that there are signs that the factory system is beginning to seize on the improved human material turned out by the modern elementary school. We know from the same authority that it could be affirmed six years ago that "not more than 5% of the youthful portion of the industrial population was touched by anything in the shape of recreative agency." And now comes Sir George Newman's report, which warns us that the war has made the immediate problem more urgent than ever, for the

160

special conditions have taken some fifty thousand children, on a modest estimate, out of the schools at an abnormally early age. Lastly, a most important conclusion has now been established by experience. It is this. The best material for an army is not produced by military drill. What is wanted in young men is the full development of their limbs and minds, giving carriage, tone, muscle, and readiness. Military drill kills interest and spirit in boys; it becomes wearisome and monotonous. Routine drill is necessary in an army, but it puts on the finishing and not the creative touches. It is not educational in itself, for in some sense it tends to cramp the mind; nor is it the best means of training eye or hand or muscle. If, therefore, we want to produce men who will make good soldiers quickly, we cannot do better than give them a generous and well-considered system of physical training in adolescence, in which marching, drill and rifle drill would be a very subordinate element. In the Army, it must be remembered, Swedish exercises are an important part of military training. Hence, whether we are fearing war in the future or preparing for peace in the futue, wisdom and prudence call for the same measures.

It was commonly said before the war, when this or that reform was proposed, that the taxpayer could not stand it, or industry could not stand it, or public opinion was not ready for it. The war has shown us how hollow many of these objections were, how timidly we had estimated our powers and resources, and it has brought home to us the sovereign importance of the quality of a nation's life. We cannot repeat that mistake to-day. "If we are determined to rear a healthy and virile race, of high capacity", says Sir George Newman, "we must, from a physical standpoint, begin earlier and continue later than the hitherto accepted period of education. What is needed, indeed, is an effective supervision and a sound practical training of the body from the end of infancy to adolescence. It is said sometimes that, in the interest of economy, the State cannot afford such a complete scheme. My submission is that in the interest of economy, the State cannot afford to neglect a complete scheme." That is the spirit in which the nation has to face its future. We count our youth with feverish anxiety to-day, for our boys of eighteen are not the property of this or that employer, or the disused and discarded instruments of this or that wasteful trade, but the arm of a nation fighting for its life. How shall we think of them tomorrow? Will we think of them again as van-boys, errand boys, piercers' or riverters' boys in whom the nation takes no interest, for whom it feels no concern, for whom school life and its games and its ambitions come to an end as soon as an employer can find a use for their fingers or their muscles. Or shall we think of our youth as boys and girls, the promise of men and women, whose minds and bodies no nation can afford to squander? On the answer to that question it depends whether democracy can win those greater battles for which civilization has to prepare on larger playing-fields than those of Eton, an Army which is not a class but a whole people.

Recreation and the War

T. Dinsmore Upton, Superintendent of the Division of Recreation, Grand Rapids, Michigan, speaking on *Recreation and the War,* said in part:

There never has been a time in the world's history when we have needed organized play for the younger generation as we do today—in the midst of a world war. The terrible social and economic effects of war are not now so noticeable as they will be in a decade, yet already the juvenile delinquency in the warring nations of our allies has increased fifty-three per cent since the war began. The one greatest combating influence against the terrible effect of war on those too young to take part, is training along the right lines with regard to games, and playing them fairly.

The greatest product of autocratic rule, as regards the playing of games, is the losing sight of all fairness in an effort to win by any possible means. Four years ago, before this war began, a splendid Olympic athlete told me that German athletes thought first and foremost of winning—by any means. That is the same spirit which was evidenced when German autocratic powers pronounced a treaty not worth the paper it was written on.

I cannot conceive of an American, a Frenchman nor an Englishman firing upon an enemy after showing, or while showing, a flag of truce. · I cannot conceive of their ravaging the defenseless, nor restoring to the means autocracy has used, to gain her ends. Why? Why, because their sense of fairness, ingrained in them by proper training in the playing of games, doesn't allow them to conceive of it..

When the Japanese champions in tennis returned to Japan from America, they bore home wonderful tales of the American idea of sportsmanship. In my estimation, there could be no finer compliment payed to any nation. The splendid English idea of fairness is as proverbial as their bulldog tenacity and courage. What fostered it? Primarily their love of a generous winner and a courageous loser on the playing field.

We are engaged now in the most terrible of all wars, for the reason that the government of a nation doesn't know what fairness in the playing of the finest of all games—life—means. Isn't the true spirit of democracy, the "fair play" spirit?—the spirit of every man's playing for the team—not for the glory of a single leader?

I have heard it said that in times like these we should not think of joyous things—of play, of song, of laughter. There never has been a time since God's original dawn when we just had to have these things as we do now. The very preservation of the future of our nation depends on the things we teach the men and women of tomorrow. What shall count as much as the true spirit of manliness and womanliness taught in the playing of games, where the sense of fairness—of courtesy to the loser, of right feeling toward the winner, shall be taught.

The world is to be won for democracy. And democracy means oneness and fairness in playing the game of life. Democracy needs that the younger generation play and prepare.

Twelfth Annual Conference of Boys' Club Federation

The Twelfth Annual Conference of the Boys' Club Federation was held at Philadelphia, May 21-23, in Houston Hall, University of Pennsylvania, and was the largest attended conference in the history of Boys' Club work.

Emphasis was laid upon the demonstration of practical Boys' Club activities, and the most up-to-date methods in physical work was demonstrated by instructors in physical education of the University, with Older Boy Delegates as the class.

163

A demonstration of the work of the Woodcraft League was conducted by Ernest Thompson Seton, its founder. Other demonstrations were made of debating and dramatics in Boys' Club work, and of storytelling to boys.

Among the addresses creating much favorable discussion was one by Dr. F. B. Kelley of New York City on *Teaching History and Civics in Boys' Clubs.* Illustrating his lecture with lantern slides Dr. Kelley presented an activity that appealed greatly to the Boys' Club workers assembled. He pointed out that the objective in this type of work was the development of a clear understanding of government, and an appreciation of its problems. To be most effective such ·work must be personal and original, and a greater latitude allowed than is possible in the activities of a classroom. Historic spots in each city may be visited and studied, steps taken to make them better known, if obscure, and plans made for their preservation. Literature has been issued giving sugggestive programs for several types of clubs working along these lines.

A study of the *Relation of the Boys' Club to the Home,* by Fred K. Zerbe, Superintendent of the Syracuse Boys' Club, was very helpful. Mr. Zerbe emphasized the need of a far closer cooperation between the Boys' Club and the home than has hitherto prevailed, and strongly advocated the employment of a friendly visitor in every club to bring this about.

The Third Annual Conference of the Older Boys' Association of the Boys' Club Federation was held in conjunction with the Federation Conference, and was attended by delegates from as far west as Chicago and south as Nashville. The sessions of the Older Boys' Conference were characterized by the most thorough and frank discussions of the subjects assigned.

Particularly interesting were the conclusions arrived at in the discussion of *Self-Government in Boys' Clubs,* and *Locked Doors on Sunday.* In the former the attitude was taken that to most perfectly carry out the aim of Boys' Club work—defined as character building for citizenship—it is essential that·the plan of self-government on the basis of the national, state or municipal form of government be introduced into the Boys' Club. The reason for this is that only by actually performing the duties of citizens and themselves carrying out the theory of government can the members of a Boys' Club fully and early comprehend the meaning of citizenship. In the long discussion of this topic there was not a dissenting voice, and a resolution was adopted, urging the introduction of self-government into the Boys' Clubs of the country.

There was a greater difference of opinion with regard to *Locked Doors on Sunday.* The general conclusion, however, was that the needs vary in the different communities, and that where it can be shown that the need exists for the Boys' Club to open on Sunday, there should be no hesitancy about opening it. Whether the activities should be the same on weekdays or not created considerable discussion, and it was finally settled by a motion to the effect that this question be left to the discretion of the superintendent.

The closing banquet, given by the Curtis Publishing Co., in their building, was attended by both the adult and Older Boy delegates. A feature of the banquet was a series of stunts given by delegates from the various sections of the country. The speakers of the evening were Cyrus H. K. Curtis, President of the Curtis Publishing Co., and Allen D. Albert, Past International President of the Rotary Club.

Hopedale's Glorified Mill-Pond

ANOTHER PRIZE ARTICLE IN THE BEST THING IN YOUR TOWN CONTEST

JAMES CHURCH ALVORD, Littletown, Massachusetts

Hopedale, Massachusetts, has been "done to death," in the stock phrase of those who write and those who publish. After living in the village for four years I found that it was known by Germans, Italians, Englishmen and Frenchmen for its model homes, its paternal government, its famous strike against some of the conditions appertaining to paternalism. But there is one thing which, strangely, has never been cataloged abroad—this is its glorified mill-pond.

A mill-pond is an ugly spot, God wot. Never was an uglier pond than the bare, bulrush-shored, mucky stretch of bog and water which nestled, up to 1898, right in the heart of this community. From this dingy morass clouds of mosquitos arose each night to swoop down upon the unhappy inhabitants.

But in one famous day and year at the annual town meeting

* Courtesy of the Independent

a few progressive souls advocated, as they had for a decade, "the purchase of about five acres for a town park" and succeeded. The town annually appropriates $2500 for the care of the park, and the sale of trees brings in five hundred or so more. There has always been at the head of the work a scientifically-trained forester. The present man has held his place for thirteen years and is an artist in his line. His one ambition has been to keep the park with so carefully careless a grace that the casual visitor shall declare "nature did it all." Nature did—mighty little.

The first care of the committee was to attend to the immediate needs of the community; so an extra appropriation of twenty-five hundred was voted. The worst part of swamp-land, immediately under the noses of the villagers, was drained with catch-basins, a hedge of shrubbery was set about, and a field for football and baseball, as well as a bandstand, was built. An annual field day for athletic and aquatic sports has increased the interest of all in this portion of the park. Gradually too this end, into which a bit of orderly, artificial, decoration was allowed to creep, was fitted up for the recreation of the toilers. There is a bath-house, a shore of imported seasand, and wharfs for boats and canoes. Unfortunately a group of small boathouses have grown up, sheds of the shed-iest type; but their days are numbered.

Then slowly with the years began the work of transforming a hideous muck-hole to a lovely plaisance. The lakelet was drained, dead trees removed, boulders blasted; but the artistic sense sufficed and an ancient stone-fence, cutting under the waters, has been left. In a drought it makes an exciting bit to negotiate in a boat, yet is so lovely, so odd, that nobody complains. Huge lilies, a pink-stained variety and native to the pond, were encouraged; the lotus has begun to bloom in sheltered nooks. The townsfolk gather these blossoms by huge armfuls every morning, every social occasion overflows with them, and the two pulpits droop under their burden every Sabbath; but the supply never fails.

The appreciation of the people for their own work is immense. They own boats and canoes almost to a man—and a woman, and vote enthusiastically for the efforts at mosquito-extermination, while the attempt to induce the wild natives of the woods to seek refuge here is encouraged by everybody. The result is that squirrel, pheasants, quail, rabbits, as well as all the common, and uncommon birds have learned that in this park is safety from the volley of the gun.

166

From the nearer end of the water pleasant glimpses show the huge factory looming up like some medieval factory and houses "beside the pond" are in wide demand. Only the very fortunate obtain one right on the shore and, having obtained one, never let it go.

The whole morale of the village is raised and transfigured by Hopedale's glorified mill-pond.

Please mention THE PLAYGROUND when writing to advertisers

The Victrola in Open Air Calisthenics, Benton School, Kansas City, Mo.

Sailor Drill with the Victrola, Field Day, Evansville, Indiana.

The Efficiency of a Nation

requires that its citizens must be physically fit.

In the Golden Age of Greece, the city of Athens was supplied with ample playgrounds and gymnasia for the training of its youth.

The schools are the laboratories for future citizenship. Every American boy and girl is entitled to correct and carefully supervised bodily development as a part of his school course.

The Victrola and Victor Records

furnish music which makes Physical Education more attractive, and which makes pupils more responsive in rhythmic feeling.

Have you tried these selections in your school?

Marches and Rhythms

18209 { **Boy Scouts of America**—March (Sousa) **Victor Military Band**
10 in. 85c { **Blue-White March** **Victor Military Band**

18253 { **Motives for Skipping** (Kindergarten Rhythm) **Victor Band**
10 in. 85c { **High Stepping Horses and Reindeer Running** **Victor Band**

35228 { **Eros**—Scherzo Valse (Martin) Butterfly Dance) **Victor Orchestra**
12 in. $1.35 { **Golden Trumpets**—Schottische (Rollinson) **Sousa's Band**

35532 { **Cupid and the Butterfly**—Intermezzo (Claude d'Albert) **Victor Military Band**
12 in. $1.35 { **Dorothy Three-Step**—Mazurka (J. B. Lampe) **Victor Military Band**

Folk Dances by Victor Band

18331 { **Arkansaw Traveler**—American Country Dance (Burchenal)
10 in. 85c { **Soldiers' Joy**—American Country Dance

18004 { **Black Nag** (2) **Grimstock** (From "Country Dance Tunes," Sets III and IV) (Cecil J. Sharp)
10 in. 85c { **Newcastle** (2) **Sweet Kate** (From "Country Dance Tunes," Sets III and VI) (Cecil J. Sharp)

17158 { **Dance of Greeting**—Danish Folk Dance (From "Folk Dance Music") (Burchenal and Crampton)
10 in. 85c { **I See You**—Swedish Singing Game (From "Folk Dance Book")

Ask any Victor dealer to play the above selections for you. For further information, write to the

Educational Department

Victor Talking Machine Co.
Camden, N. J.

Victrola XXV, $85
specially manufactured for School use

When the Victrola is not in use, the horn can be placed under the instrument safe and secure from danger, and the cabinet can be locked to protect it from dust and promiscuous use by irresponsible people.

Victrola

"HIS MASTER'S VOICE"
REG. U.S. PAT. OFF.

To insure Victor quality, always look for the famous trademark, "His Master's Voice." It is on all genuine products of the Victor Talking Machine Company.

Richmond, Mass.

THE PAGEANT OF THE PIED PIPER—THE HAPPY VILLAGE
OF HAMELIN

Richmond, Mass.

THE PAGEANT OF THE PIED PIPER—THE PIED PIPER
MAKES HIS BARGAIN

The Playground

Vol. XII No. 4   JULY 1918

The World At Play

Thrift Stamp Day. — The first of every month is to be observed as Thrift Stamp Day, upon which everybody is urged to buy more and yet more of these small life-savers.

"I Hear America Singing." —C. C. Birchard and Company, Boston, Massachusetts, announce a book of fifty-five songs and choruses for community singing, compiled and published under the authority of the National Conference of Music Supervisors.

Watch Out for the Play Wagon!—Western New York State will see this summer play wagons sent out from the larger towns to the hamlets and villages about. Each wagon will contain swings, baseball bats and other play apparatus. A play leader and one or two assistants will accompany the wagon. Arriving at a "corner," the leaders will requisition a suitable lot and call upon volunteers to help lead and carry on the work when the wagon departs. Twenty-five district s c h o o l teachers have already volunteered.

Miss Maria Knight is the originator of the scheme, which found immediate favor with school boards because of increased mischief and juvenile delinquency made m a n i f e s t since the beginning of the operation of the draft in these rural districts.

Kindergarten Drive for the Children's Year.—The Bureau of Education in cooperation with the National Kindergarten Association, among other activities of the children's year is promoting the establishment of a kindergarten in every school. Many valuable articles from mothers who have been kindergartners are being sent out as propaganda. Only about 500,000 of the 4,300,000 children of kindergarten age in this country have kindergartens available.

At Play in the Canal Zone.— *The Panama Canal Record,* the official bulletin of the Panama Canal contains an article about the playground at Balboa. Two

171

directors are on the ground during the hours when the weather is cool enough for play, the little children in the morning and the school boys and girls after school hours and in the early evening. The usual activities are carried on for all groups.

Better Use for the Money.— Granville R. Lee, of the Recreation Commission of Portland, Maine, recommended that instead of the trophy cup usually presented to the winning team of the Grammar League the money be given to the Red Cross and the trophy consist of a receipt bearing the names of all the players. This could be framed and take its place in the trophy hall. Mr. Lee felt that American boys would be happy and proud to accept such a trophy in war times. The money might also be spent for War Savings Stamps or go toward some other war need.

Dramatics for Getting It Over.— A thousand girls from the Julia Richman H i g h School in New York City costumed to represent the schools' activities, c a l l e d upon the Mayor and asked for a new building and better equipment. The pageant appeal to the eye, the ear, the sense of rhythm ought to make the need unforgetable.

Many Players; Little Equipment.— In the course of a month's psychological study of children's play needs in the State orphanage at Davenport, Iowa, Dr. Mary L. Neff, Phoenix, Arizona, a member of the State Council of Defense, developed the *Davenport hoop game*. Little equipment was available except for volley ball, but Dr. Neff reports that even in a month a noticeable change in the atmosphere of the institution was evident. The hoop game may be obtained from Dr. Neff or from THE PLAYGROUND.

Rehearsal for Life.— "If 'all the world's a stage,' then," says some one, "'most of us need more rehearsals.'" Recreative activities in physical education serve as such rehearsals. There is no opportunity elsewhere in education to compare with that of the physical educator in the matter of 'rehearsing' pupils for the smaller or greater emotional and moral crises of life. It is not in book or laboratory instruction or even formal drills that are to be found opportunity for the exercise and direction, for the 'rehearsal' if you will, of the deep-seated human passions that in the last analysis control human conduct—love, hate, desire, fear, anger, resentment, disgust, grief, depression, re-

172

morse, elation; or for the instinctive expression of rivalry, risk, sense of justice, self-assertion, cooperation, sacrifice, loyalty. Our education is perhaps weakest in this matter of training the emotions. Recreative activities, since they hark back to old foundations, to old roots of both body and soul, and involve the instinctive and emotional elements I have mentioned, offer almost our only field in school instruction, where with reference to the deep emotional elements of character, we can give our pupils opportunity to become 'doers of the word and not hearers only.' With what deep and conflicting emotions does a football player, for example, see an opponent in 'the great game' bearing the ball for repeated gains towards the goal, threatening decisive and final defeat? A college player was once making such gains; finally upon being tackled and thrown with arms and ball beneath him, his face unprotected, the opposing fullback rushing down the field towards him, plunged and thrust his knee squarely upon the fallen player's face, crushing his nose. The offending player, of course, was promptly put out of the game, the injured player remaining and actually making the play that won the game. As he entered the dressing room after the game, the ejected player approached him, the tears fairly streaming down his face, grown man that he was, and in pitiful mental suffering begged for forgiveness. He had met one emotional moral crisis and been defeated; he met another and was victorious. Can one doubt that this experience was a genuine rehearsal for life? No classroom or laboratory experience, formal gymnastics or military drill, stirs a big boy's soul thus to its depths."—George Ellsworth Johnson in *Mind and Body*

London Welcomes American Soldiers.—The House of Commons has organized a hospitality committee of its leading members, who will give one afternoon each week to entertaining American soldiers at the Houses of Parliament. Tea will be served on the famous t e r r a c e overlooking the Thames.

The American Committee of Engineers, largely composed of men who worked in Belgium for the relief committee before the United States entered the war, has rented one of London's largest theatres for a rendezvous and dormitory for American soldiers and sailors. Allies will be welcome as well.

Another committee known as the British Committee for Entertaining American Soldiers is planning public entertainments and arranging home entertainment for three days or more for men wounded or on leave.

British Rotary Opens Homes for Americans.—The councils of the twenty-one Rotary Clubs in the United Kingdom are organizing a scheme for entertaining in the homes of the country American soldiers on leave from the front. The guests will be introduced by American Rotarians or recommended by American commanding officers. They usually come in groups to one "English Mother" who "sizes them up" so as to fit them into the most congenial home. The hostesses call for their guests and thereafter a daily cup of tea or "war rations" at the various homes helps the days to pass —all too quickly—and widens the circle of hospitality. One

boy said to his "English Mother," "Don't you worry about the food, ma'am. Why, even if we only have bread and water at your table, with you smiling and looking like you *care*, it will make happy chaps of us all."

Other efforts besides this extended hospitality are being made, by the Rotarians, a notable one being an adequate map and list of places of interest of the City of Liverpool.

Entertainment for Convalescent Americans.—The seaside cities of England which are to be used as convalescent camps for American soldiers are using something of the methods of the War Camp Community Service in this country. The first soldiers to arrive were greeted by the mayor and welcomed into private homes. Free amusements, among others Sunday baseball and Sunday vaudeville, a great innovation in England will be provided for the men.

Patriotic Play Week and the War-Time Recreation Drive

The Second Drive of "Children's Year"

CHARLES FREDERICK WELLER, Associate Secretary, Playground and Recreation Association of America

Eleven million women are asked to organize ten thousand communities for a Recreation Drive this summer culminating in "Patriotic Play Week," September 1 to 7. This war-time movement has been inaugurated by the Children's Bureau, United States Department of Labor and the Woman's Committee, Council of National Defense; with these Federal agencies the Playground and Recreation Association of America is cooperating. The Recreation Drive is under the direction of the Child Welfare Department of the Woman's Committee, whose headquarters are in Washington, D. C., 1814 N Street.

I. COOPERATING ORGANIZATIONS

Allied for this War-time Recreation Drive, with the Children's Bureau and the Woman's Committee, are the following national organizations which promote playgrounds, recreation centers, and leisure-time activities. At four special conferences in Washington, in June, their representatives worked out the following war-time message:

"To 11,000,000 PATRIOTIC WOMEN
IN THE STATE DIVISIONS OF THE WOMAN'S COMMITTEE, COUNCIL OF NATIONAL DEFENSE:

"For the boys and girls of this. country we appeal, through you, to all patriotic citizens to save the nation's children from the war-time hazards of increased delinquency, over-taxed nerves and weakened bodies by giving them a fair chance in the summer vacation to grow well and strong through play and recreation.

"Official reports of war-time conditions in Europe warn the United States that it is imperative that all the agencies promoting playgrounds, recreation centers and leisure-time activities for boys and girls shall be given money and personal service enough to increase, instead of decreasing, the number of young people benefited.

175

"You eleven million women are asked, each in her own community, to foster and promote wholesome leisure-time activities throughout July and August leading up to a Patriotic Play Week, September 1 to 7.

"Suggested programs will be provided through State Chairmen of the Child Welfare Committee by the Woman's Committee, Council of National Defense, Washington, D. C."

Additional allies may join later. Those who have already enlisted for the War-time Recreation Drive, by signing this appeal, include:—

> Boy Scouts of America
> Camp Fire Girls
> American Red Cross Bureau of Junior Membership
> Young Women's Christian Association
> Drama League of America
> Amateur Athletic Union of the U. S.
> Cooperative Extension Work, U. S. Department of
>   Agriculture and Colleges of Agriculture
> Community Chorus Movement
> U. S. Bureau of Education—U. S. School Garden Army
> National Storytellers' League
> Girl Scouts of America
> Educational Dramatic League
> Playground and Recreation Association of America
> American Folk Dance Society

II. Why Recreation During War?

This is "The Children's Year"—April 6 to April 6, 1918-19—the second year of America's participation in the war. It was the Children's Bureau which conceived and announced "The Children's Year"; the Woman's Committee, Council of National Defense accepted the responsibility for carrying out the program. The first drive—to "Save the Lives of 100,000 Babies"—is going forward with growing power in more than six thousand communities. Now comes the second drive—for Patriotic Recreation—to Save Childhood and Serve the State.

President Wilson endorsed the Children's Year in a special letter addressed to Secretary W. B. Wilson of the U. S. Department of Labor, and published widely.

President Wilson's personal example strengthens the second drive—for Patriotic Play. For it is through recreation—or play —that the President keeps himself fit. The second drive of Children's Year is to enable the Nation's boys and girls to follow

President Wilson's example—each to become well and strong for his Country's service.

Modern military training includes play. Every soldier in Camp Sherman, for example, has two hours of organized play, daily, as a vital part of military training. Inside and outside all the military training camps, play or recreation or leisure-hour activity, has been mobilized by agencies of the War and Navy Departments Commissions on Training Camp Activities—to develop capacity, will and daring in soldiers, sailors and marines. Opportunities for such patriotic play should now· be extended to America's children and to as many as possible of her older citizens.

No money or time can be spared from war-winning activities. But, the winning of the war depends on man-power and man-power cannot be sustained in any nation without health and wholesomeness in the children. Far worse than exhausting America's financial capital would be the exhaustion of child life— her man-power capital. To be strong for Victory, the Nation must let her children play.

England is already turning to lift war's burdens from the children and, as one expedient, is giving them a better chance to play:—she began, in January, 1917, to grant government funds to local play centers. Can America do less?

During this summer vacation time, especially—with schools closed, fathers and older brothers called to war and many mothers to war work—there is urgent need to give the boys and girls an American square deal—to "Keep the community from sitting on the children's safety valve of play"—as Jacob Riis would say it.

"Americanization" is a timely word and to Americanize all the people of each community one of the best means is play— which draws people together, children ˙first, with many parents following. To help win the war, we must Americanize the people's leisure. "The battle of Waterloo," said Wellington, "was won on the play fields of England".

III. PROGRAM SUGGESTIONS

"Patriotic Play Week", September 1 to 7, (or earlier if local schools are in session during the first week of September) is the first thing to be planned in each local community. Local organizations and individuals, men and women, interested in changing leisure hours from liabilities to assets are to be called together under the leadership of the Child Welfare Committee of the Woman's Committee, Council of National Defense. When this group of local organizers have agreed upon the program for the culminating week, they will immediately begin preparing for it by appropriate recreational activities throughout the summer. Patriotic Play Week is thus proposed as the best means by which to bring about the Recreation Drive throughout July and August.

While the first week in September is suggested, the local community may select any other week instead or may use one or more Saturdays for the demonstrations and exhibits of Patriotic Play—which may well be combined with a County Fair, Grange, Bush Meeting or other community gathering.

One way to plan the program for Patriotic Play Week is to secure the cooperation of all local agencies. In many states there are township or community Councils of Defense through which the whole community may be reached. Organizations of women are already banded together in the Woman's Committee for war work and will be ready for service. In addition, ascertain whether there are in the local community some or all of the following agencies: Boy Scouts, Camp Fire Girls, Y. M. C. A., Y. W. C. A., a Playground or Recreation organization, Park Board, School Board, a Health or Police Department or other branch of local government interested in constructive and preventive work, a Chamber of Commerce, organizations promoting Dramatic, Musical or Manual Arts, War Gardens of the U. S. Bureau of Education, Boys' and Girls' Clubs of the U. S. Department of Agriculture, or any industrial or commercial organizations interested in the conservation of leisure. Ask each of these to be responsible for a half-day, or for some specific part of the program for Patriotic Play Week. As soon as each agency accepts its share of the culminating program, it should begin practice and preparations which will fill the intervening weeks with wholesome recreation.

In city neighborhoods and other communities where competent leadership and many cooperating organizations are available, the Patriotic Play Week may include athletics, games, water sports, music—especially community singing, dramatics, various contests, exhibits, refreshments, speaking. Each of these might have its half-day or its hour in the culminating week. Or, the week's program may be organized around a "Children's Day", "Family and Community Day", "Soldiers' and Sailors' Day",

PATRIOTIC PLAY WEEK

"Fraternal Orders' Day", "Public Schools' Day", "Church Day"— the latter being either the opening or the final Sunday of the week. By this method of program planning the organizations and individuals responsible for each "Day", or each special group of Activities, would needs begin in July and August to enlist and train the children and others who are to take part.

In its simplest terms, for communities which have few organizations or individuals experienced in recreational leadership, the Patriotic Play Week may consist of only a day, or even a half day, in which the neighbors unite in a parade, or a simple pageant, or a festival with vocal and instrumental music, or a community gathering—possibly an old-fashioned picnic. Preparations and practice for one day or two, or for a half day, of organized community play in September may vitalize many leisure hours during July and August.

A patriotic pageant may be the organizing theme for Patriotic Play Week whether seven days or only one or two half-days are to be devoted to the final exercises. A pageant may readily coordinate all the features of the program. Each group participating may be costumed simply and may present such activities as interpret the contributions which the group have been making during the summer to the strength and spirit of community life. Sewing and other manual arts will be stimulated throughout the summer in the preparation of costumes, banners, floats and scenes, while neighborliness and social recreation are developed by the meetings necessary to plan and practice for the pageant.

Advice in selecting and staging a pageant may be had through the "Drama League of America," 306 Riggs Building, Washington, D. C.—whose executive secretary, Mr. C. H. Gifford, has submitted the following:

"A fitting climax of the entire summer's efforts would be a pageant staged on the last day of Patriotic Play Week. This could be made doubly effective if staged at the County Fair. It could begin with a procession or a moving exhibit of all results accomplished, from a given point to a position in front of the grandstand where, with symbolic characters participating and the real characters forming a background, could be enacted a brief drama consecrating our effort and our resources to Columbia and the cause of human freedom." Suggestions for folk dances of the United States and other allies may be had through the American Folk Dance Society,

Miss Elizabeth Burchenal, chairman, 2790 Broadway, New York.

Gardening, pig, calf and poultry raising, cooking, canning and other manual activities may be made most valuable and most popular expressions of the spirit of play and recreation. Representatives of the U. S. Agricultural Department, of State Agricultural Colleges and of the *U.* S. Commissioner of Education are more than ready to help in these patriotic endeavors. Local leadership should also be enlisted. Products should be displayed—possibly carried in the procession or pageant—and prize winners should be honored publicly in the Patriotic Play Week. Helpful pamphlets and other assistance may be had, free, from the U. S. Commissioner of Education, Mr. P. P. Claxton, and from the *U.* S. Department of Agriculture (Mr. O. H. Benson—for the North and West—and Mr. O. B. Martin—for the South—representing the Boys' and Girls' Clubs)—all three at Washington, D. C.

Exhibits—possibly in connection with a County Fair—may constitute a nucleus for Patriotic Play Week. Junior Red Cross auxiliaries may be called upon to conduct a section of the exhibit in which they can show the things they make, knit and sew for soldiers, sailors and war refugees. Canning Clubs may demonstrate their methods and exhibit their products. Stock and Poultry Raising Clubs should put on exhibition their prize chickens, calves and pigs.

Community Singing should be emphasized. "The patriotic appeal of the new war-time songs is strong and it is hoped that many singing or glee clubs and bands or orchestras may be organized during the Recreation Drive. People like to get together and sing and they should· be urged to form definite groups to provide music at the Play Week celebrations. In several States, directors of community singing have been appointed under the State Councils of Defense, whose cooperation in Play Week will be valuable. In one State an effort is being made to organize pennywhistle clubs among the little boys who might otherwise be idling in the streets." Books of war-time songs may be secured at small cost through the War and Navy Departments Commissions on Training Camp Activities, 19th and G Street, Washington, D. C.

Meals may possibly be provided during Play Week activities by the Young Women's Christian Association or by the Woman's Associations of one or more churches. Part of the expenses of the Week might be met by this means.

180

Toys, swings, sand-boxes and other facilities for children's play may be exhibited and children's games may be demonstrated. Floor games devised by H. G. Wells and other play activities for the home may be learned from a pamphlet on "Child Care," written by Mrs. Max West, of the Children's Bureau, Washington, D. C., from whom copies may be had, free, on request.

Athletic Badge Tests of Physical Efficiency for boys and girls and the awarding of national medals to those meeting these minimum standards of normal strength and skill, may well be one feature of the summer-time activities. The badge winners should have places of honor in the final celebrations between September 1 and 7.

These tests may be arranged as a simplified field meet would be. They afford practical, popular means of testing—and promoting—strength and skill in boys and girls. To stimulate the children's interest in keeping strong and in increasing their physical vigor, the badge tests may be repeated from time to time, giving an opportunity to boys and girls who are unable to pass them at first to take the tests again six weeks or ninety days later. They involve no dangers of overstrain.

Full, simple explanations of these Athletic Badge Tests may be had, free, on request of the Playground and Recreation Association of America, 1 Madison Avenue, New York City. This Association provides, without charge, blanks and directions for certifying Badge Test winners and supplies handsome bronze badges for a small sum—which winners should be allowed to pay as Phi Beta Kappa winners buy their keys.

Detailed, simple instructions for games will be provided, on request, by the Playground and Recreation Association of America, 1 Madison Avenue, New York City. See also Jessie Bancroft's useful book, *Games for the Playground, Home, School and Gymnasium*, 456 pages, $1.50, published by Macmillan, 1909.

Playground and Recreation organizations will undoubtedly supply experienced leadership for the Recreation Drive—not only in their local communities but by sending skilled organizers, on request, to nearby towns. A special letter, with a copy of this statement, is to be sent by the Playground and Recreation Association of America to these leaders in organized recreation.

The Boy Scouts may be counted upon to be especially helpful—under the leadership of Mr. James E. West, Chief Scout Executive, 200 Fifth Avenue, New York City. Mr. West has been a pioneer and very useful member of the Advisory Committee who have helped to plan the Recreation Drive.

Patriotic Play Week should exhibit and demonstrate also, the work of the Camp Fire Girls and Girl Scouts. Like the Boy Scouts, these organizations can contribute to Play Week such attractive demonstrations as their first-aid work, camp life activities, the kindling of a fire without matches and their many special war-time services.

Dr. Jessica B. Peixotto, executive chairman, department of Child Welfare, struck a key note for the Recreation Drive when she said, "Play keeps alive the spirit of youth. This spirit of youth is the very essence of that resolution and daring we need above all to carry us through this war."

IV. To *You,* ANYWHERE

ANYONE, in ANY COMMUNITY, who is willing to help in any way in the Patriotic Recreation Drive, should not wait to be discovered but should :—

First: Learn if there is a local Child Welfare Chairman or Committee responsible for the Recreation Drive and, if so, offer them all the time, resources and suggestions which the volunteer can give.

Second: If no local arrangements for the Recreation Drive have been made, consult with the Chairman of the Woman's Committee in your community, or write to the State Chairman of the Woman's Committee. If the State Chairman cannot be located readily, write to the Child Welfare Department, Woman's Committee, Council of National Defense, 1814 N Street, Washington, D. C. Report any suggestions and working powers available for local organization.

To move every local community is the giant task of the Recreation Drive. It cannot be accomplished without the help of many volunteers. Every one interested is asked to make known what aid he or she can give and to *get to work* upon the local situation.

Experienced workers in playgrounds, recreation centers, social settlements, schools, colleges and other agencies, are especially asked to report to their State Chairman of Child Welfare that they will give volunteer service occasionally to help organize their own communities or to *visit other communities* which need help in organizing. Such visiting helpers can probably have their traveling expenses paid, if necessary, by the community they visit. There are no national funds available for this or for any field service—sorely needed as it is.

Voluntary enlistment is thus the only method by which field workers can be secured. Without such leadership, it will be difficult, if not impossible, in some communities to carry on the Recreation Drive.

V. HELPFUL FORCES

An "Advisory Committee" has been organized to develop program suggestions. Such pushing power as may be had from national organizations which promote leisure-time activities is thus at the disposal of local committees responsible for the Recreation Drive. Each of these allied organizations is asked to help in the following ways:—

(1) To send to each State Chairman of Child Welfare a list of all the organization's branches or representatives within the State. State Chairmen will gladly forward promptly to each local chairman of Child Welfare a list of all these cooperating agencies or individuals in the local field.

(2) To write to all of the organization's branches and representatives urging each to look up the local Chairman responsible for the Recreation Drive. If no such Child Welfare Chairman is found, the local representative of the cooperating organization should write to the State Chairman offering cooperation in organizing the local community.

(3) To enclose in these letters from the headquarters of national agencies to their local representatives an explanation of this War-time Recreation Drive. (Reprints of this present statement are available for that purpose, free, upon request.)

(4) To prepare a brief, attractive, special statement of the ways in which the organization's forces can best assist in the Patriotic Recreation Drive. This circular should mention any helpful pamphlets or books to be had through the organization. Especially the circular should tell local people in exactly what ways they may use the organization, or help to apply its methods locally, or assist in extending its work.

VI. HOW WASHINGTON WILL HELP

Washington headquarters will prepare circulars each dealing with specific problems or with program features designed to meet the differing needs of various communities in city, town and rural regions. These little pamphlets will be sent to State Chairmen to use as they may find most advantageous. The circulars already planned are as follows:—

A Bibliography of the most serviceable books and pamphlets.

Special suggestions for *home recreation* in which whole families and small neighborhood groups may participate.

Explanations of the National Badge Tests of physical efficiency and how to operate them.

Reports of methods applied successfully in various states, cities, towns and rural regions, as the Recreation Drive develops.

It is important that correspondence and all other details shall be handled within each State and the State Chairman will naturally organize her forces with this in view. Time and efficiency would be sacrified if Washington headquarters should attempt to handle local details; funds and facilities available in the Washington office would not be adequate.

Local inquiries' or offers of help if sent to Washington, will be referred to the appropriate State Chairman.

VII. A FINAL WORD

This *Patriotic Recreation Drive* must be cooperative. To be successful it must command the services of the most resourceful, influential local leaders—men and women. The call to them is for vital war-time service—to Serve the Country by Saving Childhood and by Strengthening Health, Resolution, Team-play—in a word, the War-winning Spirit—throughout America.

Independent initiative is essential. Washington headquarters can only submit suggestions and report clever expedients devised by State Chairmen and by local leaders. Local adaptations are indispensable; no single plan or system could fit throughout the United States.

Together, we are enlisted to help win the battles of war-time and the coming conquests of peace by helping boys and girls and older folks, also, to become Physically Fit for their Best Possible Service to their Country.

CHARLES F. WELLER.

A BRIEF BIBLIOGRAPHY FOR THE PATRIOTIC RECREATION DRIVE

I. For General Information

Addams, Jane; *The Spirit of Youth and the City Streets.*

Full of human interest, very readable, the clearest, most convincing statement of the fact that neither communities nor individuals can be efficient unless young folks have opportunities for wholesome recreation. Inspired by years of intimate observation and service at Hull House, Chicago, where some of the earliest developments of playgrounds and other leisure-time activities took place. 162 pages; $1.25; Macmillan, 1909

Bancroft, Jessie; *Games for the Playground, Home, School and Gymnasium*. The most complete list of games of all kinds, fitting people of all ages and descriptions; each game is fully and clearly described in a readable way; all the old favorites are here—games which have met the tests of human need in many countries, for many years. 456 pages; $1.50; Macmillan, 1909

Curtis, Henry S.; *Education through Play*. Practical, interesting accounts of what various communities—American, English and German—have done and should do to meet the need for playgrounds; discusses the philosophy and effect of play and the ways in which play should be developed in rural and in city schools, in summer playgrounds, in camps and social centers; describes and commends "the Gary System;" tells how to play 26 games. 359 pages; $1.50; Macmillan, 1915

Curtis, Henry S.; *Play and Recreation for the Open Country*. Rural communities, their needs and possibilities in recreational lines, are treated more effectively in this than in any other work on playground subjects; suggests recreational activities for the home, for the dooryard of the farm home, the rural school and school yard; recreation for the country girl, the farm wife, the farmer; country festivals and pageants; rural social centers; country churches as recreation centers; methods of organization and leadership. 265 pages; $1.25; Ginn and Co., 1914

Gates, Herbert Wright; *Recreation and the Church*. Fundamentals of play theory and procedure; tells how to discover the specific recreational needs of a community and how to meet them—stressing the big and growing part which churches should play in organizing leisure time; reports the recreational activities and equipment of fifteen churches in various cities; an up-to-date bibliography filling fifteen pages. Mr. Gates is Director of Religious Education, Brick Church, Rochester, N. Y. 185 pages; $1.00; University of Chicago Press.

Johnson, George E.; *Education by Plays and Games*. Written by a former school superintendent, now one of America's best teachers of playground directors; "presents a curriculum of plays and games graded from infancy to the middle teens, and analyzes them to show the chief mental and physical activities developed by each; discusses the meaning of play, its relation to work, its history and its application to education; describes, with illustrations, the best games chosen from a thousand or more and graded according to the child's needs." 234 pages; $0.90; Ginn and Co

Johnson, George E.; *What to Do at Recess.* A readable little book, pocket size, describing with pictures and diagrams, the most popular games for children of various ages; very human and helpful; tells teachers and other leaders how to get the children to playing profitably; if you can own or study only one book on recreation, this may well be it. 33 pages; $0.25; Ginn and Co., 1910

Lee, Joseph (President of the Playground and Recreation Association of America); *Play in Education.* One of the best discussions of the philosophy and psychology of play and of the fundamental instincts to which play must appeal to be successful; a readable, though profound, book, illumined by humor, human insight and originality; based upon years of sympathetic observation of child life and upon pioneer experience in promoting playgrounds; really a great book—which may come to be ranked with Froebel's contribution to the understanding and enrichment of childhood. 500 pages; $1.25; Macmillan; 1915

One Monthly Magazine, *The Playground,* is devoted entirely to brief reports and practicable suggestions of recreational activities and methods; publishes an annual "Year Book" or census of all recreation associations and all playgrounds in America with brief descriptions of their activities and the names and addresses of their directors—latest "Year Book" in April number, 1918; publishes frequent reports of War Camp Community Service which this Association conducts for the War and Navy Departments Commissions on Training Camp Activities; $2.00 yearly; free to all members (subscribers of $5.00 or more) of the Playground and Recreation Association of America, 1 Madison Avenue, New York City

Free, on request, a printed catalog (pocket size) listing all of the 167 or more pamphlets upon recreational topics published by the Playground and Recreation Association of America, 1 Madison Avenue, New York, N. Y. Many of these pamphlets are available without charge; for others the cost of printing is charged —varying from five to forty cents each.

II. *For Special Information*

A. Additional Literature and Reports on their Special Work may be had on request from the following:

American Red Cross, Bureau of Junior Membership, Washington, D. C.

Amateur Athletic Union of the *U*. S., 290 Broadway, New York City

Boy Scouts of America, 200 Fifth Avenue, New York City

Camp Fire Girls, 31 E. 17th St., New York City

Drama League of America, 306 Riggs Building, Washington, D. C.

Educational Dramatic League, 105 W. 40th St., New York City

Girl Scouts of America, 527 Fifth Ave., New York City

Knights of Columbus, 110 W. 42d St., New York City

National Story Tellers' League, 3 Kennedy St., N. W., Washington, D. C.

Playground and Recreation Association of America, 1 Madison Ave., New York City

Young Men's Christian Association, International Committee, 347 Madison Ave., New York City

Young Men's Hebrew Association, 31 West 110th St., New York City

Young Women's Christian Association, 600 Lexington Ave., New York City

B. Government Reports:

Children's Bureau, U. S. Department of Labor, Washington, D. C.

U. S. Commissioner of Education, Washington, D. C.

U. S. Department of Agriculture, Boys' and Girls' Clubs, Washington, D. C.

C. Studies in Recreation Issued by Private Associations:

Russell Sage Foundation, Recreation Department, 130 E. 22d St., New York City

PATRIOTIC PLAY WEEK

NATIONAL BADGE OF PHYSICAL EFFICIENCY

Proposed for the War-time Recreation Drive and Patriotic
Play Week by the Playground and Recreation Association
of America, 1 Madison Avenue, New York City

Needed: An Army of Boys and Girls to Serve their country
by Becoming Physically Fit—that is one slogan of the summer
drive for Patriotic Play.

To measure up to National Standards of normal health and
strength should be the patriotic goal of every boy and girl.

To give every boy and girl a fair chance to do this should be
the patriotic goal of every community.

By passing the National Badge Tests a boy or girl wins the
right to wear a handsome bronze medal supplied by the Playground and Recreation Association of America. The awarding
of these badges should be part of the crowning ceremonies of the
Patriotic Play Week September 1 to 7.

Parents, or local representatives of the Child Welfare Committee in charge of the Recreation Drive, may easily use these
Badge Tests at the beginning of the summer to determine how
nearly each boy or girl measures up to normal standards of
strength and skill and to learn what each should practice during
the summer to make up any deficiencies.

Interesting activities have been chosen as the basis for the
tests, so that boys and girls like them and like to practice for
them:

A Boy to win the first medal must:

    (1) Pull up or chin himself four times.

    (2) Jump 5 feet 9 inches in a standing broad jump.

    (3) Run 60 yards in 8 and 3/5 seconds.

A GIRL to win the first medal must:

    (1) Run a Potato Race in 42 seconds, or an All-up
        Indian Club Race in 30 seconds (Simple descrip-
        tions on request).

    (2) Throw a Basket Ball into its goal twice out of six
        trials, from 15 feet away.

    (3) Walk 24 feet, balancing herself, with a book on her
        head, on the narrow edge of a fixed 2 x 4 scantling.

(For the second and third medals, these tests are made more
difficult.)

188

PATRIOTIC PLAY WEEK

The Playground and Recreation Association of America adopted these tests in 1913 after careful consideration by committees of experts. Thousands of boys and girls, in rural districts and in cities, have proven that the tests fulfill their purpose—"to provide a standardized test of physical efficiency; to promote all round physical development; to be interesting; and to be applicable in all parts of the country."

If older people will join the boys and girls in preparing for these tests and in winning the medals, the interest of the whole community will be strengthened and the nation will be served through the improved health and efficiency of her people. There are no age limits for the badge tests but no individual can be awarded more than one badge in a single year.

Pamphlets will be mailed, free, on request, describing these National Badge Tests fully and simply, with photographs, and explaining how the tests are made, how reported, and how the medals are secured.

Beautiful bronze medals have been prepared. They are safeguarded carefully so that no one can get one in any way except by having responsible people certify that he has passed the tests. (To make and distribute these medals costs the Association twenty cents each; that cost should be defrayed by the badge winner—or by a local committee.)

Wherever, throughout the United States and Canada, a Badge Test winner meets another, there is a bond of patriotic fellowship. The Badge says for its wearer; "I am making myself Physically Fit for my Highest Possible Service to my Country."

For further information, free, address the

PLAYGROUND AND RECREATION ASSOCIATION OF AMERICA,

1 Madison Avenue, New York City.

Co-operating with the CHILDREN'S BUREAU and the WOMAN'S COMMITTEE, COUNCIL OF NATIONAL DEFENSE in the Patriotic Recreation Drive of Children's Year.

Extracts from
Industrial Recreation—A Recent Phase in the Playground Movement

O. W. DOUGLAS, Anderson, Indiana

Because of the phenomenal growth of Akron, Ohio, transportation, housing conditions, school buildings, boulevards, parks, playgrounds, and other essentials, have been utterly unable to keep pace. Akron, therefore, presents a fine example of overgrowth and congestion. Recognizing these conditions as unsatisfactory, the management of the Goodyear Company saw the necessity for providing recreational facilities on an independent basis. The company employs about 16,000 people in the various departments. The daily shifts of workmen are so arranged that it is possible for a large number of employees to have an opportunity for play during practically all hours of the day. Many of the employees have families and live near the factory, and they and their children have been well provided for in the recreational plans.

About fifty acres of land owned by the company are dedicated solely to the purposes of play. This land is admirably situated in a valley, and a large hill or bluff serves as a natural amphitheater. Another elevation serves as an ideal spot for coasting and skiing.

For the children, complete playground equipment is provided, including many coaster or wave slides, seesaws, ocean waves, swings, giant strides, traveling rings, horizontal bars, ladders.

Besides using the apparatus, the children engage in folk dancing, playground ball, wading, and various children's games. For the folk dancing and many other games the large dancing floor, provided primarily for adults, is utilized during the day by the children. Sand boxes and baby swings are also provided for the little tots.

For the larger children and adults first-class facilities are provided for baseball, football, track athletics, hockey, skating, basket-ball, volley ball, tennis, cricket, coasting, skiing and dancing. The grand stand and bleachers in connection with the base-ball ground have a seating capacity of 9,000. Three thousand removable seats are supplied, which are shifted to other parts of the grounds as occasion demands. Not only are Goodyear leagues maintained, especially in baseball, basket-ball, football and track

190

athletics, but there is also a City Industrial League in which athletic teams from the various factories engage in friendly rivalry.

All of these activities are under competent supervision. A thoroughly trained physical director is in charge. He has three assistants, one male and two female, all trained and experienced. In addition, there is a superintendent of grounds always on the premises. One of the recent and most satisfactory innovations is that of community singing, in which hundreds engage under a competent leader.

Plans for the School Recognition and Credit of Home and Community Recreation Activities*

Memoranda and Suggestions from the Physical Training Bureau of the Military Training Commission, State of New York

THOMAS A. STOREY, M. D.

State Inspector of Physical Training, New York

I. Recreational requirement—in effect not later than September, 1917. (See General Plan and Syllabus for Physical Training, State of New York, pages 15-16, page 27, as corrected, and pages 195-196). "Four hours a week, at least one hour of which must be under the direct supervision of the regular school officials; the other three hours may be satisfied by equivalents accepted by the school from the home or community activities of the child."

II. Suggested list of activities that may be credited by the school in satisfaction of the requirement:

    (1) Athletics

    (2) Club activities (Boy Scouts, Girl Scouts, Camp Fire Girls, Y. M. and Y. W. C. A.)

    (3) Military drill

    (4) Manual training or agricultural classwork out of doors

* The New York State Legislature requires that four hours a week be given to recreation and Dr. Storey has suggested in this article ways of using these four hours in accordance with the New York State Law.

*Presented before the New York State Association of District Superintendents of Schools, New York City, January 18th, 1918

(5) Chores and special home work as: Wood chopping, lawn mowing, sweeping and other home activities regularly done, canning in clubs and alone, gardening, churning, milking, pitching hay, pumping and carrying water, sewing, ironing, tending chickens, carrying out ashes, tending furnace, care of auto or motor boat, berrying, fence building, plowing, wheeling baby

(6) Individual sports as: skating, skiing, swimming, coasting, bicycling, horseback riding, canoeing, tennis, walking

(7) Acquisitional sports as: Hunting and fishing, bug hunting, geology, botany trips, trapping

(8) Regular paid work

(9) Junior Home Projects (Professor Fred Griffin, Cornell University)

III. General Policy: School people should be concerned not so much with a rigid detailed plan for checking up these recreational equivalents as with ways and means of stimulating cooperation along these lines between the school and the home. Every reasonable effort should be made to influence the life of the child; foster the right sort of play; and encourage the health habit of cheerful recreation. There must be no "invasion of the home", but rather a recognition of the value of activities carried on by the child in the home and outside the school. The method of reporting and checking up recreational equivalents in a given school must be worked out by the officials of that school—the superintendent, principal (or teacher) and the supervisor of physical training.

(1) The plan must be organized and presented tactfully. The home people must not misunderstand or be given real reason to feel annoyed.

(2) The plan must be simple enough not to burden parents, teachers, and other school officials unduly with its execution.

(3) Reports and records must be frequent enough to give information while it is fresh and the memory of the activity is clear and reasonably accurate.

(4) Must include amount of time spent per week and general character of activities.

IV. Suggestions to superintendents and other school offi-

192

cials for their assistance in formulating their local plans for reporting and checking recreational equivalents. These suggestions are of use only as suggestions. Each school must work out its own plan devised to fit its own peculiar needs. No other school plan is likely to be the very best plan for a given school community. In most of the plans that have been submitted, too much emphasis has been placed on the rigid checking of equivalents. A general survey of the recreational activities of children will provide information as to what boys and girls are doing during their after-school hours. It should also supply data relative to existing recreational agencies in the community. With such information available greater emphasis should be given to the stimulation of larger participation in recreation in the case of those individuals needing such stimulation.

(1) Statement of plans that have been used or that have been suggested
    (a) Reports by pupils
        Some schools have arranged to receive written reports from the pupils at intervals of one week; other schools, two weeks; and other schools, monthly. In some places the children report to the class or classroom teacher; others, to the special teacher of physical training; others, to children who have been appointed as officers of room-clubs or health clubs in the school or recreation club. Such plans give opportunity for pupil dishonesty—but such opportunities are always present. This objection seems hardly of sufficient weight to condemn these plans. The problem of teaching good morals is always present.

    (b) Reports by parents covering recreation activities of their children and the amount of time spent in those activities
        In a number of schools, reports are requested of parents covering the nature of the activities and the amount of time spent on them. In some cases these reports are asked

193

weekly; others, bi-weekly; and others, monthly. A lack of tact and an insistence on too frequent reporting are the dangers present in this plan. It succeeds only where it is very wisely operated and really understood.

(c) Successful plans are reported in which the pupils are asked to write letters to their regular teachers or physical training supervisors, describing their recreational activities carried on outside the school for the preceding week or other period. These letters serve as bases for work in composition, English, spelling, after which they are used as records of, and reports on, the satisfaction of the recreational requirement.

(d) This plan suggests the possibility of success through written reports from pupils covering their field work in nature study, biology, woodcraft, first aid, and so on, in schools in which such outdoor activities are accepted as recreational equivalents. Such reports could in addition serve as exercises in English, in composition, as well as records of recreational activity. The recreational experiences of the pupil outside of school hours could be used, too, as a basis for work in oral English. A summary or brief of the pupil's presentation could be prepared by him for record as to his recreational program.

(e) Some district superintendents are making successful use of the following plan: Each pupil in their rural schools has a physical training note book in which the child records recreational activities that are carried on outside the school. The teacher inspects these note books frequently as does the physical training supervisor. At the close of the year one district superintendent plans to give a prize to the child who has the neatest and most satisfactory book.

V. Suggested Routine: With the above suggestions and memoranda in mind, we recommend that school people concerned with the formulation of a plan for operating Division D of the Regents' Requirement in Physical Training, utilize a routine somewhat as follows:

1. Make a survey of the recreational possibilities (a) within the school; (b) in the homes of the pupils; and (c) in the community. Tactful letters to parents and simple written questions to pupils will furnish evidence upon the recreational activities of the children. Letters to various organizations (see Division VII) will secure information concerning community recreational possibilities.

2. Work out your plan and program to fit your local needs and resources. It is recommended (but not required) that not all the recreational credit be allowed weekly for a particular individual activity, i. e., walking to and from school ordinarily ought not to satisfy the whole requirement, especially if there is no social factor present in the recreational life of the child concerned.

Not all of the outside recreational requirement should be covered by home duties that contain little or no recreational element; that is, home duties ought to be accepted and credit given on the basis of recreational content as well as the amount of physical work done; for example, sawing wood three hours each week ought not meet the full requirement, but sawing wood and piling it as a member of a group or in friendly competition with some other pupil, or member of the family, might meet the full requirement.

Club activities in which the recreational, social and physical elements are the main features, should be encouraged and full three hours' credit allowed, provided satisfactory regular reports are submitted by the club authorities.

3. Inform pupils and parents concerning your plan. Outline activities that will be credited by the school. Indicate your method of securing reports. Make every reasonable effort to secure cooperation through an intelligent sympathy on the part of the parents con-

cerned. Get report blanks to pupils or to parents or to club organizations (Boy or Girl Scouts, Y.M.C.A.) for record of attendance.

4. Arrange for receipt of reports through children or classroom teachers, or special teachers of physical training, and for a simple permanent record either in card file or in a ledger record book.

VI. School officials who develop satisfactory plans for the recognition and credit of activities carried on by children while out of school, should send a description of those plans to the State Inspector of Physical Training, Albany, New York, so that they may be placed at the disposal of other school people.

VII. List of organizations concerned with recreation, from which local schools may receive help

A number of well-organized national associations are available to the schools of the state through which this three-hour recreational requirement may be very satisfactorily met. Information concerning these organizations may be secured through conference with their local representatives, or by writing to the following addresses:

Boy Scouts of America—J. T. West—200 Fifth Avenue, New York City

Camp Fire Girls—Lester F. Scott—461 Fourth Avenue, New York City

Girl Scouts—Dr. Abby P. Leland—527 Fifth Avenue, New York City

Knights of Columbus—Albert D. Maguire, 105 W. 40th Street, New York City

Pioneers of America—Clinton, New York

Playground and Recreation Association of America—H. S. Braucher, 1 Madison Avenue, New York City

Y. M. C. A.—Dr. George J. Fisher, 124 E. 28th Street, New York City

Y. M. H. A.—Dr. A. Robinson, Lexington Ave. and 92nd Street, New York City

Y. W. C. A.—Dr. Anna L. Brown, 600 Lexington Avenue, New York City

Y. W. H. A.—Mrs. S. Schwartz, 31 West 110th St., New York City

VIII. References to literature that may be of use to superintendents and other school people concerned with the recreational activities of children:

Playground, published by Playground and Recreation Association of America, 1 Madison Avenue, New York City

Physical Education Review, published by American Physical Education Association, Springfield, Mass.

Journal of the Outdoor Life, 289 Fourth Avenue, New York City

Garden Clubs in the Schools of Englewood, New Jersey—Department of the Interior, Bureau of Education, Bulletin 1917, No. 26

Bibliography—published by Physical Education Review, Springfield, Massachusetts

Bibliography—published by Playground and Recreation Association of America, 1 Madison Avenue, New York City

Bibliography—Bureau of Education, Washington, D. C.

The Practical Conduct of Play, by Henry S. Curtis, published by the Macmillan Company, New York City

Education through Play, by Henry S. Curtis, published by the Macmillan Company, New York City

The Play Movement and Its Significance, by Henry S. Curtis, published by the Macmillan Co., New York City

Games for the Playground, Home, School and Gymnasium, by Jessie H. Bancroft, published by the Macmillan Company, New York City

Play in Education, by Joseph Lee, published by the Macmillan Company, New York City

How Do You Count Your Attendance?

We are interested in knowing how superintendents of recreation and playground directors compute attendance on the playgrounds. Many people have felt that if we could standardize the methods of computing attendance there would be a distinct gain, and that in collecting data for the *Year Book* we should have a very much better basis for formulating statements about the number of children being served by playgrounds throughout the country. Such a standardization, it has been suggested, would also help materially in promoting a basis for computing per capita costs. We are anxious to have a discussion of the subject. Will not our readers tell us the methods they may have worked out providing what they feel to be a fairly accurate basis for computing attendance?

Through the courtesy of Mr. William A. Stecher, director of physical training, and Miss Elizabeth O'Neill, we have secured the following information regarding the methods used on the school playgrounds of Philadelphia:

"Perhaps a little history of our experience in counting the attendance of our Philadelphia playgrounds may be interesting. We have used a number of methods, and for two years we have used the method of finding the median by taking seven counts during the day, which may be the best means of striking an average theoretically, but practically it seems to us (who have to deal with the reports) that it is the same old game of "guess" in a new dress. In the early days we asked our teachers to count the children at various periods of the day to estimate the time when the largest number of children were present. The attendance was found to be at the maximum in the majority of playgrounds at about 11 o'clock in the morning and at 4 o'clock in the afternoon. We then requested that all teachers record the actual number present in each playground at 11 o'clock and 4 o'clock. The cards prepared for this purpose gave date, children a. m. and p. m. and were totaled for the month. To the largest total (for either morning or afternoon), we added at the office an additional 25% to allow for children who had been present. In most instances the teachers were quite fair in estimating, while others saw through greatly magnified glasses. This method was used for some years, until criticism was made by the various officials who, in passing certain playgrounds, could never see such large numbers as those reported at the end of the month.

"Then we tried a weekly postal card with counts for four periods—10 o'clock, 11 o'clock, 3 o'clock, 4 o'clock, dividing by four to get the average attendance for each day, and then the average was computed for the week, month, and finally for the season—again one count. The amount of work entailed by such a method every Monday morning overbalanced all possibilities of continuing such a system for more than a season.

"Next we tried the method now in use for two years of getting the median attendance each day. This requires seven counts to be taken during the seven hours the playground is in session. While it has had the effect of reducing the average

198

attendance to the point where we can no longer be accused of padding our records, the method as far as accuracy is concerned is no more accurate than the records made in the early days, because everything depends just the same upon the vision and good judgment of the teacher taking the count. Teachers have so many important duties to perform in a well-ordered playground, that it is almost impossible to interrupt activities to count the children seven times a day, and reports show that most of it is "guess" between the first and last counts both morning and afternoon.

"A few years ago we took a census, from which much valuable information was gathered. It confirmed the fact that the hours between 10:30 and 11 in the mornings, and between 3:30 and 4 in the afternoon showed the maximum attendance for morning and afternoon. We took the names and addresses of those who came into each yard that day, and we found that in playgrounds having the average attendance of 125 for the day, more than 300 children had been in the playground during the day."

Working—and Fighting—Better through Play*

An evening newspaper of New York City recently told a pathetic story of a boy Kursman who was refused by the Army examining officer. Despite his appeal to Washington headquarters, his willing spirit had no redress when the papers came back with no other comment than:

"Under-developed."

Kursman was sad.

"I wanted to grow up strong," he said, "but how could I? There was no public gymnasium, no swimming pool, no place for me to train. I went around lifting granite paving blocks for the exercise, then I climbed ladders whenever I could find one. What else could an East Side boy do?"

For lack of opportunity, patriotic young Kursman was forced to bow to the tape measure when the time came for him to offer his all to the country he called his own. Spiritually, morally, and intellectually all that his country could ask, he was physically below the requirements for lack of the chance to develop as he wished.

---

* Courtesy of *Outing*

Fortunately, such conditions as he had in his boyhood have been done away with to a considerable extent, particularly in such large centers as Kursman called home. The importance of playgrounds, the results obtained from them, and also the extent of what remains to be done appears in an article by George W. Ehler, in May *American Physical Education Review*:

"Ipswich is a town of 8,000 inhabitants. It has no playgrounds, no physical training in its schools. It has a high school athletic field, many vacant lots, and the open country is in sight. On a test given to all the boys in the fifth, sixth, seventh and eighth grades, it was found that the average performance of the thousands of boys in the same grades in the schools of the Borough of Manhattan, New York City, exceeded that of the Ipswich boys, in the standing broad jump by 25 per cent; running 60 yards, 70 percent; in chinning the horizontal bar, they did five times as many."

New York has a highly developed system of play for children. The results are showing.

All of this brings us to an unavoidable topic—the war, of course. Surprising as it may seem, and revolutionary as it may be, the fact remains that one of the most successful training stunts with volunteers in Canada has been the simple playing games of youth. To specify, the game called *Three deep*, has been used extensively. Leap frog and other similar ones have proved valuable. To set a group of men in khaki at play in order to prepare them to fight is not an anomaly. It is only an axiom now that he who plays best works best. It is just as true when that work becomes fighting.

So much for the immediate question, our biggest question, just now, the best method of making our boys,—Kursmans and others—best fit to cope with those whom they must fight. As we have pointed out in these columns before, 85 per cent of military training is physical training. It is this sort of physical training that we mean. Parenthetically, may we say here that when the records of the various training camps come to light after the war, there will assuredly be great enlightenment upon the evil results of the too-intensive physical training given many college men on championship teams. There will be a renewal of the acrimonious discussion regarding valvular heart trouble and like symptoms of overstrain.

WORKING AND FIGHTING—THROUGH PLAY

**Playgrounds—
The Solution**
Those of us who are older go fishing, hunting, hiking, traveling because we like it, and because only so are we able best to do the duties before us. Not so much care is taken for the youngsters, as witness young Kursman's plight.

The children may not always accompany us upon our excursions. No need to explain why. In addition, they need far more play. They are still growing and need development. Older ones need merely maintenance, with sometimes a bit of rebuilding.

There is no such opportunity for children as that offered by The Playground and Recreation Association of America. It has done much against great odds; both in the attitude of many against it, and in lack of funds, the natural outgrowth of our carelessness.

It was as recently as April, 1906, that this movement became tangible. In that month a group of interested—and interesting—people met in the city of Washington, "to consider the advisability of forming a national organization which should have for its object a furthering of the general movement, then beginning to focus in all parts of the country, *for providing children with places where they might have real play and safe play.*"

This might almost be called a Declaration of Independence. It is true that many cities had playgrounds prior to this, Boston having begun as early as 1882. But, quoting further from the Association's records:

"It was recognized that adults must help the child to find a place . . . where he might without hindrance carry on the business of his life, which is to play, the child himself being powerless in the situation."

Poor, down-hearted, rejected Kursman's dilemma was thus foreseen.

Earl H. Lee, physical Director of the Y. M. C. A., of Spokane, Washington, presents facts which show us more nearly where we stand:

"The countries whose armies in this war are found best prepared, do not give military drill in their schools. On the contrary, they give abundant instruction in physical training. As illustrating the interest in physical training, independent of the schools, in Germany alone, in 1910, in 7,174 cities and towns there were 8,607 gymnastic societies with a total membership of 902,910, and an active membership of 416,320.

201

"Some of the pacifists of the country have said that in case of war we could raise a million men overnight, but in the light of figures from the recruiting stations over the country, a few of them would need fixing before being sent to the front."

Mr. Lee made these statements a year ago. From what we have already learned since we put some of our young men into training camps—much less the pacifistic overnight million—more than a *few* need fixing. There are too many Kursmans.

All of which brings us to the big query: Will we stick to the lessons we have learned after the war is over? *Or will we forget in our leisure what we had to learn in our frenzy?* The answer we make will determine largely how much we distinguish between the value of the immediate present and the permanent welfare of those who will make our future.

Some of what we are pleased to call "primitive" nations knew what their children needed in the way of development, physical as well as intellectual. Not merely that, but they saw to it that the means of accomplishing the desired ends were placed in the hands of those children. They knew enough to train up their children in the way they should go. We are learning; will we remember?

Book Reviews

WHAT TO DO FOR UNCLE SAM

By Carolyn Sherwin Bailey. Published by A. Flanagan Company, Chicago. Price, seventy-five cents

The call of the United States Bureau of Education for increased emphasis upon citizenship and the child's own community obligations and activities in the schools led the author to prepare this book of things boys and girls may do for Uncle Sam. Through the description of each activity runs the golden thread of the meaning of it all in patriotism. The activities described include: "health, economy, conservation, civic beauty, communication, wealth, transportation, charities, education, life saving and Junior activities through Boy Scouts, Camp Fire Girls and the Junior Red Cross."

PATRIOTIC PLAYS FOR YOUNG PEOPLE

By Virginia Olcott. Published by Dodd, Mead and Company, New York. Price, $1.25.

Nine little plays are given, of the quality and tone those familiar with Miss Olcott's previous plays would expect. The Little Home-maker and her struggle with Waste, in which Economy and Thrift helped, is a particularly charming presentation of the note so prominent in American patriotic ideals today.

BOOK REVIEWS

1917: A PATRIOTIC MASQUE

Text by Hartley B. Alexander, music by Henry Purmort Eames. Published by C. C. Birchand & Company, Boston

THE DRAWING OF THE SWORD

Together with the text of the National Red Cross Pageant, by Thomas Wood Stevens. Published by C. C. Birchard & Company, Boston

AMERICA YESTERDAY AND TODAY

By Nina B. Lamkin. Published by T. S. Denison, Chicago. Price, fifty cents

Four patriotic pageants, any one of which would repay expense and effort of production, are made available in these pamphlets. *The Drawing of the Sword,* used so marvellously by an all-star cast for the National Red Cross Pageant, is of course in a class by itself. Miss Lamkin's pageant had at the time of publication been successfully produced some 350 times. The others are less pretentious, even fifteen or twenty people with a chorus, could produce either. It is encouraging to see how much above the average peace time "pageant" is the text of these war time dramas.

ICE-BREAKERS

By Edna Geister. Published by Woman's Press, 600 Lexington Ave., New York City. Price, one dollar net

A multitude of suggestions for social occasions for men and girls at which there is no social dancing have been gathered for this little book. The author has tried out the games and stunts under various conditions—most recently at a war time recreation center near Charleston, South Carolina, "to which flocked hundreds of soldiers, sailors, girl uniform makers and the girls of the community." One might wish for something more of dignity and mental content in recreation for young people but of play as of folks "it takes all kinds to make a world."

Please mention THE PLAYGROUND when writing to advertisers

STORY HOUR FOR THE BABIES AT THE VAN LEUVEN BROWNE CAMP FOR CRIPPLED CHILDREN AT PORT HURON, MICHIGAN

BOYS AND GIRLS WHO CANNOT WALK A STEP CAN SWIM WELL AT THE VAN LEUVEN BROWNE

THE FIRST TROOP OF CRIPPLED BOY SCOUTS IN THE WORLD AT
THE VAN LEUVEN BROWNE CAMP. THE TROOP WAS
ORGANIZED IN 1913.

PART OF FIRST CAMP FIRE OF CRIPPLED GIRLS ORGANIZED AT
THE VAN LEUVEN BROWNE HOSPITAL SCHOOL, DETROIT,
IN 1913

Manila, P. I.

THE ADVENT OF AMERICAN SPORTS HAS SHAKEN OFF THE
SPANISH LANGUOR OF THE PHILIPPINES

Manila, P. I.

EVERY BOY AIMS TO BE AN ATHLETE IN THE PHILIPPINES NOW

207

Manila, P. I.
EVERY NEW SCHOOL WILL HAVE A PLAYGROUND AS AN
ESSENTIAL FEATURE

Washington, Indiana.
AN ANXIOUS MOMENT. THE RUNNER PICKS UP HER POTATO
ON A TEASPOON

The Playground

Vol. XII No. 6   SEPTEMBER 1918

The World At Play

Wm. Taylor Elgas, Montgomery, Alabama, writes of Montgomery's big Play Day: "The Playground spectacle still thrills me; the parade of the army motor trucks crowded with cheering children waving American flags was a sight worth journeying many miles to see. Down Dexter Avenue and around the fountain in Court Square swept the motor trucks, while a moving picture operator filmed the parade from a window in Bullock's Shoe Store on Dexter Avenue. Many were the predictions of direful calamity that reached my ears from parents whose children were not allowed to take part—predictions that it was impossible to handle in safety in army motor trucks six hundred children to and fro from the Capitol to Camp Sheridan, and keep them orderly and systematically at play. But it was accomplished. Mrs. Michael Cody, the chairman of the Special Committee on the Playground and Games, officially reported that not one child was even scratched.

"It was a pretty sight—this playground of 600 children in operation for one hour and a half, systematically playing games for fifteen minute periods, and responding simultaneously to the blow of the whistle. The children played in three large rectangular spaces marked with colored guide flags in juxtaposition. Two hundred children filled each rectangle— in the first, children six to eight years of age, in the second, children, eight to ten, and in the third, children, ten to twelve.

"After the flag-raising ceremony, in which the children recited the pledge to our flag, and sang *The Star-Spangled Banner,* the playground swung into harmonious action, while the little folks played such games as *Drop-the-handkerchief, Farmer-in-the-dell, Cat and Dog, Stealing sticks, Statuary, Pass-the Ball, Three-legged Races,* and *Chariot Races.* Then followed the grand May Pole Military Dance, around an immense flag staff 50 feet high, from the top of which floated the Stars and Stripes. Two hundred streamers of red, white and blue, 75 feet long, were held by children's fingers as they followed the figures of the dance—a spectacle beautiful beyond description.

"As a crowning climax, seven aviators from Taylor Field gave an exhibition of stunt flying overhead, dipping, spiraling, nosediving, Immelman-looping, flying up-side down, long to be remembered. Two aviators circled the May Pole several times while the crowd cheered wildly. Playgrounds are unknown in Montgomery, none being in operation, but five thousand people stood for two hours watching our playground. The effect upon public sentiment can be imagined."

Settlement Holds Community Picnic.—At the Community Picnic of the Irene Kaufmann Settlement, Pittsburgh, Pennsylvania, athletic contests, games, sports, a pie eating contest, a watermelon eating contest, baseball, tennis, filled the day and evening. A patriotic entertainment entitled, *The Children of the Allies* was presented by the children of the Settlement. Each child was requested to bring an American flag.

The Settlement joined in the observance of Baby Week for children's year. Notices concerning the Week were issued, asking that mothers have their babies weighed free of charge by the nurse each week on Saturday afternoon at the Settlement and find out if the baby is improving, and if not find out why from the doctor. Two prizes are offered every three months for the babies who have been weighed regularly and show the greatest improvement.

"Thrift" in Story and Play.—The National War Savings Committee tried out a number of stories and plays carrying the message of *thrift* at the Horace Mann School in New York City recently. Among others a little play called *Thrift*, presented by children under ten got its teaching over very successfully. The play is published in *The War Saver*, Metropolitan Bank Building, Washington, D. C.

Children Equip Playground.—School children of Ridgefield, N. J., under the leadership of a principal who was weary of listening to complaints of broken windows surrounding the school yard, gave entertainments to raise money for playground equipment. Then both principal and pupils turned in to make ready the ground. For ten weeks after-school hours and Saturdays were devoted to the work. When the soil was so difficult to dig that men's help was needed, the girls volunteered to sweep the schoolhouse so the janitors might help on the playground.

Three hundred dollars, all raised by the children, was expended for apparatus. Recesses were arranged for small groups at a time so all might enjoy the new playthings.

The principal hears no more of broken windows nor recess squabbles. Punctuality and attendance have improved. And the happy children are eight weeks ahead of previous years in the course of study and ten weeks ahead of last year.

Badge Tests to the Rescue.—A letter from Miss Mary Holman, Playground Director, Tyrone, New Mexico, tells of pioneer playground work:

"Tyrone is a mining camp three years old owned by the Phelps-Dodge Co. whose offices are in New York City. It is called "Tyrone Beautiful" because of its wonderful location in a valley just below the continental divide and the unusual scale on which it is being builded. All buildings have been designed by the same man who designed the buildings for San Diego Exposition — I've forgotten his name. Truly, the place is wonderfully beautiful and is being promoted by men of ability to make of it what they choose.

But the people—! ! !

"There is an eighty thousand dollar public school building in the town and the school was organized for the first time this year.

"On account of the nature of the population it was impossible to get a correct school census before the opening of the school year. Accordingly, the school board—composed of the usual hard-headed business men—provided a superintendent and ten teachers. School opened the first Monday in September with an enrollment of six hundred Mexican children and one hundred and fifty whites of a class, (for the most part), believed now to exist only in Bret Harte's and similar stories.

"School continued in this fashion for three weeks—with daily threatenings of race riot at recess periods—and then the county superintendent, Miss Isabel Eckles, whom I had met at a summer resort the previous summer, sent for me.

"So I went to Tyrone basing my anticipations on what I knew of Miss Eckles and in no wise prepared for confusion of tongues and general conditions which existed there. I was given six playground balls and bats and three balls more and the gracious privilege of proceeding the best I could. I won't attempt to tell you what ensued.

211

(Have you forgotten that I'm trying to explain *why* I sent for the badges?) Suffice it to say that I spent the time until Christmas trying to learn Spanish and to grasp the individual personality in that sea of black faces. After Christmas we began to organize and early in the spring I began to talk Athletic Badge Tests. One way and another I got the simple apparatus required but my long list of applicants for the badge dwindled terribly when they realized that the securing of it involved signing of names and conforming to law. I had advertised a play festival for May the fifteenth with the Badge Tests as one of the chief features, so in desperation I wired for the badges and extra copy of the tests that I might display both and try an appeal through the eye. It worked.

"Fifteen girls took the first tests—none qualifying. Nineteen boys tried and you have the results.

"I'm out of paper but I'm coming to New York in July to tell you the rest and solicit help for next year."

Playground Lectures in Mississippi.—The State Department of Education has engaged a lecturer to present playground theory and practice to the summer schools of the state.

Made Use of What They Could Get.—The two churches of Newfoundland, Pennsylvania, led a movement to purchase the local hotel for a community club. The bar room became a domestic science room and the barn a gymnasium.

Playground Ukuleles.—At playground No. 4 in Mt. Vernon, N. Y. the boys and girls have started to make ukuleles out of cigar boxes. Some pretty good ones have already been turned out and the boys and girls are getting lots of fun in learning to play after they make their own instruments. It will not be at all surprising to see the various playgrounds turn out representative musical organizations to cheer their teams on at their various league contests in the near future.

Miss Pearl V. Casey, Director, has kindly given the following information about this activity:

Material supplied by pupils— cigar box, any size, one piece of wood 12 inches long, $2\frac{1}{4}$ inches wide and 1 inch thick, for finger board; three blocks of wood $\frac{7}{8}$ inches thick $1\frac{1}{4}$ inches wide and 2 inches long; keys, sounding board and string base can be made from short lengths $\frac{1}{2}$ in. thick by $\frac{3}{4}$ in. wide.

Material supplied by Director—glue, varnish, two $\frac{1}{2}$ in. screws, two 2 in, screws (small size), two four penny nails, 2 violin A and 2 violin E strings.

Tools required—sharp penknife, brace, and ⅜ in. bit, screw driver, file, hammer and sandpaper.

Cut a round hole 1¼ in. in diameter in center of box lid.

Scrape all paper from cigar box and glue all inside seams.

Next carve out three sounding boards, width of box, and fasten with glue to inside of box, one on the bottom 2 in, from the end and other 2 in. from end of inside of lid, one at each end. Glue two of the blocks to each end of the box on the inside. Nail and glue the third block to one end of the 12 in. piece of wood and fasten this end of 2 in. piece of wood to box with glue and the 2 in. screws. Make string base 2½ in. long and at equal distance cut four small grooves for strings. With glue and two small screws fasten to top of lid two inches from farthest end of lid, groove side nearest end of lid. Glue lid to box making sure that the top of the lid fits evenly all around the box. Starting from box, mark off frets on 12 in. piece measuring respectively ⅜ in. ⅜ in. ½ in. ½ in. ½ in. ½ in. ⅝ in. ⅝ in. ¾ in. ¾ in. ¾ in. ⅞ in. at this point insert a small piece of hard wood so that it extends about ⅛ in. above the surface and make four small grooves at equal distance for strings.

In the remaining space bore three ⅜ in. holes for the keys. The keys are to be carved out of small pieces of wood, and have a small groove at the end to hold the strings.

Sandpaper all rough edges and varnish. After varnish dries put on strings. (The two inside strings are violin A and the two outside strings are Violin E.)

This simply constructed instrument is very popular with the children, and it is true that without the slightest knowledge of music one can learn to play it in from six to eight lessons.

War Work of Women for Women.—Columbia University offers a month's course beginning September the eleventh in the organization and leadership of recreational and patriotic activities for working girls. The course is given under the auspices of the National Council of Defense, the National League of Women Workers cooperating. Candidates must have had two years of college work or a high school diploma with some experience in social work.

Gift Playground for Saginaw.—The German Society of Saginaw has given a block of wooded ground, once a beer garden, for use as a playground. Saginaw now has grounds enough for her children though she has not yet inscribed her name on the honor roll of cities providing year-round play leader-ship.

State Aid for Gardens.— Under this heading the June PLAYGROUND announced joint aid offered by New York State and Cornell University for home gardening projects. The money Cornell offered was from a Federal war emergency fund, which has long since been exhausted, and, up to the present not renewed. About twelve directors were placed through this fund, appropriated to the *U. S.* Department of Agriculture and apportioned by the States Relations Service of the Department through the Cornell Extension Department.

The New York State law still stands authorizing boards of education to employ a director of agriculture and the State, through the Commissioner of Education, to re-imburse such a board of Education to the extent of not to exceed $600 for the salary paid said director during any given year.

Communities planning to take advantage of this law for next season should get started early enough to get the boys and girls properly started on their garden activities in the spring.

Twelve Good Games

SUGGESTED FOR THE

"WAR-TIME RECREATION DRIVE" AND "PATRIOTIC PLAY WEEK"

CHARLES FREDERICK WELLER, Associate Secretary Playground and Recreation Association of America, New York City

Without apparatus, "Playgrounds," money, or experience, anyone can use one or more of these games to vitalize leisure hours in his family or neighborhood.

Many boys and girls today do not even know how to play such games. At best they need opportunities and some help in organizing. Leadership is thus necessary.

Therefore the following games are described as the personal experiences of one adult who—in Chicago, in Lawrence, Kansas, and in a Maryland farming region—used these simple games to set the boys and girls to playing.

214

TWELVE GOOD GAMES

Hearts beat, lungs expand and muscles strengthen, while alertness, self-control and "team-play"—or self-subjection to a social purpose—are developed by these rousing old games. For all-round physical efficiency—with the qualities of brawn, brain and spirit which that involves—there is nothing better.

I. POM-POM-PULLAWAY

One evening in Chicago I chanced upon a vital discovery. I went into the street in front of our home, called together a few of the omnipresent youngsters and told them I was "It" for *Pom-pom-pullaway*.

I lined the children up on one curbstone and explained that they must run across the street to the opposite curb when I called out:

"Pom-pom-pullaway!
If you don't come,
I'll pull you away."

When I caught any runner and tagged him three times he was "It," too, and must help me catch the others. Each player tagged became a tagger until all were caught. Then the player who had been caught first was "It" for a new game.

I was so awkward at first that I fell, tore my trousers and scratched my hands. Buttons were torn off my old coat. I learned that the good old game is too strenuous for the aged, but my vital discovery was that the game would not let me remain aged. Many times since that night, thirty minutes of Pom-pom-pullaway has re-created me—physically and spiritually—and, for good measure, has won me the friends among the neighboring children.

II. TAG GAMES

Everyone knows the good old game of *Tag*, in which one player chases the others until by touching one of them he makes him take his turn as "It."

In *Cross Tag*, "It" starts after any player he chooses, but must change his course to pursue any other player who runs between "It" and the one he is chasing. Thus a fresh runner may at any time divert "It" from a tired player who is nearly tagged.

In an amusing form of the old game the player tagged must keep one hand on the part of his body which "It" touched until the new "It" can tag someone else. This is easy if the elbow was the spot touched, but not so simple if "It" managed to tag the player's ankle.

Red Light is an inactive modern form of *Tag*, which illustrates the present-day tendency away from vigorous play. My children taught me to play it with them on the sidewalk and grass plots before our house. The player who is "It" turns his back to the others or closes his eyes while he counts ten. Then he shouts:

"No moving;
No talking;
No laughing;
Red Light!"

At these words the players—who have been moving away from "It"—must "freeze" and remain motionless. If anyone moves, "It" chases him, and if he is tagged he becomes "It" in his turn.

Travelling Apes is of my own devising. One day after I had read *Tarzan of the Apes* I made up a new combination of *Tag* and *Pom-pom-pullaway* as a means of getting my boys and girls to move rapidly down the street on an errand upon which we had been sent by the household powers.

I explained that Tarzan and his brother apes travelled from tree to tree along the branches but we would modify this slightly by travelling on the ground. All the apes gathered around a tree trunk. I selected as their first goal another tree—the first, second or third tree down the street.

As the Hunter, I stood between the apes and their new goal and shouted:

"Travel, Apes!"

Any ape that I tagged as he travelled between the trees became the Hunter, while I became an ape for the run to the next tree selected further on.

To expedite our progress no ape was allowed to run back toward the houses or to stray out of the space between the curbstone and the houses.

III. Tug of War

A strong rope thirty or forty feet long has provided for two very popular games in the big old attic of our house. On rainy days or in the cold weather of winter, these games may be played on a barn floor or in any large room. But like all other play they are at their best outdoors.

Tug of War is played by dividing the company into two equal groups, each holding half of the rope, which is divided by tying a handkerchief in the middle. All the players on both sides grip the rope strongly, holding it so that the handkerchief stands at first just above a half-way point marked with chalk upon the floor.

On signal they pull as hard as they can. That side wins which pulls, and holds, the handkerchief over on their side of the line.

IV. SNAKE IN THE GRASS

This old rope becomes a "snake" for the second game. A big knot is tied in one end. The players arrange themselves in a circle and one of them, standing in the center, swings the rope around, skimming along the floor or grass at the feet of the players.

Each player must jump up as the rope nears him, so that it may pass unimpeded beneath his feet. If it touches him, the player drops out of the game. That player wins who is the last one touched or "bitten" by the "snake."

In military training camps this game is played with an iron or lead weight fastened on the end of a strong cord. I have also heard of an old book being used as the weight.

V. PRISONER'S BASE

Our family went to Grandfather Winston's at Lawrence, Kansas, last Christmas and, recalling what Pom-pom-pullaway had done for me and for the children living near my Chicago home, I spent one to three hours daily for a week playing youthful games with my own boy and girl and other children.

We played a timely war game, *Prisoner's Base*. I told the youngsters that in good old England centuries ago *"Prisoner's Base* was prohibited in the avenues of the palace at Westminster during sessions of Parliament, because it interrupted the members and others passing to and fro." It was then played principally by adults.

In Lawrence, we marked out two circles about fifty feet apart— they might have been nearer or farther. We "chose-up" sides and each of the two equal armies of players stood safely within its own circle.

Then a player from the opposing side led out from his goal toward ours and I ran to tag him before he could get back home; I was "fresh" on him, because I left my goal after he left his.

But another of our opponents left his goal after I left mine and tagged me before I could either touch the first runner or get back home. Thus I became a prisoner and had to stand in the

217

jail which was located near the enemy's goal so that their army could prevent the prisoners from being rescued.

Then the captain on my side sent his players one by one into the open to tempt the enemy to run out of their base in pursuit. Then, before the enemy could run back into their goal to get "fresh" again, my captain rushed out—"fresh" on all opposing players—tagged me in my prison and thus took me safely home to keep on playing.

Any player may slip into his enemy's goal if he can get there without being tagged. The latest player to leave either goal—his own or his enemy's—is "fresh" on all players who ran into the open before he did, and may therefore send anyone of them to prison by simply tagging him.

When you have tagged a player, both of you may go unmolested to your places—you to your home base; your enemy to prison; or your own man, if you have just rescued one from prison, to his home goal.

The latest prisoner must keep one foot or hand within the marked circle or touching the tree or post which constitutes the prison. The other prisoners form a line stretching out toward their home goal; the player who has been in jail longest stands farthest from the prison; all others in the order in which they were captured. Each must clasp the other's hand; the oldest prisoner, nearest his home base, must be rescued first.

When all the players of one side are prisoners, the other side has won the battle.

VI. DUCK-ON-THE-ROCK

One afternoon at Lawrence we picked empty tin cans out of the scrap barrel in the back yard—one can for each player. One boy, volunteering to be "It," stood his can (or "Duck") upon a larger can, or on a box (called "the Rock"). The rest of us tried to knock it off.

We threw our cans (or "Ducks"), one at a time, from behind a marked line about twelve to twenty-five feet away from "the Rock." Then each player tried to run back with his Duck to the throwing line—to throw again.

While watching for a chance to run home safely, the player must keep his foot on his Duck. Whenever his foot is off the Duck, the player may be tagged by the guardian of the Duck on the

218

Rock. But, whenever this Duck is knocked off the Rock, its owner must replace it before he can tag anyone.

When the Duck is on the Rock and its guardian tags another player, that player becomes "It;" he puts his Duck on the Rock, and all the other players try to knock it off.

Real rocks may be used instead of cans. Bean bags do nicely—especially indoors—but when a bean bag is the Duck, the Rock on which it is balanced should be an Indian club—or, in the school room, a desk or small table.

VII. Fox and Geese

Not having time enough for golf, I prefer a game like *Fox and Geese*—which Minnesota school children know as *Cut-the-pie*. Snow is best to play it in, but, lacking snow, there is no good reason why one should not mark out a big wheel, with lime or chalk, on the asphalt pavement in front of a city home or on any available space.

Mark out a circle of any convenient diameter—perhaps twenty to fifty feet. Mark the spokes of the wheel—possibly ten or fifteen feet apart at the circumference and meeting at the hub.

Make one player "It." He pursues the others, but only on the spokes, tire or hub of the wheel. When he tags another player, that one takes his place in chasing the others. Some play that the big hub is goal and a player safe while he stands there, but I think that makes the game too slow.

VIII. "Up, Jenkins!"

Aunt Adda (who is eighty-four year young) taught me to play *Up, Jenkins!* and this became the principal indoor game with which we passed the Christmas-to-New Year's evenings at Lawrence last winter.

In two opposing groups, one on each side of the bare dining room table, we lined up the children, parents and gandparents, ages five minus to eighty-four plus. One side took a silver quarter and passed it back and forth, with their hands all hidden beneath the table.

After the quarter had lodged in somebody's hidden hand, the captain of the opposing side, across the table, commanded: "Up! Jenkins," and all the hands together were raised high over the table, with all fists clenched alike. "Down, Jenkins," called the opposing captain, and all hands at one time slapped the table noisily, with fingers extended and the quarter ringing on the boards—somewhere.

Then the captain of the opposite group of players, after consulting with his men, ordered up his opponents' hands, one at a time. If he succeeded in selecting empty hands, leaving the quarter under the last hand left pressing upon the table, then his side took the quarter and its former custodians tried to win it back in similar fashion.

Obviously, this game may be played outdoors also. It gives less vigorous physical exercise than the other games described; but like them develops such discipline or "team play," and such alertness of eyes, ears and judgment as are essential parts of physical efficiency.

IX. HORSESHOES

Up among the farms and orchards of northern Maryland, where my youngsters take me nearly every summer, the only game I ever saw played spontaneously by the natives was *Pitching Horseshoes*—one may say *Quoits* if he prefers to buy them.

Everybody, old or young, can pitch horseshoes—though the youngest players would better use rope rings.

Two wooden posts about an inch and a half thick are driven into the ground at any convenient distance apart. The posts stick up about four or six inches above the earth. Each of the two or more players, in turn, stands behind one post and pitches two horseshoes, one at a time, at the other post.

When all the players have pitched, the score is counted—perhaps as follows: Nearest the post, one point; if both the horseshoes of one player are nearer the post than any opponent's horseshoe, two points; a "ringer" (encircling the post), three points. Sometimes you play that the horseshoe farthest from the post subtracts one point from its pitcher's score.

From behind the post first aimed at, the players pitch next for the other post. The game may be for the largest score or for a definite number of points, say 21. Teams of two or three players may compete or each may score singly.

In Columbus, Ohio, a resourceful organizer of recreation developed Horseshoe Tournaments into which players were drawn from all over the city. Crack teams fought for the championship for their neighborhood, or city square; and newspapers made much of the scores and personnel and skillful plays of the chief contestants.

TWELVE GOOD GAMES

X. Run, Sheep, Run

In small towns or country districts, in my boyhood, we played a kind of *I Spy* or *Hide and Seek,* called *Run, Sheep, Run.*

One player threw a stick as far as possible, shouting, "Run, Sheep, Run." The player who had previously been chosen "It" must get the stick and lean it against the goal. Meanwhile all the other players ran away and hid themselves.

While the stick was on the goal, if "It" saw any player he called the player's name, threw the stick as far as possible from the player caught, shouted, "Run, Sheep, Run," and ran to hide while the new "It" got the stick and leaned it against the goal. Thus the games really began anew as soon as any player was caught.

While "It" was searching in one direction for hidden players any player might run in from another part of the field, throw the stick as far from "It" as possible—shouting, "Run, Sheep, Run"—and thus give all the players a chance to run farther from the goal and to hide themselves more securely.

XI. Volley Ball

If a family or a neighborhood group can spare five to ten dollars they will find that a *volley ball* and net are a good investment. (A clothes line or any other rope will do instead of the net.) This is the most costly playground equipment I shall suggest, for I believe in "apparatus" and in "playgrounds" far less than in play.

"Experts" disagree somewhat as to the rules for *volley ball,* but the following may answer:

Use a tennis court, if you have one, or mark off an oblong the size of your back yard or lengthwise of your front street—about fifty feet long and twenty-five feet wide. Stretch the old tennis net, or your wife's best clothes line, across the middle of the oblong, the twenty-five foot way. Have the line, or the top of the net, six to eight feet above the ground—its height depending somewhat on the age and skill of your players.

A volley ball is large and light. You and your boys have a preliminary contest as to which can blow it up the tightest and whose "butter fingers" let the most air out in trying to tie up the neck of the inside bladder.

The players are evenly divided, half on either side of the net or rope. Any number of players may play on a side, say three to thirty. One of the players stands behind the back line—the serving

221

line which lies parallel to the net and twenty or twenty-five feet away from it—as the playground space permits. The batter, or server, holds the volley ball on his left palm, tosses it up a little and hits it with his right hand—trying to make the ball go over the net and strike the ground, within lines, on the opposite side of the court.

But the enemy are alert to knock the ball back over the net to make it hit the ground first on the server's side. No one may catch or hold the ball, but a player may strike it with one or both hands—hands always open. Good players will sometimes bat the ball from one to another on their own side of the net until they can suddenly bat it into a place where no opposing player is ready to keep it from falling to the ground. But no player may touch the ball more than twice in succession until some other player has touched it.

The server's side scores one when their opponents fail to return the ball. If the ball falls to the ground on the server's side, no one scores but the chance to score by serving the ball passes to the other side. Any server continues putting the ball in play until his side fails to score, then the opposing side get the ball and serve it. On both sides the players take regular turns in serving—a new server each time the team gets the ball.

If the ball touches or passes beneath the net or rope, the play is lost but, if the ball came directly from the server, he has a second trial. Whenever the server fails in any way to get his first ball fairly over the net, he may try once more before losing his turn to serve.

In Elgin, Illinois, I saw fifty of the leading men of town—ministers, teachers, doctors and big business men—dressed in gym suits and shoes; yelling like mad; acting and feeling like a crowd of happy boys over their semi-weekly game of volley ball. It has no equal for meeting the recreation needs of all sorts and ages of folks. Boys and girls like it all the better because adults play it, too.

None of the older boys or girls should be allowed to graduate from any school or from a summer "Recreation Drive," without proving that he, or she, has established a volley ball playing habit which is likely to help him over even such great "divides" in life as the forty-fifth year.

Eyes, head and chest are all uplifted because the volley ball is constantly flying in the air. The players strike upward.

They run, jump, turn about, hit hard, and use all their muscles snappily. More individual skill and greater team organization are called for by this game than by the others I have described, but unskilled youngsters enjoy it and it draws them on steadily toward greater physical efficiency.

XII. BASEBALL GAMES

Two modern games there are which should be universalized— *Volley Ball* and *Playground Baseball*.

Any American patriot would feel insulted at being told how to play baseball. Suffice it that *Playground Baseball* or *Indoor Baseball* (though it is best played outdoors) differs from ordinary baseball in four ways, namely: (1) A big *soft* ball is used, (2) because this soft ball cannot be batted far, a small diamond—not over 27 feet between bases—is laid out; (3) the pitcher must serve the ball underhand—that is, it must be tossed instead of thrown; (4) a base runner may not "lead off" his base, but must keep one foot on it until he runs for the next base.

Some people, girls especially, like to play this game without a ball bat—the batter striking the ball with his open palm. For this a volley ball may be used.

A game may also be played which my boyhood comrades called *Scrub*. In this game there are no organized teams, but each player works his way, in, turn, from fielder up to batter, falling back to fielder when put out at bat. There are always two or more batters. If only two, they should run only one base and home again. In this single-base game the batter's difficulties are sometimes increased by putting the one base back of the pitcher—about where a second base should lie.

Edna Geister (author of *Ice Breakers*—a recent book of social games and stunts, mainly indoors) told me that when her father took away the children's bat and ball one day they made up a "ball" game in which a piece of old garden hose about twelve inches long served as the "ball."

Home base was two brick bats far enough apart so that a player's foot could easily be kicked between them. Thus the "batter" was just a kicker. When he had kicked the rubber hose into play it was treated like a baseball and the usual rules of *Playground Baseball* applied.

Like volley ball, these games of modified baseball are far safer than basketball—for they do not overstrain the players' hearts or other physical powers. They develop all the essentials of physical efficiency more effectively—and with greater happiness for the beneficiary, boy, girl, man or woman—than any other method of physical training yet devised—even by Americans.

WHY TEACH GAMES

These twelve games show clearly the need for resourcefulness and leadership, which someone—an adult usually, or an older boy or girl—must supply. But the classic expression of playground opponents is: "It's as foolish to talk of teaching children to play as of teaching fishes to swim."

Obviously, however, children do not by instinct know the rules of games like these. Such games are a precious social heritage. In my childhood they were part of an active play tradition handed. on by adults and by other children.

At present, anyone who will watch what boys and girls are really doing in any community will usually find that they are idling or merely "fooling"—not playing an organized game which demands strength and skill and develops them.

To "teach children to play" is therefore essential—though formal "teaching" is less effective than such informal fellowship, with such suggestions, opportunities, and leadership as I have sought to portray in these "Twelve Good Games."

Other games may be drawn from young-spirited adults who can revive local play traditions, from immigrants who recall the games of their native lands, and from books like *Games for the Playground, Home, School and Gymnasium*, by Jessie Bancroft. (Published by Macmillan, 1909; 456 pages; $1.50)

If anyone doubts that the teaching of such games to boys and girls—America's future rulers—is appropriate wartime service, let him consider how Rear Admiral Carey T. Grayson, M. D., has served his country and all humankind by teaching President Wilson to keep himself FIT THROUGH PLAY.

If some of these games can be made to take root in each American community, this Patriotic Recreation Drive will have added the equivalent of many regiments to the war-winning strength and spirit of our Country.

Suggested Procession and Pageant for the Patriotic Play Week*

Conducted by the Children's Bureau of the United States Department of Labor and the Child Welfare Department of the Woman's Committee of the Council of National Defense. Prepared by C. H. Gifford, Executive Secretary of the Drama League of America, Washington, D. C.

PROCESSION AND PAGEANT †

(Designed to be staged at the county fair, or in a similar setting).

All of the results of the Recreation Drive and Patriotic Play Week should be arranged in a Procession from a given point to a position in front of the Grand Stand. The order of the Procession should be:

1. Boy Scouts
2. Columbia, with attendants, in a float
3. Girl Scouts
4. Badge Test Groups
5. Camp Fire Girls
6. Junior Red Cross
7. Boys' and Girls' Canning Clubs
8. Stock and Poultry Raising Clubs, etc., etc.

Columbia's float should be halted in front of the center of the Grand Stand. The Boy Scouts, marching to the extreme end and turning to form the front line of the background, should so arrange themselves that the line is broken in its center by the float. The other marchers pass between this line and the audience, after which they turn and take up positions, either in blocks or lines, back of the line of Boy Scouts.

When the formation is completed, Columbia and her attendants descend from the float. As she advances slowly toward the audience, her attendants dance gaily about her. Suddenly the sound of trumpets and martial music burst forth. Columbia and her attendants stand aghast.

---

† Note: This outline has been worked out with the view of meeting the needs in the greatest possible number of communities. In some cases it may be advisable to substitute real characters for the symbolic ones (except Columbia and Justice), in which case children in costumes of the various oppressed nations might be used, and participants in the Procession might respond to Columbia's calls.

COLUMBIA:

Hark! What means this discord
Of strange sounds?

(Enter Justice, followed by suffering children of Europe.)

JUSTICE:

It is I, Justice,
Fair Columbia,
And those whom I would defend
Against a tyrant's power.
We crave your protection,
Your strength and loving care.

COLUMBIA:

But, Justice,
Art thou not the law of mankind?
Then, how dare this tyrant challenge
Your sacred right?

JUSTICE:

Would that I could prevent it,
O fair Columbia;
But 'tis the voice that
Proclaims Might the law of the universe.
My throne is threatened. Except by thy help
These poor ones must forever live in bondage.

(Led by Coumbia, all sing, O God, Our Help in Ages Past)

COLUMBIA:

(As if gaining new resolve through this prayer)

I come! Justice!
In thy name,
My resources, my strength—my all—
Will be thrown against this offender.
The first aid I give thee is loving service.

*(By uplifted hand she summons, and a group of girls representing
the Red Cross dance forth and take their positions at extreme
right.)*

COLUMBIA:

That these tortured bodies may be strengthened, I give thee
food.

*(Summons repeated, and groups representing the harvest dance
forth and take their positions at extreme left.)*

COLUMBIA:

Gold ·

(Another summons, and a group representing gold dance forth and take up their positions at right.)

COLUMBIA:

Fuel and raiment!

(Summons repeated, and a group representing fuel and raiment dance forth and take up their positions at left.)

COLUMBIA:

Yet more, O Justice,
Do I give.
I draw the sword that shall never be sheathed
'Till this tyrant's power is crushed.
I give my most precious treasure—my loving sons—
To defend thee
On land *(Pause while an American soldier takes his position at her right)*
On sea *(Pause while sailor takes position at her left)*
In the air *(Pause while aviator takes place at her right)*
Everywhere! *(Pause while marine takes place at her left)*

(The action must be quick. As soon as the line is completed, the band strikes up, O Columbia, the Gem of the Ocean. All sing. During the first line of the second verse, the Stars and Stripes should be planted by two Boy Scouts behind Columbia, high enough to float over their heads.

(The band then plays one verse of The Star-Spangled Banner, while all stand at attention, the soldiers at salute. The band then plays America Forever, while Columbia, with attendants, Justice and children, enter the float, and the Procession moves off.)

COSTUME SUGGESTIONS

Columbia: Draped in white with crown and sceptre
Justice: Classic robe of purple
Columbia's Attendants: Some in red, some in white, some in blue
Oppressed Children: Draped in grey
Red Cross Group: Dressed in red or white, carrying red cross
Harvest Group: Dressed in green or white, carrying golden sheaves
Gold Group: Dressed in gold, carrying chest of gold
Fuel and Raiment Group: Some in wood brown, carrying bundles of faggots; some in deep rose, or light watermelon pink, carrying wool

227

The Use of Folk Dancing as Recreation in a Health Program

Prepared by MISS ELIZABETH BURCHENAL, Chairman Organization Committee,
American Folk Dance Society

FOR THE WARTIME RECREATION DRIVE

CONDUCTED BY

The Children's Bureau of the United States Department of Labor and the
Child Welfare Department of the Woman's Committee
of the Council of National Defense

Folk dancing is quite definitely a thing apart from other kinds of dancing, and serves an entirely different purpose if used in its traditional form and spirit. The form of a folk dance is as definite as the words of a folk song, while the manner in which it is danced and the spirit, feeling and attitude of mind of the dancers are as definitely part of the dance as are the actual steps and figures. The "folk manner" is of utter simplicity and straightforwardness, with no attempt at "grace" or "daintiness." The feeling and attitude of mind is of simple pleasure in the dance itself. It is this unstudied simplicity and naivete, together with the compelling rhythm and vigor, that makes folk dancing so appealing to and appropriate for children. Its usefulness as a means of recreation, however, is by no means limited to children, for it presents large opportunities for recreation and social enjoyment for adults.

The folk dances that lend themselves best to a recreation and health drive are those which may be classed in the same category with active games most desirable for the same purpose, i. e., those in which large groups take part, which are easy to learn and to pass on to others, and which provide vigorous action, forgetfulness of self, keen interest and pleasure, team work and the social element. A large number of such game-dances selected from among the folk dances of many countries are available for immediate and practical use by leaders who have not necessarily had previous training. For these leaders the following suggestions are given:

HINTS ON FOLK DANCING (FOR LEADERS)

1. Let the teaching of folk dances be done as informally as

228

possible, and with a minimum amount of explanation. In the main, they can best be learned by *doing* them!

2. Use dances which are full of action, simple and easy to understand and to pass on to others, and which are good fun. Choose those which have only the simplest steps (such as running, skipping, and simple and easily understood figures). Difficult steps and elaborate figures mean too much time spent in teaching, and not enough in recreation.

3. Have good and spirited music—this is an important factor in the successful use of folk dancing. Have a musician who is familiar with the dance and plays with inviting rhythm and enthusiasm; or use a *phonograph*. These have been widely used throughout public school systems and elsewhere and have been found extremely helpful in developing the use of folk dancing as play.

4. When a dance has been learned it should be used as a form of play for play's sake, on *exactly the same basis as games are played*. The leader can get best results by dropping the attitude of teacher and joining in the dance with her group.

5. The test of success in a folk dance is:
   Is it interesting, in the game sense?
   Is everyone taking part, or are some standing idle?
   Do the children enjoy doing it by themselves when the leader is not with them?
   Is it full of vigorous action?
   Do the children pass it on to others?

6. The choice of dances should be left to the players, the leader merely suggesting, and the same dance may be used as long as it retains its interest. The leader should be ready with a new dance when interest in the old one wanes.

7. Avoid any suggstion to children that what they are doing is "cunning" or attractive, or pleasing to spectators. Nothing is more interesting and beautiful than children dancing or playing, but once the "showing off" spirit is engendered the pleasure taken in it becomes that of appeal to the onlooker and self exploitation rather than that of a healthy game spirit. Bear in mind always the end in view, i. e., *health and recreation for the children,*

rather than *pleasure* and *amusement* for *spectators*. To this end, avoid solo dancing (or dancing in small groups), fancy costumes, exhibitions—especially on platform, or stage, or under conditions suggestive of anything but the playground atmosphere.

8. When a demonstration of folk dancing by children becomes necessary or advisable care should be exercised to arrange it in such a form as to make the children as little conscious of themselves as possible. The following form is suggested:

A Big Outdoor "Play Day" of folk dances and games given on a beautiful large grassy space which is kept clear for those taking part, only; and with a great number of children divided into groups dotted all over the field, taking part at the same time in every event. In this form of demonstration there is no "Grand Stand," the spectators being scattered in a thin line around the edge of the field. The space is so large and the numbers taking part so great that each group may have a happy informal play time and yet unconsciously contribute toward a wonderfully beautiful and moving spectacle. It is the size of the field, the numbers taking part and the atmosphere of happiness created, that makes this kind of an occasion the most appealing and effective of all demonstrations. The simplest folk dances and singing games such as those listed below as "Suitable for Recreation" are most successful and effective for such an occasion.

FOLK DANCES ESPECIALLY SUITABLE FOR RECREATION IN A
HEALTH PROGRAM

The folk dances listed here are from many different countries, and have been selected for their health and recreation values.

The numbers in parentheses after the dances refer to publications, in which the music and descriptions may be found. These are listed numerically immediately following the dances. Phonograph (Victor) records of all the dances named are also available.

SINGING GAMES (extremely simple)

Bridge of Avignon, The.................(12)
  (Sur le pont d'Avignon)
Carrousel ....(7), (14)
Gustaf's Skoal........................(2), (9), (14)
I See You............................(7), (14)
Nigarepolska ....(4), (14)
  ("Brownie" polska)
Our Little Girls......................(2)
Seven Pretty Girls...................(2), (10), (14)

DANCES (simple and vigorous)

Come Let Us Be Joyful...............(2)
Crested Hen, The....................(2), (5)
Farandole ....(3)
Gathering Peascods..................(8)
Gotlands Quadrille..................(2), (13)
Gossiping Ulla......................(4), (6)
Hatter, The.........................(5), (10)
Little Man in a Fix.................(5)
Reap the Flax............. ....(7), (14)
Sappo ....(4), (6)
Sellengers Round.................... (11)
Seven Jumps........................ .(2), (5)
Stick Dance.........................(5)
Tarantella ....(7)
Tinkers Dance.......................(5)
    (Especially suitable for patriotic and
    social use)
Oxdans ....(7), (14)
Arkansas Traveler...................(1)
Circle, The.........................(1)
Lady of the Lake....................(1)
Money Musk..........................(1)
Old Dan Tucker......................(1)
Virginia Reel.......................(1)

FOLK DANCES OF THE ALLIES, FOR PATRIOTIC PAGEANTS AND PLAYS

As an integral part of a patriotic pageant or play the real folk dances of the various countries represented would have a logical place if given in their traditional form. Folk dances familiar to many through use as play and recreation might thus be fitted into a patriotic community celebration.

The dances listed here are actual folk dances from the allied countries and would be recognized with emotion by natives of these countries.

The numbers in parentheses refer to the publications containing the music and description, which are listed numerically in the accompanying bibliography. Phonograph (Victor) records of the dances are available.

1. UNITED STATES OF AMERICA

The Circle............................(1)
Old Dan Tucker.......................(1)
Arkansas Traveler....................(1)
Money Musk...........................(1)
Virginia Reel........................(1)

2. FRANCE

Farandole ....(3)
The Bridge of Avignon...............(13)
    (Sur le pont d'Avignon)

3. BELGIUM

Seven Jumps...........................(2), (5)
Ladita ....(13)
    (It is not generally known that these
are Belgian dances. The latter is known
in Belgium as "Streep," but the music
and dance is the same as that known in
Sweden as Ladita.)

4. ENGLAND

Sellingers Round......................(11)
Gathering Peascods ....(8)

5. ITALY

Tarantella ....(7)

6. PORTUGAL

"Vira" ....(15)
  For the national anthems of all the Allies, see No. 16 of the
bibliography.

BIBLIOGRAPHY OF PUBLICATIONS CONTAINING MUSIC AND DESCRIPTIONS OF DANCES LISTED ABOVE

No.—Title   Author   Publisher   Price
1. "American Country Dances" (Burchenal), G. Schirmer.......$1.50
2. "Dances of the People" (Burchenal), G. Schirmer........... 1.50
3. "Farandole" (sheet form) (Burchenal), G. Schirmer.......... .20
4. "Folk Dances and Games" (Crawford), A. S. Barnes........ 1.80
5. "Folk Dances of Denmark" (Burchenal), G. Schirmer........ 1.50
6. "Folk Dances of Finland" (Burchenal), G. Schirmer........ .20
7. "Folk Dances and Singing Games" (Burchenal), G. Schirmer 1.50
8. "Gathering Peascods" (sheet form) (Sharp), Novello (H. W.
    Gray) .... .10
9. "Gustaf's Skoal" (sheet form) (Burchenal), G. Schirmer..... .20
10. "The Hatter" (sheet form) (Burchenal), G. Schirmer........ .20
11. "Sellingers Round" (sheet form) (Sharp), Novello (H. W.
    Gray) .... .10
12. "Sur le Pont d'Avignon" (sheet form) (Burchenal), G. Schir-
    mer) .... .20
13. "Swedish Folk Dances" (Bergquist), A. S. Barnes........... 1.60
14. "Swedish Song Dances" (Eastman and Kohler), Ginn....... 1.50
15. "Vira" (sheet form) (Burchenal), G. Schirmer.............. .20
16. "The National Anthems of the Allies," G. Schirmer......... .25

For further information address

Elizabeth Burchenal, Chairman Organization Committee, American
    Folk Dance Society, 2790 Broadway, New York City

Harvesting Transplanted Playgrounds

By FRED O. ENGLAND, Director of Playgrounds, Manila, P. I.

When C. M. Goethe, on his tour of transplantation, scattered the seed of American Playground propaganda in Manila he must have selected an exceptionally good quality of seed. The good seed that has been sown together with the rich and fertile soil in which it was planted have both contributed toward the rapid and marvelous development of the Manila recreation system. Manila is far in advance of every other city in the Far East in playground and recreation facilities. The Bureau of Education of the Philippines is the sturdy pioneer and builder. The preparation of the field for a system of public recreation is due, in a large measure, to the resolute and intense activity of its American employees in introducing and creating a keen desire and demand for American games and athletics. The efforts of the Bureau of Education have been supplemented to a great extent by the Philippine Y. M. C. A. Under the leadership of Elwood S. Brown, General Secretary of the Philippine Y. M. C. A. and Secretary of the Playground Committee, the Association has been of material and valuable assistance in promoting, advising and suggesting.

Previous to American occupation, Spanish customs had inculcated the idea that working with the hands was proof of low social standards, and as a result in the early days when athletics were first being introduced the well-to-do boys and girls were very loath to engage in such "common" activities as indoor baseball, basket ball, with the attendant soiling of hands, clothing, and excessive perspiration. However, the desire for play has broken all social customs and traditions. Today the average Filipino boy has two aims in life. One is to become a student and the other an athlete. There is not a corner in the entire archipelago, where the Bureau of Education is operating, that indoor baseball, volley ball, basket ball and track and field sports are not being played.

Public recreation has been made an extension feature of the department of city schools. When the playground committee was appointed by Governor-General Harrison, the city authorities were induced to set aside several school grounds, a large filled-in tract of land surrounding the old Walled City, which was a filthy moat in Spanish days, and a few other small parcels of land as public playgrounds. The city at that time owned very few schoolhouses. The majority were rented. Those that were owned by the city had not been built for school purposes, but were ordinary business structures, remodeled to serve as schoolhouses.

Playground development goes hand in hand with more and better school buildings. It is the avowed policy of the city to provide ample playgrounds in connection with all its schools. Three new playgrounds were added the past year in consequence of the three new school buildings that were completed. These playgrounds are, in the majority of cases, considerably larger than the average school yard in the States. Most of the school playgrounds are large enough for baseball and soccer football.

The most important development during the past year was the introduction of a play period in connection with the regular school program. Through the interest of Superintendent James F. Scouller in the play idea permission was obtained to try out a play period in connection with two 'schools as an experiment. The plan proved so successful that its adoption by all schools with playground facilities is assured. The plan provides for two and one-half hours of supervised play per week for every child enrolled in the schools that are affected. The school day has been lengthened twenty minutes. In addition, ten minutes which were formerly devoted to calisthenics, have been included in the play period time, making a total of thirty minutes for the period. The school day is divided into nine thirty-minute periods. The classes come out on the playground in rotation. The activities consist of marching, calisthenics, folk dancing, group games and athletics. Emphasis is placed on the recreative element.

Of the schools, at which the plan was given a trial, one was the smallest and the other one of the largest in the city. The innovation proved more successful at the small school because only one class comes out at each period. This made it possible for the playground instructor in charge to direct all the classes. At the larger school three classes come out at the same time. With only one playground instructor it became necessary to impose upon several of the teachers the burden of directing and leading their classes on the playground. The majority of the teachers lacked knowledge and technical skill in play leadership. The result was a lot of time wasted in trying to do what they had never been trained to do. With the general adoption of the plan,

234

however, enough trained instructors will be employed so that there will be one instructor for each class that comes out at the same time. The largest school in the city, containing sixty class-rooms, will require six instructors to handle the situation.

The Filipinos have very few games peculiar to them as a race. Those which they do possess have become practically extinct in congested city life. The play period in connection with the regular school program will not merely be the means of stimulating participation by thousands of underexercised children in wholesome and vigorous activities, but it will also be the means of teaching and planting an abundance of healthy, vigorous games that will eventually find their way into every home. Just recently the writer observed a group of native children spontaneously playing *Round and Round the Village, London Bridge Is Falling Down,* and *Drop the Handkerchief.*

Games and athletics have a unique value as an educational factor in this country. This factor is English. It is an undertaking of considerable magnitude to attempt to change the mother dialects of a race. It is a certainty that it cannot be accomplished in a single day. The greatest difficulty encountered by the educators in teaching English is to get the pupils to make a practical use of English in ordinary conversation. But when games taught in English are played spontaneously the American expressions crop out. Even young fellows who have never attended school will use American expressions, in ball games especially. The reason is obvious. The native dialects or Spanish do not contain such expressions as "steal home," "four balls, take your base," "wait for a good one."

A keen interest in folk dancing has been awakened. The playground instructors use them as regular activities on the playgrounds. A number of lessons in folk dancing were given for the benefit of school teachers. Between seventy-five and one hundred teachers took advantage of the lessons.

A mammoth program is in the course of preparation to celebrate Playground Day, an annual event in connection with the annual carnival. Six thousand children will participate. "The Dance of Nations," a series of folk dances representative of various nations, is the predominating feature. Five nations are represented. In addition there will be a calisthenic drill by 3,000 boys; a competitive military drill; a gymnastic dance by 500 boys; and May-pole dances by 500 girls.

235

One playground in the city is illuminated at night. It is lighted by ten 1,000 watt lamps suspended on cables stretched between poles. At the time the lights were installed the playground had a formal opening and was rechristened "recreation center." Illumination appears to be the only practical method of solving the problem of adult recreation. There is no twilight. In consequence it becomes dark between 5:30 and 6:30 the whole year round. Therefore very little time remains for the average working man for recreation from the time the day's work is ended until the sun sets. The recreation center is proving very popular. Scores of people attend. An outdoor stage has been provided and public evening entertainments are regular features.

Approximately 272,000 square meters of land comprise the playground area of the city. This area includes ten playgrounds and twenty tennis courts. The amount of funds appropriated by the city for public recreation is steadily on the increase. The city authorities are in full accord with the play idea. The Honorable Justo Lukban, Mayor of the City of Manila, is chairman of the Playground Committee. When the city has completed its extensive building program funds for public recreation will be greatly increased and more easily obtained. The prospect is very bright that the appropriation for 1918 will more than double that for 1917. It is only a matter of a few years until Manila will possess a system of public recreation equal to the best in the States.

In these strenuous war times it is an exceedingly sagacious government that has vision to realize the importance and value of investing in a policy that assures a vigorous, healthy and sturdy future citizenship.

The Physical Rebuilding of Philippine Manhood

George R. Summers, Assistant Superintendent of Schools, Manila, P. I.

"The growth of every child is the story of a 'Sleeping Beauty' in which Play takes the part of the Prince. As the Prince awakened the Sleeping Beauty, so organized play is transforming the leisure hours of the new generation into character, growth, strength and citizenship."

It may not be a matter of common knowledge yet it is a fact beyond dispute of which there are many notable examples that our young men, most of them in the public schools, are undergoing a most remarkable physical development. To be more specific, mention might be made of the 1555 uniformed and completely equipped baseball teams of the Bureau of Education. In the City of Manila itself, the thousands of spectators who weekly attend the baseball games of the Manila League notice in particular the splendid physique of the Filipino players.

The great work of the Bureau of Education in its program of "athletics for everybody" is generally recognized throughout the Philippine Islands. There are also other agencies which foster and encourage athletics and physical training. In the City of Manila there are scores of independent indoor baseball teams; tennis clubs are multiplying rapidly; and soccer football is now being introduced. Mention might be made of the physical training that the young men of the country are now receiving as a result of the organization of the Philippine National Guard. The latest report submitted by the Senior Inspector of Schools, Philippine Health Service, indicates that athletics have been an important factor in decreasing the number of cases of tuberculosis among pupils. Also on account of recent physical betterment of our young men, the physical requirements for entrance into the Philippine Constabulary have been considerably raised.

If we can say that at least a good beginning has been made in the physical betterment of the race, then the real problem before the country is to extend this movement so that it reaches the adults quite as much as it does the boys; to get away from, so to speak, the form of leisure perfumed with aristocracy. We must get away from the siesta chair. If a movement, call it what you like, can be undertaken to get the adults of this country better acquainted, the problem will be solved because when people talk together, sing and play together, the ideals of a pure democracy have been safely launched if the citizens have been trained up to have faith in humanity. To emphasize this point, I have in mind the work of various clubs and associations in the City of Manila. Pay a visit some afternoon to the Manila Y. M. C. A., the Casino Español, the Columbia Club, the Filipino Cluub, Laong-Laan, or to a number of other clubs which I might mention.

237

Here you will find army officers, business men, lawyers, ministers, government officials, and private citizens, all at play, not behind barred doors with the air full of tuberculosis germs, but out in the open playing tennis, or in the gymnasium, clad in athletic suits, playing volley ball or some of the other group games as a member of some team. The aim should be to extend this movement, not only in the city of Manila, but to the provinces as well.

The Liberty Sing Idea

Robert D. Dripps

The American people love clean, wholesome outdoor sports. There is never any difficulty in getting a crowd together for a baseball game, a football game, an automobile race or a boxing contest.

When we Americans witness athletic contests we like to show our enthusiasm and to cheer on the team we are backing, so that everyone and especially the players themselves will know where we stand.

Which of us ever witnessed a college baseball or football game and failed to be impressed not only with the cheering but with the way in which singing supplements cheering; or who can doubt that such singing has a tremendous influence on the players? Many a game has been won by the spectators.

Today, this country of ours has a team in the field. The stakes for which it is playing are such as no team ever played for before.

We who almost agonize in our desire to play on that team are for one reason or another compelled to watch on the side lines.

As we wonder if there is anything we can do to help, there comes a call from Washington for cheers and singing, to put "pep" into the contestants, to show them how intently, how eagerly we are watching them and how earnestly we want them to win.

When we respond to this call we are not singing for our own amusement, we are singing for Liberty.

As we sing we are united as never before; stirred with patriotism as never before; and as Tennyson puts it, "The song that moves a Nation's heart is in itself a deed."

2

Why Make Good Times Accessible?

The April number of *Social Hygiene* publishes several articles of interest to all thinking people in this day of increasing social responsibility and of particular concern to all who are interested in War Camp Community Service as they deal with the underlying problems which caused the War Department and the Navy Department to institute their Comissions on Training Camp Activities.

The first of these articles, *The Social Status of the Sailor*, gives a splendid interpretation of the man inside the white uniform and jaunty black tie whom we see swinging along the city streets of our seaport towns, the personality of the individual whom we carelessly regard as merely an atom in the great war machine instead of as a lively, human, fun-loving boy, who might be our son or brother.

Says the writer, Medical Inspector J. S. Taylor, U. S. N., in picturing the sailor, "The day's work is never done—he must toil early and late for the maintenance and upkeep of his perishable, floating abode, incessantly attacked by salt water and the oxidizing air, whose inroads must be neutralized by ceaseless scraping, chipping, red leading, and painting, from the double bottoms to the platform of the cage mast. If the reader can conceive himself a part of it [this life] and if his imagination can perform the still greater feat of appreciating what it means after one, two, three weeks without setting foot on shore; what it means to experience it for three months—he is prepared to understand what tempestuous craving for change, what irresistible impulse to reaction, what agitation and wild exuberance of feeling sweeps over the man-of-war's man when at last comes 'liberty.'" He adds from his own experience that the man's feeling when that glowing word comes is like that of the time-expired man.

He comes ashore as care-free as a ripple on a summer sea and twice as joyous, because he is absolutely his own master—or thinks he is. His hunger for a change of scene, craving for some fun, and his pocketful of money, says Mr. Taylor, make him an easy prey to all the sharks and harpies that infest the water front. "There is no lack of opportunity to spend his money and beguile his time. The trouble is that the easy ways of finding diversion are usually bad ways, and the companions ready to hand * * are frequently pernicious. The good influences are far to seek,

clothed in drab, with nothing to offer which compares in attractiveness with evil allurements." This latter statement is surely a
challenge to us who pursue our complacent civilian way. "The
attractiveness of evil allurements" raises our fighting spirit but we
are only just beginning to counter it. And it must be countered
by an attractiveness equally great—for the day of pious psalm-
singing has passed. Mr. Taylor presents us with the portrait of
the typical American boy when he says, "The sailor has a horror of
the tract handed to him in public, and in spite of a fundamental
respect for 'the cloth' he is not to be approached by a clergyman at
a time like this. It was not for a gospel talk that he had his hair
clipped, that he shaved to the roots, got himself as clean from
head to foot as soap and water could make him, donned his immac-
ulate undershirt and the best shore-going uniform he possesses,
drew all the money he had on the books and flung himself into the
liberty boat with his cap set at a rakish angle!" It was for a
Good Time, spelled with capital letters, that he prepared with such
scrupulous care, and the Good Time ought to be worthy of such a
preparation. That is the meaning of the many little bulletins and
cards bearing the War Camp Community Service insignia which
one sees containing advertisements of dances, concerts, "shows,"
canteens. The effort is being made to make them not only
counter but superior attractions.

Any effort to influence the sailor's behavior while on liberty,
the article continues, must be circuitous, indirect, made at long
range with infinite tact and diplomacy for he is suspicious and
keen to scent a "missionary" effort. It must be attended by a
complete comprehension of him and his needs, his strength and
his weakness. What he wants is something "different," to look at,
to hear, to eat and to do. Chiefly, it's amusement he wants and
if the best isn't easily accessible "he will compromise with something that is far below the best," which is never hard to find. If
the man has relatives or friends in the port he either goes "out
home" or immediately seeks a telephone booth to notify his friends,
who see to it that he has a good time such as he used to have at
home. But those fortunate men are few in number, by far the
majority being strangers, knowing no one in the town. For that
reason they are the more ready to make friends and are not
particular in their choice, provided a good time is in sight.
Naturally it is girls who attract them, cut off as they are from
contact with women in their daily life. Mr. Taylor says, "If our
240

sailors could step ashore to be introduced to jolly, fun-loving girls of their own station in life and could go with them to dance and skate, to a theater or a picnic, in a word if there were the disposition to extend to them the same type of hospitality that is lavished on officers; if there were homes for them to go to, a goodly proportion of the crew would take advantage of such opportunities." This is the contact the War Camp Community Service is endeavoring to establish, has established to a great extent, but vastly more remains to be accomplished. It is meeting and will continue to meet in increasingly large degree Mr. Taylor's exhortation when he says, "When we begin to make legal enactments for the prevention of vice, let us restrain first of all the *agents provocateurs* who work primarily—in the interests of men and women who openly acquire wealth by playing on the baser side of men's natures. And when we close dance halls, lewd shows, groggeries, and brothels, let us be at equal pains *to provide something better in their stead."*

The article concludes with a short heart-to-heart talk with the reader that again embodies the principles of War Camp Community Service. It is well worth a repetition. "To really accomplish anything there must be personal sacrifice. If those who are concerned for the sailor's welfare are capable of even a little personal sacrifice much good will come. Can they be moved to undertake the sacrifice? If you are dining in a restaurant, are you ready to go over and sit down to meat with some lonely, embarrassed sailor lad who after a long solitary walk has continued his efforts towards a respectable "liberty" by going to a decent place and ordering a decent meal, who may be trying to put out of his mind the dangerous allurements of the big city with its warm snuggeries, its gleaming barroom lights, its proffer of lips and arms painted and powdered perhaps out of all attractiveness and yet promising a warm personal touch in the life of the weary, friendless stranger? Are you prepared to take such a young man to your club and after a chat and a smoke to drive him down to the wharf in your automobile? Will you invite him to enter your house as your guest and send him away enriched by an increased self-respect and a feeling of noblesse oblige? If not, are you not something of a coward and a hypocrite when you resort to the law for his salvation and to acquit your conscience of guilt should he cry out in bitterness: 'No man hath cared for my soul.' "

241

Another article, *Passing of the Red Light District—Vice Investigations and Results,* expounds the new program which is dealing with the social evil, namely that of repression, the most immediate part of the program, and that of prevention. Prevention is the wider and more constructive field, which is open not only to the trained social worker but to every American citizen. With regard to it the writer, Joseph Mayer, says, "The relation of juvenile delinquency to vice is becoming more clear and child welfare bureaus are being established to cope with it and related problems. Public amusement and recreation facilities are being extended, such as social centers and playgrounds, and recreation commissions are being formed to coordinate activities. The most convincing example of both the need and efficacy of such measures is exhibited in the work of the Commission on Training Camp Activities, which is supplementing a rigorous policy of vice suppression by supplying wholesome recreational and social opportunities for the thousands of men in concentration camps." It is the first time in the world's history that a nation has undertaken to deal with vice in a constructive way and the results have already silenced the doubters.

One cannot doubt the value of work that improves the morals and morale of our fighters, and so surely as we pay now with the coin of our financial, moral and personal support for the continuance of a national policy of raising morals and morale so surely shall we receive principal and interest back to build again and better when the war is won.

Mrs. Eva Whiting White comes to the Play-ground and Recreation Association of America

Mrs. Eva Whiting White, Head Resident of Elizabeth Peabody House, Boston, represents the vital leaders of the younger group in the settlement ranks. It is such as she who give confidence that those who are sometimes called the "Old Guard" of the settlements are by no means without those in the next generation who will effectually carry forward the torch.

Mrs. White is one of the first fruits of specialized training in social work as she was one of the original graduates not only of Simmons College, where she took domestic science courses, but of the Boston School of Social Work. She has been in charge of Elizabeth Peabody House during the last ten years. Taking the leadership of this settlement in its early and struggling days, she has made it one of the most important social agencies in Boston, housed in a building admirably equipped for its work. In addition to the varied round of neighborhood service for which the settlement stands, it has a perfectly equipped theatre in which a number of interesting and promising dramatic experiments have been carried on, with a quite remarkable response from the local immigrant neighborhood.

Mrs. White has for several years past been in charge of the school centers in Boston as an officer under the school board. Undertaking this problem amid special difficulties, Mrs. White has been able to elicit a remarkable degree of local initiative and neighborly cooperation in support of the centers in many different parts of the city and under a variety of community conditions. Her experience in this service, and the very exceptional facility with which she has earned and kept the confidence and loyalty of the different local groups indicates clearly the steady and varied stimulus and help which will come of her leadership in connection with the War Camp Community Service.

She imparts to all her efforts the spirit of good sport. She plays different positions with happy excellence; her play is always fair, always for the team. She gets quickly into the game and does not seem to mind when it is uphill.

There is not only a lasting but a cumulative quality about her work and influence. Even at that, she is more than her work. She has a great liking for folks, and they like her.

Book Reviews

AMERICAN COUNTRY DANCES

Edited by Elizabeth Burchenal. Published by G. Schirmer, New York. Price, Paper, $1.50, net; Cloth, $2.50, net

Twenty-eight "contra-dances," largely from the New England States, are presented in this, the first volume in a series destined to make available our own truly national dances. These are "essentially *American* folk dances because they have grown here. Some of them are slightly reminiscent of English country-dances, and were probably suggested by, or evolved from them. Most of them, however, seem to be products of this country, and all have a typical and distinctly individual quality of their own, both in their form and the manner and style in which they are danced."

Miss Burchenal was much helped in her search for these half-forgotten dances by "Uncle Steve" Kimball, who has played the violin for country dances for over forty years.

BOOK REVIEWS

KEEPING OUR FIGHTERS FIT

By Edward Frank Allen. Published by The Century Company, New York. Price, $1.25

The various phases of the work of the twin Commissions on Training Camp Activities—of the War and Navy Departments—are presented from the point of view of the layman in such social work. Prepared with the cooperation of the Chairman of these Commissions and with a foreword by the President of the United States, the book goes forth under official sanction as an authoritative account of the work—its aims and achievements.

Speaking of the War Camp Community Service, the writer says: "An antidote for loneliness and the blues has been provided by the Recreation Association of America [Playground and Recreation Association of America], working through the various agencies that have rallied to its aid. The organization has evolved a remarkable system, a system with a personality. It proves that machinery may have a heart."

"The functions of the War Camp Community Service are almost without number. Drinking fountains have been erected in cities where formerly there were none. Atlanta, Georgia, built a comfort station at a cost of $20,000. Other cities have done the same. Money and labor have been given lavishly to keep our fighters fit mentally and morally, to keep them from homesickness and depression."

"The hours allowed for relaxation are apt to be misused. There are evil forces at work to undermine the morals and health of the men who are to fight our battles. The Commissions on Training Camp Activities have set up competitive forces with which to combat them, and this is one of them—to give the men healthful, interesting recreation while they are away from camp."

THE BOOK OF SCHOOL GAMES

Edited by C. E. Hodges, M.A. Published by Evans Brothers, Ltd., Montague House, Russell Square, W. C. Price, 3s 6d

Many games not frequently played in America, as well as many played under another name, are found in this book. A large section is devoted to devices for introducing the play element into school room history, geography, arithmetic. Descriptions are given from the point of view of formal discipline, which it is to be hoped most American play leaders have outgrown. The illustrations show boys and girls at "Attention" while waiting turns in leap frog, three deep, potato race!

AN INTRODUCTION TO RURAL SOCIOLOGY

By Paul L. Vogt. Published by D. Appleton & Company, New York. Price, $2.50

A very close and detailed study of rural conditions is presented, with attention to the many phases of life economic, moral, social and the present status and possible development of the church, the school, farmers' organizations. Professor Vogt notes that the rural community is gradually yielding to urban ideals as to recreation, self-entertainment giving way to professionalism and commercialized places of amusement taking the place of private social affairs, led by volunteer social leaders. Discussing limited social groups such as the farmers' clubs of twelve families, the author raises the question of the value to the community of such exclusiveness, if carried to exaggeration.

244

Washington, Indiana

THE WORK OF NIMBLE FINGERS FOR THE CHILDREN'S FAIR

LANGDON SWIMMING POOL, PORTSMOUTH PLAYGROUND

A STREET-SHOWER BATH, TO BE SEEN VERY FREQUENTLY DURING
THE SUMMER TIME IN CERTAIN SECTIONS OF PHILADELPHIA. THE
POLICEMAN TURNS ON THE FIRE-PLUG TO FLUSH THE STREET,
THE CHILDREN GET A BATH

THE PAGEANT OF THE PIED PIPER—THE PIED PIPER
CHARMS AWAY THE RATS

246

CRIPPLED LADS CLIMBING TREES AT THE
VAN LEUVEN BROWNE CAMP AT PORT
HURON, MICHIGAN

High School Cadets Drilling to the Music of the Victrola, Santa Barbara, Cal.

America's Slogan: Freedom, For All, Forever!

Now is the time for all American children to hear and learn to sing the stirring patriotic songs of our country,—the music which is inspiring the boys of Uncle Sam's Army and Navy, who are helping to win the war.

Now, if never before, our boys and girls should know the good old folk melodies of America, and the wholesome, hearty country dances of our pioneer forefathers:

Many old American Country Dances, recently revived by Elizabeth Burchenal and featured, with full directions, in her new book on "American Country Dances" (Published by G. Schirmer), have been recorded by the Victor Company under her direction.

The Victrola and Victor Records

are the *best* means by which these old American country dances may be brought into your school and community festivals. They are simple, tuneful, charming, easily taught, and have a truly American flavor.

Ask to hear the following records played by the Victor Military Band, at your dealer's:

18490 { Old Dan Tucker / White Cockade

18491 { Green Mountain Volunteers / peed the Plow

18356 { Lady of the Lake / Old Zip Coon

18367 { Hull's Victory / The Circle

18331 { Arkansaw Traveler / Soldier's Joy

17160 Pop Goes the Weasel

Any Victor dealer will gladly play the above for you, and supply you with a copy of "A New Graded List" and the Victor Catalog of Records. For further information, write to the

Educational Department
Victor Talking Machine Co.
Camden, N. J.

HIS MASTER'S VOICE

Victrola XXV, $85
specially manufactured for School use

When the Victrola is not in use, the horn can be placed under the instrument safe and secure from danger, and the cabinet can be locked to protect it from dust and promiscuous use by irresponsible people.

Victrola

LUTHER HALSEY GULICK, 1865-1918, FIRST PRESIDENT OF THE
PLAYGROUND AND RECREATION ASSOCIATION OF AMERICA

The Playground

Vol. XII No. 7   OCTOBER, 1981

DR. LUTHER HALSEY GULICK

A Pioneer in the Play and Recreation Movement

Dr. Luther Halsey Gulick, loved of all in the play movement, died August 13, 1918.

Throughout all his years of useful public service, Dr. Gulick labored that all might have a more abundant life. A pioneer ever in all he did, Dr. Gulick saw before most of his associates the need of physical education and gave this movement a great impetus through his own special contribution of service to it. After working for boys and young men in the Y. M. C. A., he turned to apply the same principles to all boys. In the New York Public Schools Athletic League, associated with other leading citizens, he helped to work out a demonstration that play could be used to bring more all-around development, not alone physical, but mental and moral, and life development as well for all the school boys and girls of a city than which no city in the world is more difficult for such an experiment.

When the leaders of the play movement came together in Chicago in 1906 Dr. Gulick was the natural choice as President of the new Playground Association of America. As the delegates talked together, swam together, played together, all felt his inspiration. After the work of the Association was well started he insisted that he be relieved of the responsibility of the presidency, but he always remained a great power behind the Playground and Recreation Association, as it had later come to be called. The particular needs of the girls gripped him, and with the help of Mrs. Gulick, who was ever by his side working with him, he developed plans for the Camp Fire Girls of America which will have a lasting influence on the young womanhood of other countries as well as our own. No painting has greater beauty than the ideals which he made so attractive to the army of young girls who were thirsting for beauty and adventure.

Dr. Gulick saw the community, the brotherhood of men living and working together, as few in his generation have, and wrought to bring the community and the neighborhood to have the respect, affection, power and place which would make each citizen proud to be a citizen.

Returning from a trip to France to report on the conditions surrounding our soldiers there, his mind at once leaped forward to the conditions that should surround our troops when they return to our own country after the war. He suggested large plans to make America as attractive and as wholesome for the returning troops as the camps in France have been made under the United States Government.

Throughout his public life, Dr. Gulick commanded the affection of men who differed radically from him. He rejoiced to stimulate other men, to arouse them from the ordinary routine by some challenge which called to new tasks. Always his friends knew that by his enthusiasm, his never-dying youth, his breadth of vision and personality, he would carry to success seemingly impossible tasks. He so lived that his friends, still under the spell of his forward-looking vision, glad for the years during which they enjoyed comradeship with him, cannot be sad and heavy-hearted even when he has gone.

H. S. BRAUCHER

LUTHER HALSEY GULICK

Dr. Luther Gulick died at South Casco, Maine, on August 13th, in his fifty-third year. Community workers owe to Dr. Gulick more than any one of them can fully appreciate. His direct contribution to public recreation and to the community center movement was important and his indirect contribution, growing out of a life work of more than thirty years, was momentous, not only to the community center movement but to the development of American social policy.

I do not know how to put in words the thoughts which crossed my mind on the day of his funeral at Springfield, Massachusetts. Dr. Gulick was endowed with the comic spirit and with a powerful feeling for the real. He therefore was not sentimental, and there was no sentimentality at his funeral. He had suffered much but was always gay, and at his funeral there was no sadness of the ordinary kind. He was one of the few men whom I have known who was truly possessed with inward religious convictions, including a belief in the effective reality of God and the immortality of the soul, yet at his funeral there was no preachment about a life hereafter, no appeal to an invisible Power for a compensation to make up for the shortcomings of this world. Nothing about his funeral had been prearranged, but the little group of friends who met there seemed to be possessed with a spirit that had little in common with the more lurid hopes or despairs of past ages. Dr. Gulick had lived here and now the intense life which our ascetic religions had taught us we would live in some hereafter world. Through his life, many interests of old time had been given a new meaning and a new birth, and some things had been brought into consciousness which will not be the common property of men for centuries yet to come. Those who spoke at his bier used simple language and the entire ceremonial had about it a quietness and majesty, and a joyousness, such as one feels in pine forests on a sunny afternoon, when the wind is breathing faintly.

I try to give this impression of Dr. Gulick's funeral because it suggests the meaning which his life takes on, when revealed in the sudden blaze of cold light that death brings. In some way, through some narrative or statue or poem, this unique quality of Dr. Gulick's personality and life ought to be preserved for the youth of America.

In this short memorial article, only fragmentary things can be said. Dr. Gulick came up within the Christian tradition, which in America is an ascetic, puritanical one. Through his entire life he held fast to the values of this tradition, and yet he made into a science and art the subject of physical training. He went further and translated a social movement into esthetic symbols—the outcome was the organization of the Camp Fire Girls.

Dr. Gulick might have been faithful to the Christian tradition and he might have contributed as he did to the Hellenic tradition of a whole man, whole in body as well as mind, and he might still have remained an individualist. But long ago, before social psychology was recognized as a branch of science, before social anthropology had begun to yield significant fruit, Dr. Gulick found his way to the thought of the *group* and the *community*. He formulated the doctrine that social values are collective, not personal, that the community transmits social heredity, that the dynamics of human behavior are to be understood through contemplating human relations rather than isolated human beings.

253

He did not pause long in the theoretical aspects of this momentous idea, but passed to its application in terms of public schools athletic leagues, playground associations, and school community centers.

Dr. Gulick lived by a theory which to the philistine mind is not an attractive one. He never did anything if he believed that someone else would do it anyhow. He never stayed with any institution after he had made that institution successful. He was essentially a frontiersman. In addition, he worked so hard that there was little time for writing, and his books were relatively casual products. Thousands of pages of unorganized manuscript, some of it profoundly significant, exciting and inspiring, lie in his storage rooms. He never took time to get them in shape for the printer.

A word should be said about Dr. Gulick's family life. Most men who are creative, who are absorbed in public affairs, live the best part of their lives outside of their homes. Dr. Gulick reversed this present-day habit. It was never possible to determine where his home ended and where his world's work began. They were confluent. Much of that life attitude, which no phrases can describe, which was eternally reborn in him day by day, will be carried forward as a part of the very nature of Mrs. Gulick and of their children.

During the last twelvemonth, Dr. Gulick had been identified with the war work of the Y. M. C. A. This policy-forming work, having to do with sex hygiene and with the broader question of morale, to which he gave literally the last hours of his life and for which he knowingly surrendered years of a life which with justifiable prudence he might have prolonged, will survive in the fabric of national betterment which the ordeal of fire is bringing to our country.

He was of the race of Thomas Davidson, Charles Sprague Smith and above all, William James. His was a "life with one cold unchanging gleam imbued." He required for America something more than contentment and the well-being of the flesh. Call it adventurousness, romance, splendor, religion, the search for deep waters and for further horizons. A significant intensity of life, a passion of hope and of deed, and withal a passion for scientific method and for the application of science to the adjustments of personal life and the making of social programs. There is no "social worker" of our times, at least in America, who for

254

vision, for scientific equipment or for audacity of thought can be compared with Luther Gulick. His industry and tenacity were equally phenomenal. What he wrote or uttered, he executed in life and in work. A horizon-builder, he was yet almost fiercely practical.

It is these things that Luther Gulick symbolizes to us of the younger generation who owe to him nurture, a vivified ideal of self-criticism, an intimation of great forces to utilize and great problems to solve which are in wait for us out beyond the frontiers of conventional thought. At this moment of time, individual lives, institutions, whole peoples fade away, and their going is hardly more noticed than the passing of a shadow. But when all is summed up, there are only two things known to us humans which are real, undying. Of these two things, one is personality. The other is achievement—the discovery and mastery of energies cosmic, social, psychic. Let us pause for a moment, and take into ourselves the life meaning of this *true* creator, this energetic and disinterested friend of so many. Because he has lived, life is more believable, personal values are more real to thousands. And because he has discovered, innovated, achieved, our humanity will sooner come to the promised land.

JOHN COLLIER

Members of National Finance Committee, War Camp Community Service ·

JOSEPH LEE

Joseph Lee is a member of the Commissions on Training Camp Activities of the War and Navy Departments as well as president of the War Camp Community Service and a member of its National Finance Committee. He has been president since 1910 of the Playground and Recreation Association of America which was asked by the Commissions to undertake the work of War Camp Community Service shortly after the United States declared war.

Mr. Lee was born in Brookline, Mass., March 8, 1863, went to school in Boston, and earned his A. B. in Harvard in the class of '83, and his A. M. and LL. B. in the Harvard Law School class of '87. He was admitted to the bar that same year, but almost immediately took up philanthropic work with especial reference to leisure time recreation and athletics.

He was captain of his school football teams, played on his freshman team at Harvard, rowed on the Sophomore crew, and won the middleweight boxing championship in his junior year. His son, Joseph Lee, Jr., 17 years old, who is attending the Country Day School in Boston, is already winning races in fine form.

In his social work, Mr. Lee has carried out the idea that the element of competition in athletics ought to be complemented by a minimum standard of "things that every fellow ought to be able to do." He established national standards of this sort of three grades. "The boy without a playground," according to Mr. Lee, "is the father of the man without a job."

As the organizer and president of the Massachusetts Civic League Mr. Lee has been instrumental in obtaining much social legislation. He brought about the first Probation Commission in Massachusetts, and became a member of it, and was chairman last year of the Boston School Committee of which he had been a member for nine years.

At all times he has promoted the playground movement and the opening of further evening play centers. In 1906 he was successful in obtaining the passage of a bill for medical inspection in the schools, and an annual test of sight and hearing. He has pushed hygienic measures, including improvements in the care of children's teeth, promoted continuation schools in Massachusetts, and succeeded in increasing the number of classes for backward children in Boston from 8 to 60.

In addition to the foregoing work Mr. Lee lectured at Harvard for two years before the war on *The Place of Play in Education,* and is the author of *Constructive and Preventive Philanthropy,* published in 1902 and *Play in Education,* published in 1915, in addition to many articles in the school and philanthropic magazines. He is writing at present about War Camp Community Service for some of the popular magazines of large circulation.

MYRON T. HERRICK

The marvel about Myron T. Herrick, Ex-Governor of Ohio, and former Ambassador to France, is how he does it all. He is not only chairman of the National Finance Committee of the War Camp Community Service, but, among other things, one of the

256

Joseph Lee, President War Camp Community Service

MYRON T. HERRICK, CHAIRMAN NATIONAL FINANCE COMMITEE,
WAR CAMP COMMUNITY SERVICE

Cleveland members of the Financial Committee of Seventy of the National Association of Owners of Railroad Securities, representing the owners of $4,000,000,000 worth of these securities, one of the incorporators of the Committee for Armenian and Syrian Relief, president of the Cleveland Chamber of Commerce, president of the American Committee for Devastated France, and president of the Society for Savings in the City of Cleveland. These are only a few of the financial and war relief activities in which Governor Herrick is interested.

It is his belief that these two lines of activity are inseparable. "Our first business," he says, "is to win the war. The directors of any corporation who at this time put ordinary business first should be ashamed of themselves. All other matters can wait. Any line of activity that will help win the war is worth while. Any line that does not contribute to that result is a handicap."

Governor Herrick was born at Huntington, Ohio, October 9, 1855. He attended high schools in Huntington and Wellington, was a student at Oberlin College and Ohio Wesleyan University, and was admitted to the bar in 1878. The latter university granted him the honorary degree of A. M. in 1899, and after his return from his splendid work as Ambassador to France, leading universities such as Harvard, Yale, Columbia, Princeton and Union granted him the degree of LL. D. This work was so egregious that Lord Northcliffe said of Governor Herrick in Cleveland last year:

"I had the honor of meeting Ambassador Herrick in almost the earliest stages of the war, when between one and two millions of Germans were marching on Paris, and when Paris, with almost twice the number of inhabitants of Cleveland, was panic-stricken and they were fleeing from that city. And it was largely due to a man from Cleveland that that panic did not extend so far that the whole population would have left and the Germans marched into Paris. That feat of Ambassador Herrick is one of the most remarkable achievements of any one man during the war, and it has been acknowledged by our Government and King and by the Republic of France."

It was at the instance of Mr. Henry P. Davison of the Red Cross as well as many of his friends already engaged in the work of War Camp Community Service that Governor Herrick, who has served on its Budget Committee since the beginning of the

259

WILLIAM B. JOYCE, VICE-CHAIRMAN, NATIONAL FINANCE COM-
MITTEE, WAR CAMP COMMUNITY SERVICE

war, accepted the chairmanship of its National Finance Committee. He has been in turn a successful lawyer, banker, business man and manufacturer, and is an officer or director of many of the larger corporations of the country. He has been associated with a great number of nationally known financial enterprises, but during his entire business and professional career he has devoted a large share of his time and energy to things not for profit.

WILLIAM B. JOYCE

Although William B. Joyce is now the President of the National Surety League at 115 Broadway, New York City, he has never forgotten that thirty-seven years ago he sold newspapers in Grand Rapids, Michigan. Moreover he is proud of it. When he was recently engaged in raising money for the Newsboys' Club Building Fund he said:

"I used to get up at four o'clock in the morning and shout myself hoarse before I ate my breakfast, hawking the old *Michigan Times* and *Michigan Democrat* in the principal streets. Both papers are dead now but the old Michiganites remember them. There weren't any newsstands in those days and it was all up to the newsboys.

"I wouldn't wipe out that experience for thousands of dollars. Quick character reading, the essential principles of salesmanship, power of initiative and the realization that honesty is the only policy sum up my own psychological profits from my career as a newsboy."

Mr. Joyce like Governor Herrick insists that "the war comes first and all other business comes second."

"I believe," he said, "that one of the wisest moves which the Commission on Training Camp Activities has made was to appoint the War Camp Community Service to carry on its work in the communities outside and adjacent to our great camps, cantonments and naval stations.

"Invaluable as is the work of its other agencies inside the camps, this personal attention to our soldiers, sailors and marines while they are on leave and away from military discipline will do more than anything else to show them that the nation as a whole is backing them up in every way."

Before Mr. Joyce accepted the vice-chairmanship of the National Finance Committee of the War Camp Community

261

Service his financial interests had occupied the greater part of his time. He was born in Utica, New York, on December 28, 1866, the son of Henry Manwaring and Mary A. Joyce. He was educated in the public schools and on January 19, 1889, married Miss Lucy Natalie Curley of Louisville, Ky.

From 1891 to 1904 he was first western manager of the National Surety Company of Missouri and then of the National Surety Company of New York. In the latter year he became and still is the President of the New York Company. He is director of the American Light and Traction Company, Kerr Lake Mining Co., United Gas and Electric Corporation, Tennessee Copper and Chemical and the American Sumatra Tobacco Company.

He is an Episcopalian and thirty-second degree Mason and a member of the following clubs: Bankers', Recess, Metropolitan, and Sleepy Hollow Country.

(Other members of the National Finance Committee may be found on page 325.)

United War Work Campaign

LETTER OF PRESIDENT WILSON

"The White House,
"Washington, Sept. 3, 1918

"My Dear Mr. Fosdick:

"May I not call your attention to a matter which has been recently engaging my thought not a little?

"The War Department has recognized the Young Men's Christian Association, the Young Women's Christian Association, the National Catholic War Council (Knights of Columbus), the Jewish Welfare Board, the War Camp Community Service, the American Library Association, and the Salvation Army as accepted instrumentalities through which the men in the ranks are to be assisted in many essential matters of recreation and morale.

"It was evident from the first, and has become increasingly evident, that the services rendered by these agencies to our army and to our allies are especially one and all of a kind and must of necessity, if well rendered, be rendered in the closest cooperation. It is my judgment, therefore, that we shall secure the best results in the matter of the support of these agencies, if these seven societies will unite their forthcoming appeals for funds, in order that the spirit of the country in this matter may be expressed without distinction of race or religious opinion in support of what is in reality a common service.

"This point of view is sustained by the necessity, which the war has forced upon us, of limiting our appeals for funds in such a way that two or three comprehensive campaigns shall take the place of a series of independent calls upon the generosity of the country.

"Will you not, therefore, as Chairman of the Commission on Training Camp Activities, be good enough to request the societies in question to combine their approaching appeals for funds in a single campaign, preferably during the week of Nov. 11, so that in their solicitation of funds as well as in their work in the field, they may act in as complete cooperation and fellowship as possible?

"In inviting these organizations to give this new evidence of their patriotic cooperation, I wish it distinctly understood that their compliance with this request will not in any sense imply the surrender on the part of any of them of its distinctive character and autonomy, because I fully recognize the fact that each of them has its own traditions, principles, and relationships which it properly prizes and which, if preserved and strengthened, make possible the largest service.

"At the same time, I would be obliged if you would convey to them from me a very warm expression of the Government's appreciation of the splendid service they have rendered in ministering to the troops at home and overseas in their leisure time. Through their agencies the moral and spiritual resources of the nation have been mobilizing behind our forces and used in the finest way, and they are contributing directly and effectively to the winning of the war.

"It has been gratifying to find such a fine spirit of cooperation among all the leaders of the organizations I have mentioned. This spirit and the patriotism of all the members and friends of these agencies, give me confidence to believe that the united war work campaign will be crowned with abundant success.

"Cordially and sincerely yours,

"Woodrow Wilson"

263

WAR CAMP COMMUNITY SERVICE

MEMORANDUM OF AGREEMENT BETWEEN THE COOPERATING ORGANIZATIONS

(Adopted September 4, 1918)

It is agreed by the National War Work Council of the Young Men's Christian Associations, the War Work Council of the National Board of the Young Women's Christian Associations, the National Catholic War Council (Knights of Columbus), the Jewish Welfare Board, the War Camp Community Service, the American Library Association and the Salvation Army

1. That there shall be a joint campaign for funds during the week beginning November 11, 1918.

2. That by *joint* campaign we mean, so far as it can be brought about, a campaign undertaken through the agency of consolidated committees rather than seven separate campaigns in the same week.

3. That each society will adopt a joint pledge card.

4. That the committee organization now installed throughout the country for the collection of funds be disturbed as little as possible, and that the policy of addition rather than of elimination be advised.

5. That in so far as the campaign has a name it shall be called the "United War Work Campaign" followed by the names of the seven organizations participating.

6. That Mr. Cleveland H. Dodge be the national treasurer and that the moneys collected in the states be paid to him for proper distribution among the societies.

7. That all funds collected be distributed on a pro rata basis among the seven societies participating in the campaign; that is, the funds received shall be divided among the participating organizations in such proportion as the total budget of each organization bears to the sum total of the combined budgets. The budget estimates and percentages are as follows:

National War Work Council of the
  Young Men's Christian Associations..$100,000,000..58.65%

War Work Council of the National
Board of the Young Women's Chris-
tian Associations .... $15,000,000.. 8.80%
National Catholic War Council
(Knights of Columbus).............. $30,000,000..17.60%
Jewish Welfare Board.................. $3,500,000.. 2.05%
War Camp Community Service........ $15,000,000.. 8.80%
American Library Association.......... $3,500,000.. 2.05%
Salvation Army .... $3,500,000.. 2.05%

8. That specified or restricted subscriptions shall not be asked for, but if given, shall be credited to the particular association, such amount to be a part of the total and not an addition to it.

9. That the advertising which each organization has planned for itself proceed as planned but that some advertising be advised in the name of the United War Work Campaign.

10. That the expenses incurred in joint work in connection with the drive be paid on a pro rata basis.

11. That Mr. George W. Perkins and Dr. John R. Mott for the Young Men's Christian Association; Mrs. Henry P. Davison for the Young Women's Christian Association; Mr. John G. Agar and Mr. James J. Phelan for the National Catholic War Council (Knights of Columbus); Mr. Mortimer L. Schiff for the Jewish Welfare Board; Honorable Myron T. Herrick for the War Camp Community Service; Mr. Frank A. Vanderlip for the American Library Association; Mr. George Gordon Battle for the Salvation Army; and Mr. John D. Rockefeller, Jr., Chairman of the Great Union Drive for New York City, and Mr. Cleveland H. Dodge as Treasurer ex officio, act together under the chairmanship of Mr. Raymond B. Fosdick of the Commission on Training Camp Activities of the War Department, or their alternates, in settling any questions between the seven organizations participating in this agreement or in handling any arrangements which have to be dealt with jointly, and, at the invitation of the Secretary of War, to discuss and adjust matters relating to the work of the several organizations which might involve duplication in the expenditure of money and effort at home and abroad.

The War Camp Drives

JOSEPH LEE, President of War Camp Community Service

These seven seek your suffrage and support
For work with soldiers, sailors and marines:

First that society which, having learned
Its ministry behind the fighting lines
In France and England, China and Japan,
In Russia, Germany, and Mexico,
And by the streams that nurtured Babylon,
Now brings expert assistance to our arms
From first line trenches to the training camps,
Extends its expert aid to Italy
And helps bewildered Russia in her need;
Thus speaks in service the Y. M. C. A.

Next comes a sister company to lend
Its woman's aid to woman in this war—
Its hostess houses for the soldier's wife
Or sweetheart when she visits him in camp,
Its raising of the flag of womanhood
Above a thousand Patriotic Leagues,
Calling our girls to show what love can do
In sending forth our sons to victory.

Then come in shining panoply the Knights,
Bearing the spirit of the old Crusades
Across the storied battlefields of France—
The lightning rescue stroke of chivalry,
The knightly help to suffering or want—
The message of the Catholic War Board
To all of every nation, race or creed.

Next we present the Jewish Welfare Board,
The modest helpmeet of its brother bands,
Aiding through them the sons of Israel
Who march beside the soldiers of the cross
To the great Armageddon of the world,

While here their fathers represent the race
By giving aid to others, asking none.

Now, with the cheery note of fife and drum,
The glad Salvation Army comes in view;
Unto this last its message, and the stone
Rejected of the builders claims its care
In peaceful ministration, but in war
To battered trenches bringing aid and cheer
With homely housewifery and simple things
That touch the heart and win the soldiers' love.

Then an Association bringing books—
A book for every fighting man—to make
A reading army to maintain a world
Where mind shall hold inevitable sway
Despite the frantic thrashings of the brute.

And last there comes, bearing a newer word,
The War Camp Service in Communities,
Whose grateful task it is to mobilize
The cities' heart of hospitality.
A club that is his own, the church, the home—
The mother voices, the evening meal,
The family gathering around the hearth—
The sanctioned meeting place of youth and maid:
These are the means it uses, and its aim
To keep alive in each enlisted man
The pure white flame of all that he defends,
That in each bayonet thrust America
Shall speak, and shall not need to speak again.

These all to each and each to all are leagued
To bear your purpose toward your hero sons
At home and on the battlefields of France.
And now in mutual comradeship they seek
The grateful evidence of your support,
Trusting their work has proved their worthiness.

War Camp Community Service

JOSEPH LEE, President of War Camp Community Service

BUDGET SONG

Here is the tale of the expenditure
Of War Camp Service in Communities—
In twenty cities, thirty villages,
More than two hundred towns, contiguous
To where your soldier boys lie encamped.
These are the things your money did for them—
Three and three-quarters million up to date
(Or will accomplish by September first,
The destined end of this financial year.)

First, none of it was squandered in the cost
Of its own raising—a twice helpful friend
Provided generously for such expense
Before the fight began. So every cent
A grateful public gave (except seed corn
For such another harvest, should it chance
Such friend may not be found a second time)
Has sped the cordial message to its goal.

Some sixteen hundred fourteen thousand served $1,614,000
To furnish soldiers' clubs—and soldiers here
Stands equally for sailors and marines.
Half was for building and for fitting up
With various kinds of things a soldier wants:
With fireplaces, sofas, easy chairs;
With beds and billiards, bowling alleys, baths;
With soda fountains, cafeterias,
And rooms to meet their sisters, mothers, wives
Or sweethearts—as the special need might be;

The other half for rent and for expense
Of carrying on these hundred rendezvous
(And half as many more by careful count)
Where, unmolested, the enlisted man
May smoke or read or loaf—nor apprehend
An omnipresent uplift breaking in.

WAR CAMP COMMUNITY SERVICE

Two hundred three-and-seventy thousand more.   273,000
Provided a variety of shows,
(Each item bears the overhead expense
Assigned in due proportion to its kind;
For exact figures see appended sheet).
Partly in the communities themselves,
Part found in the communities and sent
To help amuse the soldiers in their camps.

Of all kinds were they: concerts, movies, bands,
Orchestral music, high class vaudeville,
Dramatic presentations; and their range
Reached from a boxing match to William Taft
Explaining that the country is at war.
Yet all were censored (save as Taft perhaps
Needed no expurgation) and were such
As might refresh and strengthen, not seduce.

Forty-four thousand dollars builded booths $44,000
Of information to the soldier when—
Seeking such sport as it may have to show
Against the dull monotony of camp—
He comes to town with pay and liberty,
When first suggestion counts for weal or woe.
These, eked with "joy books" or directories,
Spread by the hundred thousand in the camps,
Tell where the movies are or soldiers' clubs
With other best resources of the place—
And serve as sign-board to his wayward thoughts.

For swimming pools—or more, for bath houses   35,000
Beside some wooded shore of lake or pond
Or the cool depths of ocean near the camp—
Thirty-five thousand welcome dollars helped.
Eleven thousand furnished football games   11,000
Between the soldiers and the townspeople,
(Or baseball, haply, or athletic sports)
The proceeds buying further bats and balls
Our men might carry with them into France.
Some eighty-seven thousand rendered aid   87,000

WAR CAMP COMMUNITY SERVICE

To travelers at the stations near the camps
Which—acting with the information booths
And other agencies we set on foot—
Have helped, in finding out some place to sleep,
The soldier's stranded relatives and friends,
Coming perhaps across the continent
For that last word and look before he sails.
Another two and thirty thousand gave   32,000
Rest rooms and comfort stations to small towns
That could not grapple with so large a cost.

For Patriotic Leagues and other clubs
To organize the girls in helpful work,
For the Red Cross or otherwise—to show
Their sense of woman's mission in this war—
One hundred and eleven thousand served.   111,000
And in mere justice we do here record
Our admiration for Y. W.
C. A., Our generous friend who furnished us
Its workers' service at its own expense—
Without whose aid our work had not begun
So promptly nor so well among the girls.

To forward these and many other sorts
Of hospitality between the camps
And the community, helping out
The Masons, Knights, Odd Fellows, Shriners, Elks,
Kiwanis, Boards of Trade or Rotary
(The last not least in pep and helpfulness)
And other throng of live societies,
With names of their own members in the camps
With correlation, push or stimulus—
The city's self perhaps
Thro' live committees made articulate
Its soul arising at the need of soul—
Six hundred seven-and-thirty thousand wrought; $637,000
(Though in such service, to discriminate
Which dollar went to which is difficult—
This was the aim of our most cherished work,
And precious by-product of all the rest).

270

And never money, so we dare affirm—
For so have soldiers' words emboldened us—
Bore gifts more precious to the homesick wight,
More consecration to the warrior,
Nor better omen for the manners brought
By our young Galahads returning home.

$3,750,000

If in this statement we have used the "we"
And seemed to claim the work that you have done,
You citizens of camp communities,
Such claim is really farthest from our thought.
This work of ours lives not for itself
Nor building of an institution up,
But rather triumphs most where it is least;
Its only full success is when it dies
And leaves the citizens fulfilling all.
This is the people's war. The church, the home,
The grace of womanhood, the people's love,
The institutions of America—
These are the forces that we liberate
And in such liberation lies our hope.

To the Workers in the 270 Communities Organized for War Camp Community Service

MYRON T. HERRICK, Chairman National Finance Committee, War Camp Community Service

"There are," said Napoleon, "four great elements in every successful army—armament, military technique, numbers and morale, but three-fourths of the whole is morale".

Napoleon, perhaps better than any other man who ever lived, knew how to rally an army to his standard; how to organize it from the standpoint of technical efficiency and to instill into the forces a *vir* and *elan* that made his ragged regiments irresistible upon the battlefields of Europe. It is significant that present day commanders are not at all inclined to question the emphasis placed upon morale by Napoleon.

271

The problem in our day in this connection is to state the essence of morale in the terms and standard of our generation. What is morale?

It is perhaps as impossible to answer that question within the compass of a single sentence as it is to paint the rainbow using only one color. Morale is the purely human element in the war. Its strength consists of all of the strength inherent in our social fabric. Its weaknesses are those that are found in our social fabric even when it is functioning at its best.

Morale is more than patriotism. It is more than love of home. More than consecration to the service of the nation; it is all of these unified and strengthened by a common determination,—a determination worthy to achieve in behalf of our individual and national ideals. Morale is a thing of spirit. It stands for the soul of the people.

Just as it is impossible to state within the compass of a single sentence all that morale represents, so it is likewise difficult briefly to summarize all of those agencies and factors that maintain and sustain morale. A grip of the hand—a smile in passing— a word of welcome—an act of hospitality—kindly and friendly interest heartily expressed—are all factors that link civilian and soldier and make them unconsciously one force working out a common problem.

It is a mistake, of course, to assume that we are concerned only about the morale of the army. Civilian morale is equally important. We can do for the soldier only those things that we are able to do for ourselves. To make the soldier our friend we must be his friend. To cause the soldier to rejoice because of our hospitality we must first be ourselves hospitable. After all, the soldier is merely ourself placed in a military rather than a civilian position.

War Camp Community Service is in a peculiar way the conscience not only of our military but of our civilian morale as well.

In a broad way, what is the task War Camp Community Service sets for itself? Its business is to do for the soldier all of those things that our people would do themselves and on their own account if they had the opportunity. War Camp Community Service is the agent of all those millions of our people who, distant from war camps and from war camp cities, are without frequent opportunity to establish contact with the soldiers. It is a striking fact that after all W. C. C. S. does nothing for the soldier that it would not be worth while to have the community do for itself. Those engaged in the activities are twice blessed. They cannot help the soldier without helping themselves.

It is the duty of W. C. C. S. to make it certain that wherever our soldiers, sailors and marines may go while in this country they will find not only a town wide open for hospitality, but a community wide open for decency. And is not that what we desire upon behalf of our citizen population?

We are, of course, impressed with the fact that welcome accorded our soldiers should not be saved up, as it were, against the time when they return to us victors. They will not need us then, those conquerors. Nations will acclaim them. Rulers will pay them tribute. They will be welcomed with great acclamations; with magnificent pageants. Individual welcome may count for little then, but the individual welcome,—that personal touch, that expression by means of familiar institutions of our interest in the soldier, counts for a great deal now.

It is the business of W. C. C. S. to express in action those human qualities that make life worth living. W. C. C. S. represents individual and community hospitality. It deals with human elements—wives, mothers, sisters and sweethearts. The institutions it calls into being are destined to serve the end of these people who have so suddenly been brought into new relations.

W. C. C. S. would be worth while if it were only a present thing. But through W. C. C. S. we are building for the future. We are stabilizing democracy;—we are giving a new meaning to the word hospitality. We are giving a proper place in our scheme of things to the elements that make home life and community life worth living. Our work requires vision fortified by an abiding faith in humanity. Vision and faith in humanity I believe you have in abounding measure.

War Camp Community Service---Its First Year

Scarcely a month after the United States of America entered the world war, the Secretary of War appointed the Commission on Training Camp Activities, immediately followed by the appointment of the Navy Department Commission by Secretary Daniels.

To Joseph Lee, a member of the Commission and President of
the Playground and Recreation Association of America, was delegated the task of "stimulating and aiding communities in the
neighborhood of training camps to develop and organize their
social and recreation resources in such a way as to be of the
greatest possible value to the officers and soldiers in the camps."
Nobody knew just how this could be done but the Association
utilized the machinery and equipment it possessed to make the
start. How that start developed, how new ideas and developments
came from everywhere to be melted down into win-the-war
material is a story as wonderful and thrilling as the pioneer building of the great west. Nights and days of arduous service on the
part of many patriots have developed this new method of upbuild-
ing the morale of an army by extending the atmosphere of home
across a continent. Approximately three hundred communities
have been organized by the two hundred seventy-four workers
sent out. The report of the first year can but indicate the various
channels through which these organizers have worked to help
every community in the vicinity of a training camp to do its bit in
the great adventure in friendliness.

Linking Up Camp and Community One of the earliest activities of the War Camp
Community Service was the taking of a census
for the purpose of linking up the camp and the
community. The taking of this census was made possible through
the courtesy of the commanding officers. In some cases the taking
of a separate census by the War Camp Community Service was
made unnecessary by the personnel officer's tendering the use of
his records. The cards filled out by the men indicated their
church, fraternity, college, professional and trade affiliations and
made it possible to put them in touch with the groups in the cities
with which their former interests would naturally tie them up.
The cards also disclosed a man's favorite form of recreation or
hobby and with this knowledge the local committees were better
able to plan their programs. The information on the cards made
it possible for the churches to extend personal invitations to their
members, for lodges, clubs and fraternal orders to entertain their
brothers in camp, and gave a personal touch to all the work.

With the present greatly increased movements of troops it is
impossible to continue this form of census which was of great use
where the men were stationed in a place for a fairly long period of
time. But the last few months have shown the development of

274

another kind of census that is being used extensively in all the cities making it. In St. Paul, Minn., a reference card file has been prepared wherein are registered all local organizations, churches, fraternal organizations, benevolent and civic clubs which may be called on for service. A file is also being prepared of people who are able to render services in the way of entertainmnt such as musicians, dramatic readers and actors. Washington, D. C., likewise has a census of all amateur and professional talent available in the district for service in providing entertainments for the soldiers. A card index has been made, showing the name and address of each performer, when and how often he is available, and what he can do. Rehearsals are held daily of those volunteering, and only those who come up to a fair standard of excellence are accepted. The Federation of Women's Clubs in Washington is making a census of all homes available for the entertainment of government civilian employees, soldiers and sailors.

Buildings and Roads Have Been Provided Early in the year many of the cities were unwilling to appropriate money for the installation of drinking fountains and comfort stations but as the need grew it was recognized and the cities responded generously. Additional benches in the parks and along the sidewalks have been provided for the men who have but little to do when they come to town but watch the passing crowds. Little Rock, Ark., has increased the attractiveness of a park by erecting a bandstand. And Belleville, Ill., has met a crying need by undertaking the construction of a good permanent road between the camp and the city. Hattiesburg, Miss., and Macon, Ga., have each built a much-needed city auditorium. Several cities have added swimming pools to their recreation facilities and two have built athletic stadiums. Such equipment, made necessary by the presence of great numbers of soldiers and their guests will remain valuable additions to the cities' facilities for community life long after the military necessity has vanished.

Living Accommodations A rooming and boarding house bureau almost invariably forms a part of the service rendered men in uniform, their friends and relatives by the War Camp Community Service, as there is no more urgent problem than that arising from inadequate sleeping and eating accommodations for the thousands of people who visit the camp cities. The problem is especially acute in the small communities near the large cantonments where there are practically no hotels and few eating places. In an effort to meet the needs, in practically all the cities, an Accommodations Committee has been organized as a sub-division of the main Board. The listing of rooms—the first essential—is done in several ways. Where the community is small in population and available rooms are scarce, appeals have been made to the public to open their houses as a patriotic duty. The request for rooms has been made by ministers from their pulpits and through the newspapers. In many cases coupons have been inserted in the papers so that the people desiring to list rooms might easily do so by filling out the blanks and sending them in to the bureau. In some cities thorough house-to-house canvasses have been made. In all cases the rooms are investigated before being listed. The filing of the rooms on the list is done in several ways—according to accessibility and price. In Junction City the rooms are being classified according to the character of the accommodations, in order that the more desirable rooms may be filled first. Persons to whom rooms are recommended are asked to report as to whether they take the rooms or not, and the people letting rooms are usually ready to report when their rooms are vacant. This process of checking up is carefully maintained in order that the work of the bureau may be of the most value. San Antonio reports five specific things accomplished by its Housing and Information Board.

1. Erection of a central information and housing bureau in the most central part of the city
2. A paid housing clerk in charge of the work—approximately 30 people a day accommodated
3. A paid investigator and information clerk—approximately 50 people a day directed
4. An employment bureau established in connection with this department because of evident need
5. Protection—both financial and moral—afforded in information rendered, accommodations recommended; employment obtained

Large and important as is the work of providing living accommodations for those coming to the camp city it is equalled in importance by the work of providing sleeping quarters for the men themselves when they have over-night passes. Many of the camp cities are too small to accommodate the men in large numbers. In other cases the hotel charges are higher than the average

276

enlisted man can afford to pay and the cheaper houses are undesirable. To meet this latter condition it has become customary in many of the larger cities to supply sleeping and breakfast accommodations for men in uniform at a nominal charge of usually twenty-five cents to fifty cents. This work is carried on by the Service Clubs established by the War Camp Community Service, the Y. M. C. A., Y. M. H. A., Masons, Knights of Columbus, and some of the churches which have placed cots in their social rooms. At Cape May, N. J., the War Camp Community Service has rented an entire hotel to be used as a lodging house for men in uniform. In New York City the W. C. C. S. took over a hotel and operates it as a club for men in uniform. It has sleeping accommodations for about 875. At the week-ends the building is used to the limit of its capacity and it is always well patronized. During the month of June .17,727 men used the sleeping accommodations. A charge of twenty-five cents a night is made. Washington, D. C., has several Soldiers' and Sailors' Sleeping Clubs. These are places where men in uniform may find a night's lodging with breakfast whenever they want it for the sum of fifty cents. Pajamas, clean linen, two blankets, a mattress and spring cot is the standard equipment.

The eating house problem is closely allied to the rooming house problem but does not appear to be so serious. Many cities have relieved the congestion by opening additional restaurants and still more have established canteens in connection with the Service Clubs. Suppers on Saturday and Sunday nights, when the largest numbers of men are in town, are also served at many of the churches. At Ayer, Mass., the Girl Scouts have undertaken a new phase of service. They prepare home-cooked food and sell it in small portions to the soldiers' and officers' wives and others who are doing "light housekeeping." The W. C. C. S. in Washington operates portable canteens which serve the soldiers, sailors and marines and also government employees. They consist of motor trucks which go about from place to place in the city, where ever there are crowds of men in uniform. Food is served in the fashion of the lunch wagon. The fact that they can be moved from one place to another according to the hour and the demand is of great advantage in solving the food problem in the over-crowded capital.

The question of transportation between the camp and the city is second in importance only to the rooming house problem.

Relatively few of the camps have trolley service and consequently jitney fares are high, while the train schedules are not adequate. The War Camp Community Service is working to alleviate this. In Dallas, Texas, free transportation has been secured on Saturday afternoons through the services of the Automobile Club. At Deming, N. M., a motor line of seven and five passenger cars has been started between Deming and El Paso. A line of automobile trucks seating about fifty has been instituted between Camp Cody and Deming. The fare is ten cents each way. The War Camp Community Service has been instrumental in perfecting arrangements with the military authorities for this special transportation. In many instances this service has helped to reduce jitney fare to camp from twenty-five cents to ten cents. A Service Car Association has also been formed in Deming which will include all jitneys and service cars. It will work toward bettering conditions of the roads in and around town. Several cities have found it practical to build or extend trolley lines to the camp. The American Automobile Association provides a volunteer service to accommodate relatives of men at Camp Upton.

A Guide to Strangers
The information bureau probably plays a larger part in the service rendered by the War Camp Community Service than any other single agency because it touches all other agencies and becomes contributory to their successes. It serves the initial needs of soldier and citizen and affords comfort and allays anxiety. The information bureau serves in the important capacity of a rooming-house bureau in most cities as well as in its usual capacity of information dispenser regarding city facilities, car lines, points of historical interest, location of lodges, and all the points which are so essential for the stranger to know. In many of the cities the information bureau is located at the offices of the War Camp Community Service or at the railroad station, and in addition some of the larger cities have one located in some conspicuous part of the business district.

Another phase of the work of the information department is that of printed information, including bulletins, placards, handbills and newspaper publicity. Practically all of the camp cities issue weekly bulletins which are posted at the camp announcing attractions and entertainments and where they can be found. A number have also published and distributed hand-book guides to the city and all local points of interest. Huge banners swung

278

across the street announce the location of the War Camp Community Service and placards posted in prominent places direct the soldier to the information bureau and service clubs. Handbills or small cards distributed to the men arriving on trains perform the same service. Boy Scouts in Chillicothe, Ohio, receive their highest points for assistance at the information bureau and serving as guides to strangers on Saturdays. Atlanta, Ga., has a novel plan for giving information. Every Saturday and Sunday each member of the Atlanta Real Estate Board wears a conspicuous button, two inches in diameter reading "Atlanta Real Estate Board— I live here—ASK ME." In Tacoma a series of lantern slides displayed at the Liberty Theatre advertise the Soldiers' Club to all men in camp. The San Francisco information bureau has a very business-like information sheet, on which the inquirer writes his question, a space being provided for the answer, and also for his name and address to which in case the answer cannot be determined at once, it will be sent. In Buffalo, posters were printed to put on the wind-shields of cars which read, "Soldiers and Sailors, have a lift as far I go." The response to this appeal, made through the newspapers, was most satisfactory. Requests even came from nearby towns for these posters. The information booth at the City Hall Plaza in Philadelphia had a unique expression of appreciation of its services. Knowing that some French seamen were to be sent to America and very likely to Philadelphia, some of our departed seamen (who had been stationed there) directed their French friends to the City Hall Plaza Booth and told them to get acquainted with Mr. Basford, who would direct them to places of wholesome amusement. These French seamen did call on Mr. Basford and he was very much pleased to know that our boys "over there" still appreciated the services that the Philadelphia Committee was able to render them. Much information of interest to the men is published by the newspapers, from train schedules to church suppers, and the success of many entertainments is due to the good advertising given by the papers. Ayer, Mass., reports that since the publication of its weekly bulletin attendance at out-of-camp activities has greatly increased and in some cases has been more than doubled.

What Would the Fellows Do without These Clubs The supplying of information was only one of the first steps in W. C. C. S. and the provision of material comforts led naturally to the provision of clubs. The work of the War Camp Community Service

279

in establishing clubs which are exclusively for the use of the men is one of the most widely known and best patronized phases of the program. Everyone recognizes the need for some place which the men can make their headquarters when they are in town, and as most of them are total strangers there is nothing for them to do but visit a restaurant, a movie show, or hang around the street corners. No matter how cordially they may be invited, into clubs and homes they do not like always to be beholden to others for favors. The establishment of clubs that should be specially for them met that difficulty and provided a place where they might feel entirely at home. The clubs supply all kinds of facilities from writing paper to ladies who will sew on buttons and mend clothing. They are fitted with reading, writing and lounging rooms; shower baths and swimming pools; sleeping dormitories and ball-rooms; barber shops and boot-blacking stands; cafeterias and stages for dramatics; in fact everything that the men could wish and the War Camp Community Service afford. In addition to all this material equipment the War Camp Community Service supplies the human touch in the presence of men of the city who will smoke with the men in uniform, mothers who will chat with them and girls who will play games and sing and dance with them. The existence of the clubs has been made possible by local campaigns, the generosity of Rotary or commercial clubs, women's organizations and fraternal orders. The management of the clubs is usually turned over to the War Camp Community Service, though occasionally the institutions maintaining them operate them, having a paid secretary in charge and a committee of volunteer workers. In some cities the men themselves share in the management of the club, the commanding officers appointing certain ones, or the men electing certain of their fellows to serve on the governing board. Spartanburg, S. C., operates its club in this way. The cities using this plan report that the men show an increased pride in the club and have a greater feeling of proprietorship in it.

There are hundreds of these clubs, all of which deserve special mention for their attractiveness and splendid facilities. The Soldiers' and Sailors' Club of Seattle is perhaps one of the most complete. The club occupies an entire seven-story building. On the first floor, besides executive offices, are the shower and steam baths, and the swimming tank. Any soldier or sailor wanting to swim or take a bath is given a bath towel free of charge. On the second floor are eight pool and billiard tables (for the use of which the men are charged two and one-half cents a game), together with a card and game room in which there are facilities for writing letters. On this floor there is also a boxing room and a medical department under the supervision of the Chief Medical Officer at Fort Lawton. This medical department occupies two rooms, and two men are detailed there at all times of the day and night. The large reception and lounging rooms are on the third floor, and splendidly equipped with easy chairs, sofas and writing desks. Opening off of these social rooms is a large gymnasium, where dances, smokers, and entertainments are held. On the fourth floor, there is a large dormitory which will accommodate about eighty men. The other floors, with the exception of the top one are also used as bed-rooms. On the top floor, the National League for Women's Service has an office, and reception rooms where women may meet their soldier and sailor friends. A cafeteria and dining-room have also been installed.

The Coddington Point Naval Club at Newport, R. I., was one of the first of the clubs to be opened and is of particular interest, being situated on a peninsula, in the heart of a grove, and connected with the island naval training station by a bridge built by the men themselves under government direction. The house itself is a large one of fifty rooms, surrounded by extensive grounds. The one hundred and seventy-five feet porch is generously furnished with arm-chairs and a canteen supplies the wants of the hungry or thirsty sailor. The grounds have been laid out for baseball, football and other field sports. The grove is lighted with electricity and hammocks are supplied. A sylvan theatre made by the erection of a stage in a natural amphitheatre is the scene of many entertainments and vaudeville shows, the programs being provided by the men themselves. This club with its many diversions satisfies much of the leisure time of the naval reserves and apprentices at the Newport Naval Station.

Chicago's newest service club located on Washington Street occupies a four-story building, and is connected by covered ways with a restaurant and a ball-room. On the main floor are located the lounging-room, office, ladies' reception and dining-rooms. In the basement are lockers and smoking rooms. The second floor is entirely taken up with a large open room for entertainments. The third floor accommodates reading, writing and game rooms, a cigar counter and soda fountain, while on the fourth floor are found an exercise room, showers, lockers and a barber shop.

281

WAR CAMP COMMUNITY SERVICE

East St. Louis boasts a club wherein everything that has been done for the comfort of the soldiers has been donated by organized labor. The painting of the club rooms was done by the Painters' Union; the entire building was repapered by the Paperhangers' Union; the plumbing was done by the Plumbers' Union; and the furniture and equipment were donated by other organizations. Memphis likewise is proud of its club in which everything was given, the cost of the equipment of the club to the War Camp Community Service being only $7.50.

The Corpus Christi, Texas, Soldiers' Seashore Club is unique in being built out over the Gulf at the end·of a long pier where even in the hottest weather there is always a breeze.

The churches have shown their eagerness to help in the War Camp Community Service in many ways, not the least being the tendering of the use of their buildings as clubs. Nine of the churches in Chillicothe, Ohio, provide reading and club rooms for soldiers as do seven of the down town churches in Charlotte, N. C. One of the churches in New London, Conn., made its newly completed plant, built at a cost of $90,000, available for the use of the soldiers. It contains three large rooms, a number of smaller ones, a gymnasium and kitchen. The Christian Federation House at Ayer, Mass., was presented by the war council boards of the various church denominations for use as a club for the Camp Devens men.

The men enjoy these clubs and often crowd them to the limit of their capacity. The Tacoma representative of the War Camp Community Service reports that on Saturday, the first day the club was open, "the men began coming early and kept coming all day. Those who came, many of them, would go out and bring in others. By six o'clock the 100 beds now installed were rented and until one a. m. we were sending men out to other places to sleep. At two a. m. I went down by the big fireplace and found twenty men listening eagerly to the stories of a returned Canadian soldier."

The presence of colored troops in some of the cantonments has complicated the problems of the neighboring cities. The establishment of clubs specially for them has been the largest factor in its solution. Des Moines was one of the pioneers in work for colored soldiers and is becoming increasingly well known for its splendid work for the negro troops at Camp Dodge. What is one of the first and finest of Army Clubs for colored soldiers was opened in December in a conveniently located school building with a negro secretary in charge. Besides a music room, library and auditorium for the men, there are special club rooms for the officers and a pool room and canteen are operated by concessions the receipts from which are turned into a music fund, to pay for the band concerts held there every Sunday afternoon and one evening during the week. Immediately upon its opening all activities for the colored men concentrated in the club. Often 1000 men attended the Sunday concerts and the Saturday night dances, and entertainments sponsored by a committee of responsible negro women are very popular. Special parties are frequent affairs and one emergency occasion the club was able on very short notice to mobilize forces to feed 400 soldiers. What is true of Des Moines is true also of other cities near which there are colored troops. Battle Creek, Mich., has an especially attractive club for the colored men, with an excellent restaurant service. Army City, Kansas: Chillicothe, Ohio; Little Rock, Ark.; Louisville, Ky.; Washington, D. C.; Tacoma, Wash., are among the cities having clubs specially conducted for colored soldiers.

While the cities expend most of their efforts on providing clubs and entertainment for the enlisted men, a few of the cities have seen the need for clubs for the officers. Spartanburg, S. C.; Alexandria, La.; Seattle, Wash.; Portland, Ore.; Palo Alto, Cal.; Washington, D. C.: Hoboken, N. J.; New York City, have found that the officers greatly appreciate and continually use the clubs provided for them. Practically all of the cities extend membership to the officers in the various town and country clubs free or at a reduced monthly rate.

In some of the communities near the training camps it has been found desirable to maintain community clubs where the enlisted men may mingle with the town-people, rather than strictly Army-Navy service clubs. Among the first and most notable of these is the Community Club at Junction City, Kansas. Early last fall the citizens of Junction City, realizing that something must be done for the comfort and convenience of the troops stationed at Fort Riley, at the urgent solicitation of the local War Camp Community Service representative subscribed about $9,000 to the work and a temporary building 50 x 140 was erected, designed as a place where the boys from the camp and the citizens of the town could gather. It was even a greater success than was anticipated. During the first few weeks the attendance was fifteen hundred a day during the week and on Saturdays fully four thousand took advantage of its facilities. Everything is done to make the place informal and inviting and there are no "don't" signs anywhere. The card tables, checkers and chess games are in constant demand, and the three ten foot writing tables provided with special writing paper are much used, but the really important thing about the place has proved to be that there the soldiers can get away from the purely military environment and meet "folks who look like home folks." The men and women of the city patronize the building and the officers' wives and relatives of the men make it their meeting place. Most of the social activities of Junction City for the soldiers center in the Community House and there are general social evenings, programs, dances, concerts and sings.

Chillicothe also has a community club as do Kansas City, Mo.; Manhattan, Kans.; Leavenworth, Greenville and San Antonio. The newest soldiers' club in Indianapolis is conducted on the lines of a Community Club, and Charlotte, N. C. and Newport are each planning to build one.

A very important part of the work of the clubs is that of providing sleeping quarters for the men at reasonable rates. Many of the towns are too small to accommodate the large numbers who are often there and in others the men cannot afford to pay the price asked by a respectable hotel. The service clubs, therefore, fill the want by supplying cots, making dormitories of the upper stories of the clubs. Here a bed may be obtained for from twenty-five to fifty cents a night. A canteen service is important for the same reasons. A lunch counter or cafeteria is an essential part of the club equipment. Occasionally a concession is let for the canteen but more often it is managed by the women's committee of the War Camp Community Service or the National League for Women's Service. Much of the food and service is donated and the canteens serve excellent meals at very low prices; frequently at cost. The canteen in the Soldiers' Club at Atlantic City has gained splendid support from the hotels, which take turns doing the laundry work free of charge and many have promised donations of silverware, food and pastry of all kinds. Three have given $100 apiece to buy delicacies for the Canteen on weekends. From Washington, D. C., comes the report that one man permanently stationed there said that with the money he could save by eating at the United States Service Club Canteen he had found the way clear to buy another Liberty Bond.

A man may not be able to take his home relations with him when he goes to one of the training camps but he is able to find the same fraternal interests with which he was affiliated at home and they are anxious to extend the hand of good-fellowship to him.

The Fraternal Hand-clasp The activities of the fraternal organizations hold a large place in the work of the cantonment city. In general they are divided in two classes —opening club rooms for service clubs to all men in uniform, and providing entertainment for soldier members and their friends in the lodge rooms. A number of the fraternal organizations have opened special club rooms for the soldiers and others have turned their own buildings into service clubs. The Elks' Lodge of Miami, Fla., is maintained as a regular club for men in uniform. A recreation hall at Fort St. Philip was erected in one day by the Elks of New Orleans. The idea for this hall was initiated by the War Camp Community Service in New Orleans and the Elks turned it over to them after its completion. The Masons and Knights of Columbus are also active in providing club accommodations for the men. Occasionally the management of the fraternal soldiers' club rooms is turned over to the War Camp Community Service, in the smaller places, but in the majority of cases they are administered by the organizations promoting them, who frequently maintain paid secretaries specially for this work. Everywhere the lodge rooms have been opened for the use of soldier members and frequently for any man in uniform. Country, athletic and other private clubs extend membership by reducing the fee, or free of charge, to officers and often to enlisted men. The boat club of Richmond provides facilities for fifty men at a time on Saturday and Sunday and allows the use of boats, launches and swimming facilities. In San Antonio the fraternal organizations offer special membership rates to soldiers wishing to join. College fraternities or alumni associations in Alexandria and Deming as well as in other cities have been successful in drawing their members together and providing them with entertainment. Masons, Elks, Odd Fellows, Woodsmen, Rotarians, Knights of Columbus, Knights of Pythias and many other organizations welcome the men with a practical demonstration of the principles of brotherhood for which they stand. They provide every imaginable kind of entertainment in-

285

cluding receptions, banquets, open house, smokers, picnics and dances, which seem of all forms of entertainment the most popular. In Hattiesburg, Miss., the fraternal organizations joined in a fraternal community picnic on the Fourth of July. The Knights of Columbus in Macon, Ga., serve Saturday night suppers to the men at cost. The Dramatic League of New Orleans invited soldiers and sailors to attend one of its performances. At Douglas, Ariz., the girls of the Patriotic League are entertaining groups of soldiers during the summer at picnics. In San Diego the Federation of State Societies is meeting with great success in drawing together men from the same states. A local club in Kalamazoo sends a thousand copies of one of the daily papers to camp every afternoon. Thirty-six hundred soldiers were entertained at the various clubs and lodges after the Municipal Christmas Tree celebration in St. Louis. Several of the lodges provide temporary sleeping facilities and one runs a Saturday and Sunday canteen. Banners and bulletins advertise the location of the lodges and announce special meetings. In Columbia, S. C., the weekly War Camp Community Service bulletins include notices of various lodge meetings. In these and a hundred other ways are the fraternal organizations living up to their name and performing services of inestimable value.

The Church Welcome
.
The churches have been very eager to do their part in making the life of the soldiers pleasanter not only by furnishing clubs for them but by developing their activities along many lines. Foremost in their efforts have been their plans for making the church services attractive to the soldiers. Camp pastors sent out by the various denominations in many cities have been helpful in forming the link between the camp and the church in town. Members of some of the congregations take their cars to the camp and bring the men to church, or meet them at the station and conduct them to the church of their choice. It is not uncommon to find the church choir composed of soldiers or even to see a man in uniform in the pulpit. Several churches have accommodated their morning services to the hour that is most convenient for the men to attend. Some of the Catholic churches serve breakfast to the men attending early mass. Several of the churches in Miami, Fla., send motor busses to the camp gates to get the men. The success of the war program of the churches in Washington is attested by the fact that there is a larger percentage of church goers in the

camps in the vicinity of Washington than there is in the civilian community. This result is accounted for by the fact that the churches of Washington have been organized for soldier service in a large way.

The churches do even more to provide for the time of the soldiers on Sunday afternoons and many of them attract large crowds to their evening services. In Manhattan, Kans., the six churches combine to give a program followed by a supper. This summer they have made a new departure that has proved very successful. Bleachers were erected around an open grassy space in the City Park, a speaker's stand and a truck with a piano being brought up at the base of the oval. Following a program the churches unite in an evening service after which the citizens present open up basket lunches on the grass and gather soldiers around them in family groups for the picnic supper.

One of the Des Moines churches provides a social hour at five o'clock on Sundays. Soldiers drop in and become acquainted with members of the church. At six supper is provided free to the soldiers, at which they are not isolated at tables by themselves but are mixed in with people of the church. Following the supper, the young people's society has its regular meeting.

Experience has shown that refreshments and programs are not the drawing cards at these entertainments so much as the opportunity of talking with people, especially girls and women.

Many of the churches provide a light lunch on Sunday evenings preceding the evening service and others hold an informal reception after it in the social rooms, frequently serving refreshments.

The rector of one of the Atlanta churches sends an interesting report of the Sunday afternoon and evening program followed by his church. "The accessibility of the All Saints Church to the Camp and Aviation School suggested the possibility of making the church's Sunday school rooms of use to the soldiers as a club room on Sunday afternoons and evenings. The plan was suggested by the rector to the chairman of the Women's Guild and met with their enthusiastic approval. It was determined to keep open house every Sunday afternoon and evening, providing facilities and material for reading and writing, and serving a simple supper from five-thirty to seven. The Women's Guild is divided into twelve chapters of approximately fifteen members in charge of a chairman appointed annually. Each chapter will-

287

ingly undertook to act as hostess on a Sunday. The members of the chapter decide on the menu, which has consisted as a rule of potato salad, chipped ham, rolls, pies or cakes, pickles and hot coffee. A liberal supply of cigarettes is also provided. The attendance varies from 100 to 300. The necessary funds are secured by assessing each member of the chapter on a pro rata basis and there is no difficulty in securing contributions from men in the congregation who have no wife, sister or daughter in the Guild. The chapter in charge not only supplies and serves the supper but some members are on hand at three o'clock to welcome any soldiers who drop in and they see to it that there are a number of married women and young girls on hand throughout the evening to assist in the entertaining. No set form of entertainment is attempted. On the first evening two pianists were present, but it proved a useless provision as there are always some soldiers who want to play and who play well. Usually the piano in each room is in use and seldom is there a pause in the singing in which everybody joins and which is one of the most delightful features of the affairs. So many of the soldiers return again and again that we feel sure that they must find some enjoyment in these informal occasions and it is very certain that their hosts do. Women and men seem to find a genuine joy in making the soldiers feel at home. Many of them are on hand every Sunday and more than likely some staid business man may be seen with dish towel in hand washing plates and cups and saucers when the rush is too great for the colored sexton to adequately handle the situation. Indeed it may be truly said that never has anything stirred up such general and enthusiastic interest among the members of the congregation. Its influence is felt in all other activities of the parish. While no specific effort is made to induce the men to attend the church services, nevertheless a fair percentage do attend and on the Sunday just past the color tone of the entire congregation was decidedly khaki."

During the week the churches provide many entertainments for the men. As before mentioned a large number of them have turned their social rooms or parish houses into reading and club rooms for the soldiers. These rooms are the scene of many popular parties and entertainments. The Presbyterian Church in Mt. Holly, N. J., gives very successful socials. They are announced from the pulpit on the preceding Sunday and old and young are urged to be present. A committee is in charge of the arrangements which in the main include provision of light refreshments and a rather informal program of songs, games and the like. The boys on entering are given little slips of paper on which to write their names. This slip is pinned on the uniform and one of the committee introduces the new arrival who is made to feel very much at home. After chatting for a little he is invited to join one of the games and he usually is delighted to take part—in fact he needs only half an invitation—in such games as *Going to Jerusalem, Drop the Handkerchief* and other children's games. The Virginia reel is used also and the church people enter with a will with the soldiers. So attractive are these socials to the boys that though there is a public dance going on down town they prefer to stay at the church social, once there.

One church in Syracuse, N. Y., gave a Saturday afternoon automobile excursion to Oneida Lake, on which 100 soldiers and the Twenty-third Regiment Band went as guests of the church. Dinner was served at a hotel at the lake and the afternoon spent at baseball and other sports.

Church suppers are an important factor in the program of the churches and fill a great need—that of serving a good meal at a low cost. Three churches in Chattanooga serve Saturday night cafeteria suppers. Hattiesburg, Miss., solved a real difficulty with its Saturday night church suppers as the restaurant facilities were entirely inadequate to accommodate the number of men coming to town. In Battle Creek the Congregational church serves a supper to the boys on Wednesday nights for fifty cents, providing free smokes and a dance at which the men meet the best people of the city.

Many of the churches carry on individual activities that cannot be classed under any general head. In Manhattan, Kans., an additional Traveler's Aid worker is maintained by the Home Missionary Society of the Methodist Church. One church in Mount Clemens, Mich., chartered a moving picture theatre and gave a free performance for soldiers. A Community Church House was erected by the Federal Council of Churches of Deming at a cost of $10,000. The Methodists in Fort Worth built a hotel near the base hospital for the use of relatives and friends of the soldiers. In Louisville, Ky., the Church Federation promotes a movement for the preparation of men who are to be summoned in the draft. It gives a course of three or four talks in schools in various parts of the city consisting of facts and information needed by the men preparing for camp. Each of the churches in Battle Creek has a special soldiers' secretary and donations of food supplies and money which are sent to them from organizations all over the State are amounting to thousands of dollars. St. Paul's Catholic Church in Spartanburg presented its club house just completed to the War Camp Community Service for use. Churches in several of the cities give courses in French and one gives a course in Spanish. Several churches have met housing emergencies in the city by putting cots in their social rooms for the use of the men.

The Home Touch It has been but a step from entertainment in the churches to entertainment in private homes which has been inaugurated largely through the efforts of the churches. The famous "Take a Soldier Home to Dinner" slogan was the first phase of this work and in every city the effort is made to see that all men attending church are invited home to dinner by members of the congregation. The first dinner forms the basis for further acquaintance and opens the way for extensive entertaining. In many cases acquaintanceships formed in this way have developed into real friendships and the man has been invited to consider the home as his own whenever he is in the city. Chattanooga is famous for this, as many families have "adopted" a boy and given him a latchkey that he may come and go as he pleases. Keeping open house is a popular form of entertainment, being informal and permitting the hostess to extend her hospitality to a larger number of men than would be possible otherwise. Many men are entertained over the week-ends varying in numbers from one in the spare room of a neat little bungalow to thirty or more at some large country house.

The people are responding well to this form of service and from many cities comes the word, "there were more invitations than there were men who could accept." Leavenworth, Kansas, is forgetting its old prejudice against the regular army and getting the habit of filling up the empty seats in its automobiles with soldiers and taking them for an evening ride. The War Camp Community Service in St. Paul reports that invitations to private homes are being placed at the rate of 500 to 1000 for every Sunday, in addition to mid-week invitations. Indianapolis reports that the various Business Men's Bible Classes entertained over 1000 men in private homes during the month of May.

Various methods of conveying the invitations from the hosts

to the men are used. Frequently a file is kept in the War Camp Community Service office containing the names, addresses, telephone numbers, of people who wish to entertain men at dinner or for the week-end. Men desiring to be entertained in homes report to the office and receive a card introducing them to one of these homes. In this way both the homes and the men are protected. For specific entertainments men are often picked by a chaplain or the army Y. M. C. A. One of the churches in Camden, N. J., invites men to socials at which they meet hostesses and are invited to spend the night at their homes, attend church the next day and enjoy the hospitality of the home. In Columbia, S. C., men attending Saturday night socials at the First Baptist Church receive invitations for Sunday dinner.

What is true of ordinary weekly entertainment is true in vastly greater degree at holiday times. At Thanksgiving and Christmas the cities outdid themselves to provide homes for the boys who were released from duty for the day but were unable to go home. Thanksgiving day 200 men from the Aviation Field at Rantoul, Ill., were entertained by farmers living in the vicinity who came to camp in automobiles and brought the men back to camp in the evening. At both Thanksgiving and Christmas the men who were entertained in private homes were numbered by the thousand in many cities.

The camp cities are not content to be represented entirely by their individual citizens in entertaining the soldiers but wish to show their official hospitality by community entertainments.

The Community —The Host These are largely in the form of holiday celebrations, which draw thousands of spectators.

A community Christmas tree occupied a prominent station in most cities and was the scene of Christmas festivities in which the singing of carols played a large part. In San Diego the program was opened by Mme. Schumann-Heink singing *The Star Spangled Banner* at the first note of which the tree was lighted. St. Louis had a community celebration in honor of the soldiers on December 29th. It was staged in front of the Municipal Christmas Tree and consisted of carols, patriotic songs and a pageant entitled *The Nativity*. The street was closed for a block and colored lights were strung on either side directly over a long row of Christmas trees, between which were draped the Allied flags. At one corner of the square, was placed a very large beautifully lighted and decorated Christmas tree. After the celebration at the tree the men were taken to the various clubs for further entertainment. Portsmouth conducted a Christmas celebration for the men at the Naval Hospital to which the entire community contributed. A tree was placed in the recreation room of the hospital and a program of carols and speeches was given, followed by the distribution of fruit and cigarettes to the men able to be present. After a social hour a stocking of bright colored material filled with fruit, candy, nuts, chewing gum, tobacco and a game was given to each man in the hospital. All Portsmouth had contributed time, money or articles for the Christmas stockings and the men were very appreciative. Deming became famous for its New Year's banquet at which 10,000 men were seated at a table a mile and a quarter long. At intervals along the table signs were posted bearing the State names and colors. Boys from Minnesota volunteered their help in assisting to arrange the eatables. Truckloads of soft drinks, cases of fruit and thousands of pies and cakes covered the board. After the program and the reading of the greetings of the Governor and Adjutant General of Minnesota the boys poured in by thousands to find their places under the banner of their home States—Minnesota, South Dakota, Nebraska and Iowa. The banquet was made possible by contributions of dimes from people all over the country and many of the good things were cooked by "Mother" and sent all the way to Deming. Washington's Birthday was celebrated with community programs in many cities, and athletic carnivals were the order of the day on July Fourth. Pensacola featured an aquatic meet on Independence Day and Petersburg was treated to a real Wild West Show by the men at Camp Lee.

"Hospitality Week" was featured by several cities to welcome the men in uniform to the camp community. Dayton gives regular community dances and Battle Creek gave a community farewell reception to four companies that were leaving for Texas. Norfolk has formed a plan for entertaining Colonial troops passing through the city. Committees of the Home Guard have been asked to cooperate so that on six hours' notice the armory may be secured, with the help of the company which ordinarily uses the armory on that night as well as the cooperation of the committee of hostesses, in giving a reception and dance to these troops.

One other feature of the entertainment program that may be looked on as community work is that of sight-seeing auto trips. Washington has had probably the largest celebration of this kind.

There were in the parade 1000 cars—all pleasure cars volunteered for the occasion by the automobile owners of the city, who followed the lead of the President, the British Ambassador and other prominent residents of the nation's capital in lending to the War Camp Community Service their cars. It was estimated that about 7,000 men of the Army, Navy and Marine Corps were driven over the most beautiful roads of the District and shown the public buildings and other points of interest. The military officials were enthusiastic about the trip, having been attracted by the slogan, "Show the defenders of the nation the capital of the country for which they are to fight."

Churches, fraternal organizations, individuals and communities have united in the effort to provide hospitality for the men in uniform and to forge a bond of good feeling between the camp and the community in making the men a part of the life of the city. Social entertainments of every kind form the medium of exchange for this hospitality and the basis for acquaintanceships between the men in uniform and the townspeople. Dances, picnics, receptions, concerts, community sings, church suppers, automobile rides, dramatics, athletic tournaments and holiday celebrations are but a few of the many activities which are promoting friendships and mutual respect so essential to the morale of our Army and Navy.

Dancing Ever Popular
One form of entertainment seems to be a source of never-failing enjoyment and reaches the largest number of men. Dancing is in great demand, from the few informal moments after a program or a small group gathered around a piano, to the large and brilliant affairs known as military balls. The clubs which cater to men in uniform all report a larger attendance on dance nights than on any other and the number of them which are held weekly attest to their popularity. Most cities seem to have at least three dances a week scheduled—usually two for enlisted men and one for officers. San Francisco has seven. These regular dances do not include special affairs given by various organizations, private dancing parties, or the ones arranged by military companies. In general the dances are small, the regular ones accommodating about 200 couples and the special affairs from 25 to 200 couples. The consensus of opinion is that these smaller dances are more successful and they are advocated by the W. C. C. S. The smaller dance usually gives a pleasanter time to all present and is more

easily supervised, the men being invited in groups of company formation or personally selected by the chaplain, or an officer, and the girls receiving personal invitations. Yet a few of the cities continue to give very large balls. Occasionally the San Francisco dances include a thousand guests, but can hardly be called public dances as they are all strictly invitational affairs. Norfolk gives large dances regularly to about 3000 and succeeds in regulating them by requiring the girls who attend to present their invitations which must be signed by their sponsors, who are chaperons at the dance.

Any place where the soldiers gather is the place for a dance. This of course includes the soldiers' clubs, which, in most of the cities, have at least one dance a week in their large rooms. Usually they are under the auspices of the W. C. C. S. and no admission, or a very small one, is charged. The members of the local committee of the W. C. C. S. in a few cities are opposed to having the Board sanction dances by promoting them but do not object to having other organizations manage dances to be given in the soldiers' clubs. This is frequently done even when the W. C. C. S. assumes direct control. In such cases the National League for Women's Service, the D. A. R., or some local organization plans and carries through the dance. It is quite customary now for the chaperons and girls to be supplied through the W. C. C. S., not only for dances in the soldiers' clubs but for many of the others given by fraternal and by military organizations. The fraternal societies are active in entertaining the men and have found that dancing is the most appealing form of recreation. The Masons, Elks, Knights of Columbus and other organizations cooperate with the W. C. C. S. in arranging a dance schedule. The Masonic dances in Baltimore are excellently conducted. Every girl attending must present a ticket bearing her name and the name of the Mason vouching for her. No soldier is allowed to take a girl home. A few of the churches have dances for soldiers in their parish houses. Private clubs, town and country clubs, golf clubs, provide dances for the officers, though in some of the camp cities it is not uncommon to see officers at an enlisted men's dance. This is dependent on the attitude of the commanding officer toward mingling of officers and privates and seems to be more common in the western cities. The third class is that of dances arranged by the men of various companies, battalions or other military units which are given either in the city or at the camp. Almost invariably these are charming affairs as the men take a special interest in decorating, planning extra features and in every way making the dance a success. They are well chaperoned and the girls attending are of a high class. A report from Fort Worth says, "These military dances are vivid reflections of the patriotism of the American women. Mothers willingly act as chaperons; dozens of them may be seen sitting through the entire evening in order that the men may spend a pleasant evening. The girls first pledged themselves to attend the dances as a patriotic duty, then it became a pledge of faithfulness, of loyalty, and a desire to make the soldiers happy. And now the dances are one common pleasure enjoyed by the girls quite as much as by the military men." In Montgomery, Ala., when a company wishes to give a dance the Women's Central Committee of the W. C. C. S. always assists. Ten members of the chaperon committee are asked to secure ten girls. The girls gather at their chaperon's home where the soldiers meet them and escort them to the dance. The girls return home with the chaperons, who are the finest women of the city. Dances at the camps are a rather new departure but are conducted in much the same way as the ones in town. Usually the girls are personally invited by the chaperons and taken to and from the dance by them.

At Nogales, Arizona, the camp dances are sponsored by officers' wives. In La Jolla and San Diego charming outdoor dances are given on several of the tennis courts which are specially finished to permit of dancing. Several cities conduct classes for the men who wish to learn to dance. These are of great value in standardizing the form of dancing. Commercial dance halls, which will be discussed further in another place, exist in many cities but in most cases do not compete with the more attractive private dances conducted under other auspices. A report from Ayer, Mass., says, "So many men are signing for dances in the Dance Registry at the Ayer Soldiers' Club that it is becoming difficult to send invitations to all. One man stated that the chief reason why the men greatly prefer attending one of our dances is the certainty that there will be absolutely no promiscuous dancing. He said that while a man might occasionally attempt to 'put something over,' in his heart he appreciated the fact that we are trying to maintain high standards and enjoys the dances all the more for that reason. Certainly no invitations are more eagerly sought for than the invitations to dances held in the Ayer Soldiers' Club."

In most cases the dances are free to enlisted men, those at the soldiers' clubs, fraternal lodge rooms and small private dances being purely social affairs. Of course there are frequent benefit dances for the Red Cross or some other philanthropy and the men themselves occasionally raise funds for athletic equipment or for the mess fund by admission charged at their dances. Usually the organization promoting the dance donates the refreshments and the music is frequently furnished by a military band.

There is a real problem connected with the operation of dances and many people have objected to them. But the desire to dance is universal and cannot be stamped out by the refusal of the better class of people to countenance it. In one city where the ministers seriously objected the War Camp Community Service representative showed them that dancing is an established institution, that it is demanded by the youth of both sexes, and that it lies with the thinking people to determine whether it shall be conducted upon the highest possible plane, or whether they can justify themselves in remaining aloof from it and allowing it to degenerate for want of proper control. The ministers agreed to go and take their wives to the dances conducted for the soldiers. It is true that dances must be controlled and there are two ways—by law, which at best is a limited means and makes for self consciousness, and by public opinion, by which all things may be accomplished. The most effective means of regulation, as before said, is that of public opinion. Public opinion must give its approval to dancing and set the standard for it. The most effective way of doing this is through the persons attending the dance. It is therefore necessary to see that questionable characters are excluded and that the best type be urged to be present. It is absolutely essential that some way be devised for seeing that respectable and nice girls are present to serve as partners for the men. This way has been discovered in practically all of the cities, which have adopted the invitation system. The plan is essentially the same though differing in details in various cities. The San Francisco committee had to meet the problem of deciding whether the soldiers should be allowed to bring their own girls. A report says, "We do not allow this except under restrictions, viz.: he must make application or request before the affair—otherwise we would have no check on him and anyone undesirable might stop him on the street and ask him to take her in. Moreover our affairs are strictly invitational for both men and women and therefore adding an indefinite number of girls would be disruptive to the occasion and detrimental to the pleasure of the girls especially invited to the dances." In Columbia, S. C., girls are admitted only by tickets which have to be signed by their chaperon. Girls and chaperons are provided for dances by the War Camp Community Service. It is a general rule that girls under eighteen are not admitted. The women of Deming, N. M., are invited to attend the dances at Camp Cody and are required to register their names upon arrival. They are then given a number which admits them to the dance floor. These numbers are collected after the dance. Boston has issued a folder, *Dances, How to Conduct Them,* the recommendations of which have been adopted by 500 Boston girls as their standard of dancing. The Patriotic League and local girls' organizations are active in giving dances which are in every way successful. For small dances and private dances the men also must be vouched for, either by the Y. M. C. A., the chaplain or an army officer.

There can be no question of the desirability of having dancing as a part of the recreational program for the men, for what gives pleasure to the largest number raises the morale of the largest number. With the present system of regulation in force in all of the cities the undesirable factors are being eliminated and practically all criticism has disappeared.

Plays, Pageants and Players One can scarcely imagine the person who is not charmed with the scene across the footlights and certainly the man in uniform is no exception. Professional talent is always well patronized and the production of amateur theatricals has received a great impetus. The men like to see a good comedy and are not at all opposed to taking part themselves either in an impromptu affair arranged on the spur of the moment or in an elaborate production staged in the city's largest theatre. The local branches of the Drama League are doing excellent work in presenting clever plays for the men and in assisting them to put on their own productions. The Drama League in Minneapolis has charge of all entertainments put on at the camp.

No form of theatrical entertainment draws greater crowds than the minstrel shows and vaudeville programs given by the men themselves. The Dixie Division Greater Minstrels gave a performance in Macon that was highly creditable, the singing of the men being excellent, the vaudeville given by soldier profes-

297

sionals, and the scenic and lighting effects most artistically and completely carried out.

The Camp Gordon minstrel show netted about $1000 which is to be used for the Atlanta Rotary Soldiers' Club.

Pageants are being given more extensively than ever before and are attracting wide attention. Houston enthusiastically says that the three performances of *The Torchbearers* were the best things ever put on there. The Patriotic League in the various cities has been active in presenting pageants. New London has a plan for a series of masques that is unique. Ideal little outdoor theatres have been discovered in the great doorways, balconies, wide steps, abutting windows, raised lawns of the schools, churches and public buildings of the city. Masques are to be given in them to celebrate each feast day in the year—Thanksgiving, Christmas, New Year's. The masques are to be impressive but simple and brief, the purpose not being to provide an evening's entertainment, but to develop the spirit of the feast day and elevate the mood of the people in the same way as does the community Christmas tree.

Music and Community Singing Up to the time the United States went into the war we, as a nation, had done a good deal of talking about social service and infusing the community spirit, but with the majority of us it was scarcely more than the facile use of terms whose significance we did not understand. Our entrance into the war and the establishment of the War Camp Community Service have been instrumental in putting meaning into those terms and in developing the community spirit. The whole program of the War Camp Community Service makes for community effort of which community feeling is the product and probably no part of the program has done more to develop this spirit than that of music and singing. In addition to binding the community together it is doing more to create a feeling of unity between the men of the service and the civilian population than any other agency. The man next to you seems no stranger after you've both sung *Swanee River, Tipperary, Onward Christian Soldiers, The Long, Long Trail* and other nationwide favorites with him. For some reason singing together produces more of the "getting together" feeling than any other activity, perhaps that is why it is so strongly advocated by the War and Navy Department Commissions on Training Camp Activities at this time when the nation must be one. Special musical features

298

and community singing are among the accomplishments of the War Camp Community Service in all the cantonment cities and are universally popular. Many of these cities up to the coming of the War Camp Community Service had thought of community singing only as an abstract idea so that it had to be initiated as something entirely new. Back in September, 1917, the music committee of the War Camp Community Service in Augusta, Ga., announced the first real attempt at community singing in the city. The first song fell flat—nobody would sing. But by the conclusion of the program the whole audience was taking part and went from the theatre whistling and humming. The next Sunday the theatre was packed at the opening and several hundred people had to be turned away. The War Camp Community Service representative in San Francisco at first thought it would be impossible to develop community singing there, but upon attending one of the municipal orchestra concerts concluded that it might be tried there. The concert was a good one and fairly well attended but there was "room for several thousand more" in the audience. So the program for the concert the next month was made to include singing by the audience and was very extensively advertised. When the representative arrived at eight-thirty he found every seat taken and chairs placed along the sides filled. He has since reported that the "work of the Music Committee in stirring up interest in community singing is perhaps the most important piece of work done in San Francisco." In most cities no period of education or development in community singing was necessary but once tried it was instantly successful.

Practically every city has at least one musical event a week on its program of activities. Sunday afternoon seems the most popular time to hold a community sing though in some cities Saturday or one of the other week nights is used. The program at these Sunday afternoon entertainments usually consists of instrumental music by a military band, several numbers of community singing and one or two special numbers—solos, readings or even amateur vaudeville. These feature numbers are often supplied by talent in the town but the audience—soldier and civilian—is never happier than when they are furnished by men in uniform. The community singing is usually led by the camp song leader, who is teaching the men in camp the power of song to strengthen courage and will.

That the programs are popular is shown by the fact that in

299

order to assure seats to the soldiers it has been necessary in many cases to reserve the entire lower floor for them admitting civilians only to the balconies. At Fort Worth 1,000 people were reported to have been turned away from one of the Sunday concerts for lack of standing room. In Fort Worth also the summer session of the sing-songs began with an attendance of over 4,000, one-third of whom were soldiers. In Houston a negro community concert was given by negro singers and a band from Camp Logan. *Illinois* in combination with *Dixie* and *My Old Kentucky Home* by the band and an extra corps of buglers was the hit of the afternoon. An audience estimated at 3,000, many of whom were white, attended. In Atlanta 6,000 to 8,000 people, a large number of whom are soldiers, attend the Sunday afternoon entertainment of free motion pictures, community singing and organ recital. In Augusta the song leaflets provided for the Sunday sings have been donated to the Army Y. M. C. A., Knights of Columbus, and chaplains as stereopticon slides with the words of the songs have been supplied for community use. Oakland, Cal., took hold of the community singing idea so enthusiastically that a "week of song" was made a feature of the Liberty Loan campaign. Not only was it carried out in Oakland but in all the towns of the county. "Motion picture slides of the words of fourteen songs were made and sent to 100 motion picture theatres and for five nights, audiences in practically every theatre in the county were treated to ten minutes of singing led by one of our directors or groups of school children. Thirty-five or forty churches began the week on Sunday evening with patriotic song services. Almost every public or semi-public gathering in Oakland was also covered in this way during the week. The Chamber of Commerce and Rotary Club luncheons were given over to singing. Twenty-five thousand programs containing the words of the fourteen songs were distributed to various gatherings during the week. On Friday evening, the week ended with a song festival in the auditorium arena attended by an audience of 8,000 people. The feature of the evening was the singing of 600 sailors from Yerba Buena Naval Training Station. The effect made by the singing of these boys was tremendous and the whole community is talking about it."

San Antonio is making an effort to teach everyone to sing *The Star Spangled Banner* and to learn the words.

Waco, Texas, had a musical festival in the spring consisting of a military band concert and sing in the afternoon and a concert in the evening at which a chorus of women and soldiers sang parts of *Faust*.

At Christmas many of the cities had special musical celebrations with singing around the community Christmas tree. The soldiers at Camp Fremont were wakened Christmas morning by the people of Redwood City who motored about the camp singing Christmas carols, to the surprise of all but the commanding officer, and the men were delighted with the novelty of the occasion. In Washington thousands of people, including President Wilson, gathered on the steps of the Treasury building to sing carols, after which the children from the playgrounds went to the Army and Navy hospitals to sing. But important a place as community singing holds in the program of the War Camp Community Service it does not by any means crowd out other forms of musical service for the men in uniform. Organ recitals and concerts of both sacred and secular music are held regularly in the churches in some towns and in a number union services held outdoors in the parks have been tried and found successful. "Pleasant Sunday Afternoons" bring together the soldiers and civilians in some communities for a little music and social intercourse. The musical societies are usually found to be eager to cooperate and ready to invite as many men of the service to their recitals and concerts as can be accommodated. In the larger cities many men have been admitted to the opera and symphony concerts by free tickets issued through the War Camp Community Service, and enabled to attend concerts by notable artists without charge. The representative of the War Camp Community Service in St. Louis secured tickets for 500 men for each of two performances by Harry Lauder. Very frequently the music committees supply musical talent at the War Camp Community Service clubs on certain days. These little programs are generally informal and often end in the men's gathering around the piano for group singing. A special point is made in a great many places of sending frequent programs to camp, special arrangements being made with the military authorities, Y. M. C. A. or Knights of Columbus as the case may be, as the furnishing of entertainment within the camp is properly their sphere. Usually local talent is used but sometimes outside artists are brought in and such notable stars as Mme. Schumann-Heink, Nora Bayes, Christine Miller and Freda Starr have contributed their services. The committee

301

for the coordination of camp activities at Camp Kearny, of which the San Diego War Camp Community Service representative is chairman, has secured, among other artists, Mme. Melba, Mme. Schumann-Heink, Godowsky and Florencio Constantino for recitals at camp. Concerts for the men at Camp Sherman and their friends are given several times a week, the Columbus, Ohio, Red Circle committee alone sending two each week. The Columbus committee meets the expense of transportation for its artists by the proceeds from a series of "Governor's Morning Musicales" given in various cites of the state.

The Fascination of the Military Band There is yet much of the child in all of us and as a child is delighted with a brass band so are we eager to hear the military bands. While on the one hand the communities have made music a big factor in their plans for the entertainment of the soldiers, the regimental bands, on the other hand, have been most generous in giving concerts for the civilians. Two and sometimes more regimental band concerts in town a week are no uncommon thing. Easter Sunday was the occasion for a mammoth concert by eight of the Camp Funston bands on the college campus in Manhattan. The event was in every way a success. The ministers of the town gave up their Sunday evening services in order to give their support to the concert and the attendance was estimated at over 10,000 people, more than the population of Manhattan itself. The members of the band were admitted free to a song recital given earlier in the afternoon by Oscar Seagle and after the concert the people opened their homes to the men.

In developing musical contact between the camp and community, the War Camp Community Service has tried to make its program sufficiently catholic to please all tastes and arouse general and popular interest. It has tried to merge the music of the army and the music of the people in such a way that the slogan adopted by San Antonio may indeed prove true—"Back of the Singing Army—A Singing Nation."

Games and Sports The American soldier wouldn't be a real, live American boy if he didn't love athletics and all kinds of outdoor sports. Much of his leisure time in camp is spent with a bat and ball or football according to the season, and athletic facilities provided by the cantonment cities never go begging. The cities have found that there is nothing in

302

the line of sports that the men don't like to do and they have supplied them not only with contests to witness but with all kinds of equipment for their own use. High school and club gymnasiums have been thrown open as have bowling alleys, roller skating rinks and tennis courts. In a number of cities new facilities have been built such as additional swimming pools and baseball diamonds. In Deming an old reservoir has been turned into an athletic stadium. The War Camp Community Service has assisted the camp athletic directors in arranging basketball and baseball leagues, schedules for football and soccer games, tennis, bowling and golf tournaments, and boxing and wrestling matches; one or two cities have even made provision for and found trapshooting popular. Funds raised by athletic games and carnivals are usually turned over for the furtherance of athletic programs or for the provision of athletic equipment for the men in camp. In Boston the $11,592 proceeds of the Army and Navy Carnival went to purchase equipment for the men in the service. A boxing exhibition with professionals featured was given in San Francisco under the auspices of the Palo Alto War Camp Community Service, at which $22,000 were realized, the use of the Civic Auditorium being donated without charge. The money was apportioned among the various regiments for a boxing glove fund, with the exception of $7,000 which was retained by the Athletic Council (composed of the War Camp Community Service, Y. M. C. A., and Knights of Columbus) for the construction of bleachers in the camp.

Of course the great American game holds first place in the hearts of the men during the summer season, and the number of baseball games played in camp and out, between local camp teams, between camp and town teams, between local camp teams and camp teams from a distance would be impossible to estimate, but the interest in them never flags. The War Camp Community Service in Hoboken has been instrumental in organizing the Soldiers' Major Baseball League composed of eight teams. In many places it has supplied baseball equipment to the men in camp at the request of the commanding officer.

Popular as is baseball, swimming runs a close second and the War Camp Community Service has been able to do a great deal in the way of opening private pools to the use of the men or in the construction of new ones. A pool has been given by a private individual to the War Camp Community Service of Nassau and

Queens Counties, which accommodates 3,000 men a day and around which a club has been built. At Deming a ranch owner gave permission for the men to use his irrigation tank as a swimming pool. A natural hot springs swimming pool was secured for the use of the men one day a week during the winter in Salt Lake City. Ingenuity also developed a very satisfactory pool for the soldiers near the camp at Salt Lake City. A chance exploring expedition led to the discovery of an abandoned ice pond. Further exploration disclosed the inlet and outlet and nothing was left to do but divert the water, cut away the weeds, build some simple dressing quarters and toilet facilities and within a week a real swimming hole was ready for use.

San Diego has constructed unique swimming facilities for the men stationed there. As the seaside resorts, with their splendid ocean and bay bathing are several miles from the city of San Diego, making it inconvenient for men in the Service to enjoy a salt outdoor bath on account of its being necessary to take either the trolley or both trolley and ferry to reach these places of amusement, it was decided by the War Camp Community Service to install a swimming plunge in San Diego Bay at the north end of the bulkhead, being only a few minutes' walk from the center of the city. This swimming plunge is a large crib with a graduated floor with a depth of from three and one-half feet at the entrance, to seven and one-half feet at the outer wall, surrounded by a promenade, and approached from the bulkhead by a gangway. This crib permits clean bay water to circulate continuously, and at the same time provides protection for inexperienced swimmers desiring to bathe in the bay. The War Camp Community Service provides an expert lifeguard and swimming instructor, who teaches the men in this floating plunge how to swim, after which they may swim in the enclosure surrounding the plunge, which has been assigned by the City of San Diego for this purpose. This area is enclosed by booms and piles for a twofold purpose, first, to keep out the fishing boats and other traffic, to keep the water clean and to protect the area; secondly, to keep the service men and those enjoying the privileges thus afforded them, inside the area so they may be controlled by the Military Police who are on guard. In this area, several pontoons are placed in various locations for the accommodation and protection of swimmers. Spring boards have been installed at different heights for those who wish to dive. The Service Swimming Plunge was opened to the Service men on May 29th, with a large swimming meet, participated in by some of the most noted swimmers on the coast. The band from the Section Naval Base furnished music during the afternoon, and a large number of civilians and men in uniform attended the opening. A temporary dressing-room has been erected at the extreme end of the bulkhead, equipped with shower baths, toilet facilities, benches and other accommodations. Bathing suits are supplied to all men in the service free of charge. Their clothes and valuables are checked and cared for without cost,—the only expense being five cents for the use of a towel, which covers the cost of laundering. In connection with the Swimming Plunge, is a large area of reclaimed tide lands, which has been leveled and is to be used as an athletic field. Two or more baseball diamonds, two soccer ball courts, volley ball and other outdoor games will be provided for on this field. Games will be scheduled here regularly, the men participating getting the advantage of both the athletic and swimming accommodations.

The Fall season naturally finds football occupying the main field of interest and soldiers and civilians alike throng to the games. The War Camp Community Service arranged the Thanksgiving Day game between Camp Cody and Fort Bliss at El Paso which was attended by 14,000 soldiers. The representative reports, "It was a great day, a great game and a great crowd, and was decidedly the biggest athletic event that has ever been staged in El Paso." Soccer has also received an impetus and has become popular in many places.

In the winter skating is popular in the northern camp cities. Lowell, Mass., reports that ice skating and coasting are favorite sports there. This of course is the season at which boxing and wrestling flourish at their best. In many cities an evening of boxing either by professionals or by the men forms a regular part of the weekly entertainment program.

Tourneys and Lists The provision of facilities for athletics has been the forerunner of the many athletic carnivals, track meets and tournaments which have been staged in a number of the cities, usually as a part of the Fourth of July or some other holiday celebration. San Francisco's Fourth of July program included an athletic meet and a military ball and was received with enthusiasm as was the Columbus

Day athletic tournament at which the men in uniform gave a demonstration of their ability in competitive drills, bayonet and tent pitching contests, trench digging, hand grenade throwing and races of all kinds. In San Diego the Stadium was turned over to the War Camp Community Service for the use of military organizations on Wednesdays, Sundays and two Saturdays each month for the year of 1918. The Seattle athletic committee has an elaborate program of athletic events including football games, an athletic carnival, water carnival, ice carnival, track meet and relay carnival.

Playgrounds Open to Men in Uniform All branches of city activities have tendered the use of their facilities to the men in uniform. One of the most practical donations has been that of the use of public recreational facilities, such as playgrounds, swimming pools and athletic fields and the provision of seats, platforms, bandstands, in parks. All the recreation plants of the District of Columbia Department of Playgrounds have been placed at the disposal of the War Camp Community Service and a soldiers' playground has been started in Federal Park. The Playground Commission of Los Angeles has made a very useful contribution to conveniences for the soldiers in supplying one recreation center with shower baths with hot and cold water and laundry and clothes pressing facilities which are open to any man in uniform from nine in the morning till ten thirty at night. The playgrounds at La Jolla and San Diego are used constantly by the soldiers and sailors, dances and special entertainments being provided continually.

It is not the sphere of the War Camp Community Service to establish recreation commissions and open playgrounds but its presence seems to have stimulated civic interest in recreation problems in several cities which have voted to establish such work. In Charlotte, N. C., 5,500 circular letters urging a campaign for the safety of the children were distributed, and Battle Creek is planning to open two playgrounds.

Service within the Camps Serving the men within the limits of the camp lies within the province of the Y. M. C. A., Jewish Welfare Board, K. of C. and other forces; but some phases of their programs are so closely linked with the community that the War Camp Community Service has been asked to cooperate in executing them.

306

Educational Classes

Such is the case in the educational work carried on by the Y. M. C. A. The educational committee of the War Camp Community Service has been asked in many of the camp cities to procure teachers of French, English, history, higher mathematics and also the elementary branches for the classes conducted within the camp. In Jacksonville the committee was asked to arrange a simple text-book of French as the Y. M. C. A. had no funds for the purpose. There are now four thousand officers and men in Y. M. C. A. French classes using the text pamphlet printed by the War Camp Community Service. Dayton supplied one hundred technical books to the McCook Field School.

In addition to supplying teachers to the camps the committees have organized classes in the town, most of them being held in the Soldiers' Clubs, though in one or two cases classes in French and Spanish are conducted by churches.

A newer development of the work of the education committee is that of securing lecturers for both the camp and the city. This is being done in many places, the committee securing prominent members of the faculties of the various colleges and universities in the state.

Waco has perhaps the most unique organization fostered by the education committee. The Soldiers' Sketch Club was organized, with regular meetings, for men who wish to keep up their art work. The commercial art men work on subjects which can be used by the dealers in town, the work being laid out in the form of a contest for which a prize will be given each week, the prize winning production to be used as advertising material by the dealer giving the prize.

Books and Magazines for Barrack Rooms

The library committee of the War Camp Community Service has been helpful to the Y. M. C. A., Knights of Columbus, chaplains and base hospitals in collecting books and magazines for use in the various buildings. It has also supplied them for use in the service clubs. In Charlotte a troop train passing through the city was supplied with magazines. Mobile furnishes reading matter to ships of the merchant marine stopping there. The city libraries have been very helpful in acting as clearing houses in the work of collecting the books and in classifying them. Many of the city libraries are remaining open during the evenings and Sundays for the accommodation of the men in uniform. The Twentieth

Century Club in Washington is to establish a club room for soldiers in the Public Library. The American Library Association has established branches of the cantonment libraries in many of the service clubs at the request of the library committees of the various cities. In San Francisco the library committee has extended its work of collecting reading matter to that of collecting games for use at the camps. The Augusta Committee makes a point of supplying the principal daily newspapers from every State in the Union to the Soldiers' Club.

Entertainments at Camps Concerts and musical entertainments given at camp have been mentioned already. They have been one of the forms of entertainment supplied to the Y. M. C. A. and Knights of Columbus at the camps by the War Camp Community Service. These organizations have been glad to gain the cooperation of the communities in planning their weekly programs and at most camps they book at least one evening a week for entertainers supplied by the War Camp Community Service. The Atlanta War Camp Community Service supplies fourteen to seventeen entertainments to Camp Gordon each week, and the entertainments supplied by the Richmond Committee are estimated to reach forty-five hundred men a week. These programs are largely musical interspersed with readings and given by local talent, though concerts by famous singers and players are not uncommon. Other evenings are devoted to dramatics when local amateurs present plays. The War Camp Community Service has even secured professional companies as at San Diego where the *Miss Springtime* Company, the *Bird of Paradise* and the Ruth St. Denis dancers played to capacity houses. Through the courtesy of the manager the entire bill from Keith's vaudeville was taken to Camp Meade and proved the most popular entertainment that had been supplied. The players from the Pantages Theater go to the fort hospital at Salt Lake City every Friday morning to entertain the men who are ill.

Many of the cities took Christmas entertainments to the camps and hospitals. Trees were donated and decorated, programs rendered and gifts presented.

It will be remembered also that the War Camp Community Service supplies girls and chaperons for affairs that the men themselves give at camp. The Engineers entertained at a banquet and dance at the Post Gymnasium at Leavenworth, the War Camp

Community Service providing the vaudeville and musical program and two hundred and fifty young ladies.

From Atlanta comes the account of one of the entertainers of an experience that was indeed heart-warming. "The first trip I made out to Fort MacPherson was to play for the men in the hospital. About dusk the men in one of the wards sent us word that several men in there were not expected to live through the week and one might not last the night out, and would we please come in and play to them for a while. Two of the girls and I carried in some soft stringed instruments. Some of the men were asleep so we began to play very softly some of the simple and familiar old airs. Every man woke up, and one lifted his hand like this————. They said we never could know what that night meant to them. They asked that the low light might be left on longer so that we might play more. We all came out with our hearts overflowing."

Hospital Service

One of the newer activities undertaken by the War Camp Community Service is that of hospital work for men in the base hospitals and for the nurses. This work is carried on by the War Camp Community Service in the absence of a local chapter of the Red Cross or in cooperation with the local chapter. A committee of the War Camp Community Service appointed for this work provides for visits to the hospital, entertainments, the sending of delicacies, games and reading matter to the hospital, and taking convalescent patients for automobile rides, and providing automobile rides and entertainment for the nurses. This work is done directly by the committee or by churches and clubs who are responsible to the committee.

The hospitals are visited at least once each week by women who come to talk to the men, play games with them or read to them, and who bring jellies, jams and other delicacies that are pleasing to a sick soldier's palate and are a welcome addition to the meals prepared for them. Victrolas, Victrola records and pianos have been furnished to many of the hospitals as have also books, magazines and flowers. Many florists have donated flowers from their greenhouses and private gardens are stripped of blossoms for the wards. Entertainments are provided at the base hospitals for convalescent soldiers regularly and occasional features are taken into the wards where the men are confined to their beds. In Salt Lake City the commercial entertainment committee sends two of the Orpheum Theater headliners to the hospital each week. Automobile rides prove to be one of the most beneficial things that can be done for the convalescent soldiers. These are provided regularly each week, the automobile association being requisitioned for this service or a motor corps being organized to perform it.

In Corpus Christi, Tex., teas are given at the hospital for the convalescent patients to bring them in contact with the ladies of the city. The Women's Club also conducts vesper services at the hospital. In Deming the school children sang Christmas carols in the wards of the base hospital and distributed flowers. El Paso was among the cities taking entertainment to the hospitals on Christmas. A group of El Paso women under the auspices of the El Paso War Camp Community Service went out to the base hospital on Christmas Eve, and provided plenty of fruit, candy and popcorn for the soldiers who gathered around a huge log fire, in front of which large Indian rugs had been spread, and listened to exciting tales of adventure told by an old Indian scout. After the stories, games were played. Eight trees were decorated and placed in the wards for the men who were too ill to be up, and tarletan bags of candy, fruit and other dainties were distributed. There were also presents, puzzles and different kinds of games for the men in the contagious wards. One hundred stamped postal cards were distributed to the men in the wards so that they could send Christmas cards home.

In Palo Alto grass seed was donated and $3000 worth of plants and flowers set out to beautify the grounds of the base hospital under the direction of a landscape gardener who gave his services. An open air theatre presented by an individual was built in the inner courtyard of the hospital. At San Diego the Federation of Women's Clubs opened a hotel for the use of women relatives visiting sick soldiers, and the Open-Air Tuberculosis Society has arranged to treat tubercular soldiers who have been discharged from the service. Several ladies in Birmingham, Ala., asked the chairman of the base hospital committee at Camp McClellan to find for them six or eight boys in the base hospital in whom they might take an interest not only here but when they go to France. Chattanooga sends a committee to the hospital each day to mend. The trips for convalescent patients and their nurses in Jacksonville are receiving the highest praise from the doctors at the hospital as they are proving very beneficial. The

310

men are taken for a weekly boat trip on the river, with lunch served at a beautiful wooded place in the country. On the way home the men are presented with souvenir cards showing that the trip was held under the auspices of the War Camp Community Service.

The Nurses Not Forgotten Entertainment for the nurses has just been inaugurated and is developing along the lines of home entertaining and automobile rides. At Yaphank a dance was given for the nurses and a group of officers, which was greatly appreciated as it was the first thing that had been done for them.

Community Problem Community problems have increased with the coming of thousands of men who have been sent to the training camps. Some of them have been comparatively simple problems requiring merely the provision of adequate facilities for their solution, while others have involved old and fixed traditions and convictions of the people, or old situations aggravated by new conditions. Complete success in their solution is an ideal to be hoped for, to be worked for and the W. C. C. S. is doing much to help the communities to attain it.

Commercial Relations Committee and Profiteering Profiteering at the expense of the men in uniform has unfortunately been rife in many communities, reports showing that there has been over-charging in forty-six cities since October, 1917. Some few merchants, from patriotic motives, may resist the chance to increase their prices but so many have taken advantage of the men in uniform that some of the cities have gained a bad reputation with the soldiers and sailors. This practice of profiteering has included exorbitant rates charged by merchants, shop keepers, moving picture men, tobacco dealers, tailors who make alterations, overcharging for rooms at hotels, restaurants, and soft drink establishments, and excessive jitney rates. The W. C. C. S. is endeavoring to combat profiteering and has been able to do a great deal of good, though of course it has not been able entirely to solve the problem, which can be done only by the honesty of the dealers themselves.

The W. C. C. S. has found that wide publicity is the best way of controlling overcharging. Articles in newspapers discouraging profiteering have their place but the most satisfactory weapon is a threatened "black-list" to be posted in the barracks at the camp. The threat of posting it has usually been sufficient to bring the offenders to terms.

In Little Rock where the jitney drivers were overcharging, the Adjustment Committee posted placards in all the barracks informing the soldiers of the correct fare. It was also arranged with the military and civilian authorities to cancel the license of any violator. Cases of overcharging soldiers' families who were stopping at Louisville over the week-end were taken up by the Commercial Relations Committee which adopted the policy of insisting upon an absolute refund of cash wherever an overcharge was made or legal action would be taken through the Legal Committee. The Cincinnati Committee began work by considering a definite case of overcharging by a certain hotel. All the hotel men of the city were brought together and a system of charging worked out. The hotels have agreed to place a definite price on every room and post it conspicuously in the room. A final program was reached in this city on the matter of profiteering. This provides that all merchants in the city will plainly mark on price tags the cost of each article exhibited for sale and submit a monthly retail price list to the W. C. C. S. office. The W. C. C. S. furnishes to each merchant carrying out this program a card to display in store windows containing the insignia of the W. C. C. S. and bearing the words "This Store Is Cooperating with the W. C. C. S." The W. C. C. S. sent circulars to the camp to be posted on the bulletin boards and hand circulars to be distributed among the men containing the statement that all stores where this sign is displayed may be relied on to give soldiers a square deal.

Sunday Recreation

Probably the average religiously-trained American is opposed to the term "Sunday Recreation" for men in uniform with all its implies of Sunday theatres, excursions, crowds and peanut shells. He feels that the Sabbath is a day for rest, for quiet, for religious observance. All of which is true, but the average American must meet the present situation. He knows the facts—that thousands of soldiers, sailors and marines come to town on Sunday for their one day's leave in the week. They have been living a life of iron routine and monotony. They are looking for a change and a good time. They are going to get it. The Average American can't retire to his Sunday afternoon nap and say it's no affair of his. He can't vote that the soda-water fountain, cigar stores and moving picture houses be closed and do nothing himself to pro-

312

vide the recreation which the men in uniform seek and need. He can not be blind to the fact that if there isn't something decent and attractive for the men to do the forces of evil which he as a church member deplores will have a rich field in which to work havoc. He has seen the crowds of boys on the street corners with nothing to do and "waiting for something to turn up," the hundreds wandering idly along the streets and looking in the store windows. And the Average American being at heart a good citizen gives up that Sabbath institution, the afternoon nap, and shoulders his responsibility.

In the first place he endeavors to see that the morning service in his church is made as attractive as possible to the men in uniform. He may even take his car out to the camp to bring in a capacity load of men to attend the service. The War Camp Community Service starts a campaign to "Take a Soldier Home to Dinner," to which he responds. Perhaps the first Sunday the boy he has entertained is bashful and leaves early saying he has to go down town. The Average American thinks he may get that nap after all but suddenly the thought bothers him—what is that boy going to do? He has admitted he doesn't know anyone in town and the Average American knows that he has voted to put on the "Blue Laws." It sets him thinking and he concludes that while "Blue Laws" may be all right for civilians who have homes in which to spend Sunday the case is different for the men in uniform who are far from home, and that he must do his part to provide proper Sunday recreation for them.

Such is the situation in most of the cities near the training camps. Most of them have been opposed to commercial recreation on Sunday but have realized the necessity of giving the men something to do on their one day in town. They have accepted Sunday athletics and have consented to Sunday moving pictures. But they have put their hearts into providing concerts, auto rides, open house at clubs and church entertainment of all kinds.

Sunday baseball draws large crowds of soldiers as do the moving pictures. Many cities have agreed to open the latter, often arranging special free performances for the men in uniform. Some of the southern cities which were most violently opposed to commercial amusements have agreed to have the motion picture theatres opened to men in uniform only, no admission being charged, but a contribution box being placed near the door, the

313

proceeds of which go toward paying the expenses of the performances. In Chicago a series of large theatrical entertainments, free to men in uniform, are given in the leading theatres on Sunday afternoons. The W. C. C. S. in New York City has a theatre where Sunday performances are given to men in uniform, the actors being professionals of note who give their services.

The W. C. C. S. clubs for men in uniform are usually well filled on Sundays. In some cities the various organizations take turns supplying a light lunch at the club rooms or afternoon tea when the ladies of the town are present to talk to the men and to lend a more homelike atmosphere. The Girls' Patriotic League is active in most cities in keeping open house Sunday afternoons and evenings at the Y. W. C. A. or Women's Club.

The churches are active in providing for the men on Sundays. Many of them keep open house in their social rooms and serve supper before the Sunday evening services, or hold informal receptions after them. In Petersburg, Va., nearly all the churches serve coffee and sandwiches at six thirty, drawing from 200 to 400 men per congregation. The lunch is followed by a social hour, a thirty-minute song service and the usual evening church service. The Danish church in Tacoma has Sunday evening dancing which the men greatly enjoy. The churches in many cities have united in arranging Pleasant Sunday Evenings. San Antonio conducts these each Sunday during the summer in Brackenridge Park, at seven o'clock. The program consists of a band concert, a brief address, musical features, patriotic songs and hymns. The program is not pronouncedly religious in character.

One of the very pleasant activities for Sunday afternoon and one which the men greatly appreciate is automobile rides. It is a frequent sight in any camp city on Sunday afternoon to see many private cars filled with men in uniform touring the town. As Rock Island conducts these automobile rides about seventy-five cars go to the Arsenal to get as many men as they can carry. On one Sunday afternoon they stopped at the community sing which was being held in one of the parks, then visited the Blackhawk Watch Tower, had refreshments at the Inn and finally went for a ride in the country.

It is by such efforts as these that the camp communities are endeavoring to make the men feel at home on Sunday and the Average American frequently finds that the keen pleasure of the boys he has helped to entertain repays him for his efforts.

314

Colored Troops a Problem of Adjustment The policy of the Government of placing negro battalions in each of the camps has created a problem in the neighboring communities which the W. C. C. S. is endeavoring to solve. Most of the cities have been destitute of recreational facilities that are suitable for the colored soldiers and were confronted with the necessity of adjusting Northern negroes to Southern cities and vice versa. The W. C. C. S. is meeting with a good degree of success in handling the situation and is providing the men with the forms of recreation which they most enjoy.

Several of the southern cities have formed parallel committees for W. C. C. S., one being for work among the white people, the other among the colored. The colored committees work along practically the same lines as do the white and practically the same activities are conducted. The majority of the cities have as a branch of the W. C. C. S. general committee a sub-committee on colored cooperation. In all the cities the effort is made to have the people of their own race undertake the management of the work, in so far as possible, as well as the actual entertainment of the men.

Several of the cities conduct rooming house bureaus for the furnishing of rooms to the wives of the men. A number have installed additional comfort stations. Practically all have opened clubs and many of them employ a special worker for work among the colored women and girls.

The supplying of a club seems to be the best single answer to the problem of recreation for colored troops. Not only does it serve as a headquarters for them but also most of the activities for the men seem naturally to center about it. This is highly desirable as affairs so concentrated can be better regulated. The men are greatly pleased to have these clubs and the cities report a large regular attendance at them. Des Moines was a pioneer city in establishing a club for colored soldiers. Permission was secured from the school board to use the two upper floors of one of the school buildings which is attended by negro and foreign children for the club. The upper floors are shut off from any connection with the school rooms and there is an entirely separate entrance and stairway. The club is managed by a negro advisory oard with the help of a house committee of soldiers. Concessions were let for the cafeteria, pool rooms and canteen, ten per cent of the proceeds going to the W. C. C. S. for a music fund

315

to provide band concerts every Sunday afternoon and once during the week. The attendance at the club averages about 300.

The negro soldiers at Camp Gordon were asked what kind of recreational facilities they would like to have; among the things were a club, writing facilities, a victrola and a piano, sleeping quarters, an opportunity to attend church and to spend several hours and take a meal in a respectable home. The club itself supplies a number of these things but in addition the colored entertainment committee arranges for parties, dances and programs at the camp. A number of the cities have given the colored draft men large farewell receptions, parades and a big "send off" at the station. In Mobile a farewell service was held in one of the colored churches. The draft men were told about the W. C. C. S. and the colored soldiers' club, parties and church services in the camp city to which they were going and each man was given a book and a letter of introduction to the W. C. C. S. organizer in the camp city. The colored entertainment committee of Washington arranged for 400 men, who came in a body, under military orders, to attend a production of *The Servant in the House* by a professional negro company. They also saw that 250 colored soldiers from Camp Meade were entertained in private homes for dinner New Year's day and later were sent to special entertainments arranged for them. The School Board in Charlotte has done good work in establishing colored community centers by granting permission to the W. C. C. S. to install equipment for games on the playgrounds adjoining the three colored schools. Committees were formed among the colored young men to prepare the grounds for tennis, croquet and similar sports. Collections were taken up among the colored people for funds for sandpiles, see-saws and other amusements for the younger children.

Community singing seems specially adapted to the colored people and they keenly enjoy the concerts which are held. Concerts given by them seem the best way of creating a common bond with the white people. The community singing and review of colored troops at the Des Moines stadium did more to change the attitude of the people toward the colored troops in the city than any other single factor.

One of the most important parts of the work of the committee on colored cooperation is organizing work among the young girls and supplying protective workers. Heretofore practically nothing has been done in most of the cities to organize the leisure time of

316

the colored girls. Patriotic Leagues are now being organized among them with great success; special girls' workers are employed in a number of cities to work with them. Houston has secured a large well-equipped room for constructive recreational work among the colored girls and young women. In Columbia, S. C., a colored dance hall inspector was appointed by the mayor on the recommendation of the colored committee. The inspector is paid by the dance hall manager.

Each month the work for colored troops becomes better organized and the results are increasingly encouraging.

Commercial Recreation Social entertainment features in the community occupy a generous share of the leisure time of the men in uniform but by no means all of it. The W. C. C. S. in many cities has a commercial recreation committee which functions with regard to commercial amusements—seeing that places are sanitary and have adequate fire protection, endeavoring to see that the number of commercial amusements is adequate to the demand, and, what is most important, maintaining a proper standard of manners and morals. The chief forms of commercial recreation with which the committees have to deal are moving picture houses, vaudeville theatres, various forms of physical recreation, such as billiard and pool halls, bowling alleys, roller-skating rinks, swimming pools.

The local committee on commercial recreation investigates all places charging an admission fee and determines whether they are properly ventilated, whether the seating capacity is adequate or whether they are over-crowded, whether the laws of fire protection are complied with, whether there is a need for additional amusement features in the town, and whether the conduct of the men and girls visiting the various amusements is satisfactory.

The committee also makes arrangements for free passes to be supplied to a number of men and for reduced rates of admission to be extended to all men in uniform. The committee in San Francisco has made arrangements whereby about 2,000 passes to seventeen theatres, vaudeville and moving picture houses are supplied to the W. C. C. S. for distribution each week. In St. Louis a large number of passes are supplied to the big league baseball games, for which the soldiers are required to pay only the war revenue tax. At Deming the

317

committee arranged with the military commanding officers to have tickets to carnivals and amusement places, sold through the Post Exchange at Camp Cody, allowing five percent on the sale of these tickets to the Exchange and five percent to the W. C. C. S. In Deming, also, ten percent of the weekly gate receipts of the Turner Amusement Park go to the W. C. C. S. The committee at Little Rock found there were many men at Camp Pike who had little or no money to spend on amusement because their pay was practically all used in allotments, Liberty Bonds or insurance. The committee therefore arranged with the local theatres and with the commanding general to issue tickets which would be accepted in the principal theatres. These passes are given out through the captains to those men who are without means of coming to town for any amusement. The captains are chosen to distribute the tickets because they know the amount of money which each man under them draws. In one or two places where the moving picture houses were overcharging they lowered the admission price because of action from Division Headquarters. In many places the committee has succeeded in interesting the managers of moving picture houses and theatres to the extent that they have given special performances free to men in uniform. In other places the commercial amusements have agreed to admit soldiers, sailors and marines at half price.

The most important phase of the work of the commercial recreation committee is seeing that a high standard of entertainment is maintained and that the conduct of men and girls is satisfactory. In many cities the commercial recreation committee has a sub-committee on censorship which visits the moving picture and vaudeville theatres to see that a good grade of performance is given. In most cities the managers of these theatres have proved very willing to cooperate and to present only such performances as the Board will approve. In one city the lists of films to be shown during the week is presented first to the W. C. C. S. for its approval. The National Board of Review of Motion Pictures has been active in corresponding with the managers of motion picture theatres, urging them as a patriotic duty not to present certain types of pictures and in supplying them with lists of particularly desirable films. A number of cities have ruled that no licenses shall be granted to commercial amusements until the applica-

318

tions have been referred to the committee on commercial amusements for investigation. In Lawton, Oklahoma, the committee on commercial amusements suppressed the many lottery schemes that had been rampant in the town previous to the organization of the committee.

Girls' Work

The Young Girl The problem of the young girl is no new one but it has become much more a problem with the construction of the training camps near many cities and even near the home town of the girl. The presence of thousands of young men, many of them very handsome in their khaki and all of them appreciative of her prettiness, is enough to turn her head. It has been called "the lure of the khaki," which is perhaps the best name for it. The uniform spells to her bravery, daring and heroism and she admires it and its wearer with all her impulsive youth. That in itself would be harmless, if properly controlled, but she does not know it should be controlled and if she did, would not wish to do so, for youth is blind to the dangers it runs. In the terms of sixteen, she is "thrilled to pieces" when the troops come to town. Being "thrilled to pieces" is a delightful, excited state but scarcely one to be trusted to its own chaperonage. Consciously or unconsciously the men react to her enthusiasm. She is attractive and ready to be friendly—remember everything in uniform is a hero to her—and they from motives innocent or otherwise, for unfortunately everything in uniform is not a hero, are quick to offer advances. And there is the problem—to keep the relations between them as near normal as possible, for even innocent ardor sometimes runs away with itself.

The War Camp Community Service was quick to recognize this problem and took immediate steps to counteract the emotional excitement of the girls. Their admiration for bravery and heroism might be directed to patriotic channels with care and tact. This, in general, is the way in which all the organizations interested in work for girls are endeavoring to meet the "lure of the khaki"—turning that spirit ever so gently over to one of loyalty and patriotism and providing definite things to be done to work off excess energy and enthusiasm. Incidentally

319

it is needed work and work which will better equip these women of to-morrow.

The Patriotic League is probably the largest organization working for these ends. The Patriotic League reaches girls of all creeds and classes, and its emphasis lies on patriotism, the pledge which every girl takes beginning, "I pledge to express my patriotism." Loyalty to the nation is expressed by the organization of groups for Red Cross activities, knitting, sewing, first aid classes. Classes in domestic science, telegraphy and stenography have been organized. The girls try to keep themselves physically fit and gymnasium classes and hikes form a part of the program. The various units in each city are bound closer together by monthly rallies at which there are patriotic features and "stunts," and each small group enjoys club suppers and picnics. In some cities there are classes in military drilling conducted by certain non-commissioned officers. Ayer, Masachusetts, has a nine room clubhouse which is the headquarters for all girls' activities. One room is used for socials, dances and entertainments for the soldiers. In a number of cities the girls have given successful pageants that have drawn the attention of the entire city. Though the emphasis of the work is laid on activities for the girls alone it has not failed to recognize the need of normal contact between the men in uniform and the girls. And so the girls keep open house at the club-rooms on Sunday afternoons and evenings, give parties to a selected group of men, and dances, all of which are carefully chaperoned. The club leaders instill the feeling in the girls that they are hostesses to the men and try to put that position on a high plane of courtesy and graciousness but not of familiarity. They try to give the girls a feeling of civic responsibility for the kind of hospitality extended to the men, who will write home about the way they are treated. Churches, local girls' clubs and women's organizations also provide entertainments for the girls and men.

There is a protective side to the program for girls' work. At the rallies inspirational talks are given to show the girls the need for high standards of living and idealism. Sometimes there are talks on the need of modest dressing, and in a number of cities a series of lectures have been given to girls and women on social hygiene. The work of the protective officers in the camp cities has been taken over by the Law Enforcement Division of the Commission on Training Camp Activities. Many cities supply colored protective workers for work among the negro girls and women. Policewomen are employed where needed and detention homes have been built in a number of cities. The National Travelers' Aid Society has assisted local Travelers' Aid Societies in increasing the number of workers in the camp cities, in enlarging the work to meet the enlarged need and in increasing its efficiency. A large number of the cities have engaged additional Travelers' Aid workers, these being paid often by the Young Women's Christian Association, sometimes by the local society, and in a few cases in part by the railroad and in part by the city. Most of the war camp cities now supply these workers so that girls arriving there are met at the railroad station and receive proper care, in some cases being sent back home, if it seems wise.

The War Camp Community Service in each city has a sub-committee on work for girls and women, under which the constructive work of the Patriotic League and other organizations come. The National Board of the Young Women's Christian Association has rendered invaluable aid in sending special workers to the camp cities to work with the committee, acting as advisors, studying the needs and applying the remedies. The War Camp Community Service has recently made a new departure in its work for girls. An assistant community organizer, a woman, has been sent to a few of the cities to head the War Camp Community Service work for girls and women, to centralize the work and to reach girls hitherto not included in any organization. The work of the woman community organizer in no way interferes with that of other organizations but does make for the coordination of the activities of the agencies engaged in girls' work, the training of volunteers and the supplementing of the work which is already being done.

Women and the War Camp Community The success of a large part of the War Camp Community Service program is due to the cooperation of the various women's organizations. Local clubs have given up their art study classes and bridge parties to visit the men in the base hospitals or to serve in the canteens. They have given money and time unstintingly. The larger organizations such as the National League for Women's Service and the D. A. R.

have devoted large sums of money to the community work and have adopted a national war-time program of service.

Women's organizations have been of inestimable value in war camp community service in providing entertainment for men in uniform, in visiting the hospitals, in serving as chaperons, in entertaining the men in their own homes, in equipping and maintaining clubs and canteens.

Acknowledgments The Playground and Recreation Association of America takes this opportunity of expressing its gratitude to the National Board of the Y. W. C. A., the State Divisions of the Council of National Defense, the D. A. R., the W. C. T. U., the Drama League of America, the National League for Women's Service, the American Library Assn., Knights of Columbus, Salvation Army, churches, Chambers of Commerce, Rotary Clubs, Jewish Societies, Y. M. C. A., fraternal organizations and hundreds of local clubs and societies for their cooperation in carrying out War Camp Community Service for soldiers, sailors and marines of our nation, which is a vital part of the preparation of our fighting forces.

Missionaries of Liberty

(Written exclusively for THE PLAYGROUND)

JOHN PRICE JONES, Assistant Director in Charge, Press Bureau

Publicity Department, Liberty Loan Committee, Second Federal Reserve District, 120 Broadway, New York

With the entrance of America into the Great War, American boys and girls have entered into a rich responsibility of service. The readiness with which they have accepted this responsibility and transmuted it into golden privilege has been one of the glories disclosed by America embattled.

Sacrifices have been made, and more may be demanded. But with each sacrifice offered by its youth, the life of the Republic has been enriched and ennobled.

It has been written that it is more blessed to give than to receive. But to give to America is to receive more than any of us can possibly donate.

322

A new issue of Liberty Bonds is now offered. Not a little of the success of this issue will depend on the boys and girls. They should constitute themselves missionaries of Liberty. In every home they should tell again the stories they have learned from American history of sacrifices made by those whose memories must be forever honored.

Youth is the period of grand vision, fine enthusiasm, hero-worship. Don't be ashamed of these gifts. Apply them, use them for your country. Re-awaken enthusiasm among your elders. Remind them that if a Nathan Hale could welcome death with the sole regret that he had but one life to give for his country, surely they will not regret the few more dollars that they are asked to lend to the country for which Nathan Hale died. If they say they have done all that is possible remind them of John Paul Jones and ask if it would not be more glorious to say that they had not begun to fight yet.

Think often of those things for which this war is being waged. Your President has said that it is being conducted to make the world free for democracy. That is true, but there are those who may say in your hearing that it will cost so many lives that it should be ended. Remember then that this is a war for the righteousness of the Lord.

"As for man, his days are as grass; as a flower of the field so he flourisheth. For the wind passeth over it and it is gone, and the place thereof shall know it no more. But the mercy of the Lord is from everlasting to everlasting, and His righteousness unto children's children, to such as keep His covenant, and to those that remember His commandments to do them."

That is what we fight for; that is what men, realizing how little are their lives by comparison, are ready to die for.

You do not have to die for this ideal, but there is a sacred obligation that you should live for it as good Americans. Help America, help the cause of righteousness by doing all in your power to sell Liberty Bonds.

How they Played during the Patriotic Play Week

The opening of playgrounds and play centers in connection with the schools has been one of the chief activities of the Recreation Drive. In St. Joseph, Mo., ten school playgrounds

323

that had been closed for two years on account of lack of funds have been opened for the summer. They are being financed by private subscription. Teachers of some playground experience are giving their services in exchange for very small salaries and the physical supervisor of the public schools has volunteered to act as director. The Junior Red Cross and the Storytellers' League are working at the playgrounds.

In Minneapolis, the Woman's Committee in cooperation with the Board of Park Commissioners has opened four new playgrounds and has provided supervisors and additional equipment for school play centers. One center is being equipped to serve as a "permanent monument of the Children's Year work." Outings to parks are being given to mothers and children from crowded districts.

The State Child Welfare Committee of Wisconsin has arranged for institutions to be held throughout the state for training volunteer playground workers. Mobile, Ala., has trained volunteers for playground work. The Board of Education of Dallas, Tex., has provided for playground instructors during the coming year at twelve city schools. In Hastings, Mich., the city council appropriated a sum of money for the salary of a playground instructor. In New Orleans, La., school-yards were open for play from August 26 to August 31, the week before the Patriotic Play Week. Playgrounds or play centers have been opened in Rockford, Ill., Mobile, Ala., Wahpeton, N. D., and Poplar Bluff, Missouri.

The city playground supervisors cooperated with the child welfare committees to make Patriotic Play Week a success. In Superior, Wis., August 15 and 16 were given over to exhibitions of playground activities, including the badge tests. In Nashville, Tenn., children from the various playgrounds of the city and county came together during Patriotic Play Week for a play festival. The colored children of Nashville also celebrated Play Week.

Dallas, Texas, celebrated Patriotic Play Week during the first week in September with pageants, games, picnics, water sports, community singing, athletic meets, exhibits and speaking. New Orleans had an elaborate celebration of Play Week with a pageant, a flower parade, badge tests, kite flying contests, folk dances and story telling.

Walla Walla, Wash., had a Patriotic Play Week, securing

324

the cooperation of the Sunday Schools. The Utica, N. Y., week was given over chiefly to demonstrations of the activities of the organizations interested in young people; with a playground field day, and a united field day in which all organizations joined, and daily "twilight recreation." Two Rivers, Wis., and Trenton, N. J., celebrated Play Week, and Poplar Bluff, Mo., Whitley County, Ind., Marshall, Mich., and Plattsburgh, N. Y., staged recreational activities for children in connection with county fairs. The Irene Kauffman Settlement, Pittsburgh, has recently given a special patriotic pageant as its contribution to the Recreation Drive.

Birmingham, Ala., is providing free movies in connection with the Recreation Drive and is organizing informal children's choruses. The Children's Year committee of Dallas, Tex., is also promoting "sings." Community sings are being held in schoolhouses throughout the county and a movement is under way to provide phonographs for country schools. An encampment for the girls of the canning clubs is part of Dallas' Recreation Drive. Evansville, Ind., and Salem, N. J., are also having community "sings." Minneapolis is exhibiting a "movie" showing the recreational activities of children.

Members of National Finance Committee War Camp Community Service

JOHN D. ROCKEFELLER, JR.

A man is known by his works, and his affiliations betray what sort of man John D. Rockefeller, Jr., is. In addition to being a member of the National Finance Committee of War Camp Community Service he is a member of the Rockefeller Foundation, of the General Education Board, of the Rockefeller Institute for Medical Research, of the Bureau of Social Hygiene and of the International Health Commission.

Mr. Rockefeller is active in Sunday school and philanthropic work, but he is also an extremely practical business man, and is associated in various business enterprises with his father, who endowed many of the philanthropic institutions in which Mr. Rocefeller, Jr., is interested.

Mr. Rockefeller, Jr., has been interested from its inception in

War Camp Community Service and rendered invaluable assistance to its first financial campaign. It was not until he inspected the new $22,000 soldiers' club of the War Camp Community Service in Rockford, Ill., last June, however, that he vizualized the full scope of its usefulness.

"It is delightful," he said, after his visit. "The principle underlying the work of the War Camp Community Service is right. It is bound to establish closer relations in the community and secure cooperation for the common cause. It will do the community good. I am sure every soldier will appreciate it and it ought to have unbounded success. I have enjoyed this visit because it is my first opportunity to see the actual working basis of the War Camp Community Service in which I have been deeply interested from the beginning."

Mr. Rockefeller, Jr., was born in Cleveland, Ohio, January 29, 1874. He obtained his A. B. at Brown University in 1897, and married Abby Greene Aldrich, daughter of the late Senator Nelson W. Aldrich in 1901. His reputation in this country is unique. The son of an immensely rich father who was at the head of a great corporation which has been subjected to violent attacks from many sides, no one has ever questioned his altruism or his sincere desire to do all the good that lay within his power to his fellow man.

SAMUEL MATHER

Samuel Mather, member of the National Finance Committee of the War Camp Community Service has found time in the midst of a busy life to take a keen interest in the welfare of those who need his attention and his assistance. He is a member of the Executive Committee of the National Civic Federation, a member of the Central Committee of the American National Red Cross and a trustee of the Carnegie Peace Foundation.

"The reason I am interested in War Camp Community Service," he said recently, "is because it is fundamental work for the fighting men who are going to preserve the existence of this country and of all of its useful activities, of your acitivities, of my activities, and of the activities of everyone in this country.

"The thing which will win this war is the spirit of the men who are fighting it for us. While in camp and on duty they are constantly stimulated by their officers, but what would their feel-

John D. Rockefeller, Jr., Member National Finance Committee, War Camp Community Service

ings be if they encountered nothing but indifference when they are on leave from camp and off duty?

"War Camp Community Service affords an opportunity to every citizen of this country to show our soldiers, sailors, and marines that our hearts and homes and purses are open to these men who are willing and eager to lay down their lives, if necessary, for everything that we hold most dear."

Born in Cleveland on July 13, 1851, his father was Samuel Livingston Mather and his mother Georgiana Pomeroy Woolson. His early education was obtained in the public schools of Cleveland. Later he attended St. Mark's School at Southboro, Mass.

His business life has been most active. He is identified with more than twenty-five corporations as officer or director. He is a director of the United States Steel Corporation and of the Lackawanna Steel Company. Moreover he is the senior member of the firm of Pickands, Mather & Co., miners and dealers in iron ore and coal and manufacturers of pig iron.

On October 19, 1881, he married Miss Flora A. Stone, of Cleveland.

THE RIGHT REVEREND WILLIAM LAWRENCE

The Right Reverend William Lawrence, D. D., Bishop of Massachusetts, succeeded Phillips Brooks in 1903 despite a most eloquent plea not to rob Cambridge of the rector of St. John's Chapel, celebrated by Longfellow. Since that day his work as the head of that great diocese has been greater and more varied, than even his friends anticipated. It has included, in 1915, his temporary removal to New York City to raise a pension fund of $5,000,000 for the Episcopal Clergy.

Born in Boston in 1850, he came of a line of merchants. His father was Amos A. Lawrence, eminent in Boston commercial circles and influential in the early history of Kansas. The city of Lawrence, Kansas, and Lawrence University, Wisconsin, took their names from him. His grandfather was Amos Lawrence who, with his brothers, gave the family name to Lawrence, Massachusetts. His mother, born an Appleton, was the daughter of another great Boston merchant and politician.

Bishop Lawrence was graduated from Harvard with the class of 1871 in which were Senator Henry Cabot Lodge, William E. Story and Charles J. Bonaparte. He received his divinity

Samuel Mather, Member National Finance Committee, War
Camp Community Service

.degree. at the Episcopal Theological School, Cambridge, in '75 and became assistant rector of Grace Church, Lawrence, Mass. Here began his keen interest in humanity. No parish of the wealthy was his, but hard, continuous work among the mill operatives. They were more than his parishioners, they were his friends and he was as popular among them as, later on, he was with the cultured people of St. John's Chapel. In 1874 he married Miss Julia Cunningham, in 1884 he became Professor of Homiletics in the Episcopal Theological School, and in 1888 Vice Dean and then Dean. In 1889 he was made preacher to Harvard University. A writer, summing up his career once wrote: "In social relations he is a thorough democrat equally at home upon an Admiral's flagship or in the cottages of the poor."

The Bishop has said he is not a money raiser, but his friends say that as one of the Board of Fellows of Harvard he raised $2,250,000 for that institution. He became acting President of Wellesley College and within a week occurred the great fire there. The sum of $2,000,000 was needed and he gave himself ten months in which to raise it. At 11 p. m of the last night there was a considerable shortage but in the morning's mail there was between $30,000 and $40,000 more than the amount.

His war activities have been both varied and effective. Besides being a member of the National Finance Committee of the War Camp Community Service he became chairman of the War Fund Commission of the Episcopal Church which raised $600,000 for work with the troops this year, and started a campaign among churches of all denominations to provide chaplains of regiments called into service with units consisting of a motor truck, a big tent and a motion-picture machine.

EX-SENATOR W. MURRAY CRANE

Politics and finance occupied most of the hours in the busy life of Ex-Senator W. Murray Crane of Massachusetts until he transferred part of his financial activities to the War Camp Community Service. He is now a member of the Natonal Finance Committee of which Ex-Governor Myron T. Herrick is chairman.

Senator Crane has, with Senator Henry Cabot Lodge, controlled the destinies of the Republican Party in the state of Massachusetts, which during those years was equivalent to guiding the destinies of the state itself. His political life began in 1897

THE RIGHT REVERENED WILLIAM LAWRENCE, D. D., MEMBER NA-
TIONAL FINANCE COMMITTEE, WAR CAMP COMMUNITY SERVICE

Ex-Senator W. Murray Crane, Member National Finance
Committee, War Camp Community Service

when he was elected Lieutenant Governor. This position he filled for two years.

One year later he became Governor, holding office until 1902. On October 12, 1904, his successor appointed him United States Senator to fill the vacancy caused by the death of George F. Hoar; at the succeeding election he was chosen to fill the three years remaining of Senator Hoar's term. In 1907 he was elected for the full six-year term and upon its expiration in 1913 he announced his permanent retirement from active politics.

Senator Crane has long been a prominent figure in the National Council of the Republican Party. He was a member of the Republican National Committee from 1892 to 1900 and again from 1904 to 1916. He was a delegate at large to the National Conventions of 1892, 1896, 1904 and 1908.

Senator Crane was born at Dalton, Mass., on April 23, 1853, and he still makes his home there. His father was Zenas Marshall Crane and his mother Miss Louise Laflin. He was educated in the public schools and at the Williston Seminary. In 1897 he received the degree of Master of Arts from Williams College and Harvard made him LL. D. in 1903.

CHARLES DYER NORTON

Charles Dyer Norton, vice-president of the First National Bank in New York, is a member of the National Finance Committee of the War Camp Community Service because this work is in line with everything else that he has undertaken in his extremely busy life.

He was born in Oshkosh, Wis., March 12, 1871, and obtained his A. B. at Amherst in 1893. Many other men have accomplished this feat, but comparatively few have done so on money earned by themselves as Mr. Norton did. He made the money to complete his education by going into the insurance business at the early age of sixteen.

After working in the editorial department of Scribner's Magazine for a short period, Mr. Norton had to devote his time to the pursuit of health until he joined the forces of the Northwestern Mutual Life Insurance Company in Chicago in 1895. There he quickly won his way to the position of General Manager at a salary of $50,000 a year.

In 1909, Secretary of the Treasury Franklin MacVeagh asked Mr. Norton to become his assistant at a salary of $4,500 a year be-

CHARLES DYER NORTON, MEMBER NATIONAL FINANCE COMMITTEE,
WAR CAMP COMMUNITY SERVICE

cause he knew what sort of man Mr. Norton was. The offer was promptly accepted at a loss in salary to him of $45,500 a year, but a gain to the country as he saved a full two million dollars his first year of service for the Department of Fiscal Bureaus.

His next step in the public service was to become secretary to President Taft, which office he held during the years 1910 and 1911. He then accepted his present position as vice-president of the First National Bank. His duties as vice-president of this institution, however, are not the measure of his work and responsibilities. He is also a director of the First National Bank, the First Security Company, the Bankers' Trust Company, the Baldwin Locomotive Works, the Equitable Life Assurance Company, Montgomery Ward & Co., the Adams Express Company, and the Delaware, Lackawanna and Western Coal Company, as well as trustee of the American Red Cross, the American Academy in Rome and the Charity Organization Society.

With all these multifarious duties Mr. Norton has found time to devote part of his brains and energy to the affairs of War Camp Community Service because he believes that the work which it is doing for our soldiers, sailors and marines in this country is not only fundamental but essential for creating and maintaining among them the morale which is going to win the war.

BEN B. LINDSEY

Judge Ben B. Lindsey who has presided over the Juvenile Court of Denver, Colorado, for eighteen years, recently returned to this country from England where he had spent several months at the invitation of the British Ministry of Information and of local organizations concerned in the moral and social welfare of young men both during the war and thereafter. In referring to his experiences on the other side of the Atlantic, Judge Lindsey spoke feelingly of the insight his visit had given him into conditions which have grown out of the war and especially of the influence of War Camp Community Service in caring for the men in service after they had left their homes and in bidding them God-speed on their trip across the ocean.

"The fine spirit and the wholesome life of these young men," said the Judge, "as well as their disposition to avoid the temptations besetting them in a foreign land, are undoubtedly due in a large measure to the lasting influence of the hospitality extended

335

Judge Ben B. Lindsey Who Is on a Speaking Tour for War Camp Community Service

to them in the towns near their camps and especially to the excellent care of War Camp Community Service both at home and at or near their port of embarkation.

"My years of service on the bench in so directing youths that they want to become good men and useful citizens have given me, I am confident, a clear understanding of them. And I want to say that not once, in England or in the trenches in France, have I seen among our men any sign of 'mollycoddling' by the home folks or the War Camp Community Service.

"On the contrary, I have seen nothing but universal evidence of fine character. The boys over there are more cheerful and are better all-round soldiers from every angle—especially that of manliness, because of the work done for them by the War Camp Community Service. That service has made all this possible and without it we should have had a very different kind of soldier."

Judge Lindsey was elected to the bench on January 7th, 1901. Since then he has been reelected eleven times and on each occasion received both the biggest vote and the largest majority at the election. Since he became Judge, he has written one hundred and four separate items into the Colorado laws dealing almost exclusively with the protection of women, children and youths. Many of these have been adopted in other states and abroad.

The Judge was born at Jackson, Tennessee, on November 25th, 1869. His father was Landy Temstall Lindsey and his mother, Miss Letitia Anna Barr. He was educated in the public schools and admitted to the bar in 1894. On December 20th, 1913, he married Miss Henrietta Brevoort, of Detroit. He is the author of *Problems of the Children, The Beast and the Jungle* and *The Rule of Plutocracy in Colorado.*

Book Reviews

THE CHILD'S FOOD GARDEN

By Van Evrie Kilpatrick. Published by World Book Company, Yonkers-on-Hudson, New York. Price, forty-eight cents

This small book covers a great deal of ground, telling the story very simply and from the standpoint of the child. It could well be put into the hands of children eight or nine years of age or those of any age whose knowledge of gardening is elementary for it begins at the beginning.

The Playground

Vol. XII No. 8   NOVEMBER 1918

Courageous Stand of Otto T. Mallery in Philadelphia

BOARD OF RECREATION

PHILADELPHIA, PA.

September. 18, 1918

To THE EDITOR:
The Playground
Cooperstown, N. Y.

DEAR SIR:

The following information may interest you as a topic for your magazine. At a recent meeting of the Board of Recreation of Philadelphia, Pa., held in Room 587, City Hall, a reorganization took place. The following members were appointed and officers elected: Honorable Raymond MacNeille, Judge in the Municipal Court, President; Robert Smith, Vice-President; Edwin O. Lewis, Secretary; James A. Hamilton, Louis N. Goldsmith, authoritative writer on Athletics and member of the Board of. Managers of the A. A. U. and Thomas J. Meagher, Robert Smith and James A. Hamilton were members of the incumbent Board. Judge Mac-Neille, Mr. Lewis, Mr. Meagher and Mr. Goldsmith were appointed by Mayor Thomas B. Smith to fill the unexpired terms of Hon. Ernest L. Tustin, Miss Sophia L. Ross and William A. Stecher.

Immediately following re-organization, the new Board elected Mr. Eduard R. Gudehus to the position of Supervisor of Recreation for the City of Philadelphia.

Very truly yours,

GENEVIEVE CARR,
In charge of Publicity

WAR CAMP COMMUNITY SERVICE

To the Editor of The Playground:

The above news item is of but little interest except for the series of events attending the re-organization announced. Two statements are made: the reorganization of the Board of Recreation and the appointment of a Supervisor of Recreation. On these two statements hangs a tale and an unsavory one in the history of playground activities in the City of Philadelphia.

In 1915, the Playgrounds Association of Philadelphia, recognizing the urgent need of a supervisor of playgrounds, procured the services of Mr. J. Leonard Mason, a capable man, trained and experienced in recreational activities. As no provision then existed for this position our Association paid his salary for some eighteen months until Councils created the municipal office of Supervisor of Recreation. Last May the position became vacant through Mr. Mason's resignation. The caliber of man to succeed him was naturally of great interest to us, realizing as we did the unusual qualifications necessary.

Notwithstanding the fact that an efficient and experienced temporary incumbent was secured and that the Mayor of Philadelphia was requested by the Board of Recreation to postpone further action till Autumn, announcement of an examination for applicants for the position of supervisor was made on June 6th.

The following text of an affidavit made by Mr. Otto T. Mallery, a tax payer and Treasurer of the Playgrounds Association, on which a warrant was issued for the arrest of Thomas B. Smith, Mayor of Philadelphia, on the charge of misbehavior and misdeameanor in office, concisely explains the controversy over the appointment of Eduard R. Gudehus and the occasion for the warrant of arrest.

Otto T. Mallery, being duly sworn according to law, deposes and says that he is a citizen of Pennsylvania, and resident and taxpayer of the city of Philadelphia, and that Thomas B. Smith, of the said county, being then and there Mayor of the city of Philadelphia, did, within one year last past, *commit the crime* of misbehavior and misdemeanor in office, which crime was committed under the following circumstances and in the following manner:

"The said Thomas B. Smith, being Mayor as aforesaid, did appoint certain citizens of said city to the post or office of member of the Board of Recreation, to which said board or office he was

340

by law entitled to appoint. Among the citizens so appointed were Ernest L. Tustin, Henry Berkowitz and Sophia L. Ross.

"That by virtue of his office of Mayor, the said Thomas B. Smith was also a member of said Board of Recreation. By reason of the resignation of J. Leonard Mason, who held the post of supervisor of recreation under said board, a vacancy existed in said position of supervisor, which it became the duty of the said board to fill by the appointment of a competent and proper person to the post.

WHAT POST REQUIRED

"That by the provisions of the by-laws of said Board of Recreation, the duties of the person filling the said post of supervisor were such as to require that he should have practical experience in connection with the work of recreation, playgrounds and physical education, and with organizations or boards conducting such physical education, and to be generally competent for the post of supervisor by character, knowledge and previous practical experience.

"The vacancy in said post was temporarily filled by the said board in accordance with law by the appointment of William H. Welsh. In order to make a permanent appointment to said post, it was necessary under the law that the Civil Service Commission of said city should by public notice, advertise a time for an examination of applicants for said position and certify the names of at least four applicants for said position, who had successfully passed said examination and were eligible for appointment.

"Without the knowledge of a majority of the members of the Board of Recreation, the said Civil Service Commission, on June 6, 1918, did issue and advertise a notice for an examination of applicants for the position of said post of supervisor, to take place on the 28th day of June, 1918, and did advertise in accordance with the duties required of said supervisor by the by-laws of said Board of Recreation, that applicants 'would be required to have had experience in recreational activities and have had responsible contact with such work.'

ABUSE OF POWER

"Nevertheless, the said Thomas B. Smith, desiring and intending to have *Eduard R. Gudehus, an incompetent and unfit person,* passed by the said Civil Service Commission and certified to the

341

Board of Recreation as an eligible person for appointment to said position, did *wrongfully and in abuse of his official position and power,* induce, require, and compel William H. Kreider, secretary of the said Civil Service Commission, to cancel the said notice so advertised and to advertise in its stead another notice under date of June 12, 1918, for said examination on the 28th day of June, 1918, and to omit from said notice so advertised the requirement of practical experience above referred to as a necessary qualification for applicants for said post.

"That the sole purpose of the said Thomas B. Smith, Mayor, in thus procuring the cancellation of the first notice advertised for said examination and the advertising of said second notice with the omission of the qualification of experience above referred to, was to enable him, the said Thomas B. Smith, Mayor, to secure for the said Gudehus, notwithstanding his unfitness and incompetency, by reason of his lack of practical experience, the appointment to the post of said supervisor *as a personal reward for services rendered to the said Mayor personally,* said position carrying with it a salary of three thousand dollars per year.

PROTESTED TO MAYOR

"That the action of the said Thomas B. Smith with respect to said second notice of examination was wholly without the knowledge or consent of a majority of the members of said Board of Recreation, and that the said Ernest L. Tustin, Henry Berkowitz and Sophia L. Ross, aforesaid, did personally protest to the said Mayor against his said action, whereupon the said Thomas B. Smith, Mayor, did state to the said members of said board that he did have the said change made in the qualifications for said position by the said secretary of the Civil Service Commission of his, the said Mayor's, own motion, and because the said Gudehus did not possess the qualification of practical experience, and that he desired to reward the said Gudehus for personal services rendered to him, Thomas B. Smith, by having him, the said Gudehus, appointed to said post as supervisor, and that as he could not pass the examination required by law and be so appointed under the requirement of practical experience on the part of the appointee to the said post of supervisor, he had personally instructed and directed the said secretary of the Civil Service Commission to cancel and revoke the said first notice, and to advertise in its stead a second notice of examination omitting

342

the said qualification of practical experience on the part of an applicant for the said position of supervisor.

WANT OF EXPERIENCE

"The said members of said board last above referred to objected to said action of said Mayor and told him that they could not conscientiously vote for the said Gudehus for the post of supervisor because of his unfitness and want of experience, even though he passed the said examination under the second notice advertised by said Civil Service Commission as above set forth, and that *the action of the said Mayor was against the public interest and would be injurious to the work* of the said Recreation Board, and that the appointment of said Gudehus as supervisor would *be injurious to the public interest, harmful to the work of said board, and to the detriment of the educational system* established by said board and the welfare of the school children of said city.

"Notwithstanding said protests and objections by said members of said board, the said Thomas B. Smith, Mayor, did state that he would expect the said members of said board to vote for and appoint said Gudehus to said position if he passed the said second examination, and that if they did not do so he would remove them from their offices and appoint in their places and stead other persons who would vote for and appoint said Gudehus to said position of supervisor.

RESULT OF EXAMINATION

Afterward, the said examination having been held, the said Civil Service Commission did certify to the said Board of Recreation, that but one person, to wit: said Gudehus, had passed the said examination with an average of 71 (70 being the minimum average required by said Civil Service Commission, to entitle an applicant to be placed in the list of eligibles for appointment), and that seven other persons who took the examination at the same time, most of whom had had practical experience in connection with the work of said Board of Recreation itself, had failed to obtain an average of 70, and were, therefore, not certified as eligibles to said Board of Recreation.

"Subsequently, the said Mayor did again communicate with the members of the Board of Recreation above referred to, and did demand that they should vote for and appoint the said Gudehus to said position, of supervisor. Whereupon, the said members of the said Board did again protest to the said Mayor that *they could not in good conscience vote for or appoint the said Gudehus because of his incompetency and unfitness,* and because they were entitled by law, before making an appointment, to have a list of at least four eligibles certified to the Board of Recreation by the Civil Service Commission, from which list of eligibles a competent appointment might be made.

DEMAND BY MAYOR

"And the said Thomas B. Smith, Mayor, did again state to the said members of said Board that he would require them to vote for the said Gudehus, as he personally desired to reward the said Gudehus, and had promised to give him an appointment on the city payroll as a reward for personal services to him, the said Thomas B. Smith, and again did threaten the said members of the said Board that if they did not vote for the said Gudehus he would remove them from office, and appoint others in their stead who would vote for the said Gudehus, and thus enable him, the said Thomas B. Smith, to reward the said Gudehus for personal services done for him, the said Thomas B. Smith.

"And the said Henry Berkowitz did, in a letter written to the said Thomas B. Smith, Mayor, set forth his conscientious official objections to the appointment of the said Gudehus because of his want of qualification and fitness and to the course of the said Mayor in endeavoring to have such said appointments made, and other citizens, also interested in the welfare of said City and the education of the public school children of said City, did, in writing and otherwise, personally protest to said Mayor against his action in endeavoring to compel the said Board of Recreation to appoint the said Gudehus to said office of supervisor, notwithstanding the members of said Board were unable in good conscience, because of the incompetence and unfitness of said Gudehus, to vote for his appointment.

CALLS FOR RESIGNATIONS

"And the said Thomas B. Smith, Mayor, did thereafter demand that the said members of said Board of Recreation should resign their offices because of their said refusal to vote for said Gudehus for the post of supervisor and in order that the said

344

Mayor might appoint others in their stead who would appoint said Gudehus.

"The said members of said board did not comply with the demand of said Mayor that they should resign their offices for the reason aforesaid, and thereafter held a meeting of said Board of Recreation on the 16th day of July, 1918, at which they passed a resolution requesting the said Civil Service Commission to hold an additional examination and certify to the said Board of Recreation, as required by law, a list of at least four eligibles for the said post of supervisor, from which list the said board might make a lawful selection and competent appointment.

"Whereupon the said Thomas B. Smith, Mayor, in execution of his threat to remove the said members of the said board if they did not violate their official consciences and make an appointment believed by them to be unfit and improper, did, in the unlawful, wrongful and abusive exercise of his discretion as Mayor, remove the said Ernest L. Tustin, Henry Berkowitz and Sophia L. Ross from their offices as members of the said Board of Recreation aforesaid.

"UNLAWFUL PURPOSE"

"And thereafter, the said Thomas B. Smith, in further pursuance of his *unlawful purpose* to put the said Gudehus upon the public payroll in reward for personal services, and secure his appointment as supervisor aforesaid, did thereafter, as Mayor of said city, appoint to fill the places of the members so removed other persons as members of the said Board of Recreation for the *sole purpose of carrying out his unlawful purpose* aforesaid, and the said members so appointed by him did, carrying out the purpose for which they were so appointed by said Mayor, vote for and appoint the said Gudehus to the said post of supervisor aforesaid.

"Whereby, the said Thomas B. Smith, Mayor, by reason of his unlawful acts aforesaid, and by reason of his illegal, wrongful and abusive exercise of his official power and discretion, against the public interest and to the detriment of the public services, and solely with a view to the accomplishment of said personal unlawful ends and objects, *did commit misbehavior and misdemeanor in office, contrary to the peace, good order, public economy and law of the Commonwealth of Pennsylvania.*"

The Playgrounds Association in its endeavor to support those

345

members of the Board of Recreation loyal to the interests of the children of Philadelphia, did everything in its power by petition and protest to prevent the introduction of politics into the administration of the playgrounds. Time will tell whether methods such as were employed in the appointment of Supervisor will be tolerated by the citizens of Philadelphia.

Thanking you for your courtesy in granting me the space to place the entire situation before your readers, I am,

Very sincerely yours,

JOSEPH WOOD WAGNER,

October 8, 1918 President

State Legislation for Physical Training*

THOMAS A. STOREY, M. D., PH. D.

Professor of Hygiene, College of the City of New York

Inspector of Physical Training, Military Training Commission, State of New York

CHRONOLOGICAL ANALYSIS

Since May 15th, 1916, seven states in this country have enacted physical training laws. The first of these became a law on May 15th, 1916, when Governor Whitman of New York signed the Welch Bill. The New Jersey law was introduced February 13th, 1917; Nevada, adopted March 21st, 1917; Rhode Island, April 19th, 1917; California, May 26th, 1917; Maryland, introduced March 22nd, 1918; Delaware adopted April 10th, 1918.

Illinois The State of Illinois possessed a law on physical training which was signed by the Governor of that State on June 26th, 1915. This law of Illinois, therefore, antedates those of all these others. It provides for physical training in all of the public schools and in all of the normal schools of the State.

So far as I can discover, no special provision has been made in that State for the operation of the law; no appropriation for the development of a program or the publication of a syllabus, and no resource for the employment of state supervisors, inspec-

* Presented before Physical Directors' Society of the Y. M. C. A., Springfield, June 3, 1918
* Reprinted from *Physical Training*, September 1918

tors or other administrators of physical education. I understand that the people of the State are not satisfied with the law and that efforts have been made to amend it so that it may serve a more useful purpose.

New York The New York law, approved May 15th, 1916, and amended at this last session of the legislature, provides that "all male and female pupils, above the age of eight years, in all elementary and secondary schools of the State, shall receive, as a part of the prescribed courses of instruction therein, such physical training under the direction of the Commissioner of Education, as the Regents, after conference with the Military Training Commission may determine during periods which shall average at least twenty minutes each school day." . . . . "Similar courses of instruction shall be prescribed and maintained in private schools of the State and all pupils in such schools above eight years of age shall attend upon such courses; and if such courses are not so established and maintained in any private school, attendance upon instruction in such school shall not be deemed substantially equivalent to instruction given to children of like ages in the public school or schools of the city or district in which the child resides."

The administration of this law in the State of New York is a function of the Regents of the University of the State of New York, that is, of the State Department of Education. A bureau of Physical Training has been established as a subdivis'on of the State Military Training Commission. The State Inspector of Physical Training, the chief officer of this Bureau, is required, in accordance with the law, to observe and inspect the work and methods described under the provisions of the Education Law relating to instruction in physical training. The State law in New York also provides that all public schools in the State employing special teachers of physical training, qualified and duly licensed under the regulations of the Regents, may receive financial support from the State to the extent of half the salary of each teacher so employed, provided that half the salary does not exceed $600, and the law further requires that "The Board of Education or trustees of every school district in a city, and every union free school district regularly employing ten or more teachers, shall employ a teacher or teachers qualified and duly licensed under the regulations of the Regents to give such instruction; in every other

347

district of the state they shall require such instruction to be given by the teacher or teachers regularly employed to give instruction in other subjects or by a teacher or teachers qualified and duly licensed under the regulations of the Regents.

At the last session of the legislature, the sum of $60,000 was appropriated for the purpose of enabling the Education Department of the State to provide for the supervision and special instruction in physical training of teachers of other subjects who are assigned or designated, as required by law, to give instruction in physical training.

Pursuant with the enactments of 1916, the Regents of the University of the State of New York and the Military Training Commission of that State, produced jointly a State Program and Syllabus of Physical Training, which in published form covers about 300 printed pages. In this program and syllabus, physical training is interpreted as covering: (1) "Individual health examination and personal health instruction (Medical inspection) (2) Instruction concerning the care of the body and concerning the important facts of hygiene (recitations in hygiene) and, (3) Physical exercise as a health habit, including gymnastics, elementary marching and organized supervised play, recreation and athletics."

The program and syllabus now operating in the State of New York requires six hours a week in physical training from every pupil who comes under the provision of the law.

New Jersey The physical training law of the State of New Jersey was introduced before the legislature of that State February 13, 1917. This law requires that "there shall be estab'ished and made a part of the courses of instruction in the public schools of this state (New Jersey) what shall be known as 'a course in physical training.' Such course shall be adapted to the ages and capabilities of the pupils in the several grades and departments and shall include exercises, calisthenics, formation drills, instruction in personal and community health and safety and in correcting and preventing bodily deficiency and such other features and details as may aid in carrying out these purposes, together with instruction as to the privileges and responsibilities of citizenship, as they relate to community and national welfare, with special reference to developing bodily strength and vigor and producing the highest type of patriotic citizenship, and in

348

addition, for female pupils instruction in domestic hygiene, first aid and nursing. To further promote the aims of this course any additional requirements or regulations as to medical inspection of school children may be imposed."

The New Jersey law prescribes that the State Commissioner of Education, with the approval of the State Board of Education, shall prepare a course in physical training in compliance with the State law and that experts may be employed to assist him in preparing such courses of instruction and in putting those courses into operation in the public schools of the State.

All children physically fit and capable of doing so, are required to take the course in physical training as provided by the State legislature and such course is made by law a part of the curriculum prescribed for the several grades. It specifies that the conduct and attainment of the pupils shall be marked as in other courses or subjects, and the standing of the pupil in connection therewith shall form a part of the requirements for promotion or graduation. The time requirement in New Jersey is "at least 2½ hours in each school week." The law further requires that all students in the state normal schools of New Jersey shall receive thorough instruction in physical training and that such instruction shall be provided for all students in attendance at the State summer schools as shall elect to take such instruction.

Instruction in courses of physical training in New Jersey are subject to the general supervision and direction of the Commissioner of Education, who is authorized by act of the Legislature to appoint such expert assistants as in the opinion of the State Board of Education shall from time to time be necessary to carry out the purposes of the State law. Local Boards of Education are authorized to raise money for the support of the local expense attending upon operating the State Law of Physical Training, but no special provision is made by the Legislature of the State of New Jersey for State support in local school systems. The general law governing the distribution of money regarding apportionment to teachers is, however, effective in the case of physical training supervisors and teachers.

The original bill provided the sum of ten thousand dollars for the purpose of enabling the State Commissioner of Education and the State Board of Education to carry out its provisions and made it a law that the sum of $12,000 be provided in the annual appropriation bill for the purpose, for the year 1918.

Pursuant with the provisions of this law, the Commissioner of Education and the State Board of Education of New Jersey, have produced and published a State Program and Syllabus of Physical Education.

Nevada The physical training law for the State of Nevada was approved on March 21st, 1917.

This act reads in part as follows:

"Section 1. It is hereby made the duty of all school officers in control of public high schools in the State of Nevada to provide for courses of instruction designated to prepare the pupils for the duties of citizenship, both in time of peace and in time of war. Such instruction shall include:

(1) Physical training designed to secure health, vigor and physical soundness of the pupil; (2) Instruction relative to the duties of citizens in the service of their country. It shall be the aim of such instruction to inculcate a love of country and a disposition to serve the country effectively and loyally.

"Section 2. All Boards of Education or Boards of School Trustees of county or district high schools offering a four years' high school course are hereby empowered to employ teachers of physical training who shall devote all or part of their time to physical instruction for boys and girls.

"Section 3. In order to assist in the payment of salaries of said physical training instructors, there shall be levied on the passage of this act an ad valorem tax of five mills on the hundred dollars of assessed valuation of all the taxable property of the State."

The Superintendent of Education for the State of Nevada has issued a program and syllabus for physical training, pursuant with the provisions of this law.

This Nevada law has the advantage of providing an assured income through its ad valorem tax for the assistants of the various high schools and the payment of salaries of their teachers of physical training. It apparently does not provide any administrative machinery whereby the State Superintendent of Public Instruction may more effectively direct, supervise and inspect the operation of the State Program of Physical Education. The law unfortunately leaves out of consideration the elementary schools of the State in which physical training is even more important than in secondary schools. I am informed that this deficiency is met in part at least through the authority of the State Department of Education which has made physical training a requirement in the elementary schools of the State.

Rhode Island On April 19th, 1917, the Governor of the State of Rhode Island approved a law to provide physical training for school children, which reads as follows: "All children above the age of eight years, attending public schools or such other schools as are managed and controlled by the State, shall receive therein instruction and the practice in physical training under such regulations as the State Board of Education may prescribe or approve during periods which shall average at least 20 minutes in each school day. No private school or private instruction shall be approved by any school committee . . . . as substantially equivalent to that required by law of a child attending a public school in the same city and town, unless instruction and practice in physical training, similar to that required in the public schools, shall be given.

"For the purpose of preparing and introducing such course of instruction, the sum of $500, or such sum thereof as may be necessary, is hereby appropriated . . . ."

Pursuant with this act of the Legislature, the State Board of Education has issued a syllabus for physical education in the schools of Rhode Island.

This syllabus is concerned with (1) The provision of the health and sanitary environment for pupils (2) A personal health examination and instruction for each pupil at least once a year by a physician and specialist and daily by the parent and teacher. (3) Class instruction concerning the important facts of physiology and hygiene for all children and all grades. (4) Exercises including such motor activities as marching, gymnastics and supervised play and recreation.

The general plan and syllabus of physical education for the schools of Rhode Island covers 110 printed pages.

There seems to have been no provision made in this law for the expense of enforcing this requirement in physical education by the Board of Education in the State of Rhode Island; no provision for state support of local school systems for the employment of special teachers; and no provision for administrative machinery for supervision, direction, or inspection of the operation of the law. Unless some such support is given, the proba-

351

bilities are that the law will not be particularly productive in Rhode Island. These deficiencies in this law seem to have been supplied partially at least by already existing resources within the office of the State Commissioner of Public Schools. The following memorandum from that office is reassuring:

"The physical education law will be codified with other laws dealing with provisions for the safety and health of school children. The law·is mandatory, has been put into effect and is being complied with throughout the State. It is to be regretted that a section of the original bill carrying an annual appropriation for special state supervision and inspection was not enacted into law. A state supervisor devoting full time to supervision and inspection, could do much to accelerate progress."

California On May 26th, 1917, an act providing for physical education became a law in the State of California.

This law provides that the school authorities in the public schools of the State, elementary and secondary, shall prescribe suitable courses of physical education for all pupils, except such as may be excused from such training on account of physical disability.

The aims of physical education are stated in the California law, as follows:

"To develop organic vigor, provide neuromuscular training, promote bodily and mental poise, correct postural defects, secure the more advanced forms of coordination, strength and endurance, and to promote such desirable moral and social qualities as appreciation of the value of cooperation, self-subordination and obedience to authority and higher ideals, courage and wholesome interest in truly recreational activities; to promote a hygienic school and home life, secure scientific sanitation of school buildings, playgrounds and athletic fields and equipment thereof."

The California law makes it a duty of the superintendent of schools in every county or city, and of every board of education, board of school trustees or high school board, to enforce the courses of physical education prescribed by the proper authority, and to require that such physical education be given in the schools under their jurisdiction or control.

In the elementary schools the time requirement in California shall "average 20 minutes in each school day," and in the secondary schools "at least two hours each week, while that school is in session."

352

This law requires that if the number of pupils in a given school system is sufficient, there shall be employed a competent supervisor or such special teachers of physical education as may be necessary. The enactment further specifies that the State Board of Education shall require a course in physical training in all the normal schools of the State and provides that the State Board of Education shall prescribe a course in physical education for such schools and shall make the completion of such course a requirement for graduation.

Under this law, it is the duty of the State Board of Education: (1) "To adopt such rules and regulations as it may deem necessary and proper to secure the establishment of courses in physical education in the elementary and secondary schools in accordance with the provisions of this act; (2) To appoint a State Supervisor of Physical Education . . . . (3) To compile or cause to be compiled or printed a manual in physical education for distribution to teachers in the public schools of the State."

The sum of $10,000 was appropriated for the purpose of carrying out the provisions of the California law.

The California program has not yet been printed. Some advance information has been given out and there is every evidence that Clark Hetherington will produce for that state a thorough and carefully developed curriculum. The present emphasis in California seems to be directed toward the training of teachers, which is without doubt the most important factor necessary for the successful development of a state-wide program of physical education.

In my judgment, the California plan will be handicapped because of inadequate financial assistance, unless the legislature does better than $10,000 a year for the supervision, direction and administration of physical education throughout the State.

Maryland   The physical training act which is now a law in the State of Maryland was introduced before the Senate of that State on March 22, 1918.

This law reads in part as follows:

1. "There shall be established and provided in all the public schools of this State and all schools maintained or aided by the State, physical education and training for pupils of both sexes during the following minimum periods: A. In the elementary public schools at least 15 minutes in each school day and also at

353

least one hour of directed play outside of regular classroom work in each school week. B. In public high schools at least one hour in each school week and also at least two hours of directed play or athletics for all pupils outside of regular classroom work in each school week."

The law of Maryland provides for the appointment of a supervisor of physical education whose duties shall be to direct and carry out the provisions of the State law under the direction of the State superintendent of schools. The State Board of Education is further authorized and directed to appoint such other assistants, both clerical and professional, as may be recommended by the State superintendent of schools as necessary in the administration and supervision of physical education.

The law further provides that the state supervisor of physical education immediately after his appointment "shall organize his work and shall formulate the necessary and proper plans, courses and regulations for carrying out the provisions in the State Law of Physical Training.

The Maryland program has not yet appeared. The time obviously has been too short for the organization and publication of a program and syllabus for application in the schools of that state. In view of the great resource which Maryland possesses in its highly trained and public spirited citizens prominent in the health educational movements of our nation, it is to be expected that Maryland will produce an effective and far-reaching plan for the physical education of her school children.

Delaware On April 10th, 1918, an act was approved by the Governor of the State of Delaware "prescribing physical training for the school children of the state and creating a physical training commission to inaugurate a system of physical training for school children."

This law reads in part as follows:

"That from and after the passage of this act, the school children of this State shall receive physical training, the character and methods of which shall be prescribed from time to time by the State Board of Education and a commission is hereby created to be known as 'The Physical Training Commission,' whose duties shall be to devise a system of physical training and inaugurate the same in the schools of this State, subject to the direction of the state board of education.

354

"The said Commission shall consist of the Governor and four suitable persons, to be appointed by the Governor, who shall serve without pay. The functions of the said Commission shall cease when a system of physical training shall have been inaugurated as provided in section 1 of this act."

So far as I know, the personnel of the Physical Training Commission provided for in this act has not yet been made public. It is obviously too early to anticipate the character, the scope or the possibilities of physical training in the State of Delaware consequent on this law. It is to be expected, however, that in face of the acute realization of the importance of physical education which is now gripping the world, Delaware will make full use of her opportunity.

THE OBLIGATIONS WHICH THESE LAWS BRING TO THE TEACHER OF
PHYSICAL TRAINING

It is obvious from a review of this recent state legislation that the field of physical education has grown enormously here in America within the last two years. Never before in the history of this country has there been such a remarkable growth. The demand for expertly trained and competent teachers of physical training exceeds the supply by a greater margin than ever and this demand will inevitably increase with the better organization and operation of physical education in the states in which these laws have been recently enacted, and in those other states which most certainly will follow. Massachusetts for two consecutive years has attempted to secure a State law in physical education. We are told that efforts in the same direction have been made in Connecticut, Pennsylvania, Illinois, Ohio and Colorado. It is inevitable that other states will make the same effort and that physical training will, within the not distant future, become a requirement in every state in the Union. Federal laws with this end in view, are even now being devised and formulated so that the time may soon arrive when our national government will support physical education in the states of this country just as it now supports vocational education through the action of the Smith-Hughes law.

All this means an increasingly heavy and a continuously growing demand for teachers especially fitted to do this work, and it means that the time will soon come when every teacher, no matter what he or she may teach, will have been trained in the elements of physical education just as every teacher is now trained in the elements of English or arithmetic.

With these facts before you, and with the memory of your own observations and experiences during the last three or four years, you must be asking yourselves just as I have asked myself why it is that the importance of physical education has impressed itself so rapidly and compellingly upon the great public and its legislative representatives. And I know that you have given answer with as little delay as I have. I know that you realize that the great war has emphasized and driven home truths which appealed to us as specialists in physical education before this war was declared and at a time when many of us thought a war among civilized nations was an impossibility. This war has wakened the world to the importance of the human being as a national resource; to the importance of man power and woman power; to the stability and continuity of the nation; and to the importance of vigorous and enduring health as a solid basis for national conservation and national defense.

This enormous expansion in physical education brings serious problems for the specialist in physical education to settle; problems that involve an analysis of our work in the past and a construction of programs for the present and for the future.

We dare not be satisfied with the products of physical education of yesterday. The value of that physical education has been grimly measured and mercilessly tested since we entered this great war. If you accept the standards of our first draft, you must admit that a rejection of 30 or 40% of our young men because they were physically unfit for military service would seem to show that our physical education has been only 60 or 70% effective. If you accept the standards of the Life Extension Institute you will have to admit that our physical education has failed to produce a sound body in 50% of our fellow-citizens. If you accept the standards set by the regular army, you will have to admit that 80 or 90% of the men who are applying for service there are unfit and, militarily speaking, must be thrown into the scrap heap because physical education for them has failed.

In the face of the facts that have been produced in England, France and America, no specialist in physical education today would dare maintain that it is desirable to continue the standards of effectiveness that existed yesterday when these men now being rejected at the draft were being conditioned in our schools and through our systems of physical education for the demands of citizenship which they are now facing.

We must not be—we cannot be—contented with the sort of work that has been done in the past; with the extent of that work and with the number of specialists who have been engaged in its operation. It is your duty, and my duty, as long as we remain in physical education, to bend every energy, to be more usefully productive, to encourage the entry into physical education of competent young blood and to stimulate all those who are now occupying responsible positions in which they come in contact with the boys and girls of today to redouble their efforts so that those boys and girls may be ready for the demands which are going to be made upon them tomorrow.

The most important thing today is victory. Nothing else counts but success in this war. But this war will not be ended soon. Are you going to permit it to happen that the boys in your hands today will be thrown, 30% of them, or 50% of them, or 90% of them into the scrap heap because they are not ready physically for the demands of military service when those demands are made upon them? You and I are now training future soldiers in a pre-military period in which immense armies have been lost in the past because of poor training. In that same past, from the standpoint of our regular army, only one boy out of every seven has been conditioned, while a boy, so that he was physically acceptable when a man for military service. When I realize that future battles may be lost because of inadequate and inefficient pre-military training right now, it makes me wonder that every state and every country and every district in this whole land of ours is not spending its greatest energy to conserve the lives and vigor of their boys and girls.

You men and the men and women that are working with you in physical education have a responsibility that is second to that of no profession, and no group of men and no group of women anywhere in this world, in your relationship to the army that is going over there next year and the year after next and throughout the sequence of years that this war is going to last. Upon you rests a responsibility which I am afraid you have not realized, which I am afraid thoughtful men and thoughtful women in this country do not adequately realize, and with every persuasion which I possess I would urge you to consider your responsibilities and your opportunities most seriously.

For these are days of serious thought; days when every man of us plans to do for his country the thing he can do best; days when we challenge the things we are doing and test them in terms of patriotic service. What are you doing? What am I doing for the support, the success of this nation in its period of peril and critical need? I heard the Honorable J. Sloat Fassett the other day ask in language which I cannot reproduce: "These young men are giving all they have; their hopes of home and family and their plans for success and happiness, even their lives— for you. Are you worth it?"

And I heard Harry Lauder say one day last winter: "If they over there are willing to die fighting for you, you over here should be willing to die working for them."

And we search our souls each day to find the answer?—"Am I worth it?" "Am I working for them?" "Am I doing the thing I ought to do?" "Should I be in the army, the navy, building ships, in the Red Cross, with the Y. M. C. A., or with the Recreation Commission?"

The affairs of yesterday seem so commonplace, so ordinary and so inappropriate. The things of today are so dramatic, so spectacular and so immediately and critically and seriously appropriate. The urge to forsake the occupations of yesterday; to go into the objective things and the applications of today is well-nigh compelling. The relative values of the two appear at first to be wholly unequal. But sober judgment insists that we analyze the things we do; that we examine into our activities and weigh their deeper values in relation to possible national and international utilities before leaving them for newer activities and applications.

Some of us *must* go into new work. Some of us will find our best service somewhere in some new job and in some new field. Who is it that must stay "on the job?" What kinds of work—the old work of yesterday—are essential to the future integrity of our nation? Who are they who should wait?

It is harder each day to answer these questions. The pressure from many sources raises the question anew each morning after every answer that led us last night, sleepless, to decide that it is our patriotic duty to stay with our work—to "keep the home fires burning." And on every new day every man of us reopens his case.

Fortunately for the safety of our decisions there is a growing accumulation of evidence that bears upon the essential national importance of physical education. Voices are being heard and judgments are being rendered that assist the civilian not of the age of conscription in his decision.

You who are specialists in physical training must give ear to the judgments of the great public through its professional men, its educators, its legislators, its military men, its congressmen and its President. As I interpret these judgments they go a long way toward making it your patriotic duty to stay with your work, to see it with a larger vision and to do it with a greater vigor and a deeper conscious patriotism.

I have told you that the legislatures of New York, New Jersey, Rhode Island, Nevada, California, Delaware and Maryland have passed laws establishing physical education in the schools of their states, and you know that like bills are pending now in other legislative bodies in this country.

If you have read "The Wasted Years" that appeared two years ago in the *Nation*, a publication issued in London, you will have noted that England will never again let it be said that she cared for her boys only when she needed them for war. For England has determined to make physical education a compulsory part of her national educational program. France has reached the same decision and there are strong factors at work here in America, as I have told you, that must lead our own country to a universal requirement in physical education.

We have public statements from General Wood, General Crowder, Secretary of War Baker and President Wilson, that insist upon the fundamental values of physical education for military citizenship as well as for civic service. No wise military man today will fail to tell you that military training should be superimposed upon a physical training that has produced a strong vigorous body.

On every hand we find evidences of dissatisfaction with the high percentage of men rejected at the draft because of physical deficiency and with our high morbidity and mortality rates from preventable and postponable diseases.

Intelligent citizens are everywhere considering ways and means for the more effective conservation of our national resource in man power and woman power. Our city and state boards of health and boards of education, our national security organizations and defense leagues, our educational, medical and health societies, are recording themselves more and more insistently for the more effective acquisition and for the more thorough conservation of national health.

Physical training or physical education, or whatever you may choose to call this thing you are doing, is finding itself. The specialist in physical education who thought yesterday that his concern was only with muscles, finds today that he has been and that he must be engaged in building men and women; that he cannot limit himself to a part of the great problem; and that his duty, now a patriotic duty, brings him face to face with every influence that bears upon the physical, mental and moral health of the citizen of the present or the citizen of the future now under his care.

The men who have made physical training laws in seven of these United States interpreted physical training as a health process. In no single state in which such laws have been enacted or proposed, has the conception been limited to a vision less broad or to a field less fundamentally comprehensive.

My analysis of physical training as it is revealed in the departments of physical training in our schools, colleges and universities, and as conceived and stated by our state and federal law makers, leads me to define it as a program for the acquisition and conservation of health made up of divisions concerned with health examination, health information and the establishment of health habits; and it is wholly satisfied by no less a quality of health product than that represented by the normal growth and the normal function of each and every organ of the human body.

These State laws on physical training that I have been disussing here were enacted in order to conserve human life—the chief and most precious asset of the State. Universal physical training when it comes, and it must come, will come for the same compelling reasons and for the same state and national purposes.

And you specialists in physical education are engaged in an essential and patriotic service. If you are ready, as Harry Lauder urges, to "die working for them over there," if you are putting the best you have into your work, you are doing a service that is preparing the nation for successful battles of war over there and for successful battles of peace over here. You are concerned with a physical training that is not satisfied with a degree and quality of human health that is represented by being merely well or by the man or woman who is able to be out of bed and eat three meals a day and get about without an abnormal temperature. It is your job to add an enormous resource to the man power and the woman power of your country; to reduce and perhaps remove entirely the great percentage of young men thrown into the scrap heap by the draft; to save hundreds of thousands of young men for the armies which we must have in the years that this great war is going to last; to stop our staggering annual losses in working time through sickness and accident and provide thousands and millions of working days now lost for the construction of our fleets and munitions to supply the needs that will be larger and more insistent in these coming years; and to give to the nation not only the lives of men and women saved from preventable and postponable death, but the lives of men and women made more productive, more physiologically useful and more enduring.

Think again of the armies you are training. Think of the armies you are conditioning! Think of the armies you can save for tomorow—for the tomorrow when our country will need all the human resource, all the man power and all the woman power here and abroad that we and our Allies can produce, to win the victory we must have.

In the State of New York, as in every other State in this Union, we are short of teachers, short of nurses, short of medical internes and short of physicians. Five hundred thousand boys in that State should reach the age of twenty-one in the next five years. Are we getting them ready? Of those who live to reach that age, will thirty percent or fifty percent or eighty per cent be physically unfit? And whose fault will it be?

If you are in this work; if you are preparing boys and girls for the demands of life—if these are the noble purposes of your work, keep it up! Don't leave it uncovered! Work harder! We must win this war! Nothing else matters! Without this service we lose!

Boys and Girls to Help Win the War

THEY WILL JOIN IN A NATION-WIDE
EFFORT OF SERVICE AND SACRIFICE.

America's boys and girls are to have a chance this fall to help win the war. Seven great organizations engaged in providing for the comfort and happiness of our soldiers and sailors the whole world over have joined to give the young generation this opportunity to do its share.

The Young Men's Christian Association, the Young Women's Christian Association, the National Catholic War Council (Knights of Columbus), the Jewish Welfare Board, the War Camp Community Service, the American Library Association, and the Salvation Army, in their *United* War Work Campaign to raise $170,500,000 for the continuance of their war activities, will challenge every boy and girl in the country to serve and to sacrifice in the "great cause." A separate division of the campaign, that of the Victory Boys, will have for its goal the lining up of "a million boys behind a million fighters." The girls too will have a separate division to be known as the Victory Girls.

Those enrolling in either division must pledge to earn and give an amount to be individually determined for welfare work among our soldiers and sailors; and this means that no boy and girl can give any money he or she has not earned.

The war has called half our workers away from their ordinary peace-time occupations, leaving much work undone in the homes and in the home communities. As the boys and girls will find their tasks in these now neglected fields, their united effort will go a long way toward helping us keep our affairs in order over here, while the giving of money earned will make for the comfort and morale of our fighters.

Community Organization Versus Institutionalism

Opportunity and Danger for War Camp Community Service

CHARLES FREDERICK WELLER, Associate Secretary, Playground and Recreation Association of America

"If it hadn't been for the war I'd never have known you nor Mrs. Sutton nor Mrs. Alderson and her daughter. You wouldn't have stood for my grammar and—everything." So said a young jackie to Miss Hinman, his hostess at the Soldiers' and Sailors' Club in Chicago. Then he went on to ask what seems to me one of the profoundest questions of the War.

"Say, Miss Hinman, I could go right up to Mrs. Sutton's door and ring the bell and go right into her home and talk to her, couldn't I?" "Yes, surely," said Miss Hinman. "And I can talk to you anytime, can't I?" "Yes." "And to Mrs. Alderson and her daughter?" "Yes, indeed." "And I dance with these ladies and the swell girls at your dances, don't I?" "Yes, Jimmy."

"Well," said the sailor boy, "You know I used to go to Dreamland and those other dance halls. And, say, I used to think those girls there were mighty cute and all. And last week Bill Gregson he said to me, 'let's go to Dreamland.' And I remembered the good times I'd had there and the pretty girls and we went. Well, say, do you know what happened? They made me tired. Those girls couldn't talk or nothin'. And I used to think they was some swell girls. I just had to get out and leave 'em."

"Now what I want to know is—after the war—can I know you and Mrs. Sutton and such folks? Or, have I got to go back to the Dreamland crowd and all?"

Do you agree with me that this is one of the profoundest questions which the war has yet raised; namely, will our new and nobler democracy persist when peace returns? If you feel this as I do you will also see why I believe in retail rather than wholesale hospitality for our soldiers and sailors. Why I care chiefly for the human touch, for warm human interest in the uniformed men as men and brothers. Therefore, institutions do not seem to me to fulfill our War Camp Community Service. In contrast to institutions I put my faith in organization, in Community Organization. For six years I have thought of Community Organization as America's next and greatest need. Now I am asked to explain my conception in its relation to the congenial principles and achievements of War Camp Community Service.

I

Club houses for soldiers and sailors have received during the past few months about one-third, I imagine, of all the strength and funds of War Camp Community Service. These clubs are the most popular, because most tangible, of all our activities. We must have them. They are safer in our hands than in the control of institutionalized groups. Yet, I believe these clubs represent also our gravest danger—the danger of ossification and of arteriosclerosis of our movement and for the fundamental issues of democracy which we represent.

Money and power are always dangerous, always liable to become deadening. Club houses are especially dangerous because they are so necessary, so beneficial, so practical, so apt to make commmunities regard them as the glorious end and purpose of our War Camp Community Service rather than as one of its incidental, subsidiary means.

Unless we make these Club houses serve as meeting places, bridges, occasions for outreaching fellowship between civilians and soldiers, we shall or should, regret the day they were conceived.

One way to minimize the danger is suggested by the work of the hospitality man at our Earlington Hotel and club center in New York City. He says it is impracticable to fill directly from the camps our invitations for home dinners, dances and other civilian-soldier activities and he has made the New York club houses effective as open doors to these contacts with community life.

In Chicago, too, our leaders bring women and other civilians to parties, entertainments and dances at their great Soldiers' and Sailors' Club purposing that natural acquaintanceships formed at the Club shall lead the uniformed men out of segregation into abundant fellowship with community life.

"The Jolly Tar" at Waukegan, Illinois, near the Great Lakes Naval Training Station, is a club house so inspired by warm human interest that the old "family mansion" seems like a shabby, hospitable *home* with the fewest possible traces of Institutionalism. Here the Illinois Congress of Mothers and Parent-Teachers' Association give the sailor boy a cat to pet, a kitchen stove on which to cook candy or to get himself a little luncheon, a sewing machine, electric flat iron, typewriter, victrola and some cots in the attic with home-made bed coverings—no two alike. I hope the "Jolly Tar" will never grow big, fine and wealthy because it seems now to be a close approach to the old free-and-easy home life for which many lads must be lonesome.

We must defend our souls against Segregation as distinguished from Fellowship; against Machinery in contrast with the Human Touch; against Wealth and Power displacing humble Service; against providing Static Comfort instead of Activities; against methods which are Wholesale rather than Retail.

II

That real dangers are involved is indicated by our recent experiences in a wholesome camp community of some twenty thousand people where a board of splendid men and women was organized for War Camp Community Service. Before undertaking any actual work they submitted a budget including subsidies of $10,000 to the Knights of Columbus; $600 to the Masons; $12,500 to the local Y. M. C. A.; $1,500 to an independent work for girls; $1,200 to the Jewish Board of Welfare work; $10,000 to one local club for uniformed men; $1,950 to another; and $5,000 for public bathing beach developments under management independent of the War Camp Community Service. They asked for $62,000 altogether, including $42,750 for subsidies to independent institutions.

It has been difficult in that city for our experienced community organizer himself, as well as for his new Board, to understand that their chief service to the uniformed men in the nearby camp, must be such as money cannot buy—cannot, sometimes, even see. Rumors have been circulating generally in this city to the effect that large sums were available; that other communities having fewer men in camp had been promised larger amounts; that the Government, with a big G, would either start a new great institution or greatly strengthen existing club houses. So our people fell naturally into the pratical businesslike view that coordination and control are to be brought about by financial appropriations. Some of their leaders said, "Why, if we don't build new club house facilities or extend the three existing clubs, we shall be doing nothing at all for the men in uniform." Here, pressed to some of its logical conclusions was the Institutionalism which has its dangers, I believe, for all of us.

To help arouse these good people from their institutionalism I prepared a list of twenty summer-time activities requiring little or no money. Instead of funds, these activities require vision, organizing power, the stimulation and coordination of existing resources. As these suggestions for summer can be had by anyone for the asking, it were wearisome to repeat them here. They include plans for developing vacant lots as play centers; little-used asphalt streets for dances; neglected water fronts for swimming; outdoor sports; hay-rick and auto rides; hikes; camp fires and marshmallow roasts; lawn fetes and old-fashioned picnics; athletic contests; old-time and newer games; music; open-air services; special vacation-time activities for girls; auto rides and other friendly services for convalescent soldiers; and the development of appropriate help from schools, colleges and other institutions, from commercial agencies and, especially, from parks and playgrounds. To discover, enlist and extend such normal resources and relationships is Community Organization and this is distinctively the field assigned to War Camp Community Service. For the original resolution by

365

which War Camp Community Service was established read as follows:

> "The War Department Commission on Training Camp Activities asks the Playground and Recreation Association of America to be responsible for the work of stimulating and aiding Communities in the neighborhood of training camps to develop and organize their social and recreational resources in such a way as to be of the greatest possible value to the officers and soldiers in the camps." (May 5, 1917)

III.

One reason why Community Organization is preferable to Institutionalism is because Community Organization cannot confine its benefits to men in uniform. Institutions, like our club houses, can be limited narrowly. They may exclude girls, women, all civilians. One of our promising new clubs, conducted by a fine group of public-spirited men, proposes to limit their club house strictly to men because it is believed that the soldiers and sailors will feel freer if women are not around. Of our Chicago Club, too, soldiers have complained that there are too many sailors in the place; sailors have complained there are too many soldiers.

This liking for segregation and exclusiveness seems to be normal with many good people. (I hate it heartily.) But my point here is simply that the truer we are to Community Organization, the more inclusive and democratic our activities become.

Starting with Community Organization for soldiers, we extended the service, step by step, to sailors; to marines; to the merchant marine; to the girls of communities near the camps; to the families of enlisted men; to young men on the draft lists; to industrial workers in a few selected centers.

Where should we draw the line? Nowhere. Our distinctive emphasis is upon *"Community* Service." We are not in uniform. We are civilians. We are preparing already for social reintegration after the war. Ideally our task is to weave the fibres of social relationship from uniformed men to every soul in the community and—from the obverse point of view—to help organize every member of every community into war-winning efficiency, into realization of that new and larger democracy for which we fight; which also fights for us.

What do you suppose was the first reaction when I suggested to our War Camp Community Service groups in Rock Island, Moline and Davenport that the 9000 industrial employes of the Government in the Rock Island Arsenal should receive some of the same services we had been extending to the 1400 soldiers? Some community leaders said of the war worker in blue overalls what they had said a few months earlier of the man in khaki: "He is different from us, usually inferior; we have no tastes or tasks in common. Even if we were willing to welcome him into our homes, clubs and social parties he would not care to come. He likes to live on a different plane." Nonsense!

If there can be any adequate compensation for the heaped up anguish of this war it is in our growing recognition of this fact—the hidden pearl of all human experience—that normal human differences are unimportant; that we are all engaged together in a crusade great and glorious enough to lift us out of petty provincialisms; that separations based on differences in occupation, culture and opportunity are simply so much of death and dissolution for the man or for the state which they infest.

Eighteen industrial workers, leaders among the nine thousand munition workers in the Rock Island Arsenal, met our community organizer. They responded eagerly to his suggestion of club house centers, social activities and, especially, to the plan of joint committees in which the industrial employes would work in democratic fellowship with the best people of the tri-cities.

From the civilian side, one man, a veteran of the civil war, a member of our Moline committee, surprised us by his response to the suggestion of War Camp Community Service for industrial employes. "This is the most important service," he said, "that has ever come to Moline. We need it to help win the war; but we need it even more for times of peace. It points toward a solution of our labor problems." I would add that it promises democracy—for real democracy has not come until it prevails, not politically alone, but in industry and even in social intercourse.

Thus, while we emphasize the Community organization

367

features of our War Camp Community Service, its field broadens. If the war lasts three years longer—which, pray God, it may not—we shall share worthily in that democratization of industry, of education, of religion, of social service and even of so-called "society" which America and the whole world need.

IV.

Consider Community Organization, now, not simply from the viewpoint of war and of training camps, but from the standpoint of my own home neighborhood in "Hyde Park," a wholesome section of Chicago.

We live near the University of Chicago in a favored community between Washington and Jackson Parks, only five blocks from Jackson Park with its wealth of baseball diamonds, tennis courts, golf links, boating and other recreations including one of the most popular bathing beaches I ever saw. A summer playground is also operated in Jackson Park at a point eight blocks from my home. We are thus environed by the famous South Park System which leads the world in small-park playgrounds. In the magnificent Hyde Park High School, eleven blocks from us, are all the modern school facilities plus a successful "Community Center." A philanthropy called "Hyde Park Center" with a playground and other social settlement activities is only six blocks away. One of the best equipped public grammar schools of Chicago, occupying a former high-school building, with gymnasium, ground-floor auditorium, large yards and a social-spirited principal, stands one block from my back gate. A Catholic parochial school housed excellently in a former public school building is less than two blocks distant. The Hyde Park Y. M. C. A. with a separate boys' building and other modern facilities inspired by a splendid spirit of service is four blocks from us. Of churches—most of them with chapels or social buildings—we have eight within a radius of four blocks.

Neighborliness, however, is no more—in our community as in others. A family living on the third floor of a three-apartment building learn through crepe upon the door of the second floor that a neighbor has died whose name and existence were unknown though he lived within twenty feet of their household. Here are the nomad cliff dwellers, the restless flitting families who characterize all modern flat building districts. Here are many lonesome, heartsore people, lost in the un-human wilderness of human beings; reading their newspapers, killing time at the movies, hardened by feeling that they are unknown and unneeded among their neighbors. Except through industry they have little or no relation to society. Their leisure time, with its vivifying, democratic, unifying possibilities, is dead.

Only by re-vitalizing some of this wasted leisure can we mobilize the community's resources for service to the men in uniform. A big camp nearby might help to do this for our neighborhood. But the small group of soldiers located in our midst (housed in an abandoned telephone building while they attend classes at the University) serves only to show how dead our neighborliness is, how ill-prepared to assimilate any neighbors—new or old—uniformed or civilian.

Such conservation of leisure as our community needs, has been attempted usually through institutions, not through organization. People have thought of playgrounds and of playground apparatus rather than of play. Such institutionalism has been in evidence throughout the field of social service; the "Good Neighbor" seeking life more abundant for his community, has been speedily institutionalized into an Associated Charities or a Social Settlement. Now we need Good Neighbors who shall not be walled-in. It is not enough to have static agencies like playgrounds, community centers and Y. M. C. A's.

Instead of buildings and places to which the community is expected to come—but, largely, doesn't come—America needs a community organizer for each group of twenty to two hundred households—in city, town or country.

This community organizer should become acquainted with every member of all the neighborhood families. Without preconceived notions as to the activities to be developed, he should be resourceful, adjustable, with a large repertoire of social activities. He should be familiar with the methods of modern social service; with games, dramatics, vocational developments, educational and philanthropic agencies and with the methods by which resourceful individuals or civic forces may be moved to appropriate action. Among the families with whom he becomes acquainted he will find specific needs to be met and he will stir to action the social agencies appropriate to these needs.

369

For the girls of the community, dramatics, dancing, study and patriotic services should be organized, not neglecting opportunities for wholesome fellowship with boys. Especially, recreation should be emphasized which brings family groups together. For families or households, instead of segregated individuals, should be the units in some of the community's recreations.

Specialists in various fields of social integration may be needed to help the community organizer in the larger communities. Folk dances should be taught to one group of leaders; games, dramatics, orchestral and band music to others. Boy Scouts, Camp Fire Girls, the Women's Suffrage Movement, churches, University Extension and Correspondence courses, parks, community centers, people's forums—and other social service methods or agencies should do their appropriate share toward the organization of the community.

For each group of twenty to two hundred households there might well be a community organizer whose salary and working funds would total about as much as the budget of one of the eight or nine local churches—(which probably reach an average of less than one hundred families each and have comparatively small effect upon the lives of even this small number of the least needy people).

One danger which a community organizer should avoid is the danger of officialism, the danger that men and women who should be the volunteer leaders or centers of neighborhood groups will leave the employed organizer to serve alone. That would mean that the community organizer would soon have his entire time and resourcefulness occupied by a few definite clubs or organizations. Instead, he should aim constantly to make himself a disappearing quantity, to enlist volunteer leaders and to establish activities so that they will go along of themselves, while he passes on to the inauguration of others.

Here is the basic principle;—as the scientist begins with the life and material which occupy his field and works with the laws and tendencies he discovers, so we should begin, not with preconceived institutions into which the people are to be fitted, but with the people themselves. We must first know the people, all the people, the boys, girls, youths, men and women, and know them, not as segregated classes and not as individuals alone, but in families and in other natural groups. The instincts and desires of these neighbors, their possibilities and powers of social service, their relationships and aversions, must be followed out into activities which fit the people and give them the self-expression they desire.

Leisure time is clearly the key to the situation. "Recreation" simply means attractive leisure-time activities. A large contribution which the Playground and Recreation Association of America makes is through its emphasis on recreation or leisure-time organization. Other social service agencies have been too serious-minded; they have overlooked the fact that leisure time is the only time which the people have left and that recreation, with its emphasis upon social coordination and upon the expression of natural human instincts, is the key to the development of life more abundant in any community. Our War Camp Community Service must not lack any of this vision, any of this wisdom bred of experience, which has characterized the Playground and Recreation Association of America.

V.

Lorado Taft, the social-visioned sculptor, summarized these suggestions of community organization in the following letter to his immediate neighbors on a dead-end street which runs only a block and a half from Jackson Park to the Illinois Central Railway. When Mr. Taft discussed this letter with a group of us at his home, he had not yet decided to send it out. Do you think he should?

"I have been thinking of the lost art of neighborliness. The pioneers in our little, sawed-off street tell me that once they knew everybody here and that they had a happy community life of their own.

"I have lived in my house among you for eight years and know few of you by sight. I have a nodding acquaintance with certain celebrities across the street and a much prized friendship with my immediate neighbors; the rest are merely good-looking strangers. Perhaps the fact that, these days, I am working at my studio from 8 a. m. to 10:30 p. m. may explain in part, if it does not excuse my neglect!

"The other day I remarked to my wife that we were certainly fortunate in having such friends as the Riggs and the Childs, on either side of us. She agreed heartily but informed me that the Childs were moving away! Isn't that just like life?

"After a fit interval of silent mourning, I had another thought; if the rest of the people in this street are as nice as these—and the Smiths and the Codys—we are losing a great deal by not knowing them.

371

"(Business of profound cogitation)

" 'Let's get acquainted.'

" 'Perhaps they do not care to.'

" 'Let's try anyway.'

"Now, the sensible, normal thing would be, having taken this resolution, to start out and call at each house and flat and—see what happened.

"But I have not time to do this until next September when my big job will be done—and nothing more in sight— and, besides, the old man still retains somewhat of boyish bashfulness; I don't know what you would do to me! You might think I was trying to run for Alderman or soliciting aid for the Lake Shore Drive, or who knows what! Besides Ada Bartlett, my comfortable little wife, is even busier than I—and thinks I am funny anyway.

"I guess there is no doubt about the correctness of her judgment, for I have just had this absurd idea. Let's have a basket picnic and see if we cannot get acquainted! We of our sacred enclosure, I mean. If it goes well, Jackson Park, at our door is the place to have it; but for the first time—just to make sure that we do not forget it, let's sweep clean that west end of our protected little street and set our table right there in the presence of our enemy, the Illinois Central, and eat salad and cinders in sweet converse.

"When?

"The first warm pleasant evening.

"If we need an excuse, we can call it a farewell to the Childs and others who are leaving us.

"Thus we can bring 'flowers to the funeral,' even if we have never paid such attention to the living!

"Awful thought; maybe all the rest of you are acquainted and play whist together every night. Maybe I am the only deliquent. Then *wouldn't* my cheery proposition come with good grace?

"If so, please forget my effort at neighborliness and let me subside, concealing my retreat under appropriate blushes."

Can such community organization go far, last long, or even begin at all, in most communities, without employed, professional leadership? I think not. To supply such leadership—with vision, resourcefulness and organizing power, with adequate time for the work, and with the help of specialists in various departments— this is the opportunity and obligation of the Playground and Recreation Association of America—now, through the War Camp Community Service and, after the war, in Community Organization, as distinguished from Institutionalism, for every city, town and rural region in America.

WAR CAMP COMMUNITY SERVICE

Launched as a drive for $170,000,000, the United War Work campaign became in its early stages a drive for $250,000,000, a figure the forces in the field set for themselves as the minimum amount they would consider as a sum that took them over the top.

The campaign, scheduled to begin Monday morning, November 11 and end Monday, November 18, united seven war work organizations. As approved by the representatives of the government at Washington, the budget of $170,500,000 was divided as follows:

Young Men's Christian Association....................$100,000,000
Young Women's Christian Association................ 15,000,000
National Catholic War Council (including Knights of
    Columbus) 30,000,000
War Camp Community Service...................... 15,000,000
Jewish Welfare Board............................... 3,500,000
American Library Association........................ 3,500,000
Salvation Army..................................... 3,500,000

It was realized that these budgets made necessary a curtailment of many features of the essential work being done by the seven organizations. No sooner was the campaign projected into the field than there arose a demand that the United War Work Campaign be made one that signified the intention of the American people to "stick by the boys to the end."

It was with the approval of President Wilson that the announcement was made to the country that the minimum aimed for was $250,000,000. So many states rallied to this readjusted figure that it was made the definite goal.

The United War Work Campaign is the first drive in which there has been a complete union of the forces that have been ministering to the mental, moral, spiritual and material needs of the soldier, sailor and marine in and out of camp. It was this union of forces that early made it evident that the home folks were really insistent that there be no "tapering off" as far as essential war work was concerned. Every one of the seven organizations was therefore able to get into the drive on the theory that America was determined not only to see the war through but likewise determined that the hour of victory should find the American public quite as attentive to the essential needs of the millions of men in the national service as it had been during the dark hours of the war. For that reason the United War Work Campaign became a "victory drive" bent upon maintaining for the days of peace the morale so potent from the beginning in the task of winning the war.

May Pole, Grammar School,
Freehold, N. J.

Fifth Grade,
Woodstown, N. J.

Public School No. 51,
New York City.

Teachers' Class,
Springfield, Mo.

The Victor *serves* indoors, outdoors, winter or summer, rain or shine, in work or play

The Victor in the schools is "An ever present help in time of trouble" in every phase of school work. Always ready, never weary, pleasing and serving little children, big children, teachers and parents alike.

Christmas with the boys in the trenches is just a bit hard to contemplate, but the lives of the children must not be darkened by the War Cloud. The Victrola will brighten many gloomy hours if it is systematically used. Is there any other single thing that can do so much, please so many, and contribute so richly to education?

For full information, write

Educational Department
Victor Talking Machine Co.
Camden, N. J.

"HIS MASTER'S VOICE"

To insure Victor quality, always look for the famous trademark, "His Master's Voice." It is on all products of the Victor Talking Machine Company.

Victrola XXV, $90
specially manufactured
for School use

When the Victrola is not in use, the horn can be placed under the instrument safe and secure from danger, and the cabinet can be locked to protect it from dust and promiscuous use by irresponsible people.

Victrola

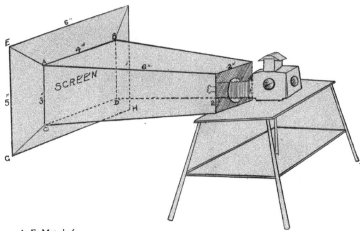

A. E. Metzdorf

STEREOPTICON SCREEN FOR USE OUT-OF-DOORS IN
BROAD DAYLIGHT

A. B. C. D.—Screen through which picture is shown. To be made of transparent
white tracing cloth. 3′x4′.

E. F. G. H.—Projection out beyond screen into which audience looks. Screen
to be at least 2 ft. back into the projection and 5′ from the lantern,
the whole 8ft. long. The sides of the projector are of heavy black
cloth tacked to a frame and fastened together by screen door hooks.

Los Angeles, California

THREE RACES—MEXICAN, WHITE, NEGRO—PLAYING WITH
BUILDING BLOCKS ON A PUBLIC PLAYGROUND

The Playground

Vol. XII No. 9   DECEMBER 1918

The World at Play

Works for Recreation in Russia.—Graham Romeyn Taylor, former Secretary of the Chicago Playground Association, and one of the leaders in the national recreation movement, has just returned to Russia, planning to do all he can to stimulate the play movement in Russia. He has asked that a special exhibit be prepared to aid the Russian people in their community and recreation developments. It is hoped that the public schools of Russia may become centers of community organization for democracy.

Play in the National Parks. —Mr. and Mrs. C. M. Goethe, passing through Canada, write of a well developed national recreation center in connection with the government's Rocky Mountain National Park. Mr. and Mrs. Goethe came as they left the forest trail rather suddenly upon a group of Canadian children at play in the park.

. Letters are continually received from friends of the Association telling how the play idea is taking possession of the national and state, as well as local government agencies. Mr. Goethe found a central recreational center with a big fire place all around the main hall and with a kitchen area for picnic parties, many of which come from Calgary and other points. More and more, the national governments are working in terms of the happiness of their people.

Gift Playground in Newburgh, N. Y.—Mrs. Frederic Delano Hitch presented a recreation park to the citizens of Newburgh, as "a community center dedicated for the recreation of every man, woman and child in Newburgh regardless of race, color or creed." Appropriate dedication exercises were held at which the Mayor accepted the park for the people and a flag was run up on the new flag pole presented by the manager of the Newburgh ship yards.

Mrs. Hitch has been an active supporter of the field workers of the Playground and Recreation Association of America in their efforts in Newburgh.

His War Garden.—"Mon-

375

day—Worked in the garden all day, raking, hoeing, spading.

"Tuesday—Worked in the garden two hours after luncheon.

"Wednesday—Worked in the garden fifteen minutes then went to a ball game.

"Thursday—Went out after dinner and walked around the garden.

"Friday—Looked out of the kitchen window to see if the garden was still there.

"Saturday—Forgot all about it."

And we might add Sunday—took one more look at it, saw how dried up and brown it was, how the bugs had eaten everything; and even the few tomatoes that had set were "measley, dried up specimens," and decided it wasn't worth while. If Monday's example had been followed through the week, Sunday's reflections would have been entirely different.—Extract from Forest Hills (N. Y.) Bulletin.

Children's Dramatics.—The children of the Forest Hills, N. Y., Playground gave two performances of *The Spirit of Autumn,* a little play telling the story of a country boy who grew tired of digging and hoeing, and so decided to go to the city. But, the spirit of Autumn with her children, Potato, Apple, Corn, Berry, Wheat, Grass and Pumpkin come to visit him. They

tell him their ideas of the city and thus make him soon change his mind and decide to stay in the country.

The proceeds from the play and lemonade table amounted to $14.22. This was turned into the Playground Fund to buy a basketball and football.

"The Torchbearers."—The patriotic pageant written by Miss Lotta A. Clark, of Boston, has been successfully produced in a number of war camp communities. In Houston, Texas, soldiers were admitted free and the general verdict was "the finest thing of the kind ever given in Houston." The Minneapolis performance by the Civic Players for the benefit of the Jewish War Relief Association and the Women's Council of National Defense enlisted over a thousand participants and netted $12,000 for the beneficiaries. Moving pictures of the pageant are being sent through the West.

All England "Blighty" for American Lads.—A widespread impulse of hospitality has thrown English homes open to Americans on leave or convalescent. Information bureaus arrange for invitations to be conveyed to the visitors. Many English people whose sons have fallen fill the vacant chairs with American guests. Clubs and organizations of all sorts vie with each

376

other in providing athletics and other entertainment for the lads from across the seas.

Wanted—S o n g s.—Admiral Rogers has suggested to Mr. Jackson of the Navy Department Commission on Training Camp Activities that songs be written for the navy inculcating the national objectives in the different lines of the navy's effort in the Great War. The objectives Admiral Rogers sets forth as:

Transport of American troops and munitions

Transport of allied supplies (food, etc.)

Deprivation of enemy of necessary supplies

Freedom of the seas and sailors' rights

The methods by which these objectives are to be attained are:

Defeat in battle of German high seas fleet

Blockade of German coasts

Destruction of U-boats

Admiral Rogers feels that if these ideas could be put into catch words and music, it would be a great advantage for naval education and morale.

Boxing Required. — Boxing has become so important a feature of the life of one camp that the Colonel has issued orders that every officer in his command must take the boxing course.

Officers as Song Leaders.—Commanding officers at many of the camps have issued orders making periods of instruction in singing as compulsory as military drill. They are even modifying drill schedules for this purpose. As the following order indicates, officers are being detailed as song leaders:

"1. The Commanding General directs that each Infantry and Artillery Regiment in this camp detail an officer to act as 'Regimental song officer,' also, that one officer be detailed in each company who will act as the company song officer.

"2. All regimental and song officers as detailed under the provisions of this order will report to —, Army Song Leader, at Y. M. C. A. building 605, in the 10th Inf. area, at 11:00 a. m., Monday, the 16th inst.

"By command of Brigadier General—."

The Future of W. C. C. S.

R. S. Hubbard, War Camp Community Service representative at Rochester, New York, writes of the meaning of the work: "Sometimes when we are inclined to feel that the part we are playing in this great fight for a great principle is not the biggest thing we can do, I wonder if we all realize the permanency and far-reaching effect of the community work we are engaged in. Most of our men in service will return after the war, to take their places in community life, fired by higher ideals and trained to fight for principles they had given little thought to before. It is a source of inspiration to know that just as we are now putting behind our men an organization that is increasing their morale, so then after other war activities have ceased, *we* shall *continue* to put behind them an organization *already prepared* to back them in their fight for a more virile, civic conscience."

The Muse to His Aid

A woman who has been helping in one of the War Camp Community Service clubs received the following poem from one of the soldiers who is serving in the Aviation section of the army:

When I am feeling lonesome,
And the world just looks all blue,
Right then I hie myself away,

Making straight a path towards you.
Only one step through the doorway,
Then your smiling face I see,
Having its wealth of sunshine,
Ever ready to greet lone me.
Really! I thank God for the blessing,

Of sending you to us boys,

May he always be most gracious,
In filling your life with joys.
Need I add more lines to convince you,
Every word is sincere and true,

And written for just this reason
My Mother is like you too.

Adult Recreation as a Social Problem*

EDWARD ALSWORTH ROSS, University of Wisconsin

The increasing poverty of modern employments in elements which stimulate the instincts accounts for the amazing growth in our time of the passion of recreation. What the "stale" worker covets is not *rest*; else why not lounge away his holiday on his back porch? Nor is *change of activity* all he craves; else why does not the hotel clerk spend his vacation as stevedore, the physician as teamster or piano-mover? If it is relaxation he is after, why does not the tired brain-worker spend his summer holidays in gymnasium, bowling alley, and shooting gallery? No, what ails the slave of desk and clock, of client and customer, is what ails the horse pawing in his stall, the wolf restlessly pacing his cage. *He needs experience that will feed his famishing instincts.* Hence the great recipe for recreation is "back to nature"—raw nature, so rich in simple and racially familiar things! In a wilderness trip the novice thinks it is the big outstanding features that do him good—canoe paddling, swimming, fishing, or shooting rapids. The fact is, most of his benefit comes from a lot of little things which he scarcely notices, but which register in his subconscious mind. Such are green-clad hills, tossing seas of verdure, the sparkle of sunlight on stirring leaves and rippling water, the mirror magic of still lakes, the soughing in pine tops, the shadow dance of sun falling through foliage, the challenge of precipitous trails, the sense of little peering furry creatures all about one. Thick woods, darkness, and queer night noises stir the wild self in us just enough to afford a delicious tingle. The fact that after a night passed close to lapping waves or a waterfall one wakes fresher than after a still night may mean that the subconscious self was recognizing grateful sounds. Anyhow, from sleep in a hotel near to train sheds or to a busy traffic corner one wakes weary.

Stimulating Deep-Seated Instincts The priceless gift a summer camp offers to city boys is not fresh air and exercise so much as the stimulating of deep-seated instincts, which find no outlet in the regular round of home, school, and street. It is full of challenge to the prying, roving, hunting, collecting,

---

Courtesy of Social Hygiene and University of Chicago Press.

379

contriving, and vying tendencies. The woods appeal to youth as catnip does to cats. "I have often," says Professor Puffer, "in taking cross-country walks with boys attempted to switch out from among the trees into open meadows or pasture land to save distance. Over and over again, however, have the boys protested. " 'No, don't. Let's stay in the woods,' they have entreated."

One who watches himself closely learns that very little things get a rise out of his original nature. Plodding through a drizzle is depressing, but there is exhilaration in battling a gusty rainstorm or blizzard. The canoeist notices the adverse waves by rousing his fighting instinct are easier to paddle against than a current or a head wind. The angler cares more for fly-casting and bait-casting than for still-fishing, because a thrill in him answers the "strike" of the fish. This is why he seeks out the "gamy" species, that seize his lure with a rush and fight hard when hooked.

Certain vices get much of their power from men's desperate desire to escape from the humdrum of a life bare of recreation. Says the Philippine Opium Commission:

What people on earth are so . . . destitute of amusement as the Chinese, both rich and poor? There are no outdoor games in China, or, indeed, any games except in a gambling sense. Absolute dullness and dreariness seem to prevail everywhere. As these two demons drive the Caucasian to drink, so they drive the Chinese to opium. As an individual may by habitual toil and attention to business become incapable of amusement, so a race of almost incredibile antiquity, which has toiled for millenniums, may likewise reach a point in its development where the faculty of being amused has atrophied and disappeared, so that all that remains is the desire to spend leisure in placidity. And nothing contributes so much to this as opium.

To Do—Not to Look On That morally the bullfight has been a millstone tied about the neck of the Spaniards, Mexicans, and Peruvians is doubted by no one who has ever seen it. In the beginning it was a knightly sport, but with the coming on of generations which had drunk in the gory sights of the bullring almost with their mother's milk it degenerated. Today the onlooking multitude shows a quite depraved taste for seeing living flesh torn and blood gush out. The riding out of blindfolded old horses for the bull to vent his rage upon is obviously no part of the fight, but a sop to the bloodthirst of the crowd. The devotees of the bullfight insist that it fosters "manliness," but what is the manliness of the spectators who from their safety cry, "Nearer!" to the *matador,* compared with that of the aviator or mountain climber who seeks his thrills by risking *his own* life, not that of another? Noting the children about the bullring, noting how even the boys in the street play bull and *matador,* one preceives why the history of so fine a strain as the Celt-Iberian is stained with mistreatment of domestic animals, the use of torture, cruelty to the fallen foe, and ruthlessness to political adversaries. A few years ago a Mexican governor addressed his people with the prophetic words: "Diaz is old. When he is gone, what will happen? I say as long as your recreation centers in the bullfight, so long as your little boys and mothers with babes at breast flock to these places, so long will Mexico be a land of revolutions. While the strong hand of Diaz still supports you, commence now to find a substitute in character-building recreation."

The prize ring differs from the arena in that the combatants are free men and their weapons not deadly. It appeals, however, to instincts as primitive as those which found satisfaction in the duels of gladiators. President G. Stanley Hall testifies:

In witnessing great pugilistic contests, which I sometimes permit myself to do as a student of human nature, the three surprises are: first, my own tense and absorbing interest that makes me want to shout and yell like a wild Indian as the rest do and perhaps leap into the ring; second, a kind of cathartic refreshment after the brainstorm, which like a thunderstorm clears the air; and third, that I see so many other respectable people there whom I know, but who do not wish me to recognize them.

Refreshment from indulgence in old prehistoric states of mind there is, no doubt, but, were the prize ring open to children and youth, it would brutalize as the bullring brutalized. What keeps pugilistic encounters from becoming rougher than they actually are appears to be, not the squeamishness of their devotees, but the sentiment of the outside public. The disgust of "fight fans" at a "tame" bout, their joy in "bare knuckles" and a fight "to the finish," indicate that but for society's veto a revival of gladiatorial combats would be a money-making venture in the great cities of today.

In the conflict type of recreation it makes a great difference morally whether a man gets the sharp tang of excitement by

381

struggling himself or by watching others struggle. In the latter case he is a spectator, not a player, and has his elation without effort, pain, or danger. But so fine a thing ought not to be had on such easy terms. It is the man willing to put on the gloves and "take punishment" who has earned the right to enjoy the boxing of others. The chief reason why national sport degenerates is that, after people have become lazy and soft, they will not make their own fun, but have it catered, allowing to be spilled the cheap blood of beasts, slaves, criminals, captives, gladiators and *toreadors,* because they are too canny to risk their own skins.

The parasitic onlooker is to blame. for the monstrous and demoralizing excess that presently shows itself in sport. The amateur sportsman is held back from such excess by the price he pays in danger and pain. The spectator knows no such curb; dulled by familiarity, he demands sights ever more sensational and shocking to thrill his jaded nerves. Thus in the course of two centuries the Roman populace became gluttons for blood. At a single spectacle Trajan produced eleven thousand animals, while Claudius staged a sea fight in which nineteen thousand gladiators butchered one another till the waters of the lake were red!

Among us, multitudes who want, not to *play,* but to be *amused,* participate by inner imitation in the contests of professionals when they should be at games of their own. One who hunts, fishes, canoes, rows, sails, climbs, golfs, or skiis, despises these flabby athletes by proxy. The "fan" who is nothing else is a hanger-on of the play of others. Least athletic of men, he never plays at anything himself but is content to be a mere spectacle-hunter. His crowd hysteria and partisanship disgust true sportsmen and throw sport into the hands of those who play for the money there is in it.

Suppression Alone Fails to Eliminate Demoralizing Sports For dealing with demoralizing sports and amusements there are three policies—viz., *suppression, substitution,* and *sublimation.*

No policy has been so thoroughly tried out as *suppression.* Religion naturally dreads whatever unleashes the beast in man and hence has taken a critical attitude toward recreations. The early Christians turned with horror from the arena. The mediaeval church sought to solve the problem of popular recreation by herself providing pageants, plays, festivals, and like means of brightening the drab existence of the masses. The Puritans uprooted the old loose communal diversions of "merrie" England, closed the playhouses, and destroyed the people's pleasure fields. Macaulay's gibe that they stopped the bear-baiting, "not because it gave pain to the bear, but because it gave pleasure to the spectators," will equally fit the foes of bullfighting, cockfighting, or any other demoralizing sport, for they are more shocked by the lowering of men than the suffering of animals. Various Protestant groups long ago took alarm at the moral flareback from recreations and proceeded to lay their ban on gambling, dancing, the theatre, the circus, and the novel.

Such a yoke may be assumed by the elect, but it cannot be imposed on the people as a whole. Even the religious groups have had to give up much of their old-time strictness. Instead of recreation being cut down in volume, there is every reason to anticipate that it will greatly expand. As our daily occupations become more specialized, more methodical, more routinary, fall completely under "scientific management" and lose much of their creative gladness, as the hotter pace of modern life brings upon the higher brain centers a constant and severe strain which must be offset by longer intervals of rest and relaxation, the demand for recreation will become more general, more imperious, and more justified.

Substitution of Higher Forms The substitution policy goes on the theory that for every low and demoralizing sport some fine and wholesome substitute may be found which will in the end prove just as satisfying. This in turn rests on the psychological principle that each of our tendencies may be brought into play by a variety of situations. Detective stories and Boy Scout maneuvers afford gratification to the hiding and hunting instincts, as well as playing *It* or *I spy*. Marchings, crew rowing, and choral singing give the pleasure of rhythm no less than seesaw and dancing. Our political contests certainly stir and refresh us, and if the Romans had stayed democratic, as the Athenians did, they would have hankered less for bloody games. Patriotic festivals, political barbecues, and ecstatic religious revivals are as truly emotional "sprees" as prize fights and lynchings, besides being innocent.

The experience of the last fifteen years opens a wonderful vista for substitution in the sphere of sports. The thirty-three hundred supervised playgrounds in the United States, looked after by eight thousand professional leaders and supervisors, have weaned great numbers of lads from mischief-making, broken up "tough" gangs, and overcome slum tendencies, athletic contests

have driven the bullfight from Hispanic peoples under American influence. The Filipinos are finding their excitement about the baseball diamond rather than the cockpit: the chocolate-colored Malay
lads took to playing our national game and talking its slang before
they were able to speak English. Under the lead of American officials the wild Igorrotes of Luzon have learned to divert themselves
with athletic contests and dancing instead of head-hunting. At
first the savage bystander would stone the too-skilful pitcher of a
visiting team and match games often broke up in a free fight;
but the onlooking Americans and the police checked such tendencies
and now the Igorrotes are said to be good sportsmen. In China,
as opium smoking declines, sport comes in with a rush and thousands of Chinese make long journeys by train in order to attend
the national meets. In the light of experience it does not seem
rash to anticipate that bullfight and cockfight, opium debauch and
vinous "spree," every ghoulish orgy of religious fanaticism and
every obscene or bloody rite in Asiatic temples, may be displaced
in a generation or two by ball games and track meet, folk-dancing
and symbolic pageants, if only in public supervised recreation
centers all the children are bred to merry and wholesome plays.

Sublimation Lifts Sport into Art   *Sublimation* occurs when the original demands
of our natures accept purely imaginative grat-
ification or become blent with culture elements.
This leads to the enjoyment of art, which is quite a different outlet from play. Music touches and rouses instinct after instinct, but
not in a way to threaten the poise of the civilized man. In the
theatre our emotions are fed with the situations presented by love,
war, diplomacy, crime, adventure, and politics. The flight instinct,
after childhood quite suppressed in real life, causes us to hang
breathlessly upon the motion-picture representation of the hunted
animal or hunted man. The maternal instinct is stirred by the
representation of the waif, the hapless victim, the stricken hero.
The well-made plot of novel or drama is a challenge to the instinct
of curiosity, like a puzzle or a riddle. The fighting spirit is never
neglected, for, in the language of President Hall, "Every drama
and romance pivots on a conflict ending in the triumph of one
and the defeat of the other force or person, and the zest of it
all is that the conflict is more intense and the issues more clearly
drawn and palpable than in real life about us."

There are signs that society, which has recently been converted
to the policy of making provisions for play, may yet be brought

to do something for music and art. Municipal bands and orchestras are not uncommon, and the Puritan horror of the theatre is nearly gone. Educators recognize the socializing power of good drama, and a stage is often provided in the newer school building. The social settlements have taken a hand in producing good plays, and their successors, the public social centers, may offset the evil tendncies of the commercial theatre.

Perhaps half a century hence it will be as much a matter of course for the community to maintain public playground, recreation field, and stage as now it is a matter of course for it to maintain a public school. For if it is wise for society to care to feed the intellect, why is it not equally wise to provide the agencies which tend to preserve a balance between primitive cravings and the humane and social feelings?

Suggestions and Proposed Regulations for Soldier, Sailor, and Marine Dances

Dancing makes its appeal, not only as good exercise, and as a necessary factor of education, but also as a socializing recreation, and its most essential and elusive quality is joy—the quality that has the power to interest and unify people of all ages and nationalities.
Mary Wood Hinman

The following suggestions and regulations submitted by Miss Mary Wood Hinman, of Chicago, have been found of value in the conduct of dances in some of the cities engaged in War Camp Community Service. They are printed with the idea that they may be helpful to other cities.

REGULATIONS

(1) DRESS: Afternoon gowns—bright colors preferable. No transparent waists or low cut evening gowns

(2) DANCING POSITION: Woman's left hand on partner's *arm only*

(3) TIME: Hours of opening and closing should conform to the time of the men's leave. It has been found best to close evening parties between eleven and twelve o'clock.

SUGGESTIONS

HALL: The hall should be large, well ventilated and well lighted with no dark corners or dimly lighted side-rooms. A hall 40′ x 60′ will accommodate 50 couples; the number of persons should never exceed the seating capacity of the hall. It has been found advantageous to limit the average party to 150 couples or less.

A sufficient number of chairs should be provided for all guests.

An adjacent room for smoking may well be provided whenever possible. Smoking should not be permitted in the room where the dance is being held.

When possible a room adjoining the dance hall should be provided for the use of those who do not dance, where games may be played, or a class formed for those desiring to learn to dance. A volunteer dancing teacher can readily be secured to take charge of this work.

Dressing rooms and toilets for both men and women should be conveniently situated.

CHECKING OF WRAPS: A good checking system is necessary, as uniforms can be confused easily. One or two experienced attendants should be in charge. All hats and wraps of both men and women should be checked. Hats should be fastened securely to coats or extra hat check issued. A printed check in duplicate is suggested. It has been found helpful to use a celluloid button for the young women because they have no place to keep checks.

No re-admission or return checks should be permitted.

WRAPS: It is suggested that no one be permitted on the dance floor with coat, hat or wraps. The habit of wearing hats at dances gives the appearance of a commercialized dance, hotel or tea dance, and we are striving to give something beyond price—home hospitality.

The custom of spectators looking on from ante rooms, wearing street costumes is to be discouraged, as it suggests the commercial dance hall.

ORGANIZATION: All forms of entertainment, including dances, should be organized to be as regular as circumstances permit, if the best results are to be secured. The chairman, the hostesses, the chaperons, the young girl guests need systematic training to do their part efficiently. All have a definite part to play in any well organized party, and accumulated experience is the ingredient needed to insure. only constructive results upon the men. Sustained, carefully guided, well organized recreation, brings about the best results. The strain of a party coming every week is too great for any one individual to carry. Therefore sustained entertainments in the way of dances, or games for uniformed men, when given to groups of from 25 to 150, are most easily handled, and have the best results when given by organizations.

The following outline offers a good working basis for the giving of dances by an organization and gives a clear statement of the responsibilities and privileges of all participants.

The president of the organization giving the party may appoint a chairman, who is responsible for the entire party. Since she is responsible for the success of the party she should be an energetic, tactful woman, not afraid of hard work and one who works easily with women. She may find it desirable to appoint to assist her a sub-chairman on refreshments. This chairman is absolutely responsible for everything in the way of refreshments and selects her own committee. Refreshments of orangeade, ice cream, cake, cookies or sandwiches are very popular, and when possible it is desirable to serve hot chocolate, cocoa or coffee. It is well when possible to have a choice of coffee and chocolate, or coffee and milk. At one club where a choice of coffee and chocolate was offered, the chocolate pot was emptied three times to one of the coffee. Many of the boys are young and have not been allowed coffee in their own homes, and chocolate or milk means home diet to them. Fresh drinking water should be accessible at all times. In all probability the chairman will wish to appoint a sub-chairman on music who is responsible for everything in the way of music, and appoints her own committee. Good music with even rhythm is essential. Loud and blatant music encourages boisterousness and therefore should be avoided. A "jazz" band atmosphere should be tabooed. A good program to observe is to have the dances from four to five minutes long, including encores, followed by two-minutes intermission.

The chairman also selects two small groups, to serve on the floor or reception committee. One committee may consist of two women and one man who remain in the dance hall and promote the good time of the party in every way possible. The other small group may consist of two women and a man who are stationed outside the dance hall to receive the guests as they come to the building. They show the young people where to place their wraps, they prevent undesirable guests from obtaining admission; they see that the guest tickets are taken up, if this is the desire of the hostess, and they also see to it that the guests register, if this is desired.

If the party is given for 50 to 100 men, the chairman appoints five hostesses. These hostesses in turn each invite two women (thus making ten women) who will act as chaperons. Each chaperon will bring to the party either five or ten girls as the hostess dictates. These young girls must be known to her personally and selected because she feels them well fitted for service of this kind, and each girl is directly responsible for her conduct to her chaperon. Each of the ten chaperons inviting five girls will make a party of fifty girls. (Should 100 be required, each chaperon would bring ten girls). Should a greater number than this be desired, the guests may be increased by augmenting the number of hostesses originally invited and through them the chaperons.

RESPONSIBILITY OF PARTICIPANTS: The chairman is responsible for the entire party. She is the supreme hostess. It is her responsibility to see that every hostess, chaperon and young girl guest knows her respective duty. It is her pleasure to keep them posted on every suggestion coming from headquarters and to stimulate and guide them. It would be well if she suggest to the chaperons and hostesses the inadvisability of standing in little groups or looking preoccupied with their knitting, and suggest that each one join in the activities and further the hospitable and social spirit of the party, keeping the guests of the evening and their pleasure ever uppermost in their minds.

The hostess is responsible for the good time of the *men*. It is her pleasure and duty to see that every man has a partner or is not repeatedly urged to dance when that is not his wish. She introduces the men to her chaperon when this seems the friendly thing to do, although no chaperon, hostess or young girl guest should hold back from any act of hospitality for lack of this formality. Every young man, however, likes to be introduced by name when possible—his individuality is taken from him so thoroughly by his uniform, that it is a pleasure to him to be individualized. This should be borne in mind at all times.

The chaperon has the care and is responsible for the conduct of her young girl guests, and is required to remain until all the girls in her charge leave the hall. She must see that each girl dances a fair number of times and is not left out or overlooked. On the other hand she must see that certain girls do not dance too often with the same young man. To accomplish this tactfully takes the social gift. Therefore the chaperon should be chosen with this in view.

SUGGESTIONS AND REGULATIONS FOR DANCES

Young women may be requested to come to the party with their chaperons and to return home with them.

Young women may return to their chaperons at the end of each dance, should they so desire. This helps to relieve the situation when the young man has not acquired enough social technique to release himself at the end of a dance.

Admittance for the young women should be by card issued for the given date and not transferable.

It has been found advisable that young women taking part should be twenty years or over.

An effort should be made to have an equal number of men and women.

The chaperon must be sure that the regulations and suggestions made by the War Camp Community Service regarding position in dancing, the request about hats and the necessity of remaining absolutely quiet during the playing of the National Hymn have been made clear to every girl in her little group of five or ten.

The hostesses and the chaperons should possess the faculty of seeing possibilities in their guests that they hardly realize themselves, and of bringing the right people together with a "send-off" that will make them friends.

Young girl guests may come to the parties unattended if it is still light but arrangements must be made for the return home, as the men in uniform are not supposed to fulfill this duty. Because the girls live at varying distances and the men have limited hours of leave, it has been found best to install the custom of the young girl guest going home with her chaperon, or of having her parents or escort call for her at the close of the party.

It has been found helpful to bring the young women together at a luncheon or tea before the dance and talk over with them the matter of dancing position, dress and other details; or they may be informed either by letter or through their chaperons.

It is desirable to have these parties as near the type of the private party as possible and the young ladies are expected to give the same attention to all the young men as they would do if their mothers were giving the party.

In the event of any young woman unwittingly disregarding the requirements, her attention must be called to it by the chaperon responsible for her.

Following is a copy of a good card of admission for the use of chaperons and young girl guests.

BLOOMVILLE WAR CAMP COMMUNITY SERVICE

DANCE

at 15th Regiment Armory, Main Street

Admit...

as chaperon

Invited by...

Hostess

Date................   7 to 11:30 o'clock

(over)

Reverse

Every Chaperon is responsible for the conduct of her girls. Every Chaperon is required to remain until all girls in her charge leave the hall.

BLOOMVILLE   WAR   CAMP   COMMUNITY   SERVICE

KHAKI AND BLUE DANCE

15th Regiment Armory, Main Street

Admit as...

Dancing Guest

Invited by...

Chaperon

Date..................   7 to 11:30 o'clock

(over)

Reverse

NO ADMISSION WITHOUT TICKET

Please report to chaperon when entering and leaving the hall. Kindly check your hat and wraps, write your name on back of your hat check and give it to your chaperon.

DIRECTORS: It is well to have a director responsible for the dance itself. This director may be supplied by the chairman of the volunteer Dancing Teachers' War Service which may be a sub-committee of the hostess committee.

SUGGESTIONS AND REGULATIONS FOR DANCES

Men not in uniform are expected to remain off the dancing floor unless invited to dance by the Floor Committee.

Any irregularity occurring upon the floor should be reported to the director, not to the hostess or chaperon, nor to the person offending.

Should the irregularity occur among the men, the director will adjust the matter directly with the man, but should it occur among the young women, the director will speak to the young woman's chaperon.

Directors should see that the entrance and doorways are kept clear, and spectators—as far as possible—should not be permitted.

A director may have two assistants who may introduce cotillion figures most successfully, and games whereby new partners are found—to prevent one couple dancing too many times in succession.

MISCELLANEOUS SUGGESTIONS: The introduction of novel features promotes sociability and friendliness.

It has been found convenient for both men and women to wear small cards bearing their names legibly written.

The Flag Game has been found most helpful in promoting the sociability of the dancing parties. As the guests enter the hall, three little paper flags are pinned on them which they are told they will forfeit if they say "yes" or "no" to anyone during the evening. This instantly results in a ready excuse to speak to one another in an endeavor to secure as many flags as possible. (The little flags may be procured at any five and ten cent store by the hundred.) This game may be played also by giving each guest four pins; anyone using the word "I" forfeits a pin to the one being addressed.

It has always been found helpful to introduce a program of general singing for ten or fifteen minutes, not longer, and when possible to display the words of the songs on a screen or blackboard. Song leaflets should, if possible, be supplied.

Dancing contests for proper position are popular, or dancing contests for rhythm. It is well also to introduce short amateur specialties to bring out the talent of the group.

A pleasant way to meet the hostess is by a general march after all are assembled, marshalled by ushers, directed by the committee or director.

Many succcessful parties close with the National Anthem, and during the playing of the anthem, every person in the room stands at attention facing the music. Every young girl is specially requested by her chaperon to stand without moving.

Cotillion figures furnish an attractive feature for dancing parties. The following are simple ones :

1. Single circle: grand right and left. At signal, dance with the one whom you are with.

2. March in fours: two outside lines take one step out: two inside lines face and make arches. Outside lines forward march, meet in couples and march under arches to end of line, then dance. When outside lines have passed through arches dance together.

3. Couples march in circle. At signal men right about face, girls continue marching forward and all continue marching. At second signal, dance with opposite.

4. Even number of couples on both sides of room, facing forward. Girls from both lines forward march and grand right and left down opposite lines of men.

5. Men on one side of room, girls on other: (men with backs turned). Girls, forward and take a partner.

6. Two circles, one at each end of room. One couple of first circle makes an arch; other circle is led under arch inside of first circle. Dance with opposite.

7. March in eights; circle in eights, grand right and left in own circle.

8. March in fours, separate as though to march in eights. Fours continue half-way down either side of room, come toward each other in center. Grand right and left down the four lines.

9. Basket figure—Two circles, girls inside, men outside. Men make arches, girls circle with hands joined step back under arches. Leader winds line in serpentine. Girls step out and form single circle. Leader unwinds girls, and taking the last girl winds them in again. Dance with opposites.

THE FOLLOWING FIGURES ARE USEFUL WHEN THE FLOOR IS CROWDED

10. Six couples dance. At signal, they find new partners from those seated. Twelve couples are now dancing. Repeat until all are dancing.

11. Lucky number contest. All are given numbers. Every few minutes music is stopped and leader draws six or eight numbers. Those called must be seated; this is repeated until but one couple remains. At an informal afternoon party, this

392

couple is sometimes given boxes of candy which may serve as refreshments for the group.

12. Robber dances. Extra men sometimes given small paper bags which are blown up and burst on the back of the man whose partner he chooses. Girl must be surrendered to new partner.

13. Extra men in center. At signal, all leave present partner and take one nearest.

14. Three Graces. When an extra number of men are present at a party, the following is a good suggestion to keep them interested. All extra men join hands in short lines of three. These lines dash out on the dancing floor and try to surround any one couple by joining themselves into a circle around them. The girl of the couple thus captured must choose a new partner from the circle, and her deserted partner takes his place in the line, and the Three Graces start afresh.

STREET DANCES

A simple, inexpensive way of providing recreation for an unlimited number of uniformed men is to give a street dance. This kind of dance permits the entertaining of large numbers of men but offers much greater problems in chaperonage and supervision. Committees desiring to undertake a street dance should thoroughly understand this. Permission is first obtained from the mayor or council for the use of the street and orders issued for the washing of the street, police direction and the roping off of the space. In selecting the site for the dance try to find a block of asphalt pavement. The lighting of the street is one of the most important factors. This can be done by stringing three or four lights across the street or by having the automobiles block the street at each end and face in with their lights burning. This provides an astonishing amount of light in a simple way. The band is stationed in the center of the block on the porch of one house overlooking the street. The house forms a natural sounding-board and also provides a little shelter for the men from wind. It is advisable to rope off the street. Any man in uniform is invited to dance and civilians, too, provided there is room. The girl question is taken care of as far as possible by the usual hostess methods, and every effort should be made to regulate the dancing. The street dance is one of the best means of entertaining on short notice and gives a surprising amount of pleasure to an unlimited number of participants.

As It Looks to One of the Girls

Mrs. James Madison Bass, of the Social Department of the New York War Camp Community Service, received the following letter from one of the girls who attends the dances for soldiers and sailors:

Dear Mrs. Bass:

You have asked me to tell you something of the spirit in which I attend the Khaki and Blue Dances, given each week by the War Camp Community Service. I suppose it's because I *have* gone every Saturday for almost a year—and because I am just a plain "sure-to-goodness" American girl that you want this letter. Anyhow I know that my feeling about your splendid work is just like that of the other girls who are trying to help you—and that means trying to give some of our Boys a good time in New York.

"To make the boys fit for fighting—and after" is the way Raymond B. Fosdick, in charge of all War Camp recreation work, defines his job. That's why, he says, they have Y. M. C. A. huts and Knights of Columbus shacks in the camps—and moving picture performances and dances and entertainments for the boys.

That's why we girls are glad to attend these War Camp Community dances—to give the lads in khaki and blue some fun, in normal, wholesome surroundings while they are on their "off time."

They are home boys—every one of them. They are the brothers and cousins of girls like us. And because these girls are too far away to entertain the boys, we've got to take their places I have a brother in the Service. He's only nineteen—tall and blond and blue-eyed—just like so many other American crusaders. And I like to feel that some nice girls are doing for him—where he is stationed—just what I'm trying to do for their brothers, here in New York.

I think we all realize this one thing—that the girls are the hostesses at the War Camp dances. That we must make each dance just as much like a big "home party" as we can. That we must be nice to the boys—to all of them, without discrimination.

It's the girls who set the standard. If we allow "twosing"— pairing off—and that sort of thing, the boys will "play up" of course. But—the nicer the parties are, the nicer the boys will be. And the better the time they'll have. That's been proved—not only by the enthusiastic things they say—but by the fact that they come week after week.

One little sailor who came to the first two parties—where he learned to dance—was on the U. S. S. B—. His ship sailed the week after that second dance. One day in July—seven months later—I heard that the B—was back in New York. And the next Saturday the lad was at the dance when the doors opened!

Another sailor wrote to a girl—just before he left for a long trip—"Carry on at those dances. You've no idea what good work you girls are doing."

Oh, there are too many stories to quote—and anyhow the attitude of the boys is an established fact now. The War Camp Community dances have the reputation of being "the best ever"— and I am proud as proud to be even in the tiniest way identified with them.

The question has been brought up: is it fair to the boys to allow them to see the girls home? Of course, they *want* to, and we're proud to have them ask us. But—we also realize that some of them must go long distances afterwards, and then snatch just a few hours' sleep before going on duty in the morning.

We know, too, that the boys are young, and very impressionable. Camp and ship-board life makes even the most level-headed of them high-strung. Many of them don't see girls, except àt the dances. So we have always gone home from the dances with other girls, or our chaperone. And the boys go back to camp or ship, as they came, "with the crowd." We can take care of ourselves, of course, otherwise we wouldn't be invited to the dances. It's for the boys' sake we try to be unselfish.

Perhaps I've talked too much, Mrs. Bass, in my enthusiasm. Perhaps I could have said it all in just one sentence—That I am heart and soul for and with the Khaki and Blue dances— because I am an American girl, because I wear a Service Pin, because I am eager to do my bit "to make the boys fit for fighting—and after!"

Sincerely yours in the service of our America,
ELLEN McLOUGHLIN

War Camp Community Service Among Civil Service Employees

One of the important tasks of the War Camp Community Service representative in Washington has been to aid in improving living conditions for civil service employees. More than 60,000 more clerks were employed during the first year of the war than formerly, most of them young girls from eighteen to twenty-one years of age. Inadequate lodging and lunch facilities, mechanical work assignments, lack of recreation and channels for making new friends combine to lower the morale and in their lonesomeness and ofttimes illness the girls leave the service. Such departures amounted to more than 12,000 in a period of four months—they gave up—not because they were slackers but because the amenities of life provided in such abundance for their brothers in uniform, passed them by.

One of the ways of helping was through the organization of the Government Recreation League with representatives from every department, headed by Major George P. Ahearn, Secretary of the Army War College. Information, suggestions, entertainers are provided, hikes, tennis matches and river trips arranged. Block dancing parties have been popular. The lunch wagon has helped meet the needs of the inner woman and made efficient afternoon work possible. Many club and educational provisions are contemplated for the winter months, making use of school buildings and churches for gathering places.

Community Christmas Celebrations

Again the jingle of the bells of the jolly saint is heard and at this writing it looks as though the happiest Christmas for many years might be celebrated. Something approaching a community Christmas is possible throughout the land. Not all may have elaborate celebrations but through the aid of light and song, drama and dance the atmosphere of good fellowship may be generated

Last Christmas the City Council of Los Angeles presented the Playground Commission with $500.00 for ten Christmas celebrations. The United States Forestry Department presented the trees and local groups looked after each program.

Bloomington, Indiana, enjoyed a series of living pictures with well-known hymns as interludes. The First Christmas, Christmas at Valley Forge, Christmas in Belgium, 1913, and 1917, Christmas in America, 1917, were represented.

San Diego, California, began its cooperation with securing the tree. The Playground Board and the Federal State Societies initiated the idea, the Cuyamaca Water Company gave the tree, the Southern Electrical Company illuminated it and the State Societies decorated it. The Superintendent of Playgrounds with a gas company truck searched the woods for a record-breaking tree and brought back one seventy feet high. Madame Shumann-Heink opened the program with *The Star Spangled Banner*. The various churches of the community held services around the tree on the nights between Christmas and New Years.

La Jolla entertained 1,500 soldiers on the great playground. Lady Gregory's *Hyacinth Halvey* was produced by a cast of soldiers and townspeople at three; athletic and swimming contests were held at four; at five Christmas carols were sung about the tree; at six supper was served to the children in the Community House and to soldiers on the playground and from seven on there was dancing on the tennis courts to the music of a band made up of picked men from Camp Kearny.

Public Recreation—How Furnished and How Supported*

A. A. FISK, formerly Superintendent of Parks, Racine, Wis.

There is at the present time much thought being given to public recreation. Yet, when the definition of the term is requested, we more or less become confused. This I believe is true because public recreation has not yet become standardized in a national way. So for this reason we find every city is a law unto itself. Each city provides its particular brand of recreation; it insists that the community shall accept the brand.

Public recreation is passing through the same stage of development at the present time that public education passed through about a half century ago. The free public school came into being, not with a bang, nor was it altogether accepted—it was to many a new idea. Some people even said that they would not give their children a pauper brand of education. But our educational policies have become standardized in a national way. The free school is everyhere accepted, and furthermore, it is the best type of a school which we have today. This vast system of education is paid for by the people. These institutions belong to the people. Because of this, they have become democratic and because of the same fact they shall remain so. You do not have to have children to pay school taxes—we all pay school

* Courtesy of *Parks and Recreation*

taxes whether we use the schools or not. We all pay once and that is when we go down and pay our taxes every year.

Public recreation is now in a formative period and we are fast approaching the acceptance of a policy which shall afford free play or recreation. All of the facilities, the major equipment such as ball fields, golf courses, tennis courts, swimming beaches and swimming pools, shall be furnished to the community without additional charge. I say additional charge, because the community has paid for the service once when the citizens paid their taxes. I am not unmindful that there are those in every community who have forgotten how to play—they may object to paying for another's fun, as they would say. Yet they do not object to helping to house and feed the convicts in our state and federal penal institutions. Of course you say they can't pay. Accepting the truth, I grant the reason for not making them pay is a good one, but life's derelicts must be taken care of, so we go on.

Let us look at the question from an economic point of view. We often hear the statement—"Let those pay who play."— Let us analyze this statement and I think we will discover that it is nothing but a catchy play of words. Suppose we tried to develop this great country of ours along these lines, how far would we get? We would have to place the burden for building our public highways upon those who actually used them. Yet who will deny that my property is greatly enhanced in value because it is surrounded by good roads. I may live in a very remote section of the country and may never have seen the property. I may never have seen the State University; I may have no children to send to this institution, yet it is not worth while to live in a country where we all believe in these institutions and where we all share pro-rata in their up-keep and expansion, dedicated to the proposition, as we are, that the product of these institutions is better citizenship and life more abundant? As we are somtimes taxed indirectly, so are we indirectly the recipients of benefits.

Yes, the old toll road is a gone-by institution; the private school is in the passing. They have not lasted because they are economically out of balance with the social principles of our democracy. We are beginning to think in terms of communities, and not in terms of the individual. The community, the state and, in a broader sense, the nation, is the unit. Society is the unit in a more universal sense. The individual is but a small component part of this unit or society. Therefore, we are more interested in the development of the entire community in a gradual upward movement, than the super-development of a few individuals belonging to this community.

As we have made our own self analysis, perhaps we have determined that horse-back riding is more in keeping with our temperament than the game of golf or tennis. But Mr. Jones does not care for horse-back riding, but does, perhaps, like golf. Now if he is willing to support your facilities for horse-back riding, then with equal justice should you not support that which enables Mr. Jones to employ his leisure time as he may have elected to do? Then again, if as a community or a municipality, we have deemed it fitting and proper to furnish without additional tax a public library, books to all who may wish to read, should we not as willingly and for the same fundamental reason furnish a bathing suit? Should we not just as ardently encourage our people to use bathing suits as library books? In its broadest interpretation does not the conservation of our leisure time embrace the development of the body as well as the culture of the mind? The recreative impulse was born with the individual as truly as a desire to improve and cultivate the intellect, and is co-important.

When our social instincts are as highly developed as our commercial instincts, it perhaps will be easier to see and to understand that the dividend which we derive from the recreative institutions which we support in a public way is the social service rendered to the community—the adequate opportunity for a fuller expression of life. It will be much easier to lose sight of the few dollars which we collect as gate receipts and our deeper concern will be that more people shall engage their leisure time in some recreative manner.

In keeping with the principles which have laid the foundations for our biggest and best American institutions and made them what they are, I believe it is fallacy and error to charge an additional tax for the opportunities for normal recreation. We must be thinking and working for a standardized policy of public recreation. By a process of education these institutions must become nationalized. They cannot grow and develop vigorously if they are supported in a dilatory manner. A would-be-free and yet half commercialized institution is but the gift of the miser. If we believe in good citizenship, if we are more interested in the normal development of our boys and girls than we are in the saving of a few dollars, let us not belie our words by our

399

acts. A yard of calico and character should not be measured with the same yard-stick, namely, the dollar sign.

In conclusion, let me say that I believe the "Park Commission" of this country is the logical organization to promote public recreation. It is admirably equipped and fitted to render this public service. I do not want to be misunderstood. I would not advocate that a beautiful landscape be marred and destroyed by building a battery of tennis cages in such a way that they became an obstruction. It is not necessary. In our large parks there are always those places where they can be located and properly screened so that no damage is done. A whole block of property can be acquired and devoted entirely to tennis courts if the demand warrants the expense. I mention this by way of suggesting a way to solve the question and yet not mutilate a beautiful landscape. Just because of these problems and the many angles involved, the never ending demands being made upon park commissions is in itself a sufficient reason why the park commission should accept full responsibility for all the recreative institutions of the community. The enjoyment of beautiful gardens and landscapes is a type of recreation. So why not accept the full responsibility and develop a standard national policy? It is a great opportunity for the park commissions. All these facilities should be furnished to the community as a part of the community equipment and no charge should be made for their use, save that which we all pay when we pay our taxes. Yes, the man who rents his house does pay taxes. He pays the taxes to the landlord on the house he lives in. Without going into a discussion on taxation, I think we can all agree that every one is a taxpayer. There never was a more opportune moment for the development of a standardized, national recreation policy under the leadership and supervision of our park commissions. Let us lose sight of the dollar sign and think in terms of service. It will pay big dividends in a better community.

Practical Aids in Conducting a Neighborhood Recreation Center

I

To all those who are trying to establish neighborhood recreation work in their own cities these suggestions will be of value because they have been found practicable in Milwaukee, a city which has realized its opportunities by opening school buildings for community use and which for a number of years has had an unusually well-organized recreation system. This article is of especial interest in connection with Mr. Harold O. Berg's address entitled "A Municipal Neighborhood Recreation Center," delivered at the Recreation Congress held in Grand Rapids, Mich., and later published in THE PLAYGROUND. Pictures illustrating the activities of these centers were published in the pictorial issue of THE PLAYGROUND in November, 1915, and have since then been made available by the Association in the form of lantern slides. For all these practical suggestions we are indebted to Mr. Berg, Supervisor of the Extension Department of the Board of School Directors in Milwaukee, who has furnished us with printed directions and forms used in the work in that city.

PRACTICAL SUGGESTIONS FOR RECORD MAKING

Method of Taking Attendance
In neighborhood centers the teachers take their count at 8:25 at the signal of a gong and place this count on the attendance card. In some centers the gymnasium classes and other activities change rooms at 8:30 and where such conditions exist it is essential that the count be taken without fail at 8:25. If the activity is an organized one as a sewing class, a class in English to foreigners, a cooking class, the teacher's count is one which appears on the weekly attendance record sent in to the superintendent by the director. Before 8:25 a door-tender counts the "outs" and after 8:25 the "ins." The sum of the "ins" and "outs' is distributed among the unorganized activities as billiard-room, active game-room, according to the directors' remembrance of their popularity that evening. On Saturday evenings when dancing classes are held from 7 to 9 and the socials from 9 to 11:30 the attendants and door-tender take the count in the usual way with the exception that the door-tender counts the "ins" from 8:25 to 10:15 after which none is admitted to the building. Those in the corridors at 8:25 are considered with the "ins." The attendance at the social is obtained from the number of tickets sold and is placed on the weekly attendance sheet. If the sum of the "ins" and "outs" is larger than the attendance at the social the difference is distributed among the unorganized activities; and if the sum of the "ins" and "outs" is less than the attendance at the social the difference is made up by deducting from the 8:25 count of the unorganized activities.

Children and Onlookers   Many mothers who attend the industrial classes, bring children with them. These children are not counted in making out attendance reports. They are not allowed in the quiet-game room as their presence there will discourage the attendance of the older boys. The rule barring school children from the evening attendance at the social centers applies with equal force to the bi-weekly entertainments and the door-tender is instructed accordingly. Many members of organized activities bring friends with them who are allowed to become onlookers. A group of boys is never allowed, however, to "squat" in an orchestra room because they do not know what to do with themselves. The attendance of onlookers is recorded in the lower half of the space in which the number of members is recorded and they are distributed between the "ins" and "outs." At the counting period a count is taken of those in the showers at the time in order that this count may not be lost. The number thus obtained is distributed among unorganized activities as are the "ins" and "outs." The figure is recorded in the upper half of the same space in which the total number of showers given during the evening is recorded.

Method for Deducing Attendance Averages   When averaging weekly attendance the attendance of the three evenings is added and divided by three or if the class meets twice divided by two. The figures in the column labelled "Weekly Average Attendance" are not added, for a class which meets only one evening a week will affect the totals. The evening school activities are divided into two classes, academic and industrial. The latter includes cooking, sewing, manual training, millinery, mechanical drawing, cobbling and hand-work. The weekly attendance report is divided accordingly, so that it is as if there were two evening schools, one academic and one industrial. In reporting the industrial classes on the weekly attendance blank the whole number enrolled and the attendance each evening is the only data required. Each teacher is requested, however, to keep an exact record of the attendance of each member of the class because a report of the average attendance of the students is required at the end of the year.

Directors having evening school activities under their charge send two reports to the supervisor at the end of each week, a regular night school report and a neighborhood center report. The combined attendance of the various activities appears on the social center attendance sheet under the heading "Evening School." These activities include the classes of English to foreigners, the academic work of the fifth, sixth, seventh and eighth grades for working boys and girls, mechanical drawing, cooking, manual training, sewing, millinery, hand-work and cobbling.

Method of Keeping the Counts   Each director is furnished with a cash receipt book. Whenever a bill is paid a voucher is filled out on which it must be stated clearly for what the money was spent, and at the end of the month these are sent to the office of the supervisor with the monthly report. They must tally with the monthly financial statement required of each director. A director is never allowed to sign a voucher. Vouchers are required for all money received and all money paid out. The financial statement is made from the vouchers and the voucher numbers are used to simplify the statement.

Monthly Reports   A monthly attendance report is made by showing the average attendance in different centers at the following afternoon activities:

Billiards, Boys' Athletic Club, Boys' Social Club, Child Welfare Classes, Dramatic Clubs, Dressmaking Classes, Entertainments, Games, High Organized; Games, Low Organized; Games, Quiet; Guardians, Gymnasium, Library, Little Mothers' Clubs, Mothers' Club, Nature Club, Nursery, Orchestra, Outing Club, Boys; Play Hour, Probationers, Showers, Swimming.

The evening activities are:

Alumni Association, Athletic Clubs, Bands, Banquets, Billiards, Boy Scouts, Business Men's Club, Central Council, Cobblers' Class, Cooking Classes, Costume Party, Dancing Classes, Dancing Clubs, Debating Clubs, Dramatic Clubs, Dressmaking Classes, Entertainments, Evening School Classes, Games, High Organized; Games, Low Organized; Games, Quiet; Glee Clubs, Gymnasium Classes, Handwork Classes, Library, Literary Clubs, Millinery Classes, Mandolin Clubs, Manual Training, Mechanical Drawing Classes, Miscellaneous Meetings, Naturalization Classes, Neighborhood Socials, Newsboys' Clubs, Newsboys' Congress, Newsboys' Glee Club, Newsboys' Trial Board, Orchestras, Parents' Social Club, Parent-Teachers' Association, Press Room Staff, Science Club, Shower Baths, Social Clubs, Swimming, Thrift Club, Wardrobe, Women's Swimming Club.

Reports of the total number of shower baths and reports of the total attendance of each center for afternoons, evenings, and for both including evening school classes are also made.

Aside from the monthly attendance report and the monthly financial statement each director must send a monthly pay roll report and a monthly towel report to the supervisor. The towel report shows the number of towels belonging to the center, the number used each day, the total number used, the number sent to the laundry daily, the number received from the laundry daily and the cash received daily.

Accidents Anyone seriously hurt at a center is taken to the Emergency Hospital and all accidents must be reported in duplicate on the regulation blanks and mailed to the office of the supervisor. The director has it understood that he is to be called immediately if an accident occurs in his building.

SOME GENERAL SUGGESTIONS TO DIRECTORS

Cooperate as much as possible with the high school principals in recording the attendance of high school students in social centers on nights other than Friday and Saturday, particularly those who are not up to standard in their daily class work.

Light is expensive; where possible have instructors attend to the lighting of their rooms upon arrival. As soon as a class is dismissed each director should turn out all the lights in his room. Do not burn unnecessary lights during center hours.

No teacher is to be excused from an evening's attendance without permission from the central office. When tardy, attendants and teachers are to fill out tardy cards which the director will mail to the central office.

Each attendant upon leaving his or her room should lock the door and bring the key to the office. No attendant should leave his room without the permission of the director. The director should not leave the building before all the patrons have left.

Night school teachers are not to waste time calling the roll but should have seat charts. In the social center activities the secretary or some reliable member of the activity should be delegated to mark the attendance.

The attendants in the gymnasium and active game rooms should dress in a costume fitting the activity. Male visitors and male spectators are not permitted in the women's gymnasium classes and active game rooms.

Bands, orchestras, dramatic clubs, glee clubs should not be

404

called upon to perform at entertainments oftener than once a month but every person joining one of these organizations should express a willingness to be called once a month to take part in a program at any center.

All employees of the social center must be over sixteen years of age.

Attendants in charge of evening schools, gymnasium classes, quiet game rooms, low organized active game rooms, afternoon libraries, are to hand in a weekly plan book each week. Plan books with the exception of those for quiet game rooms are to be kept in the office. Plan books to be of any value must be read by the directors.

Notices on the outside bulletin boards should be catchy, attractive and in large print. They should be changed often and not too much should be put on the board at one time.

Appoint an official neighborhood center reporter for the newspapers.

A Central Council should be organized consisting of one or two delegates from each activity and this Council should have set meetings. Teach and foster a spirit of self-government. Have a center yell and a center song.

Organize the alumni of the school in which you are director.

Entertainment funds may be used for buying little incidentals such as staples, wax, pool bars. No director is to spend a sum of over $5.00 from the school fund without the approval of the central office.

If you desire a picture of an activity, consult the central office. Consult the central office before beginning any new activities.

Attendants are to watch closely the temperature and ventilation of their rooms.

Check up weekly with the janitor the rooms used.

Cultivate the acquaintance of the policeman on the beat.

PRACTICAL SUGGESTIONS FOR CONDUCTING AN ACTIVE GAME ROOM

Games played in this room are to be of the class known as low-organized active games. This is the room that appeals mostly to the boy teeming with energy. Give him plenty of chance to work off this superfluous energy so that he will be ready to go to the library or quiet game room and take part in the activities there.

Encourage removal of sweaters and coats.

Suggest shower baths after strenuous play.

Handball may be played from 8:45 to 9:30. No bats are to be used.

Induce onlookers to enter into the games, speaking to those who stand in the doorway.

Guard against allowing cliques to monopolize the room and the play leader's attention.

Organize teams of various sorts. Hold contests and play festivals. Have inter-center games. Advertise contests through posters in other parts of the building. Use a score-board.

Direct games—rarely participate in them.

Sprinkle the floor as often as necessary. Pay close attention to ventilation.

Keep a close lookout for profanity. Do not allow rivalry to grow too keen. Teach true sportsmanship.

A weekly forecast is expected from each play leader. Plan books containing directions are furnished. The success of this room depends largely upon the nature and variety of the games presented. Select games suited to the age and ability of the frequenters of the room. Possess a good book on games—Jessie Bancroft's or Emmett Angell's.

PRACTICAL SUGGESTIONS FOR CONDUCTING BASKET BALL AND INDOOR BASEBALL

Encourage the formation of teams. Allow no person to play on a regular team unless he is a member of the central athletic association. Ten or more boys should be given stated times for practice games. A suggested schedule is as follows: 7:30 to 8, 8 to 8:30, 8:30 to 9, and match games after 9. These match games may be between center teams or between a center team and an outside team. All match games must have the O. K. of the director. In match games have some person placing the scores upon the bulletin board. This will keep the interest of the crowd and prevent mistakes in the scores. Encourage inter-center games. Center teams may not have a practice game and a match game on the same night.

Basket ball is a very strenuous game and particularly strenuous on the heart. There should always be an intermission in both practice and match games. Afternoon boys should not play halves of over ten minutes. Allow no person to play more than one game in an evening.

Indoor baseball practice should be limited to 45 minutes.

Rules should be strictly enforced or basket ball will deteriorate into football. Five personal fouls should cause the player's retirement from the game.

The person in charge of these games is responsible for the conduct of the audience. Legitimate applause by the audience is permissible. While a team is playing no person in the hall should be allowed to practice with another ball of any sort or rough it with another. Spectators should remove hats. No spitting on the floor should be allowed.

No one should be allowed to play without gymnasium shoes. Continuous misconduct on the part of the player or onlooker should warrant a suspension for a limited time from the center—with the sanction of the director.

The director is not only to referee but to coach.

The referee should at all times have uppermost in his mind the moral training which the games are to afford. The referee is responsible for the condition and the returning of playing materials. Balls should be blown up and mended and bats should be taped. The referee may call upon responsible persons in the hall to assist him in his duties. Referees should keep the newspapers informed of important games and scores.

Girls are to play according to girls' rules. No male spectators are allowed at girls' games. No girl should play outside games without a chaperon.

Girl spectators are not permitted in any basket ball games of the boys. The Friday evening match games are the only exceptions.

Visiting teams should receive courteous treatment. Impress sportsmanship and good behavior upon your boys before they go to play with the other outside teams.

Players should be given a locker for the season. The attendance will be more regular if gymnasium clothes remain at the center.

[To Be Concluded]

Please mention THE PLAYGROUND when writing to advertisers

"The schools must make democracy safe for the world."

The Victrola in use at School No. 25, Indianapolis, Ind.

MUSIC is the one great universal language understood, loved and used by every Nation engaged in the great struggle—friend and foe.

MUSIC is the greatest single factor which will soonest heal the wounds of strife and bring the whole world into a new relation of real brotherhood.

The schools of all Nations, but especially those of free America, must teach the new lesson of "Each for All, and All for Each"—and MUSIC, the common tone in the new harmony of Nations, is more valuable than text or sermon, bell or book, treaty or diplomacy in reaching the hearts of all our citizens, old or new, and helping all to sing a mighty paean of praise for our great Nation.

Let the children sing for the *Victory* of "Liberty Enlightening the World."

The Government has made MUSIC an integral part of all Student Army Training Schools. The 66 selected songs are nearly all on Victor Records.

Do your children know them?

The VICTOR will bring all the songs of America and her Allies, and all the old beautiful music of all lands right into the school rooms, the seed beds of our future democracy.

Are the children in *YOUR* School receiving this training for life? If not, why not?

For full information write

Educational Department
Victor Talking Machine Co.
Camden, N. J.

Victrola XXV, $90
specially manufactured
for School use

When the Victrola is not in use, the horn can be placed under the instrument safe and secure from danger, and the cabinet can be locked to protect it from dust and promiscuous use by irresponsible people.

Victrola

The Playground

Vol. XII No. 10　　　　　　　　　　JANUARY, 1919

Happenings in the Field

The call for delicacies for soldiers ill with influenza in Wrightstown, New Jersey, was answered by volunteer contribution,—no drafting was necessary. Fifteen thousand glasses of jellies, three thousand baskets of fruit—gallons of hot chicken broth, were sent in to help the men recover.

Quarantine in Allentown isn't so hard to bear when W. C. C. S. breaks the monotony with delightful vaudeville ' entertainments. A special entertainment at Camp Crane for quarantined men helped probably as much as anything else to ward off sickness—at any rate, the men highly appreciated this opportune diversion.

A serenade by Sousa's Band does not fall to the lot of many of us; but this sign of appreciation was given W. C. C. S. workers in Baltimore by the musicians after they were entertained for luncheon and dinner at the W. C. C. S. Hotel. The Band was playing in the city in the interest of the Liberty Loan Campaign.

Plans are being made for club rooms that will be placed midway between Fort Banks and Fort Heath near Winthrop, Massachusetts. W. C. C. S. will be responsible for the activities of the sick and wounded who may be sent to the Fort Banks hospital. Since these are prominent forts, the work started here now may be maintained after the war.

A unique concert to inspire the sick and the not-so-sick was planned by the Waynesboro Band. A sort of bass choir composed of the bass instruments was formed and on a high knoll from which the sounds would carry the band played sacred music, national airs and camp songs.

Two units are set aside in New York City expressly for French soldiers, although of course they are welcomed at every other club. But these have

411

French names—the "Rendez-vous des Poilus" and the "Cercle Lafayette"—and are perhaps more attractive to our French allies on that account.

British, as well as Americans, are recipients of favors and services from the Officers' Department. Through this department, entrance to the most exclusive clubs may be gained with a card of introduction; the privilege of one-half rate in the most prominent hotels is given through this and the W. C. C. S. card, and also golf and tennis privileges.

Influenza throughout the camps in the country has given W. C. C. S. opportunity to do even more helpful and kindly work. In Wrightstown, New Jersey, every member of the staff has given his entire time to ameliorating the condition of the sick. The Club House has been filled with cots for the sick.

It has been found many a time that the good that men do is not so often "interred with their bones," for knowledge of actual good accomplished prompts men to speak of it to their fellows. So it is in Baltimore with respect to the W. C. C. S. Twenty-five business men, members of the Advertising Club, who have been serving in the W. C. C. S. Hotel four hours

412

a week, and have thus acquired an intimate knowledge of the good accomplished by W. C. C. S., have volunteered to speak in the various churches on Community Service.

In Wrightstown, N. J., Signor Cusamano has asked W. C. C. S. for aid in increasing the morale of the Italians and plans are being made to have the Italian soldiers put on plays written in Italian at the theatres in the towns adjacent to the camp.

At the request of the Y. M. C. A. and K. of C., the Rochester W. C. C. S. provided full equipment for a football team among the soldiers.

Seven hundred cardboard mats bearing the W. C. C. S. seal were distributed to the sick men at the base hospital at Louisville, Kentucky. They served the purpose of supporting writing material.

The services of the staff of Rockford, Illinois, W. C. C. S. and all the cars were placed at the disposal of relatives of sick men at camp.

Assistance for the sick men at camp and their relatives was given systematically in Battle Creek, Michigan, by W. C. C. S. The ward and bed of the stricken soldier was located before the pass to his relatives was issued; sleeping accommodations were found for visiting families; transportation was organized and all trains were met.

Lincoln, Nebraska, shows a fine spirit toward W. C. C. S. and the soldiers. The Mayor told them the Keys of the City were theirs; and tailors have offered to press and clean the men's clothes free of charge.

The San Francisco office is now giving out approximately five thousand theatre passes a week to soldiers and sailors.

An old clock, standing on a twelve-foot pedestal, which had not been wound for a year, proved to be an admirable agency for W. C. C. S. publicity in Austin, Texas. The W. C. C. S. emblem was painted on the face, with dots in the outer edge of the red circle to indicate the hour spaces. Underneath the dial the words, "Welcome, Soldier," and a hand pointing to the entrance of the building, is an invitation that the soldier will probably take advantage of. The clock will be kept in order by a local firm.

Blotters with the W. C. C. S. insignia stamped on them have been placed in the hotels and railroad stations in Fort Worth, Texas, and in the "Y" huts and K. of C. shacks at the camps. These blotters have been sent to Dallas, Waco, San Antonio, Wichita Falls and Lawton for distribution.

The camps near Fort Worth are not going to let the football season pass unnoticed. An interfield league has been started and W. C. C. S. obtained permission for the use of Panther Park and the Amphitheatre seats.

The "Every Dog Has His Day" principle applies to organizations and parades nowadays. In Sacramento, when the Women War Workers paraded, the hostesses of the Soldiers' and Sailors' Club appeared dressed in the Hoover uniform and carried a sign advertising the club.

All W. C. C. S. activities in San Antonio, Texas during the epidemic were directed toward assisting the city and military authorities. Automobiles were furnished to headquarters, workers were placed in the depots to care for the incoming relatives, and with the Square Deal Association, the organization assisted in the regulation of jitney service.

Daily community sings were inaugurated in seven of the large local dry goods stores in San Francisco.

413

Relatives of the sick men at camp in Alexandria, Louisiana, were pleasantly surprised and gratified to find, upon arrival in the city, that cars were waiting to take them out to the camp. This was done by the emergency motor corps, organized to assist W. C. C. S. and women drove the motors two and a half days a week, free of charge to these visiting relatives.

Women of the Women's Committee of W. C. C. S. in Alexandria, Virginia, joined the force of nurses in the fight against influenza.

In addition to sending nurses, the Alexandria W. C. C. S. obtained blankets, gave personal advice concerning the disease and its treatment, and secured information regarding the condition of the sick men for relatives at home; also assisted in the raising of five thousand dollars for the maintenance of temporary hospitals.

If a colored person of Alexandria has a relative in the army or navy, he can become a member of the Blue Star Committee. He pays dues of five cents a month and thus contributes toward the canteen for the colored soldiers. Latest reports record not only a membership, but an enthusiastic membership, of fifty. .

414

Meals in Atlanta, Georgia, that would otherwise be seventy-five cents are given the soldiers for thirty-five cents since the ladies of the Home Entertainment Committee have taken charge of the new canteen. One of the members pays the rent; the others act as waitresses, so meals are served at cost price.

The railroad authorities in Hattiesburg, Mississippi, cooperating with W. C. C. S. have cleared the station of undesirable loungers and installed a maid to call the trains.

The Key West W. C. C. S. secured fifteen hundred dollars worth of theatre tickets for the soldiers.

Information Bureaus are called upon to arrange all manner of difficulties, and no one knows what the next day may bring. In Montgomery, Alabama, a journey was so arranged for a soldier that he could save twenty hours of traveling for his furlough; and an old man, taking his son home, was grateful for a sack in which to carry home his son's effects.

The thirty-eight men from the *City of Savannah*, coaling in Southport, North Carolina, who were entertained one evening at the Army and Navy Club danced, played pool and bowled, and went on their way rejoicing.

Possibly there are no Tom Sawyers in Arcadia, Florida, for painting and whitewashing held no terrors for the boys of this town. When the dearth of workmen, due to the epidemic, delayed proceedings in the remodeling of the Old Post Office building into a community house, some of the high school boys assisted in kalsomining walls, painting woodwork, and staining the floors.

In Augusta, Georgia, all complaints on the part of soldiers against business men will in future be referred to a board created for the purpose of investigating and adjusting all claims of serious overcharge. The unique feature of this system is that the company commanders will take charge of investigating the lesser offenses, thus giving the board influence through military sanction.

The Advertising Club of Baltimore, which has pledged its support to W. C. C. S., provides slips for business houses to insert in all their bills and packages. Such queries as, "Are you doing your part to make the men in uniform contented while here?" and "Have you had a soldier out to dinner?" in combination with the W. C. C. S. seal on the slips, are potent reminders.

"When is a truck not a truck?" In Rochester the answer would be, "When it's a canteen." For here, one of the finest residences, surrounded by almost three acres of lawn and orchard, has been turned into a place of rest and refreshment for the soldier truck driver, and is called the "Truck Canteen." The hostess is there in person to welcome the boys and to give them the freedom of the place.

Patriotic jitneys in Atlantic City! The Boy Scouts distributed automobile pasters during one week and the jitney chaffeurs are making use of them— sacrificing a fare for every man in uniform carried.

Unexpected soldiers from Camp Dix as guests over the week end, even to the number of three hundred, in no way disconcerted the Atlantic City W. C. C. S. household arrangements. Plans were hastily made; extension of passes for all piers and bathing places secured; Rotarians agreed to act as guides— and Atlantic City was made very attractive to these boys, who were originally from Camp Cody.

Two hundred sixty-four dollars and fifty-five cents was collected for W. C. C. S. during the ascent by the "Human Fly" of the side of the Traymore Hotel in Atlantic City.

Allentown, Penn., has a Women's Home Guard, formed under W. C. C. S. leadership with the cooperation of Y. W. C. A. Their perfect discipline on parade attracted very favorable attention. This proved effective publicity, for a few days later two companies were formed composed of employees of one of the large shops in the town.

Entertainment in Mt. Holly, N. J., does not lag. Over two thousand soldiers dined at the Ankokas Club during the month.

Perhaps it's the six fireplaces in the fine old house in Red Bank, N. J., where the club has its quarters, that attract so many soldiers. At any rate, the men come and stay—one Sunday, one hundred thirty-seven men spent the entire day.

The Liberty Sings in Gettysburg are not only growing in attendance but are promoting sociability among the people of the town.

"Keep - up - to - the - minute" seems to be the watchword

of the Bureau on the Common in Boston. At nine o'clock every evening and every half hour thereafter every service club in the city is to telephone regarding the state of its accommodations.

War Service Day was also cooperation day in Boston, for all the military and social organizations combined with W. C. C. S. to make the event a success in the Harvard Stadium. Forty thousand spectators especially enjoyed the highly original and exciting Ben Hur race of toboggans drawn by squads of ten soldiers each, and driven by thoroughly American, khaki-clad Ben Hurs.

W. C. C. S. distributed seven hundred fifty Square Deal cards in Portland, Me.—a very liberal representation.

"Sing, and the world sings with you" is an adaptation that applies to many War Camp Community cities. Allentown community singing has enlisted the services of four choirs, four singing societies, the employees of a store and of a factory, in addition to the participation of most of the townspeople.

Publishers in Rockford, Ill., have authorized local distributors to turn over the unsold copies of magazines to the W. C. C. S. The

416

W. C. C. S. receipt, given in lieu of the covers, heretofore torn off, entitles the distributor to credit for the magazines.

The St. Louis public evidently appreciates W. C. C. S. management of athletic activities in town. In response to many requests, W. C. C. S. has appointed a committee which will develop a Community Bowling Tournament. A committee has also been appointed for basket ball, soccer and other winter sports.

In St. Paul, W. C. C. S. is planning for various classes at the public schools looking toward reconstruction work, particularly among the soldiers at the Fort. Clay modeling, basketry, Sloyd and the making of toys will be taken up.

The Board of Directors of the Chamber of Commerce in Junction City approves of a movement to open the theatres of the city free to the soldiers on Sunday afternoons.

The War Angelus in Junction City called one's thoughts to prayer for victory. The W. C. C. S., secretary secured consent of the Mayor to give orders for the siren whistle to blow at the opening and closing of the moment of meditation and prayer for the success of our armies on land and sea and for ultimate victory.

The Soldiers' Club in Kalmazoo is benefiting from the generosity of citizens. Pianola and phonograph music has been donated, and recently, a local news agency has been giving six newspapers daily, and *Collier's, The Argosy, The Literary Digest,* and one short story magazine every week.

W..C. C. S. in Mt. Clemens helped celebrate Macomb County Day. A lively and interesting program was planned, a parade with floats being one of the chief attractions of the day's entertainment. Soldiers were, admitted free to all places of amusement.

A community sing seems to be the popular starting place for all movements and meetings these days. In Omaha the forty-five hundred people who attended the mass meeting for girls sang themselves into enthusiasm under the leadership of a song leader, accompanied by an orchestra. The meeting opened the big fall campaign for the organization of girls in the Patriotic League.

Applications placed in the pay envelopes of the men at the Rock Island arsenal brought an increase in the membership of the Davenport Club and Rock Island Club.

417

It was W. C. C. S. optimism that helped the football team of the Fifth Battalion in Rock Island. They had no fund for the purchase of equipment. The W. C. C. S. furnished them with the necessary paraphernalia which will be paid for later from the admittance fees to the games.

Another big sing! In Denver, the W. C. C. S. is preparing to welcome a crowd of twenty-five thousand; the music is to be furnished by the Shriners' Band, singing led by the Municipal Chorus, Elks' Quartette and Glee Club.

A second edition of sixty thousand copies of *Patriotic Liberty Slings* is being issued by W. C. C. S. These sheets were donated by the Denver *Times.*

They greeted the boys with a rousing cheer in Bloomington, Indiana, when they arrived in town. The W. C. C. S. with a band and automobiles for the officers, escorted the men to the barracks and every man in the detachment then received an invitation to Sunday supper. In the evening the United Chorus of the city gave the soldiers a splendid song service.

In addition to the distribution of more than one thousand free tickets by the W. C. C. S. of Detroit to the soldiers for theatre performances, arrangements were made for three hundred men to attend a special production of *Hearts of the World.*

A special music committee formed by the W. C. C. S. of Chillicothe, composed of the leading musicians of the town, will direct a Choral Union of trained singers which will be coordinated later with a chorus from camp. Several programs will be presented and the finale will be a great W. C. C. S. celebration at the Community House on Christmas Eve.

A constant reminder of W. C. C. S. clubs in Columbus, Chillicothe, Cincinnatti and Dayton, is given the soldiers by means of the passes which the W. C. C. S. had printed and sent to Division Headquarters, — one hundred thousand in all. On the back of every pass is the red circle with directions for reaching the various soldiers' clubs.

All the churches of Cincinnati have united to offer all their facilities to W. C. C. S. for the entertainment of the soldiers.

When, recently, there came a call from Camp Sherman Reclamation Department to the W. C. C. S. for assistance in mending garments—about fourteen thousand—W. C. C. S. sent out an appeal by personal letter to the women of Chillicothe. A mending unit was formed, and the ninety women who came on the appointed day mended the five thousand shirts sent in. They will meet twice a week.

Trench and Camp printed an article relative to the uncertainty of shuttle trains and the consequent pecuniary inconvenience to soldiers who were compelled to remain over night in Arcadia, Fla., through missing trains. W.C. C. S. responded immediately by installing cots in the community house.

One paragraph does not suffice to do more than hint at the glories of the War Camp Community Service Day in New Orleans on September twelfth. The celebration took the place of the annual carnival, and ten organizations of the city participated in the day's elaborate program. Vaudeville in the open street, where traffic was barred, community singing, band concerts, luncheon served to uniformed men at tables accommodating thousands at a single sitting, and a parade, were a few of the features of the day. A miniature edition of the *Times-Picayune* specially edited for soldiers and sailors was a unique souvenir. The city-wide response to the spirit of the day made certain the enduring value of the celebration to W. C. C. S.

A colored soldiers' community

sing in Spartanburg, S. C., met with great success. W. C. C. S. managed the affair, the Y. W. C. A. furnished waitresses for the supper to the six hundred soldiers, and the colored people in town did their share in providing the supper

The *Twelve Lessons in Conversational French* which was compiled by Prof. Vernalede for the Jacksonville W. C. C. S. has passed its fourteen thousandth copy. W. C. C. S. shipped one thousand copies to Camp Meade.

The universal interest in the constantly changing battle line was utilized by the Jacksonville W. C. C. S. Through help of the commanding officer, the W. C. C. S. secured a soldier artist to paint a large map of the western battle front and installed this in the glass window of the W. C. C. S. club. It drew, of course, the attention of every passer-by.

The Fayetteville children bring magazines for the soldiers to school. An automobile from Stewart & Co., contractors at camp, will call for these once a week to take them to camp.

The strike against the merchants of Key West was amicably settled in a conference composed of a representative of the labor union, a representative of the merchants, and the W. C.

419

C. S. organizer, as chairman. It was agreed that the labor people would not patronize any store that did not display the W. C. C. S. emblem as a guarantee of fair trade.

Twenty-five free seats are set aside each day for the wounded marines in Norfolk, Va., at the Red Circle Theatre.

During Community Play Week in Alexandria, Va., fifteen chaplains filled the pulpits in the city on Sunday. The week featured a variety of entertainments for the community as well as for the men in uniform.

The W.C. C. S. in Beaufort, S. C. did a big thing in getting the commanding officer to issue an order to have the "Kite", a government boat, operate between Paris Island and Beaufort, on Wednesday and Saturday, for the purpose of bringing liberty parties.

Norfolk donated the use of the Armory Building for Thursdays, Fridays and Saturdays. And full use was made of it, for in one day the hall was used successively as a theatre, a ballroom and a dormitory. A matinee was given attended by six hundred people, an evening performance attended by fifteen hundred, a dance followed, and when the dancers left at eleven o'clock, cots were placed in the room for eighty-six men who slept there.

"Garden Parties" in Savannah, though literally "Asphalt Parties", are affording much enjoyment to the people of the city. W. C. C. S., taking advantage of the opportunities offered by the small parks along Bull Street, organized the parties. The city installed a system of lights that add beauty to the monuments and shaded squares of the street. Refreshments are served after the dancing or the games, by the W. C. C. S.—free to soldiers, and five cents for each person not in uniform.

The Paul English Players have furnished high-class entertainments for six weeks in Alexandria, La. These were given at the Base Hospital for nurses and convalescents, and every evening in the local Air Dome.

In Deming, New Mexico, a W. C. C. S. emblem painted at each end of the words "Soldiers Welcome," on the wall of the armory, lighted by electric reflectors, calls the attention of the crowds that pass the principal corner two blocks away.

Band concert time has become the chief gathering time in Eagle Pass, Texas. It is an occasion when present topics like Liberty Loan and War Saving Stamps are presented to the public.

In order to inform the men of the removal of the club to Main Street in Fort Worth, Texas, dodgers were printed announcing the fact. These dodgers were dropped in camp from an aeroplane.

Some soldiers in Little Rock, Ark., have had to sacrifice their Liberty Bonds. Immediately, the alert shyster tried to reap a harvest in buying them far below par—not reckoning, however, on the W. C. C. S., which arranged with the Clearing House so that the men who have had to give up their bonds will receive the market price for them.

The churches estimate that on Sunday, Sept. fifteenth, three thousand men were entertained in private homes in Little Rock.

The Houston W. C. C. S. has been instrumental in promoting Noon Day Vespers Parade, which was started by the Musicians' Union.

Freedom of the roads was permitted the W. C. C. S. party for soldiers, by the toll people, during a trip up Mt. Hood in Portland, Ore. The owner of the hotel at the base of the mountain offered entertainment gratis to the men.

When the Commandant of the Training Detachment of the University of Utah called on the Salt Lake City W. C. C. S. to provide cots and bedding for one hundred men, the organization was not dismayed nor the Commandant disappointed. The things were soon collected from generous townspeople, and one of the Red Cross units even tagged all the blankets so that they might be quickly returned to the owners.

Not with sign language but in real French will the California soldier make himself understood when in France, for the Palo Alto and San Jose clubs are furnishing lessons in French to the men. Also, foreigners in service are given information as to where they may study English, and may get information regarding the different phases of the war.

A new job was found for the San Jose soldiers recently. Many were detailed from camp, through the National Defenders' Clubs of W.C.C.S. to help in taking care of the fruit which had been damaged by heavy rains.

The W. C. C. S. Booth Exhibit at the California State Fair in Sacramento was a center of interest. The time, the place and the booth, properly combined this time, will have far-reaching value for publicity.

Donations of fruit, vegetables and general foodstuffs are promised to the Sacramento Soldiers' and Sailors' Club. The Chairman of Registration at the Club asked the people visiting the Fair from the big farming and agricultural sections to leave their names with promises of sending gifts to the Club.

Nearly two hundred colored soldiers in San Antonio, Texas, sang and told jokes in a negro minstrel show to raise money for a recreation building at the camp. The performance was given in one of the big theatres under the direction of W. C. C. S. and the Entertainment Division at Camp Travis. The profit was two thousand dollars.

No longer in San Francisco need the soldiers walk the streets at night for want of beds. Through the W. C. C. S. Hotel Bureau, men are assigned to definite rooms in a hotel directly from the Information Desks by means of direct line telephone arrangements provided for that purpose. The expense is borne by the Hotel Men's Association who are glad to relieve their night clerks.

The Austin Army Service Club, composed entirely of women who have relatives in war schools and camps in Austin, Texas, has been organized by the W. C. C. S.

Music, tea and sociability provided the Sunday entertainment given by the Adolphus Hotel in Dallas for three hundred officers, cadets and young women. Tea was served by fifty girls in white, wearing the W. C. C. S. armband.

Thirty thousand people congregated in the Band Concourse in San Francisco for a community sing. Under W. C. C. S. auspices, a gigantic community sing was held in the Civic Auditorium on the opening night of the Liberty Loan.

It's a simple matter to take five hundred and fifty men for an automobile ride on a Sunday afternoon if it's managed by the San Francisco organization. The ride was handled there by having the machines with the "Salute and Ride" motto on their windshields line up under direction of traffic police in a certain stretch of drive in Golden Gate. Under direction of petty officers, the men were assigned to machines.

There is now a club in every city in the Mexican Border district.

Labor unions composed of shipyard workers in Tacoma, Washington, have given a number of benefit dances to provide beds for soldiers.

From Cape May, N. J., comes the announcement that Sunday night meetings are held on the pier for soldiers and sailors. The churches are indefatigable in their efforts to serve the men in uniform and they cooperate with War Camp Community Service at every opportunity.

A summer pavilion that becomes successively a dormitory and a hall for entertainments and dances has become a matter of course in W. C. C. S. work. Nothing easier! New Rochelle, N. Y., provides another example. Arrangements have been made to enclose the pavilion so it may be used for winter sleeping quarters and then for dances by moving out the beds.

The first club for colored men in Philadelphia will open in December.

Even a uniform does not render a man insensible to the discomfiture of finding himself in a large department store. Perhaps this phase of masculine psychology as well as the convenience of the men led to the establishment in New York

City of a shopping bureau for officers and men in service through the cooperation of the National League for Women's Service and the W. C. C. S. The volunteer assistance of professional shoppers can be obtained through application at one of the W. C. C. S. information booths or at the W. C. C. S. Shopping Bureau, or appointments may be made by mail.

The W. C. C. S. participation in the United War Work Drive contributed much to the success of the Drive in Jersey City, N. J., through a community sing at the Armory and, on another evening, a pageant in cooperation with the Y. W. C. A.

A "Song of the Shirt" needn't necessarily be such a depressing affair as we have been led to believe. Wives of the Rock Island Arsenal Workers put quite a bit of cheer into the work, but of course it's done for the soldiers. These women meet each week to mend the shirts of the soldiers stationed at the arsenal and in the early part of November mended two dozen shirts in two days.

The attractions of the Dayton Army and Navy Club bring

at least one hundred men each evening to the club and two hundred men on Sundays.

Any doubt attaching to the meaning of the "Slacker Record Drive" which is still on in Denver may be dispelled when it is added that three thousand or four thousand records were received by W. C. C. S. in one week. And evidently a great many soldiers and sailors are enjoying the victrolas, for fourteen thousand records received to date have been distributed to local forts and cantonments as rapidly as requests have come in.

Between two hundred and two hundred and fifty men attend the Wednesday and Saturday dances at the Colored Soldiers' Club in Rockford, Ill.

Hospitality and success are becoming related terms—one doesn't hear of the former without the latter. Through the Hospitality Committee, organized in Belvidere fourteen miles east of Rockford, Ill., a week-end party for fifty men was held there. "A complete success," says the report. The committee is enthusiastic and plans to conduct these parties every week.

"More hospitality to offer than boys to accept," is almost a W. C. C. S. slógan now, in some communities. In St. Paul, Minn., the work is most efficiently organized and so many invitations poured 'in that there were not a sufficient number of soldiers to accept them.

Although regiments and armies have accustomed one to the thought of hordes of men, the fact that twelve hundred and thirty-eight men sought the privileges of the Red Circle Club in Des Moines, Iowa, during one Saturday afternoon and night until two in the morning, is an item of marked interest as indicating the extreme popularity of W. C. C. S. clubs among the soldiers.

War Camp Community Service for the colored soldiers has taken great strides lately. In Alexandria, Va., the cafeteria of the club for colored soldiers was opened on the ninth and supper served to the men there the following evening after they had been entertained in the homes of the colored people for dinner. The War Camp Community Service representative addressed a mass meeting of the colored folk on the work of the organization, and probably the strong efforts they put forth in working for the success of the United War Work Drive is partly due to the kindly interest W. C. C. S. has shown in their welfare.

A city-wide campaign is planned by War Camp Community Service in Atlanta, Ga., to provide each boy in camp and hospital with a Christmas package. Whether it is better to give than to receive will be a question between the generous civilians and the appreciative recipients.

Entertainments, free moving pictures and community sings furnish a varied program of amusement for the soldier on Sundays in Atlanta. That five thousand people were present at the first auditorium sing for the soldiers would suggest that the civilians, too, are choosing some of it for their own pleasure.

"This alone is worth the money that must be raised in this section," said a speaker in referring to War Camp Community Service when organizing the Victory Boys and Girls for the United War Work Drive in Key West, Fla.

In Anniston, Ala., five thousand soldiers visited the Red Circle Club No. 2 during the second week in November. Among the impromptu celebrations of peace which marked November eleventh, W. C. C. S. contributed its part by placing the club piano on a truck in the Square in Anniston for community singing. A Y. M. C. A. leader and a new band from camp directed the music.

What do they like for entertainment? "Moving pictures," might be the answer. Shown at the War Camp Community Service clubs they never fail to elicit approval. In Charlotte, N. C., the free motion pictures shown each night at the club are especially appreciated.

The outburst of enthusiasm for peace in Arcadia, Fla., culminated in a street dance under the direction of War Camp Community Service for the two thousand five hundred and fifty people who congregated for a celebration.

Enlisting the services of the Motor Corps, organized by the Girls' Worker, has proved an asset to War Camp Community Service, for in doing errands around Fayetteville, N. C., the Motor Corps saves dollars weekly for the organization.

The trifles that make up the sum of service of W. C. C. S. are many and varied and dependent upon local demands. At the suggestion of the organizer upon request from the

Welfare Department of a local company, a Spanish sign was placed on a colored restaurant which caters to Porto Rican trade in Fayetteville, N. C.

The negroes' lively and expressive sense of rhythm makes any community sing enjoyable. At a sing for colored people staged in Richmond, Va., the auditorium was filled and the singing was splendid—a corollary that would always follow.

On the fourteenth and fifteenth of November the club at Southport, N. C., was closed in order that all the assistance possible could be rendered several hundred sick Porto Ricans on the *City of Savannah* bound for Porto Rico, which landed at Southport. About two hundred were taken to the hospital at Camp Caswell and a search made through the town secured one hundred old garments to relieve their destitute condition.

A wary soldier remarked recently to a lady whose tireless efforts have brought pleasure to many soldiers and sailors, when she offered him a ride in her car, "I can't ride with you. I don't know you." In Sacremento, Cal., his suspicions would have been allayed for under the chairmanship of a young woman the Auto Recreation Corps of W. C. C. S. provides rides for the soldiers and sailors only through automobile owners who are listed in the registry which she maintains. No automobile carries W. C. C. S. insignia without the knowledge of the committee.

With the attendance of five hundred children from the public schools, a large number from the Morris Lasker playground, and the presence of civilians and soldiers, community singing was resumed in Galveston, Tex., on Sunday in the early part of November. A leading member of the Musical Comedy company playing at the Liberty Theatre at Camp Logan offered an added attraction to those who wanted to hear and not to be heard.

The organization of the local W. C. C. S. Committee in Marathon, Tex., where there are no social or recreational features in the town, gives promise of enlivening times to the soldiers.

Articles of sale such as candy, dolls, Mexican curios and Thrift and War Saving Stamps attracted purchasers at a bazaar held for three days at the W. C. C. S. Soldiers' Club in Laredo, Tex. Unusual features of the bazaar which was planned by the manager of the club, were a miniature cabaret, a splendid jazz band of soldiers, and a display of war relics. The amusement of trying to hit the "nigger" dolls with balls was greatly enhanced by substituting dolls representing the Kaiser for this gave a vicarious delight to many soldiers who under such inspiration acquired a more accurate aim.

War Camp Community Service floats in a monster parade in Fort Worth called attention to several activities of the organization; a dining table around which were seated several soldiers with their host and hostess; a group standing in dancing form; two soldiers playing at a game table. Behind the truck came a large car loaded with soldiers with a "Salute and Ride" placard and on each side marched a single file of soldiers.

Cooperation of a major at Camp Bowie at Fort Worth has provided good music for W. C. C. S. parties for he has detailed an orchestra of white soldiers and one of colored soldiers to play at the Wednesday and Friday entertainments.

Community Singing Grows in Popularity

The Commission songleaders are not confining their efforts to the Army and Navy. The workmen of the Brooklyn Navy Yard are to have Sings twice a week. The song leader in New Orleans is coaching men who will lead singing among factory girls.

Seattle, Washington helped to sing the Fourth Liberty Loan across by a parade of 10,000 citizens who sang as they marched through the streets of that city on September 29th. These 10,000 people, white, yellow, and black, Christian and Jew, Protestant and Roman Catholic joined enthusiastically and whole-heartedly in a demonstration of loyalty to the common cause of Democracy.

In spite of the quarantine on the New London Naval Stations a song leader went into quarantine with the boys. This was their only form of entertainment and they appreciated it.

Some of the local Liberty Loan Committees asked the cooperation of the Camp song leaders in conducting singing at meetings during the campaign. In a Kentucky town, soldier song leaders were sent to every theatre and moving picture house to teach the audiences and get them singing. They

427

gave a good account of themselves and aroused enthusiasm.

good omen of the spirit with which they will return.

Song leaders are doing splendid work in the embarkation camps. The departure of "Singing Ships" from our ports is the marvel of the military officials who see them sail and is indicative of the spirit with which our boys go over the top. At the same time they are a

It is commendable that on several occasions when lights have gone out in moving picture theatres where soldiers were assembled, the latter, conducted by one of their own number, have immediately begun to sing and continued until the lights were turned on.

Measurable Effects of Welfare Work in Industry

Now many people feel that community service presents a greater opportunity for solving certain industrial problems than what has heretofore been known as welfare work. In thinking of such community service, one does well to consider some of the desirable effects upon labor turnover, output and costs which have resulted from welfare work. Of course, far more important is the effect upon the workers, the employer, and the community at large of together working upon the common industrial problem.

The Battle Creek Sanitarium with 1,500 employees has been carrying on welfare work in an organized way since 1913. Before the welfare plan was inaugurated there was considerable friction, lost motion and inefficiency. It was discovered after the plan had been running for a short time that absence from illness had dropped from an average of one and three-fourths days per month per employee to less than one-fourth day per month per employee. A greater volume of work was handled and the work was considerably more accurate than it was before the recreation periods were instituted.

An article called *How A Man Went to Meet His Labor Troubles,* published in the *Independent* in March, 1910, describes the welfare work carried on by Caesar Cone in his cotton mills in Greensboro, N. C. It asks, "And what of the man that has footed the bill for welfare work? Well, he has an unusual dividend, the genuine love of his people, and the other dividends for which the world is clamoring so loudly have not suffered. Several of the departments in his mills have run at almost 100 per cent efficiency and some have actually got more work from the machinery than it was built to do."

In 1909 the Clothcraft Shop of Cleveland was hiring 1,570 workers a year to keep up a force of 1,060. Life in the factory was organized for health and happiness—with what result? More work was being done in 1914 by 20 per cent fewer people and the labor turn-over had fallen 66⅔ per cent. Richard Feiss, the manager of the Clothcraft Shop has said, "Welfare work is no philanthropy but a very essential part of the management."

A table in the *Monthly Review* issued by the United States Bureau of Labor Statistics in March, 1918, shows in a general way the effect of welfare work on time lost and labor turnover from a study of 431 establishments. Although this comparison of conditions was made after labor had been somewhat affected by the war, the results are very interesting. The majority of these firms began their welfare work at least ten years ago. The costs of this work as given vary from a fraction of one per cent to five per cent of the total annual pay roll. Excluding unusual contributions, a fairly comprehensive welfare program could be maintained for about two per cent of the annual pay roll. One hundred and sixty out of one hundred and eighty-nine firms reporting on effect of welfare work on time lost reported an improvement. One hundred and thirty-six out of one hundred and seventy-four reported an improvement in the stability of the force. One firm which had compiled statistics with regard to the reduction in the turnover had an increase of 13.4 per cent of employees of more than two years' service in 1916 over a similar group for 1914, due entirely, so the management stated, to their welfare work. The extent to which the output was affected by welfare work was difficult to determine as labor conditions were unusual and few companies had made a study of that point. A few firms gave it as their opinion, however, that the output had been increased by it. Boyd Fisher, in an address at the Employment Managers' Conference in Philadelphia, 1917, said, "it is significant * * * that every plant in Detroit that has reduced its turnover of labor in the last year has increased its output per man. In some cases it has doubled it." It might, therefore, be inferred from this statement that the firms which had reported reduction of labor turnover had probably increased their output somewhat.

Hours and Wages   It is universally recognized that two of the first essentials to the welfare of the employees are an equitable wage and reasonable hours of labor. The relation of output to the number of working hours is interestingly shown by the experience of the granite cutters of the United States. The first cut in their hours was from twelve to ten and the output was not reduced. In 1890 the ten hours were reduced to nine and again the output was not reduced. In 1900 an eight-hour day was secured and still the output was not reduced. Moreover, the finished product in granite cutting has not increased in price to the consumer. Mr. Cranford of Buffalo, an employer in the granite business, found from his records that the same man under identically the same conditions accomplished more in nine hours than in ten and more in eight than in nine. He, therefore, experimented upon one man, giving him the eight-hour a day wages and letting him work but seven hours. This man in six weeks increased his output from three to twelve per cent, according to the kind of work he was cutting.

Several experiments have been tried by increasing the wages of employees, where low, through additions to the regular salaries and through providing piece work, with the result that the output has been increased, in some instances doubled, and a lower price has been offered the consumer.

Type of Work Place   The aesthetic is not overlooked in welfare work —the color of the walls and ceilings, good architectural features, trees, grass and flowers. In an investigation made by the American Museum of Safety, the question was asked of the factory managers whether they had found that their experiments on these points had increased the efficiency of the workers. Seventy-five per cent of those who replied were emphatic in their declarations that the effect had been good.

Sanitation   Sanitation is another form of welfare work which has had a direct effect upon output. Mr. Schwarze, in his handbook on shop lighting, declares that the results of experiments show that the installation of a proper system of shop lighting will increase output all the way from two to ten per cent. "In a certain

430

steel plant, where an efficient system of lighting was installed," he writes "the output at night was increased a little over ten per cent." There is the same relation between output and ventilation as between output and lighting.

Clean washrooms, toilet rooms, locker rooms and shower baths are an important part of factory sanitation. Mr. Close, manager (in 1912) of the United States Steel Corporation's Welfare Bureau, has said, "This is the feature of our work for which we are most unable to show returns. When someone asks me how it pays us to put in baths for our men and playgrounds for their children, I can't exactly tell him. And yet, you know, and I know, and everyone knows that the man who takes a bath every day is the efficient man, and the child who has a place to play is the child who will grow up to be efficient." He also declared in talking of the work in sanitation, "There isn't an epidemic in any plant of the Steel Corporation. There hasn't been one since we started our sanitary work."

Much strain and irritation has been taken from workers, through insisting on cleanliness, providing rest periods, and inventing devices which make work easier and more pleasant. The result is that the workers do more work with less fatigue. A pamphlet issued by the committee on labor, advisory commission, Council of National Defense, says, "Fatigue diminishes output not only directly, but indirectly, by increasing accidents and the proportion of spoiled work and by causing sickness and absences of employees. It will, therefore, be profitable to employers, to employees and to the Nation itself, to inquire into the ways by which fatigue may be reduced."

"Safety First" The motto of "Safety first" has been adopted in many establishments because it has been found that it is good economy to conserve human life. Miss Ida M. Tarbell in her *New Ideals in Business* tells of one foundry which claims that its accidents were reduced eighty-five per cent by compelling the workers to wear congress gaiters. The results of safety education and organization in the Steel Corporation have been amazing. Fully sixty per cent of accident reduction is charged to it. In the three years of 1911, 1912 and 1913 the casualty expense of the Steel Corporation was nearly seven and three-quarters millions of dollars. In three years they made a total net saving through safety work of $2,697,115.19.

MEASURABLE EFFECTS OF WELFARE WORK

Health Movement Very like the safety movement is the industrial health movement, which includes physical examinations of employees upon hiring, lectures on health, employing of a physician and nurse to care for employees, provision of dispensaries and convalescent homes. The value of such work is evident in keeping employees fit for work. There is no phase of the Clothcraft management in Cleveland from which it is believed a more direct return in dollars and cents comes than from this medical service. Three years after this type of industrial betterment work was started in the Tennessee, Coal, Iron and Railroad Company at Birmingham, Ala., the average earnings of the employees had increased in a higher percentage than their rates of wages and the average number of working days per month had increased from sixteen to twenty-two.

Recreation It is difficult to find figures which show the effect of recreation upon turnover and output though there are many statements to show that managers believe such effects result from this form of welfare work. In the introduction to the proceedings of the Employment Manager's Conference, held in Philadelphia in 1917, Royal Meeker says, "Leaving out of account all considerations other than the maximum output of product, a proper system of labor management would provide for workers ample time and facilities for rest and healthful recreation." Mr. Feiss of the Clothcraft Shop in Cleveland says, "I can't afford to have people working in my shop who don't have fresh air and fun." He also reports that as soon as they had their lunch room and recreation grounds in working order there was an immediate reduction in the number of men patronizing the neighboring grog shops. Before long the saloons in the neighborhood had been compelled to disappear and no one has attempted since to establish one nearby. Since "a drinking man makes stability out of the question" such a result must help to make for a reduction in labor turnover and also for a lessening in accidents. Providing milk for the employees during the day and the provision of a clubhouse where they may meet together for sociability all have a discouraging effect on the saloon.

Miss Tarbell, in speaking of the recreation facilities provided by the National Cash Register Company and the United Shoe Machinery Company, says, "They pay the firm, or they would not be supported by two as hard-headed concerns as these." "The effect of all these varied free activities * * * is blessed. It breaks the intolerable monotony * * * [which is]probably the chief cause of the unstable pay roll." "What baseball is doing for health and sociability in American industries cannot be estimated."

Miss Mary B. Gilson, Superintendent of the Service Department in the Clothcraft Shops, in speaking of the noon games and recreations, says, "I think I may safely say that in conjunction with the records of work these activities furnish us the most valuable means of determining the fitness of a worker for advancement to positions of responsibility." She says further, in speaking of the various forms of recreation provided, "Many people regard such things as fads and fancies in an industrial establishment, but * * * if you could visit one of our parties * * * you would be convinced that we are not only having a 'swell' time but we are getting results."

Mr. W. L. Chandler of the Dodge Manufacturing Company, Mishawaka, Ind., in an article entitled *Conclusions from a Survey of Over 500 Employees' Benefit Association* says, "A man who is proud of the employees' benefit association or of the thrift club, or baseball team, or band, must unconsciously have a good regard for the plant and organization behind it, which, barring irritants of some form to disturb the situation, will build for a low labor turnover."

An address by John Jackson, Superintendent of Strawbridge and Clothier, telling of the Mutual Aid Associations of that concern, says, "We believe that the group of employees' mutual benefit associations would be incomplete without an athletic association. The tonic of outdoor life and sports is one that cannot be secured in any other way. The cooperation of a large number of people from the same organization and the healthy rivalry which is sure to be engendered by outdoor sports must make for personal as well as organization betterment."

Education   The subject of industrial education is too large a one to describe here. Its beneficial effects are, however, quite evident. Boyd Fisher says in his address, *How to Reduce Labor Turnover*, "It is always cheaper to transfer from a less important position an employee who has been in training for a promotion. A work force can be more certainly toned up by educating apprentices and giving a

433

continuing and broadening education to operatives than by hiring brand new men by any system of careful selection whatever. The growing demands of industry far outrun the supply of skilled workers, and not only to contribute its share of trained people but even to obtain its share, a plant must cooperate in the general educational program."

Classes in sewing, domestic science, stenography, arithmetic, literature and technical branches related to the industry, are held in many establishments. These naturally benefit the worker and the factory profits from the improvement of the employee.

Housing
Housing is another phase of welfare work which is well worth considering. Miss Tarbell says, "One of our greatest safety experts says that safety is impossible if a man is poorly housed and fed. An experimenting and successful manufacturer employing hundreds of girls declares that unhappy homes make unstable payrolls. Competition itself is forcing employers to consider the outside life of their employees. The first and most important thing they must consider is the house the man lives in." She goes on to describe the redemption of the towns of the Frick Coke Company in Western Pennsylvania. Houses were built and put in order, streets were graded, and the yards were covered with soil to enable the residents to raise flowers and vegetables. In telling of the success of this policy, she says, "This redemption is as much a part of the company's business management as the method of taking out coal or making coke. They believe that the success of their business depends more upon their laboring force than upon any other one element. To have efficient, trustworthy, and steady men you must have healthy and contented men. Men are neither healthy nor contented in wretched homes." These are undoubtedly the reasons which have prompted other employers to provide some means whereby their employees may be enabled to live in a decent and comfortable way.

Profit-sharing
Possibly the following instance will be of interest in showing the benefits of a system of profit-sharing in reducing the turnover of labor. At the Ford Motor Works in December, 1912, 3,594 of the 5,678 men hired turned out to be "floaters," "five-day men," as those who come only to go are called. A month after the profit-sharing scheme was announced, the new practices in fitting

men to their tasks installed, these floaters fell to 322. Not all profit-sharing is as successful as this. It depends upon the form and motive of the scheme.

**Provident
Funds**
Mr. W. L. Chandler of the Dodge Manufacturing Company, in giving conclusions from a survey of over 500 employers' benefit associations, says, "Capital has but recently awakened to the value of these organizations in steadying the force and in reducing some of the unmeasured 'leaks of business.'" These "leaks" are the cost of absenteeism or the loss of quantity and quality of production due to workmen's being harassed by debt incurred through sickness or to their dragging themselves around in an effort to fight off disease without proper medical attention.

Mr. John Jackson, Superintendent of Strawbridge and Clothier, says, "The distribution of more than a quarter of a million dollars in benefits by this association carries its own message and leaves no need of comment from me as to the usefulness of such work."

The Bell Telephone Company in 1913 set aside $9,000,000 for pensions and "disability and death" funds. Since 1910 the United States Steel Corporation has administered a fund of $12,000,000 of which Mr. Carnegie gave $4,000,000. At the end of 1915, it had over 3,000 names on the roll. The average amount each received was a little over $219 a year. Many smaller concerns have provided some form of pension.

Supervision
In the table printed in the Monthly Bulletin of the United States Bureau of Labor Statistics mentioned previously, it was found that welfare secretaries were employed in 141 of the 431 establishments studied. Outside agencies cooperated in 154. The administration of the work was by employers alone in slightly more than half the cases. It is repeatedly emphasized that where the employees have a part in the management, the welfare work is most successful. Where the employer carries on welfare work as a form of charity or to further his own business interests, it is seldom successful. A generous and broad-minded policy, with the help and encouragement of the employees as its aim, will invariably bring out an unusual personal interest in the business on the part of the employees, which naturally will make for a low labor turnover.

If welfare work is administered in the proper spirit, we shall find many employers exclaiming as the steel man did, when asked as to whether welfare work paid from a practical view point, *"Pay?* Well, I should say it does pay. *Worth keeping up?* Well, we're spending more and more each year on it. *Practical?* It's practical down to the last cent!"

May Day Programs

Constance D'Arcy Mackay, War Camp Community Service, New York City

Since the celebration of May Day goes back to the very beginnings of history, there is an infinite variety of ways in which May Day can be celebrated. Nature and fanciful fairy myths may be used as the basis; a Greek theme may be drawn upon or some old world theme, such as The Pied Piper of Hamelin may be used. The English Maypole legends, including the Robin Hood legend, are ever popular. Last but not least, there is an American theme—The Maypole of Merrymount, famous not only in history, but in Nathaniel Hawthorne's story of that name.

With all this vast store of printed material ready to draw upon a great variety of May Day celebrations can be had. And it may be remarked here that May Day is too often allowed to become monotonous. By using a little ingenuity and common sense the same costumes can be utilized in succeeding years, and yet a totally different and stimulating effect obtained. A few new costumes added to the costumes on hand will often help to transform a festival into a totally new thing. Thus the costumes of nature myths will do for fairy plays, and later for Greek plays; old English costumes, supplemented by Puritan costumes can be used for The Maypole of Merrymount.

If possible a different story or myth should be used each year as a festival basis. It might be well to begin with Greek festivals or with myths and work forward to an American festival.

BOOKS THAT WILL BE OF HELP TO FESTIVAL WORKERS

Festivals and Plays by Percival Chubb, published by Harper Bros., Franklin Square, New York at $2.00. *Folk Festi-*

vals by Mary Masters Needham, published by B. W. Huebsch, 225 Fifth Avenue, New York at $1.00. *The Festival Book* by Jeanette E. C. Lincoln, published by The A. S. Barnes Company, 381 Fourth Avenue, New York City at $1.60. *Plays and Games, for Indoors and Out* by Belle Ragnar Parsons, published by The A. S. Barnes Company, 381 Fourth Avenue, New York at $1.60

FOLK DANCE BOOKS THAT WILL BE OF HELP TO FESTIVAL WORKERS

The Morris Dance, edited by Josephine Brower, published by Novelle Co., No. 2 West Forty-fifth Street, New York City at $1.00. *Polite and Social Dances,* edited by Marie Ruef Hofer, published by the Clayton F. Summy Co., 64 East Van Buren Street, Chicago, Ill., at $1.00. This book is valuable for historical pageants because it has good pictures, descriptions, and music of historic dances from the earliest times to the present. *Folk Dances of Denmark,* and *Folk Dances and Singing Games,* edited by Elizabeth Burchenal, and published by G. Schirmer, No. 3 East Forty-third Street, New York City. at $1.50

NATURE AND FANCIFUL FAIRY MYTHS

Cinderella in Flower Land, by Marion Loder, published by Chas. H. Ditson & Co., 8 East Thirty-fourth Street, New York City at 30 cents. This little operetta can be used very charmingly as a May Day Festival. It tells the story of Cinderella, only in this case all the characters are flowers, and the lost slipper is the Lady's Slipper. The costumes can be very inexpensive yet very pretty. The music is bright and attractive. This operetta has already been very widely used as a May Day Festival. Any number of children can take part.

The First Spring Baskets from *A Child's Book of Holiday Plays* by Frances Gillespy Wickes, published by the Macmillan Company, 64 Fifth Avenue, New York City, at 75 cents. This is a whimsical and delightful little play in two short scenes, both of which can be given out-of-doors, or indoors if desired. There are children and dryads and fairies and wood creatures in this play and very pretty dances could be introduced. The whole play breathes an atmosphere of spring. It would need twenty-five boys and girls to give it effectively.

Blossom Time by Alice C. D. Riley, published by the John Church Co., 39 West Thirty-second Street, New York City at 25 cents. This is a festival which can be made either short or long as desired. It needs at least twenty boys and girls to make it effective but as many more as desired can be used. The festival, which is really a festival of country life, has to do with all the new life of spring, blossoms, birds, lambkins, flowers. It contains recitations, songs and music.

Spring Festival by Marie Ruef Hofer, published by the Clayton F. Summy Co., 64 East Van Buren St., Chicago, Illinois, at fifty cents. This festival is most valuable because it gives all the music for the dances, as well as a festival outline, and descriptions of costumes. It is really a pageant of the four seasons, and either the whole four seasons can be typified or one or two of them given as desired. There are leaves and flowers, sunshine and wind and rain and insects, including grasshoppers and butterflies. It is really a very delightful festival. Little children can do some of the dances, while others can be given by girls and boys of high school age if desired. No section of the festival can be given effectively with less than forty participants. The whole festival would take one hundred and fifty participants in order to do it justice.

The Enchanted Garden and a *Pageant of Hours* from *The House of the Heart* by C. D. Mackay, published by Henry Holt & Co., 19 West Forty-fourth Street, New York City at $1.20. Both these plays have been used as a basis for spring festivals. In them boys and girls can be used interchangeably. *The Enchanted Garden* is a play about flowers, with flower dances, and from twenty to forty children can be used in it. *A Pageant of Hours* has been used as a small May Day celebration. There are fourteen characters in it, but this number may be increased to fifty or sixty by the introduction of dances.

The Sleeping Beauty could easily be made into a festival by a festival worker, since there is no dramatization of this play. A version of it given as a spring festival at the Neighborhood Playhouse, New York City, presented the idea that the Princess was really the Earth awakening to the kiss of Spring.

Spring was the Prince, clad in green, and Winter was the Witch that put the Earth to sleep.

Greek May Festival from *Folk Festivals* by Mary Masters Needham, published by B. W. Huebsch, 225 Fifth Avenue, New York City at $1.00. This festival outline can be found on page 51. It is a dramatization of the old story of Proserpine. The festival would be particularly good for an all-girl cast in a normal school, high school or college. It gives full suggestions for the organizing, costuming and rehearsing of the festival. The costumes would be Greek throughout and at the very least 35 girls would be required to produce it. For a large Greek festival on the same theme two hundred girls could be used effectively in pantomines and dances.

The Masque of Pomona from the *Forest Princess and Other Masques* by C. D. Mackay, published by Henry Holt & Co., 19 West Forty-fourth Street, New York City at $1.35. This Masque has been used by colleges and normal schools as a May celebration. It has been produced by a cast of three, Pomona, Vertunnus and an Old Woman, by leaving out the chorus of vine dressers and Greek youths and maidens with which the Masque begins. For its adequate presentation the Masque should have a cast of from twenty-five to fifty participants, or as many more as desired. A number of dances are introduced and the costumes are Greek throughout. The Masque deals with a Greek fable of the Spring.

Outlines for English May Day celebrations, including material of the Robin Hood legends can be had by applying to The Playground and Recreation Association of America, 1 Madison Avenue, New York City. Material of this kind can also be found in Percival Chubb's *Festivals and Plays,* published by Harper Bros., Franklin Square, New York, at $2.00. See page 182.

The Maypole of Merrymount from *Patriotic Plays and Pageants* by C. D. Mackay, published by Henry Holt & Co., 19 West Forty-fourth Street, New York City, at $1.35. This play

439

tells the story of the first Maypole celebration ever held in America. It is not possible for children of less than the eighth grade, but eighth grade young people, high school boys and girls and colleges have acted in it. It has also been given by communities. There are sixteen speaking parts, ten men and six girls. As many extra people as desired can be used in it. The costumes are in strongly picturesque contrast: There are Puritan costumes and the somewhat gypsylike costumes of the Merry-mount Revelers in bright gay colors. The account of this actual Maypole and its strong dramatic influence can be found in *Twice Told Tales* by Nathaniel Hawthorne.

Practical Aids in Conducting a Neighborhood Recreation Center

II

HAROLD O. BERG, Supervisor Extension Department, Board of School Directors, Milwaukee, Wisconsin

PRACTICAL SUGGESTIONS FOR CONDUCTING A BILLIARD ROOM

The billiard room should be in charge of an attendant and a checker.

The player before entering the game must register with the checker, secure a ticket and await his turn as indicated on his ticket. Five players are assigned to a table. Their tickets have the same letter and are numbered from 1-5. These tickets should be collected before the game begins. The attendant is to arrange the balls with the triangles, interesting those waiting their turn to play in chess and checkers. Do not give a boy a ticket for another game while he is still engaged in one.

Do not allow any players to sit on the table to make a difficult shot. Make them use the bridge or keep one foot on the floor.

Keep a close look-out for gambling and profanity.

Admit no boys in short trousers or under 16 years of age in the pool room—not even as spectators.

Hold monthly tournaments. Take entries and post the schedule of games. Post also scores up to date. Post the highest score made each day as an indication of the contest. Advertise

440

the tournament by posters and by word of mouth. Encourage inter-center pool contests.

Various kinds of pocket billiard games may be played. If the attendance is poor, games requiring considerable time may be allowed, but as soon as the attendance picks up such games must not be permitted to begin.

Before leaving put the attendance cards, tickets, cues, and balls in order for the next evening's work. Cues to be mended after 9:30. Keep the tables in good condition. Brush them thoroughly before the beginning of each session.

The checker is to have in his index case a card for every frequenter of the pool room. On these cards are to be placed the number of the table and the number of the card given. Particulars for these records will be found in the record books provided for that purpose.

Neither the attendant nor the checker should take part in any game. On the other hand the billiard room attendant cannot afford to be a chair warmer. The job if done right allows little or no time for sitting. Greet the boys as they come in and bid them adieu as they leave. Pay special attention to new-comers. Show them how to obtain the check. Invite those whom you see standing in the doorway to come in. Mix with the boys. Learn their names and their occupations. Interest yourself in the things that interest them. The pool room is the only kind of social center activity that at first attracts a certain type of boy. It should not remain the only one, however. Attempt to interest him in other center activities. Your position gives you a wonderful opportunity to be an influential factor in many a young man's life.

PRACTICAL SUGGESTIONS FOR CONDUCTING CLUBS AND CLASSES

Whenever possible, activities should be organized into clubs instead of classes, as for example: bands, orchestra, glee clubs, dramatic clubs, gymnasium clubs.

The attendants and the members should be made to feel the responsibility in keeping up the attendance. Periodic parties will assist in maintaining a good attendance.

Clubs are easily formed and die just as easily. Many die because they meet too often. The great responsibility of lengthening their lives falls on the director. This is done by advising and planning with the officers the work to be carried on at the meetings.

In club life breaking bread together aids in strengthening the bonds of union. Have spreads.

Each club should have its officers, constitution, stated time for meeting, monthly fee, and delegate or delegates to the central council.

Boys and men will band themselves into large clubs; girls and women form small clubs. Foster the growth of small groups and have frequent, say monthly, union parties of all the clubs.

Athletic and social clubs should gradually be led into literary, musical, dramatic work. No activity should be permitted behind locked doors.

All activities in charge of a paid attendant must have an attendance of fifteen. If the attendance falls below, the activity will be discontinued.

Clubs and societies using the center must affiliate with it and become an integral part of the organization.

Clubs may meet on any social center night.

All members of club activities should be registered on club attendance cards which should be kept in the office. Attendants are to call for the cards at the beginning of the session and return them before leaving the building with the attendance marked up to date. The director should keep in alphabetical order an attendance card for every individual belonging to some social center activity. Attendants should report new members every evening to the directors on the enrollment slips and directors should transfer these to the enrollment cards. Each individual is to have one enrollment card on which all his activities should be registered. On it should be indicated also the date of withdrawal from any registered activity, giving cause. Keep this office register up to date.

PRACTICAL SUGGESTIONS FOR CONDUCTING A QUIET GAME ROOM

The success of this room depends largely upon the personality and the enthusiasm of the attendant.

The program according to which this room is conducted is posted in the plan book furnished to the Quiet Game Room attendants. Post a list of games on hand.

Do not give out games wholesale. When a game is given

442

out delegate someone to be responsible for its return in perfect condition. Afternoon children when entering the room should be made to take seats and come for games at the invitation of the attendant. Allow no games to remain upon the tables when not in actual use.

"Quiet Game Room" is a misnomer. A certain amount of the noise can be avoided. It takes judgment to know how much legitimate talking and enthusiasm to tolerate.

When teaching a game do not become oblivious to the remainder of the room. Station yourself so that you can see what is going on. Encourage those to whom you have taught a game to teach it to a group of others. Interest yourself in the progress and the results of all games going on in your room. Indicate this interest if it be merely by a passing remark.

Advertise tournaments by attractive posters not only in the game room but also in the corridors and in other rooms of the center. Post the names of the winners.

Organize bowling teams, checker clubs, chess clubs. Arrange inter-center contests.

Keep games and supplies in a systematic order. Label the shelves of the cupboard. Mend your games. "A stitch in time saves nine."

On the last Saturday evening of each month take a careful inventory of all the quiet game room supplies according to directons found under cover of the quiet game room inventory book.

Regular bowling rules should govern the games played on the "miniature bowling alley."

PRACTICAL SUGGESTIONS FOR LIBRARIANS AND FOR THOSE CONDUCT-
ING READING ROOMS

The library should be at all times an inviting part of the center. The personality and attitude of the librarian in charge are a very determining factor in making it such. Many times the first visit to the library is one of curiosity. If made to feel at home visitors will be sure to come again. These visits though at first almost purely social, eventually under the guidance of a tactful librarian, result in an hour's reading and even in drawing of books.

The ultimate aim of the librarian is to create a reading

habit so that those coming to the library will become borrowers and draw books for home use. Work constantly to secure new borrowers. Have on hand constantly a liberal supply of applications for library cards. Encourage children to become borrowers. Explain carefully the filling out of applications. Mention to foreigners that books may be drawn free of charge. Explain in all cases that the card you give is good all over the city. Tell about the Milwaukee Public Library system. Suggest a visit to the main library and the larger branches.

It is not difficult to induce some people to become borrowers. They are already readers but have not been brought in contact with the great privileges of a public library. Other visitors have never had a reading habit, have never been brought in contact with books. Such people do not become seized with a desire for books the minute they step into a library. They must be handled with great tact. To mention the drawing of books on their first visit will be sure to keep them away in the future. Enter into conversation with such patrons, find out their occupations, hobbies, likes and dislikes, nationality, temperament. Bring gradually to their attention short *illustrated* articles that you think will interest them. If the proper subject matter, written according to their ability is put before them, they are quite sure to become interested. A librarian must know her books and magazines, know her patrons and then use tact in bringing the two together.

Greet everyone who enters your room. When they leave invite them to come again. Comment upon their absence. There should always be a quiet dignity about a library. Avoid however an atmosphere of supression. A certain amount of talking is permissible.

Teach children in the afternoon how to use the library. Teach the proper library conduct. Instill into them a library spirit.

Keep the library looking neat. Keep tables and chairs arranged in their proper order. This must be attended to several times during an evening. Do not allow chairs to be moved from one table and grouped around another.

Do not store papers, paste jars, on top of the cases. Keep the books set up firmly with book supports. Label the shelves.

Be particular about the appearance of your desk.

Check magazines and daily papers as soon as they arrive.

444

A book is furnished each library for this purpose. Notify the newspaper offices on the following morning of missing copies. Give the director at the end of the month a list of missing magazines.

File daily papers as soon as they come. Be sure to paste in odd sheets. Keep papers on file one week.

Stamp all magazines with the neighborhood center stamp on the cover and on several pages. Keep the latest issue in the magazine covers. Keep back numbers of the magazines in a special case or cupboard, stacking like magazines together. Label the shelves with the names of the magazines belonging on them. These shelves easily become out of order. They must be arranged often. Throw no magazine away even if worn. They are to be turned in to the main office at the close of the season.

Magazines can be made a great drawing card. Advertise them. Do not call attention to the magazines as a whole but call attention to individual articles. There is something for everyone in the magazines. To use a magazine successfully requires a knowledge of its contents. Review them as they come. Advertise the magazine by personal work with individuals as well as by posters. Call attention to the arrival of the new numbers. Call the attention of the other workers in your center to the articles you may find along their lines of work, for instance, crochet patterns, articles in millinery and dressmaking, chess and checker problems, baseball stories, accounts of athletics and tricks, games, plays and recitations.

Keep the bulletin boards of the library attractive. Do not allow the material on them to become ancient history. Change it often. Put up clippings, magazine and book notices, pictures and reading lists. Display curios, Public Museum specimens, industrial exhibits which may be drawn from the office. Always accompany such exhibits with reference to book or magazine articles on the subject. The main object of the bulletin board is to create new reading interests. Simple science experiments often help to interest boys to read along new lines.

Keep books mentioned in reading lists on a special shelf or table. Indicate the articles by little paper book marks on which are written the name of the book and the page of the article. Label the special shelf or table and ask that the books be returned to it.

Acquaint yourself with the course of study of the public

445

schools and the text books used in the different grades. When working with the afternoon children, ask them their grade in school and give them books related to the work of that grade. Call on the teachers of the school in which you are working and offer to secure for their pupils books on topics studied by the class.

Explain to the children the classification and arrangement of books in a library. Teach them to do reference work.

Discourage children attending the grade school from coming for books in the evening.

Advertise the foreign books. Encourage children to take them home to their parents. In such cases, care must be shown in the selection of books. Ascertain from the child something about the interests of the one who is going to read the book. Advertise the foreign books in the evening school and naturalization classes, also at the entertainments.

Play the phonograph in the evening. Do not play continually. Have intermissions between records. Do not let any person but the librarian operate the phonograph. When through using remove and put away the crank. Only one record at a time should be removed from the carrying case and should be put back as soon as it has been played. Use metal needles only. Keep speed set at 78. Dust records with a piece of velvet before playing. In the afternoon play only the records assigned to you. Keep your circulation records very carefully as indicated in the record book furnished each library. The librarian, not the afternoon checker, should make entries in the book.

Monthly reports must be closed on the twenty-eighth of the month and mailed to the office of the supervisor the evening of the same day. Make out a duplicate report for the director.

When a book is a week overdue send a postal notice to the holder. Children will sometimes be able to act as messengers for you.

Pay at least one visit a week to the main library. Telephone to the library for books requested by your patrons. Advertise the fact that books other than those on your shelves can be obtained by leaving a request with you.

446

PRACTICAL SUGGESTIONS FOR CONDUCTING DANCING CLASSES AND SOCIALS

Dancing classes and socials are held on Saturday evenings in Milwaukee, the dancing class from 7-9 o'clock and the social from 9-11:30. No one is admitted to the dance after 10:15. The attendance is limited to 300.

The admission to the dancing class is 5c; to the social 10c for a boy and 5c for a girl. Only people who are known to the director or can be introduced to him by someone whom he knows well are to be admitted. When selling tickets the checker always demands the name of the person not a member. The door-tender, checker or any other employee may not vouch for strangers. This must be done by the director. Persons desiring to be vouched for by the director or to be introduced to him must wait for him in the lower corridor. In no such case must the director be sent for. These people are to wait until the director makes his periodic round through the building. No person under sixteen years of age is admitted unless accompanied by a parent. No boy in short trousers is admitted to the social no matter what his age may be. The attendance of parents and older people is encouraged.

Tickets are sold in advance only to people who are members of other activities and then only on the night of actual attendance in that activity. Tickets may be reserved by those whose names are recorded but must be called for before nine o'clock unless some other hour is stated when the ticket is reserved. The number of tickets sold to each sex is limited but couples coming after the limit for sex has been reached are admitted. "Stagging" is discouraged.

The director is to have the following assistants at the socials: chaperon, door-tender, checker, one or more wardrobe boys.

The chaperon should not station herself on one side of the room but should spend most of her time in the middle of the floor.

The wardrobe is on the first floor. No wearing of sweaters is allowed and outer wraps must be discarded before admittance is gained to the hall. Attention to personal appearance is encouraged.

The dancing teacher is expected to give the program of the

447

social to the orchestra one week in advance so that they may come prepared. The director, too, must be supplied with the program. Each program contains 15 numbers, dances 6 minutes; intermissions 3 minutes; after the eighth dance an intermission of 10 minutes. The numbers of the program are indicated by cards and the musicians are responsible for the shifting of these cards.

SOME GENERAL SUGGESTIONS FOR THE DIRECTOR IN CONNECTION
WITH SOCIALS

Give the young people plenty of opportunity to dance so that they will be tired and ready to go home at 11:30.

Allow no one to leave the building for smoking or refreshments.

Do not permit improper holding or improper positions of the body while dancing.

Watch very closely and carefully the conduct of the young people during intermissions.

Be sure that all class room and cloak room doors are locked.

Allow no orchestra numbers with a sensual rhythm. Do not allow songs the words of which are not in conformity with the dignity of the school. Dances should maintain the same tempo throughout.

Have a floor committee. Give them a ribbon badge, a star, or some mark to designate them as individuals vested with authority. Persons violating the rules of the socials are upon the first offence to be warned without being humiliated and upon the second offence to be dismissed from the hall.

Keep the floor in good condition. Wax it when necessary. The dance floor should be scrubbed twice a month.

Young people should not be introduced to one another by persons in charge of the socials unless both persons are known to the introducer. Acquaintances should be made in the usual and legitimate manner. The dangers of wholesale introduction are very obvious.

The social is a golden opportunity for the director to become acquainted with his people and induce them to join the other activities. Announce other activities at the socials.

Where possible give the socials the atmosphere of a party by proper decorations and names, as for example, Hallowe'en

Party, Sylvester Eve Party, Valentine Party, Washington Party, Easter Party. Commercial recreation always strives to make itself attractive by alluring decorations.

Allow no dancing after entertainments or match games.

The director should be in constant attendance at the dance except for the periodic trips through the building which he should make. This is not the time to spend in the office preparing reports. With only one activity to supervise the director has a great opportunity to do field work among those in attendance.

PRACTICAL SUGGESTIONS FOR CONDUCTING ENTERTAINMENTS

Entertainments are held bi-weekly in Milwaukee. A fee of 5c is charged adults, children 3c or 2 for 5c. All activities are to be closed on entertainment nights. Entertainments begin at 8:15 and last not longer than 1½ hours. The doors are opened about 7:40.

The audience should be limited to the number of chairs. The stair-case should be lighted and exit lights must be turned on. Halls should not be over-crowded.

All children must sit with their parents throughout the evening. No child under fourteen years of age is admitted unless acompanied by a parent. Children are not admitted if accompanied only by older brother and sister. This rule is an effort to get the parents.

Boys and men not accompanying ladies are to sit in a segregated section of the hall.

The following aids are needed: door-tender, two ushers, and a ticket taker. Where possible the ushering and ticket taking is done by volunteers, thus making the entertainment self-supporting. The film rental, the salary of the operator, and the cost of any program number is paid out of the receipts. All other help is put on the pay roll. Not over $2.50 should be spent for an outside number.

The entertainments are advertised by circulars, by indoor and outdoor bulletins, through the newspapers, by pupils of the day school and the evening school, and the afternoon activities.

Copies of the programs given at the bi-weekly entertainments and children's Saturday evening entertainments are to be mailed to the office of the supervisor not later than the following Monday. Programs are to be prepared a week or two in advance.

Ladies should remove their hats at all entertainments.

No play, recitation or song is to be given without a previous reading and censorship by the director.

Windows should be locked during moving picture entertainments. If not, the costly darkening shades are pushed out of place by the draft which causes them to get out of shape and tear. The janitor is the only one who should handle these curtains.

Numbers by groups of children and local talent brings large audiences. Children's dramatics should play an important part in the Saturday afternoon program. The principals of the neighboring schools may be asked for numbers. Group numbers appeal more than solo numbers.

The Saturday afternoon entertainment should never contain more than three reels and the children's eyes should be safeguarded by having other numbers between the reels. A suggested program is: 1. Education reel; 2. Announcements (slides and oral); 3. Stereopticon lecture (short); 4. Drama reel; 5. One or two numbers (musical, humorous, dramatic); 6. Comic reel. Boys 1:45-3:00 p. m., girls 3:30-4:45 p. m. The room should be thoroughly ventilated between 3:00 and 3:30. The numbers on the program should be short and snappy and a sameness should be avoided. Intersperse your program with brief catchy announcements regarding the center. Where a number of the program serves as a basis for an announcement of an activity take advantage of it.

Good piano playing adds to the effectiveness of moving pictures. For $1.25 an expert musician can be obtained. A senior high school girl would probably welcome the opportunity and might be secured through the high school principal.

Lectures should not be read but talked from notes in a conversational manner.

Set a stated time when your band, orchestra, dramatic club, glee club, are to furnish a number for the entertainments as this furnishes an incentive.

Study the newspapers for entertaining talent. Consult your teachers, patrons of the social center, fellow directors and principals, programs in the office of the supervisor, the normal school and other educational institutions, church organizations, and settlement houses.

Encourage applause at the close of a number and be a leader in the applause. The assistants should be coached to be enthusiastic applauders.

No tickets should be sold in advance.

Participants in the program should not be left in a room unsupervised.

While the numbers are being rendered the director should station himself near the boy's section. Ushers should be in attendance throughout the program and stand in a position which permits of close supervision. After the entertainment the director should be in such a position as will enable him to pass a word or two with the people who are leaving. The aids should be assigned to different stations on the way to the outer door, first floor landing, second floor landing, and they should be encouraged to speak to the people as they go out.

PRACTICAL SUGGESTIONS FOR DOOR-TENDERS

The door-tender is not a night watchman. He is a reception committee of one. It is he who nine times out of ten gives visitors their first impression of the center.

Be dignified, courteous and friendly. Be stern when the occasion demands it.

Put people who seem strange at ease by welcoming them. Greet those who come in and bid adieu to those who leave. A handshake goes a long way. Put forth special effort to make the timid, the aged, and the poorly-clad feel at home.

Direct people to the wardrobe. Tell them there are no charges. Encourage them to take off their wraps. Attempt to become personally acquainted with the patrons of the center. Strive to learn their names.

If you speak a foreign language make use of it whenever you see an opportunity to do so.

School children must not be admitted in the evening. Newsboys and boy scouts are the only exceptions. They must present "membership cards."

Keep out undesirables.

Insist that careless young people remove snow and dirt from their shoes before entering. Instruct young men to remove their hats.

Maintain discipline on the first floor. This can not be done by standing on the same spot all evening.

Discourage "lighting up" on the part of those leaving the building. Allow no smoking or loitering on the outside of the building. Made periodic trips around the outside of the building.

Always have in your pocket "attendance certificates" ready to be filled out on demand. Use a fountain pen or an indelible pencil. Do not give a boy his slip until he is leaving the building.

In Milwaukee the door-tender is required to report for duty at 6:45 and to remain at his post until dismissed by the director. He counts all the people leaving the building before 8:25 p. m. and after that counts all those entering. He leaves this count with the director each night to be recorded in the attendance report. He signs the vouchers for all money taken in at the entertainments.

PRACTICAL SUGGESTIONS FOR JANITORS AT NEIGHBORHOOD CENTERS

The social center janitor of a full time neighborhood center is subject to the orders of the center director after 3:00 which is the time he is due at the center. He is responsible for the firing after 3:30 until the close of the evening session.

If it is necessary to wheel coal each janitor at the close of his session is to see to it that the pile is as large as he found it. At the close of their respective sessions each janitor is to see to it that the ash pit is empty.

In a full time center, basement Active Game Rooms are to be swept twice each day, before 3:30 and between 3:45 and 7 o'clock p. m., evening centers once a day before 7 o'clock p. m. Use saw dust and kerosene.

The Assembly Hall is to be swept after being used in the evening and in a full time center between 4:45 and 7 o'clock p. m., if the director deems it necessary. If used during the day, the school janitor is to sweep it before 3:30. This hall is to be scrubbed once every two weeks and oftener if the director deems it necessary. All basement rooms and corridors are to be swept once a day.

All class rooms used by night school classes and social center activities and all corridors and stairways are to be swept after the regular day school session by the school janitor and after being used in the evening by the social center janitor.

All lights must be turned off as soon as pupils are dismissed in the afternoon and lighted when ordered by the director.

In a full time social center, the janitor or an assistant must be in constant attendance from 3:00 o'clock to the close of the session. Janitors of evening social centers are to report at 6:30 p. m.

If used three or more evenings a week the kindergartens are to be scrubbed once a week by the social center janitor, preferably Wednesday evening. According to the rules of the school board the regular day janitor is required to scrub the kindergarten once a week. Thus the kindergarten will be scrubbed twice a week.

All class rooms used for regular social center activities are to be scrubbed once every two months by the social center janitor. The rules of the school board require the regular day janitor also to scrub these rooms from four to six times a year. The rule for the social center will in no way affect this rule.

The swimming tank is to be drained every Wednesday evening and the bottom and sides thoroughly scrubbed.

If a full time center and class rooms are used from which the seats must be removed the two janitors have to cooperate. The school janitor will assist in the removing of the seats. The social center janitor in turn will assist the school janitor in the sweeping of this room and as many rooms as will make the sum total of rooms swept twice the number of rooms from which the seats were removed.

The social center janitor is to *dust* once a day all furniture used by the social center. This should be done at periods when the air is not laden with the dust from a recent sweeping.

The basement windows are to be cleaned once a month and oftener if the director deems it necessary.

The shower bath rooms and the showers are to be mopped every other day. The seats in the closed showers are to be scrubbed once a week.

The soap dispensers are to be replenished each day.

Harmony between the school janitor and the social center janitor will do much in establishing and maintaining a high standard of cleanliness in the buildings.

PRACTICAL SUGGESTIONS

The attendant is furnished with a master key for the lockers. At the request of a patron he opens a locker, permits the patron to store his clothing and then locks it again. The locker is not to be opened again except at the request of the patron.

When a patron obtains a towel, which is furnished for 1c, the attendant writes on a card the number of the locker or the shower used by him. When the patron leaves his shower or requests to have his locker opened, the attendant takes his towel and crosses out his number from the list. Soiled towels should be put into a receptacle provided for that purpose and under no conditions should they be allowed to lie around even for a short time.

Guard against the stealing of towels and see that towels are not misused. Allow no private towels to be stored in the lockers—hygienic reasons are obvious.

At the beginning of each session the director is to give the shower attendant a certain number of towels. These should be kept in a locked cupboard. At the close of the session the attendant should return to the director all used and unused towels. These must of course equal the number given to the attendant at the beginning of the session. The attendant should keep on a record sheet the daily account of the number of towels given and the number of towels used. This record should be handed in daily to the director together with the money taken in and the director should total this record each month.

Allow only one person at a time in a shower.

Explain to the patrons of the showers the danger of leaving the building directly after a shower bath. Encourage ending a bath with a cold shower. Teach warming exercises. Allow no children to take a shower bath the last half hour of the session.

Vol. XII. No. 11   FEBRUARY 1919

The Playground

War Camp Community Service

In peace as well as in war, community
service helps to make the world safe for
democracy.

Howard S. Braucher

Published monthly by The Playground and Recreation
Association of America, One Madison Avenue, New York,
N. Y. Price 25 cents a copy; $2.00 a year.

Entered as second class matter on August 8, 1916, at the Post
Office at Cooperstown, N. Y., under the Act of March 3, 1879.

The "Sign of the Red Circle" brings them here

DURING the time between a supper of good home-cooked food served at a War Camp Community Service Canteen in Baltimore, and the War Camp Community Service dance planned for the evening, these men pass the time playing billiards in a War Camp Community Service Club.

When motor canteens became necessary

IN the summer of 1918, War Camp Community Service improvised a Motor Canteen Service in Washington, D.C., to help take care of the two hundred thousand extra clerks and executives doing war work there. Through such service it was possible for them to work on a half-hour luncheon schedule.

When our Northern men are under Southern skies

EVERY soldier in Camp Greene, North Carolina, was invited recently to a picnic at Lakewood Park near Charlotte. The program was arranged by War Camp Community Service. A large swimming pool was one of the biggest attractions. Assisted by the ladies of various churches nearby, a typical Southern supper was served.

In every window appears the "Red Circle"

"WREN'S Nest," Atlanta, Georgia,
the home of Joël Chandler Harris,
author of the Uncle Remus stories, has
been turned over to War Camp Community Service, and displays the sign of
welcome to all soldiers and sailors. They
come here at all times, but especially
over Sundays.

U. S. army trucks escort soldiers to matinee

IN St. Louis, Missouri, as in so many other cities, War Camp Community Service has arranged free theatre parties for men in uniform. On this occasion, fourteen hundred soldiers were brought from Camp Scott, twenty-eight miles distant.

Outdoor sports in the Northern States

FOR the Soldiers stationed in camps up North, outdoor carnivals and athletic sports of every description are arranged by War Camp Community Service. These events are always anticipated with a great deal of pleasure.

Delightful hours in Californian orange groves

A GROUP of men from Fort McAr-
thur, California, spending a happy
day in the orange grove of a friend of
War Camp Community Service in Los
Angeles. It is a rare treat for men from
the East to go on these "Orange Excursions."

The Navy was well represented

IN San Diego, California, the Stadium was placed at the disposal of War Camp Community Service for the men in service by the Park Commissioners for three days a week, and football games have been popular. Fifteen thousand sailors and civilians attended the New Year's football game.

Soldiers taking part in a trench fight

IN the late fall of 1918, War Camp
Community Service conducted a Field
Day for Men in Uniform in the Boston
Stadium. All kinds of athletic sports were
staged. The matches between the Army
and the Navy were played with the keen-
est sportsmanship.

Thanksgiving hospitality for soldiers and sailors

THROUGHOUT the country invitations for Thanksgiving Dinner poured into the War Camp Community Service offices. Everywhere men in khaki and blue found homes and hearts open to them.

There are forty clubs for colored soldiers and sailors

WITH the help of the colored people in towns adjoining the camps, War Camp Community Service has established forty clubs for colored soldiers and sailors. This one is at Baltimore.

Making the Colorado Soldiers' and Sailors' Club famous

THE Colorado Soldiers' and Sailors' Club in Denver keeps a cookie jar on hand which never gives out in spite of the constant raids upon it by the khaki-clad. Because the cookies are "like mother used to make," this Club has become justly famous.

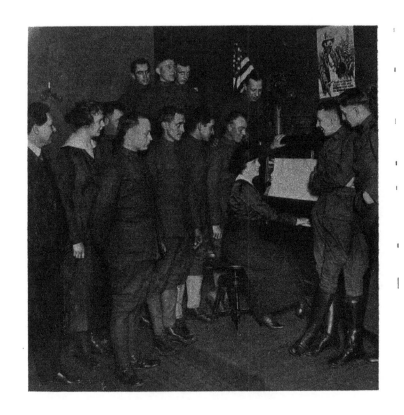

A community social in a social community

CHURCHES all over the United
States have been cooperating with
War Camp Community Service in entertaining soldiers and sailors. These soldiers
are guests of All Saints Episcopal Church
at Atlanta, Georgia. And there are many
uniforms to be seen at the regular church
services.

Did he write you a letter from here?

"IN the City of Norfolk," at the Red Circle Club of War Camp Community Service, over seven hundred letters are written each day. This mail is addressed to homes all over America. Writing materials are always kept on hand in great abundance.

E VEN in far Ha
munity Serv
and its activities
These pictures s
by The Honolulu

War Camp Com-
ias its organizer
nen in uniform.
events arranged
C. S.

Training for an Army and Navy baseball game

IN the sunny South, baseball is in season at this time of the year. Men in
blue and khaki take to baseball like
ducks to water. They are found playing
whenever and wherever possible—even
on week-end parties.

Tea and cakes and friendly camaraderie

REAL joy in a real home is the spirit
of these friendly afternoon teas arranged for Army and Navy men through
War Camp Community Service throughout the United States. To prove that
they fill a gap in a long day, the men
"come again."

Warm hearts around a warm fire

AND they hung up stockings and sat by the fireside and thought of home and told fairy tales to little brother. In this private home these soldiers weren't so lonesome after all and they certainly were made more than welcome by these friends.

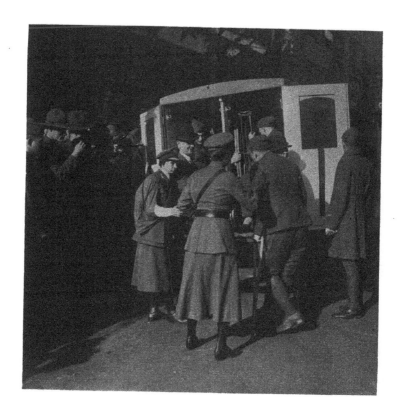

Forgetting their pain for a few hours

THE ambulances of the Motor Corps
of America carried five hundred
wounded soldiers in one afternoon from
the base hospitals around New York to
a special matinee held for them at the
Strand Theatre, New York City. This
was arranged by War Camp Community
Service.

Loving hands and tender hearts do their bit

IT took hours to wrap Christmas packages in preparation for the Yuletide
festivities held in the home of this War
Camp Community Service friend. And
the wholehearted fun when these presents were undone repaid a thousand
times the work it entailed.

Their first holiday after returning to America

IN New York City, as in so many others, War Camp Community Service planned Christmas parties and Christmas and New Year's Dances. These overseas men, not able to get home, are trimming the tree for the evening's entertainment.

Books and easy chairs and restful hours

IN Gramercy Park, New York City,
War Camp Community Service has
opened a Convalescent Hospitality Home
called "Pershing House" for Pershing's
wounded men. Coming from different
convalescent hospitals in and about New
York, the men gather in this beautiful old
house to read and write and talk and rest.

Are they hungry or just sociable?

WHEN it comes time to serve luncheon at Pershing House, the men flock to the kitchen. And they are always welcome! Often they make suggestions for "new dishes," some of which have become very popular. The National League for Women's Service, in cooperation with War Camp Community Service, serves breakfast, luncheon and afternoon tea every day.

Rainy days are quite as busy as shiny ones

ON such days more than ever War Camp Community Service workers call at the various W.C.C.S. Units to pass the hours in friendly talks and games of chess and checkers with the men who come there, who might otherwise spend a lonely day.

Storm-bound but happy in the club

THESE soldiers and sailors maintain
it is no hardship to be storm-bound
on trips between camps if such hospitality
as this soldiers' and sailors' club had to
offer is available. War Camp Community
Service endeavors to meet all emergencies with prompt action.

Scrap books for convalescent soldiers—guarantees against boredom

THIS group of workers from the La-
clede Gas Light Company are making life more pleasant for the convalescent soldiers at the hospitals to whom the
hours of waiting are so long, by making
scrap books at the War Camp Community Service headquarters in St. Louis.

Celebrating old ceremonies in new surroundings

EIGHT hundred Jewish soldiers attended a special Passover celebration at Atlanta, Ga. at which religious services were combined with special dinner festivities. The Jewish Welfare Board, which is co-operating with War Camp Community Service, entertained three hundred soldiers in the morning; in the evening, five hundred.

Where to go, eat and sleep

THESE are vitally important matters to the soldier or sailor on leave in a strange city and the thousands of information booths similar to the one erected by the Baltimore War Camp Community Service, which dot all the camp cities, represent a very practical service.

A popular dance at the colored club

THE clubs for colored soldiers which War Camp Community Service has been establishing throughout the country, have been popular meeting places for the colored troops and the civilians who are doing so much to entertain the soldiers. The Atlanta, Ga., club shown here is meeting a great need.

Please mention THE PLAYGROUND *when writing to advertisers*

Specimen page in miniature from the 52-page book accompanying each set of charts.

Specimen chart in miniature from the new Victor set of 18 charts for teaching music in the schools.

Orchestra of High School, Oakland, Cal.

Have you an orchestra in your school?

Do the pupil candidates for positions all want to play the violin or the cornet, not understanding that the oboe and bassoon, double bass and traps are just as necessary in the ensemble, even if less attractive as solo instruments? Do they know how a French horn *looks* or how an English horn *sounds*? If you started your orchestra as did a famous lady in a Western city with a "jew's-harp, mouth-harp and triangle" you will need some ocular and aural assistance in securing a balance of parts in each family of instruments.

"The Instruments of the Orchestra by Sight and Sound"

The Victor Company has just issued a comprehensive set of eighteen charts (14x22) showing each instrument in its natural *color;* and in an accompanying booklet is given a full description of the instrument, its origin, history, development and uses by composers. Two special Victor Records (Nos. 35670 and 35671) give the exact reproduction of the sound and tone color of each instrument, all three together offering for the first time complete presentation of the instruments "by Sight and Sound."

See your nearest Victor dealer for the charts and records, or write for information to the

Educational Department
Victor Talking Machine Co.
Camden, N. J.

"HIS MASTER'S VOICE"

Victrola XXV, $90
specially manufactured for School use

When the Victrola is not in use, the horn can be placed under the instrument safe and secure from danger, and the cabinet can be locked to protect it from dust and promiscuous use by irresponsible people.

Victrola

IRA W. JAYNE   (See page 530)

Hartford, Conn.

A SUCCESSFUL OUTDOOR DANCE FLOOR   (See Page 492)

THEODORE ROOSEVELT

Honorary President, Playground and Recreation Association of
America, 1906-1919

490

The Playground

Vol. XII No. 12   MARCH 1919

The World At Play

The Community Christmas Tree.—Why not keep it alive throughout the year? It is not too early in the year to begin to think about next year's Community Christmas Tree. A suggestion made by Miss Gertrude Vivian in the December number of *The Woman's Magazine* will be of interest.

"The idea of an outdoor Christmas tree that everybody in the community may enjoy has spread over America with remarkable rapidity. It was only a few years ago that New York City proudly lighted up its first community tree for its seven million inhabitants.

"The tree was a huge spruce, erected in Madison Square Park, glowing with wonderful colored lights, and crowned with a big shining star.

"The first tree in Chicago was presented by a public-spirited citizen, and decorated by the Electric and Telephone Company.

"The large cities took the lead in making the community tree an accepted yearly event. But it remained for a small town to start the latest idea in community trees.

"Flushing, Long Island, has a permanent Christmas tree that stays evergreen from Christmas to Christmas! The Park Garden Club put their heads together and decided that the cost of buying, hauling and erecting a tree each year was useless waste. Why not buy a good growing tree and plant it in a central spot, where the town could gather each year for its Christmas celebration. The initial cost would be considerable, but in a few years the tree would pay for itself by the money saved.

"So last spring the Park Garden Club bought a splendid Serbian spruce, thirty-five feet high, and planted it in front of the high school in Flushing.

"On Christmas Day it will glitter and glow for its admiring friends—and the good folk of Flushing will bid good-by to their tree with the comfortable assurance that next year

491

it will light up for them just as beautifully as before.

"What about *your* town? Can't you start a movement for a permanent Christmas tree? Begin now, while the Christmas spirit is abroad in the land. A growing Christmas tree that lasts from year to year is a good investment for any community."

A New National Habit.— From Mr. C. M. Goethe of Sacramento comes the suggestion that America ought to do far more than she has done in developing walking as a form of recreation.

Mr. Goethe's recommendation is based on a world-wide study of recreation in practically all foreign countries except South America, Australia and a portion of Africa. This study has brought to him several convictions. One of these is that the best Europe has evolved along recreational lines has been its splendid organization of hiking trips. The result of this organization is a form of recreation so inexpensive that the masses can turn to it when recreationally starved. One method is the nature-study-field excursion; another is rucksacking in such areas as the Alps, Norway or the Hartz Mountains. Still another is "wandervoegling." Europe has sensed the fact that the masses

need the inexpensive; that the incomes of most people do not permit of expensive outings; that it is only through nature study and hiking combined that they find that joy in life for which they hunger.

Mr. Goethe suggests that some way should be devised for offering the crystallized experience of Europe to America in such a way that a national habit will become fixed.

Can we not start the movement through the playgrounds by arranging for frequent walks in the course of which children can be taught in a way which will interest them permanently much bird lore and knowledge of flowers? Saturday afternoon and Sunday hikes for adults are gaining in popularity. Can they not be made to form the nucleus for the development of a new national habit?

An Outdoor Dance Floor.— Mr. S. Wales Dixon, Supervisor of Recreation, Department of Parks, Hartford, Connecticut, sends the following description of the outdoor dance floor at Colt Park, which has proved a great success:

"The floor is 86' by 126' surrounded by a row of seats, outside of which is a promenade 12' wide which goes around the entire structure; outside of this is another row of benches. Large seating capacity is thus obtained. This structure cost about six thousand dollars which we paid for during our short season. A sounding board or shell which will cost nearly three thousand dollars (and we have set aside the money for it from our earnings) will be erected in the spring which will make it possible to use the structure for a great many purposes, even for lectures. One of the best uses to which this floor has been put was the Sunday evening community sings and concerts which were largely attended. Soldiers and sailors were in evidence at week-ends.

"The floor was opened July 24th and closed the middle of October, during which time we had nearly 70,000 admissions through the gate at ten cents each, and three times that number out in the park who came to enjoy the music and the sight of the dances. The nominal charge enabled us to procure a first-class orchestra made up from the best bands in the city who each had a weekly engagement. Our smallest crowd, along at the time of closing when it was really too cold for comfort, was about 400 and our largest crowd through the gate was 2,800—which was altogether too large from many standpoints."

Americanization in Chicago. —The Chicago Association of Commerce reports gratifying results from its fifty-seven weekly classes in Americanization, held in various industrial plants. Thousands of men are reached and reduction in labor turnover, increased interest in their work and improvement in the social life of the workers are present fruits.

Another Playground for India.—Welcome news has come of the opening of a new playground in India in the management of which the Government is participating. Mr. C. M. Goethe in writing of the playground says: "Its location is in a city near the base of the Himalaya Mountains. When Mrs. Goethe and I were there our impression was that of two rival wedding processions marching simultaneously, each bidding against the other to see which could obtain the more of the available elephants. That night we slept on string beds. The next morning we breakfasted at a girls' school where all ate with their fingers out of the common dish."

It is here that the new playground is being opened.

The Need For Imaginative Recreation in the Reconstruction Period

CONSTANCE D'ARCY MACKAY, War Camp Community Service,
New York City, N. Y.

Many significant things are coming out of the Great War,
and perhaps only one of the most significant is the composite
picture of the camps and their needs—a picture of what two
million men desired in their leisure time; of what their dreams
were made of. If "we are what our dreams make us" then this
composite picture, impossible to secure in peace time, is one of
the things war-created which has an immense bearing on our
future as a nation.

Realizing the terrific strain that this greatest of all wars
put upon the soldier our Government did everything in its power
to keep life normal and sane and wholesome inside and outside the
camps. It provided dances, movies, libraries, socials, picnics,
athletics and motor rides for the men—yet there were deeper and
subtler needs than these.

We have been accustomed to think of art as one of the luxuries of life: a composite picture of the camps show that it is one
of the necessities. For art enters into all imaginative recreation.
And recreation in its deepest sense is Re-Creation.

The heavier the strain that is put on the individual the more
imaginative recreation is needed.* We hear a great deal about
What-the-Public-Wants. In the midst of war What-the-Public-
Wants was demonstrated from the Atlantic to the Pacific Coast.
It wants non-commercial imaginative recreation—wants it more,
perhaps, than any of us realize, or than we will accustom ourselves to admit. *Yet everything that has been done along the
lines of imaginative recreation in the camps has a bearing on*

*From the Central Distributing Station in Paris, one thousand
sets of costumes were issued to soldier entertainment units in France
during the month of October, 1918. The Y. M. C. A. which, overseas,
was a part of the army, stationed a man in each camp who took
charge of the entertainment needs and remained with the regiment or
division continuously. Self entertainment by the soldiers and under
soldier leadership was particularly desired and encouraged. In the
absence of established organization the Y. M. C. A. leader filled the
place of a dramatic director—From a Government report

what might be done along these same lines in civil life; for in this dawning period of reconstruction we shall need imaginative recreation more than ever before. Therefore, may it not be wise to take a brief survey of what has been done, what has been *proved,* as a basis for what *might be done,* since the past is the stepping stone of the future.

Drama and Music in Camp Life The two arts that have played the greatest part in camp life are the art of drama,* and the art of music. If you are a skeptic, and need to be convinced, step back through the portals of time to those days that now seem so far off—the days when the Great War was still being fought—and attend the Liberty Theatre at a typical camp—Camp Devens, Ayer, Mass., on an evening in late September, 1918.

You will find the theatre set in the heart of the cantonment. Before the door men are standing, men in khaki, hundreds of them—some with "Smileage Books" and some without. You enter the theatre (where no seats are reserved) and find it an immense, barn-like, unpainted structure with a sloping floor and rows upon rows of benches. Yet somehow, its very rawness is impressive. It has a suggestion of pioneer forces.

The theatre is well lighted and well ventilated. Dozens of huge electric fans are in motion; and the smell of rough, unpainted timber is strong on the air.

It is only seven-thirty, but already the uncarpeted aisles re-echo to the steady tread of feet. And presently you are aware of a mighty rustle and hum—the voices of the men as they turn the leaves of their programs and discuss the possibilities of the coming "show." The theatre is filled from the first row to the last. That means that three thousand men are present. Turn your head and take a look at those long rows of young, determined faces. What an audience to play to! Democracy incarnate!

---

*In connection with the dramatic activities fostered in the army by the Training Camp Commission it may be noted that General Yogi said at the time of the Russo-Japanese War, that for many years the Nippon Government had realized the necessity of drama as a means of maintaining the morale of the Japanese army.

General Hamilton relates that during the Russo-Japanese War he saw twenty thousand Japanese soldiers in a beautiful Manchurian valley attend a highly artistic performance given on a portable stage standing on bamboo supports. The drops and curtain, whether for interior or exterior, were draped on light bamboo rods which telescoped cleverly like fishing-rods.

IMAGINATIVE RECREATION IN RECONSTRUCTION

It is the audience and not the players that will give you the thrill of the evening.

Jock O'Dreams Reveals Himself in Song All unannounced a song leader has come out in front of the curtain, and you are on your feet hearing the *Star Spangled Banner* sung as you have seldom heard it. And then, when you have taken your seat, you are aware that another remarkable thing has happened; at a sign from the song leader the whole theatre again becomes a mighty chorus. You may have heard men sing together; but have you ever heard three thousand men sing together—three thousand men who have been trained to sing? It is something never to be forgotten. In the words of of Walt Whitman you can hear "America singing." Clear and deep and sweet the sound rises and stirs you, and you remember that the drama itself was born of song—that it grew out of rhythmic chant and chorus; out of the human need for expression.

Keep the Home Fires Burning. How they sing it! What fervor they pour into it! And in another moment they are laughing their way through the famous "chow" song:

```
"Wednesday .................S-O-U-P
 Friday .......................F-I-S-H,"
```

and next they are musically proclaiming *Oh, How I Hate to Get Up in the Morning!* And then they swing into *There's a Long Long Trail A-winding into the Land of My Dreams.* They sing it with a feeling of beauty that you would not have believed possible. Unless they really felt it no power on earth could teach them to sing it like that. And suddenly and subtly you become conscious that deep down in every man in the audience there is a Jock o'Dreams—an elusive Jock, a shy Jock, afraid to show his face, afraid he will be laughed at if he confesses how much beauty means to him. But set him singing and before he knows it he has unconsciously revealed what he thought was hidden even from himself.

The curtain rises. The evening of vaudeville begins. It is average vaudeville. Some of the "acts" are good; some of them are mediocre. Surprisingly enough, the audience, generous with laughter where there is anything to laugh at, is rather chary of applause.

And then a curious thing happens: a private in khaki appears ("From Company G," a man behind you whispers) and quite simply sings a semi-classical song. It is perfectly good English

496

that every one can understand. The unknown singer is an artist, a trained musician. That is instantly apparent. He gives what he has to give with absolute simplicity and directness in a really beautiful voice. The house, taken by surprise, is so still you can hear a pin drop. At the song's end the applause is like Niagara. It pours through the theatre, deafening, stupendous. The singer comes back and back. They will not let him go.

> "Her brow is like the snow-drift
> Her throat is like the swan."

Yes, these are the same boys that laughed so uproariously only fifteen minutes before over the acrobatic antics of Norrie, the Nut; these are the same boys that crowed with delight over a skillful "buck and wing." They wanted fun; they wanted skill; but besides all this they wanted *beauty*. The biggest, most thrilling response of the evening was made to an unheralded singer who gave the boys what they wanted—not what they were *supposed* to want. They gave a hearty response to an artillery man who did some clever imitations; they showed warm approval of a man from the depot brigade who essayed a spirited pianologue full of local hits; but it was the singer in khaki who gave them the finest work of the evening, and they recognized it, instantly and tumultuously.

They proved that the average man wants the best if he can get it easily and inexpensively.

The Unconscious Craving for Beauty in the Drama At the Hostess Houses it was not altogether the sense of quiet, and the pleasure of feminine companionship that attracted the boys, and they freely confessed it. The books, the flowers, the air of spaciousness, the good taste that lay in entire simplicity of decoration made an immense appeal. A Saturday night at one of the Hostess Houses with music and dramatic readings and good talk about the open fire was a revelation to many boys who had been compelled by force of circumstances to lead meagre, arid lives. One stormy night at the Hostess House at Camp X——— a private who in civilian life was the editor of a well-known quarterly, read aloud to the assembled men from the works of Kipling, Service, and Robert Louis Stevenson. The boys enjoyed it hugely. In the days following there was a raid on the Kipling—Service—Stevenson books in the camp library. Then came a petition for another such evening, and this petition was started by a man who, up to the time of his enlistment, had been a waiter in a New York hotel. For many men the *spoken word* holds a lure that the *printed word* does not at first possess. And drama is made up of the spoken word. That is why it is so vitally important that what the theatre offers should be of the best. The truth is, Jock o'Dreams wants something finer than either he or we will acknowledge.

In the beginning, there were only sixteen Liberty Theatres Less than a year afterwards, in response to the need for them, there were forty-five Liberty Theatres.* The price of admission in all Liberty Theatres was exactly the same—twenty-five and fifty cents. These Liberty Theatres were run without financial loss. And if these theatres could be run without financial loss, so could People's Theatres (i. e. Industrial Theatres or Workingman's Theatres †) where they and their families could see good plays at reasonable prices. At present, the working man and his family are condemned to the movies. The spoken drama is utterly prohibitive.

Self Expression through Community Drama Meanwhile, it is interesting to note that community drama (that is, drama acted by the people themselves, and in the case of the camps acted by the soldiers themselves) has flourished amazingly.

The men not only wanted to see plays; they wanted to participate in them. They participated in music; why not in drama? The word amateur really means art-lover; and as amateurs

---

* Players such as Laurette Taylor, Otis Skinner and David Warfield have appeared in the Liberty Theatres. Each camp had its favorite play. At Camp Devens the favorite play was *Daddy Long-Legs*. The most universally popular play throughout all the camps was that wholesome, "home-folks" comedy, *Turn to the Right*. Nor have the Liberty Theatres had a monopoly in the producing of plays. "Visiting talent" as well as "home talent" gave some remarkably good productions in the various Y. M. C. A.'s. In a camp near the Eastern sea-board, Anatole France's fanciful masterpiece, *The Man Who Married a Dumb Wife* proved popular, as did also Oliphant Down's *A Maker of Dreams*.
Semi-classical musical programs given by visiting artists such as Maud Powell and Leopold Godowsky drew a huge attendance.

† Such a theatre was planned by a group of manufacturers at Pompton Lakes, New Jersey, and the building was by way of being erected when peace was declared and the diminishment of the working force caused the theatre project to be abandoned. It would have been a *community theatre* with working people for its players. Its director was to have been Mrs. Pratt, formerly of the Greenwich Village Theatre, New York, and she had evolved a plan whereby the Irish workers would give plays by Yeates, Synge, and Lady Gregory; while Russian plays would be given by Russians *in English,* and so on. The ideal theatre for working people is difficult to plan for in this country since so many of our workers speak different tongues. But it can be done.

(i. e. art-lovers) the men wanted to have their share in the experience of being, if only for an evening, "some one else." They liked to be a part of the movement and color and creative life that goes to the making of any play. In other words, they wanted glamour.

The list of plays that casts of men could act successfully was so very meager that the United States Government, for the first time in its history (or in the history of any government for that matter) went into play-publishing on its own account. It published a set of one-act Service Plays which would be used only by the men in the service. These plays were distributed by the War Board, Commission on Training Camp Activities, free of charge. Each play was written by a famous dramatist especially for the camps. Amongst the authors so represented were Augustus Thomas, Edgar Selwyn, Austin Strong, Captain Rupert Hughes, and others. Barrie's tender *The Old Lady Shows Her Medals,* Yeats' whimsical *Pot of Broth,* and Lady Gregory's *Workhouse Ward* were greatly in demand as were short pieces by Richard Harding Davis, such as *The Zone Police.*

The men utilized Jewish Welfare or Knights of Columbus, or Y. M. C. A. houses as places in which to act these plays; and for fifteen of the camps the government provided experienced dramatic directors to train the men. The reports of these directors were published in the bi-monthly bulletin issued by the War Board and many of them were highly significant.

Each camp worked out its own problems individually. Camp Greenleaf, Georgia, specialized in the production of patriotic plays. *Here is a hint for social center leaders who are continually asking:* *"What shall we do to develop Americanism?"*

The Travelling Theatre Dramatic Director Rollo Lloyd of Camp Zachary Taylor, Kentucky, reported that he often used a travelling army truck as a theatre for one-act plays. *Here is an idea for sparsely settled country districts. Such a travelling theatre could easily be sent from village to village.*

The idea of a travelling theatre is not new. We are all familiar with Stuart Walker's Portmanteau Theatre. But this truck theatre, devised by Mr. Lloyd is even simpler. As to how to equip it with scenery and how to take properties along:—a clever man at Camp Hancock, Georgia, devised a travelling army theatre for use both here and abroad. This theatre and all its belongings are made of canvas. It can easily be taken apart or set up. The whole equipment, including the lighting system, can be packed up in ten small chests of locker size. There are four scenes which have first been painted and then made water proof so that the theatre can withstand all storms. This makes it ideal for use in Europe. The original theatre is to remain at Camp Hancock; and copies of it are to be turned out for use by the American soldiers across the water. *Such a travelling theatre as this would be an inestimable boon for country districts.*

Teaching English through the Drama In another report Mr. Lloyd said: "The majority of my men cannot read. Everything has to be taught orally, which is slow work. Yet everything has been well rehearsed to date."

Here is a new idea that workers among the foreign born should find of immense practical value—a wonderful opportunity to teach English even before the alphabet is learned.

In all the camps enthusiasm for community drama ran high. Dramatic Director Hackett, of Camp Dix, New Jersey, reports: —"I am deeply interested in the continual discovery of talent and the desire among so many men to give expression to their thoughts and ambitions."

One-act plays proved immensely popular because they could so quickly be learned and produced. Three or four one-act plays could be acted in an evening, with a different set of men in each play. *Here is an idea for community center workers in cities.*

The way these plays were rehearsed shows how drama can be made to seep through and through the community life of any city.

Every camp had its dramatic unit made up of one man from each regiment. This man, in turn, got together a company of dramatic recruits in the regiment he represented and under the eye of the General Director trained them. Thus, every regiment had its company complete within itself. All the plays, it must be noted, were so simple they could be given in barracks, mess halls, "Y" huts, or in Liberty Theatres.

Giving the Best in Dramatic Art At Camp Humphreys, Virginia, the Dramatic Director was Mr. Barrett H. Clark, widely known for his books on drama. Mr. Clark declared: "I do not think the soldiers here are above the average; I merely have faith that any good play that is not too subtle will succeed in any camp. There is little difference between the soldiers of one camp and those of another. I venture to say that any of the four different plays I have produced would go under similar conditions, in any of the other camps." (These plays were by Dunsany, Barrie, Lady Gregory and Yeats.) And yet there have been people who have been afraid that such plays might be "over the soldiers' heads," might be "too good." We are contemptuous of our general public because we are not acquainted with it. The one fear we should have is that the plays will not be good enough—and what is true of camp audiences is true of other audiences. *Workers interested in community dramatics in cities or country districts should take this knowledge to heart.*

The men who would be supposed to care the least about drama are often the ones who care the most about it—witness the report of Dramatic Director Boetler, of Camp Travis, Texas, on the question of interesting the South-western boy—the boy of the plains, in drama:—"I have examined very carefully into the tastes of these boys and have investigated any sort of thing which has been successful in drawing them into the theatre and I have learned that they have been brought up on burlesque and minstrelsy, and later, of course, the movies. They do not know drama * * * it is pathetic the amount of enjoyment these boys derive from our snappy shows * * * the officers tell me that the men go to bed singing after one of our shows and display more 'pep' for days afterwards."

Boys like these have to be gently led. It does not do to begin at once with the best in dramatic art; that is reached by gradations. These boys on the western plains are alertly suspicious of high-brow-ism, of "being done good to." But as Mr. Franklin Sargent, Chairman of the Department of Dramatic Activities among Soldiers, remarks: "Wherever the Directors have tested this utility of a higher grade of performance, if the material itself is worthy, and the acting is worthy, success has usually followed."

Pageantry at Training Camps At War Camp Community Service Soldiers' Clubs evenings of drama and music have served to bring camp and community together as have also the surprising number of pageants that have been produced throughout the camps. There have been pageants of the Allies, glowing with color; Historical Pageants. Pageants of Brotherhood, and Christmas Nativity Pageants. *The Patriotic Christmas*

Pageant, written for War Camp Community Service was widely used, as was the *Old English Christmas Revel.* Percy Mackaye's *Evergreen Tree* had several splendid productions. Miss Lotta Clark's *The Torch Bearers* was produced at Fort Logan with much success. Early in 1918 at Camp Devens, Mass., Thomas Wood Stevens' *The Drawing of the Sword,* a pageant of the Allies, was given in a unique manner; for the parts of the French were taken by French officers; Italians were played by Italian officers; while English officers played the parts of the English. This patriotic pageant was produced by many of the camps; the fact that it was in blank verse did not daunt its camp participants.

> "Bright is the ring of words
> When the right man rings them,
> Fair the fall of song
> When the singer sings them."

No one is proof against the magic of sheer loveliness.

Almost every camp had its beautiful *Festival of Song and Light.* In many cases this festival has been used with the Community Christmas Tree. At Camp Kearney, California, a sixty-five foot tree was brought from sixty miles back in the Cuyamaca Mountains, and the tree itself, light-spangled and wondrous to look upon, was sixty-five feet high. In one Southern camp a great singing procession marched through the streets of the camp which were filled with small fir trees, each tree hung with lights giving the impression almost of a fairy forest. *Here is an idea for Christmas in some city square or town park, where all the trees might be hung with lights; or a single block might carry out such an idea with one tree for each household. The idea of the singing procession is also a good one.*

Sailors as Well as Soldiers Are Caught by the Magic of Beauty   We already know the power of the pageant as a socializing force. The camps have proved it anew, proved that the average citizen loves color, rhythm, picturesqueness. There are people who think that art is effeminizing, whereas it is the reverse which holds true. There is nothing effeminate about our glorious army! "A singing army is a fighting army," says General Bell, and it is interesting to note that it is not only the army that loves to sing. A tremendous enthusiasm for singing exists among the sailors. Naval Training Stations, as well as camps, have their song-leaders. Indeed the music of the Naval Stations is becoming celebrated— witness the band of the Great Lakes Training Stations, which has been touring the country. Recently, Caruso wanted a pianist to accompany him at a patriotic meeting at the New York Hippodrome, and a sailor from the Great Lakes Training Stations stepped successfully into the breach.

It may be remarked, parenthetically, that the Naval Training Stations have not made as much use of drama as have the camps, it has not the hold on them that music has. Perhaps because it is a landsman's art. However, they are beginning to be interested in producing pageants, and one-act plays—particularly the plays of Eugene O'Neill, a new dramatist who has himself been a sailor, and who shows with power and veracity incidents in the lives of those "who go down to the sea in ships."

Song means so much to the sailor that hereafter for every merchant marine flying an American flag the United States Shipping Board Service has appointed an official Chantey Man to help revive the songs of the sea—for that is what chanteys are. An official Chantey Man! The very name is full of romance! It has the salt tang and smack of the waves in it. Who knows but what from the development of these chanteys we may yet have our American Kipling! Our Indian songs and songs of the Kentucky Mountains have been collected: and some one may yet collect our old American chanteys as they were sung on the sailing vessels that brought home cargoes from the Indies; and we shall hear again the chanteys of the whalers of Nantucket—bluff, hearty choruses with the long swing of the combers in them. Civilian life will be enriched because of what is being done in the folk-art of the ocean. (And is it not a joyful thought to picture our sailors singing on the seas whose freedom they have helped to win again for all the world?)

Transferring to Civil Life This New-Awakened Love of Imaginative Re-creation To take a panoramic view of what has gone forward in our camps along the line of art is simply amazing. Never before has any government taken such cognizance of the art-needs of its defenders.

"All this work," says Mr. Otto Kahn, "is getting the vast army away from the cheap and tawdry in amusement, giving a finer and wiser appreciation of art, and furnishing a higher standard of entertainment, is affording opportunity and guidance for latent talents which their owners might otherwise have never discovered. It is letting loose springs of inspiration of which these men were unconscious."

Man cannot live without beauty (and art *is* beauty) any more than he can live without bread. *Most of the art forces that existed in our camps came from the demand for imaginative recreation made by the men themselves.* Sometimes this demand was articulate; sometimes it was inarticulate; yet almost always it was there.

To men who lacked advantages our camps were like great universities. All the treasures of knowledge and art were suddenly set before them.

Now the camps are closing. The men are going back into civil life. *What is to be done with this newly awakened love of imaginative recreation?* Is it to go to waste? Are we to allow it to die for lack of material on which to feed? Will not this love, rightly fostered, result in a greater impetus of community music and community drama than America has ever known?

Already things have been done in the camps, which, turned into the right channels of civilian life, would make enormously for its enrichment in

   1—Industrial Centers
   2—Social Centers for the Foreign Born
   3—Country Communities
   4—City Communities

To turn the tide of new recreational ideas into civilian life requires no special equipment; *only a new light and a re-using of the sources at hand.*

There must be a wider development of community drama and community music in each place throughout the country, thus making for national as well as civic solidarity.

And how can this be accomplished?

By giving community drama and community music a home: in other words, by establishing in every community a Community Theatre, where choruses will be trained, where plays will be rehearsed, where pageants will be shaped, where music and drama will be more closely inter-related than they are now. Here foreign citizens should bring their arts; here American citizens should bring their ideas. Here Fourth of July and Thanksgiving celebrations should be planned; here community Christmas Tree revels designed. Here, too, should be discussed all plans for industrial recreation, for working men's theatres. Here should focus the city's or town's art-life.

The idea of such a focusing point is not a dream. Erie,

Pennsylvania, has already proved the worth of such a plan in its Little Community Playhouse. As a prospectus inspiringly says:—"The Little Playhouse is a place and an idea. The place is one of entertainment; the idea is community service. The place vitalized by the idea becomes concrete expression of civic pride.

"The Little Playhouse is the beginning of a community center and has a three-fold purpose:—to encourage and develop every kind of artistic endeavor in the city. To promote neighborliness by bringing people together and interesting them in one another. To add something to the joy of life and the presentation of good music and worth-while plays."

The Erie Community Chorus (one of the first of its kind to be organized in America) and the Erie Community Orchestra both have their home in the playhouse.

"If the salt has lost its savor, wherewith shall it be salted?" If we do not conserve what the camps have already helped to create, ours will be the loss.

We have been accused of being the most commercial nation under the sun; yet the camps have proved anew that away down deep from the heart of us the old eternal cry for beauty still wells up, as it did in the days of ancient Greece and in the days when Shakespeare was a country lad. Is it not of national import to ask how in the times that are coming we shall make answer to the cry? The government has done everything in its power to give imaginative recreation to the camps; will it not later help to plan imaginative non-commercial recreation for its lonely country districts, its toilworn towns?

Liberty Buildings

The American City, in sponsoring the idea of the erection in each community of community houses which will serve the living while commemorating the dead, has struck a note which is sounding all over the country. A number of communities are already making plans for these neighborhood centers which will express as can no marble pillar the ideal for which thousands of our men have died. Plans are on foot for converting a number of the soldiers' clubs and community buildings conducted by War Camp Community Service—which, during the war were used exclusively for men in service or as meeting places for soldiers and civilians—into community houses which will serve the entire community.

The call to action is sounded in *The American City*: "Democracy must have a home. When the war is over, the Democracy for which these men are fighting must have more adequate meeting places in the home communities. Let us all, in every city and town and village in America, begin to plan now for community houses to be erected immediately after the war. Let us call them

Liberty Buildings

and dedicate them as neighborhood gathering places for civic service and fellowship for all the people—living structures to perpetuate the democracy of the camp and to service as

Fitting Memorials to the Brave Men, Living and Dead

who shall have helped to win the world war for Democracy. From these buildings will resound through an era of peace the ringing message of human freedom.

"Let us plan our Liberty Buildings on no niggardly scale. The war has shown that the American people will give lavishly for a great cause. Let us determine the needs of our own community and plan accordingly, including such facilities for recreation, culture, fellowship and public service as a practical idealism may suggest. If we live in a large city, several such buildings may be needed; if in a village, one will suffice.

"Let the erection of these Liberty Buildings be begun at such time as may best help to tide over, in some measure, the period of readjustment when our returning soldiers or our industrial workers shall be in need of employment. And finally, in planning, financing and administration, let us make every possible use of existing commercial and civic bodies, and of the many war service organizations which have been the medium of patriotic effort in these days of strife. For if, when the war shall end, we of America can turn to constructive works of peace our new spirit and energy of public service, we shall have achieved Liberty and Democracy indeed."

In the December number of *The American City* there appears an article on *Liberty Buildings as Victory Monuments,* which gives some very practical suggestions for the construction, site, design, use, cost and maintenance of these buildings and for methods of raising money. These suggestions will be of interest to readers of THE PLAYGROUND who are thinking along these lines.

Name of the Memorial
Liberty more than any other word expresses the principle for which the war has been fought, and which is to be perpetuated by the proposed memorial. Therefore the name *Liberty* should distinguish the building: Liberty Hall, Liberty Building, Liberty House, Liberty Lyceum, or some other such name would be appropriate.

Object of the Building
The building would serve two main purposes:
1. As a memorial to the heroic dead, and to all from the local community who joined the colors during the war

2. As a community center to afford headquarters and a meeting place for such community agencies as the

Chamber of Commerce
Red Cross
War Veterans' Associations
Patriotic and Defense Societies
Local Charities
Playground and Recreation Associations
Fraternal Organizations
Farm Bureau
County Grange

Rotary Club
Civic Organizations
Women's Clubs
Boy Scouts
Boys' and Girls' Clubs
Literary Societies
Musical Societies
Study Clubs.

The Building Site
The building should be centrally located and easy of access by all means of transportation. The site should, if possible, be large enough to separate the building on all sides for at least fifty feet from other structures, and free from unusual noises. More open space would be desirable, and in some cases provision could be made for community tennis courts or other outdoor recreational features immediately adjoining the building. The site should be chosen with reference to the future, so that the growth of the city will not remove the centre of population too far away. The nature of the enterprise is such that a municipality might well donate the site or permit its erection upon ground where private buildings

would not be permitted. In very large cities several neighborhood buildings would be preferable to one central structure.

Design The building should be architecturally beautiful, featuring the best building material of the particular locality, the style to be impressive but not over-ornate. The size and cost of the building, the equipment which it will contain and the service which it will perform will depend upon local needs and local spirit. In every community some of the following facilities and equipment should be embraced in the plan:

Offices and committee rooms for the Chamber of Commerce and other local organizations

Headquarters for Farm Bureau

Auditorium for public meetings, entertainments and motion pictures

Memorial hall with engrossed records under glass, and tablets and trophies

Reading room (or complete library if the town has no public library building

Exhibit rooms for art exhibits and for products of local industries and resources

Farmers' rest room	Dance hall
Classrooms	Gymnasium
Community kitchen	Swimming pool
Dining-room	Bowling-alleys
Music room	Room for billiards and pool
Game rooms and club rooms for boys and girls	

In small towns and villages where there is no adequate town hall, it may prove desirable that the building should include headquarters for the local government, and perhaps in some cases, for the local fire department. A combination of public school building and social center will be desirable in some of the smaller places.

Use of the Building The building should be open to the whole community. It should be dedicated to community fellowship and unity, so greatly advanced by this war. Every non-sectarian and non-partisan movement to promote community progress, welfare and happiness should find sanctuary within its doors.

The meetings of the various organizations mentioned above,

lyceum courses, high schools, motion picture entertainments, dances, musicales, debates should keep the building constantly in use.

Cost of the Building For the building alone it is recommended that a minimum sum equivalent to $3 per capita in towns of 10,000 and above be provided. An additional minimum sum of $1 per capita ought to be provided for furnishings and equipment. In small communities perhaps a minimum of $30,000 for the building and $7,500 for furnishings and equipment would be appropriate. Rapidly growing communities ought to take into consideration the probable increase in population for the next ten years and build accordingly.

Raising the Money The entire cost of the building and equipment should be raised by popular subscription in a campaign conducted along the lines of a Red Cross or United War Work drive. To exact the funds by taxation would rob the building of its true nature of a thank-offering. In some cities a public-spirited citizen can be found who will donate a suitable site for the building. The building should be erected without encumbrances on either building or site. Liberty Bonds should be accepted at par from all who wish to make payments in that form.

In some cases it will be possible to secure large gifts from relatives of men who have given their lives in the war. Such a gift could, if desired, be used to provide a gymnasium, or a library, or some other special feature for which funds would not be available otherwise and which might bear the name of the donor.

Lodges or societies which are to have rooms in the building might be invited to provide the furnishing for such rooms at their own expense.

Maintenance The nature of this building and its uses place it in the class of all other public buildings and, naturally, should exempt it from taxation of all kinds.

Three methods have been suggested for the financing and maintenance of the building:

(a) An annual municipal appropriation to cover the cost of upkeep and of heat, light and janitor service; such appropriation to be made in consideration of the free use of the building by the public generally and its dedication to the welfare of the entire community

(b) The building could be made self-supporting by charging adequate rental to organizations occupying offices in the building and a reasonable charge for the use of the auditorium and of the club facilities

(c) An endowment fund to be raised by popular subscription and to be supplemented by bequests from time to time

Now Is the Time for Action While the sacrifices and achievements of the war and the conditions of permanent peace are still the main topics of public discussion, is the time for action. The project should be launched at once, therefore, and the funds pledged by the time the peace treaty is signed.

A community meeting might well start the movement. Following such meeting, a Liberty Building Committee of representative men and women from all spheres of influence might be appointed and be made responsible for the campaign. Every community now has its organization of war workers for Liberty Loan, Red Cross, United War Work and other campaigns. These organizations can, with practically no difficulty, secure funds necessary for this memorial.

The erection of these buildings will afford employment to a great number of returning soldiers and war workers, and will help in the process of industrial readjustment. The movement should be immediate also in order to preserve the splendid spirit of service that has been created in the various war activities. The spirit of unity, the subjugation of selfish interest, and the exaltation of spiritual values must be perpetuated in order to preserve the greatest fruits of the war.

The soldiers and the boys from our various communities have been enjoying in camp and in the near-by cities the facilities of the Y. M. C. A., K. of C., Red Cross, War Camp Community Service, and other agencies. They have been uplifted and ennobled by the wholesome influence thrown around them by a thoughtful government and a patriotic people. They must not return home to find sordidness and a lack of all the things that made their army life pleasant and memorable.

There should be a Liberty Building in every community by the time the last troops are demobilized.

The Campaign

As stated above, the funds to provide this building and its furnishings and equipment should be given as a thank-offering rather than exacted in the form of taxation. Not the least cause for thankfulness should be the fact that more than 97 per cent of the two million Americans who went overseas will return alive. This is a special reason why the war should be commemorated by living memorials.

To raise these funds the veterans of all the war-time campaigns should unite in one body and put into this final effort all the zeal and enthusiasm that is justified by the great victory our boys have won. The appeal can be made irresistible from a patriotic standpoint. It is also strong from a selfish standpoint, for the reason that the money can be spent at home with local contractors and dealers for home labor, to provide a structure for the enjoyment of home people and the home boys.

Community Houses

Homes of Democracy

Much interest has been aroused by the suggestion that instead of erecting monuments or statues in acknowledgment of the great debt which the American people owe their soldiers and sailors, each community throughout the United States build after the war a neighborhood house to be known as a liberty building and to be used as a center of recreation, fellowship and public service for all the people. In this way, it is believed, can best be symbolized the democracy for which so many men have given their lives and the ideal of human service for which they died.

Existing Community Buildings

Many communities are fortunate in already having community buildings which are serving as meeting places for the community and as expressions of community unity and purpose. Some of them have doubtless played important parts in shaping the ideals of many men who have fought the more gallantly for democracy because of the expression of it in which they have shared in their own communities through community centers.

Because of the present wide-spread enthusiasm over the

establishment of community houses, a brief description of a few such existing centers may be of interest.

Kentfield (Pop. 400)

Tamalpais Centre in the village of Kentfield, near San Francisco, has a beautiful and substantial recreation building costing $20,000. This building contains an auditorium of ample size with a stage, club rooms, kitchen and shop for manual work. A man qualified by training and experience is in charge. The place is the gift of the Kent family. Although Kentfield numbers but four hundred, the center is available to 4,000 people of the countryside.

La Jolla (Pop. 100)

The Community House on the La Jolla playground was a gift of Miss Ellen B. Scripps to the city of San Diego. It is provided with a large auditorium, a stage, club rooms, reading room, pool room, locker and shower rooms, offices, a hospital ward, a kitchen fully equipped, and a complete, up-to-date lantern room equipped with a motion picture machine.

Los Angeles (Pop. 503,812)

Los Angeles, like Chicago and Pittsburgh, has several playground clubhouses and recreation buildings, but in addition there is a downtown building called a "recreation center," where the playground is small and of minor importance, and the main work lies indoors. This is larger than the clubhouses and more substantially built. It is of brick and plaster, built in the Spanish Renaissance style. It was built for about $20,000 but would cost a great deal more today. It has bowling alleys, baths, call station for district nurse, club rooms, kitchen and library. The main feature, however, is a large, fully equipped gymnasium. This may be used also for an auditorium and is provided with a large stage, which is ordinarily closed off with rolling doors for use as a club room. A roof garden from which splendid views of the city and mountains may be had extends over part of the building. An artistic little five-room apartment for the manager's home completes the building.

COMMUNITY HOUSES

Nuevo Rancho

Nuevo Rancho is a little place near Los Angeles, which has a community building dedicated to the social and intellectual interests of ranchers and townsfolk.

Oakland (Pop. 198,604)

The Moss Residence in Mosswood Park, Oakland, California, was built a generation ago and is one of the best remaining specimens of the old California architecture. The city has converted it into a municipal country club, adjoining a playground and athletic field. In the south wing of the building were installed shower baths, dressing rooms, toilet and locker rooms for men, women and children. The main portion of the building contains a rest room for women, meeting rooms for clubs and societies, a branch library and tea room. Light refreshments, tea, coffee, milk and soft drinks are for sale here.

CONNECTICUT

Manchester (Pop. 13,641)

Manchester, Conn., has a recreation center, donated to the use of the townspeople by Cheney Brothers. It is a modern, up-to-date building with gymnasium, swimming pool, shower baths for both men and women, reading rooms, club rooms, bowling alleys and billiard and smoking rooms. It is under the control of a committee appointed by the school district and is maintained by membership subscription.

ILLINOIS

La Salle-Peru Township (Pop. 10,000)

The activities of the Social Center of the La Salle-Peru Township are supported by taxation and are maintained by the township board of education, under the direct supervision of a staff of six year-round workers. The work was made possible through a gift of $75,000 for a Recreation Building to be conducted in connection with the High School and to serve as a community center. This building contains a large gymnasium with a running track, a swimming pool, locker rooms, a bowling alley and four club rooms. It is used in connection with the

513

high school, containing the auditorium, which seats 600, has a stage and scenery and is modeled after the Little Theatre of New York. Just adjacent to the building lies the new athletic and play field. This contains tennis courts, a cinder running track, baseball fields and a large outdoor swimming pool. A large concrete stadium has also recently been erected, its cost being defrayed by public subscription. The Center runs year-round, night and day, seven days a week.

Peoria (Pop. 71,458)

Peoria has a fine community center, the gift of a prominent citizen, called the John C. Proctor Recreation Center and Public Baths. It has a gymnasium, swimming pool, baths, club rooms, a library, an entertainment hall, and bowling alley and billiard tables.

INDIANA

La Porte (Pop. 13,322)

In 1910 at the solicitation of the women of the town, the County Commissioners gave the old jail building to the women's organization of the city for a trial period of six months, to be used as a rest and recreation building by the town and especially by the farmers' wives and children. The building was nicely equipped at a cost of $275 and the cost of running it was about $125.00 a month. The only contribution made by the Municipality was the old jail building, the citizens of the town contributing the other funds. The building proved to be so needed and was so successful that finally on the site of the old jail the women's organizations and interested citizens built a new building which is supported by voluntary contributions.

KANSAS

Coldwater (Pop. 1,088)

Coldwater has a community building 75' by 120' which will seat 2,000 people. It has a stage and four small rooms, two dressing rooms, two shower baths, a library, a reading room and a rest room.

Marysville (Pop. 2,166)

The community house at Marysville was the outgrowth of

514

the thought and interest of two public spirited citizens, one of whom supplied the money for the enterprise. The house has a reception or living room, a library, rest rooms for men and women, office, reading and game rooms, a nursery, tub and shower baths and a gymnasium in which a race track may be used as a gallery for spectators. It also has a porcelain lined swimming pool, 20 by 50 feet with a depth running from 3 to 8 feet. Additional features which, in the estimation of the originator, might well be added are an automatic bowling alley, a shooting gallery, a moving picture theatre for educational films and rooms which might be rented to organizations.

The expenses for running the community house for seventeen months averaged $174.12 a month, part of which included initial expenses which would not be a consideration a second year. Membership dues are paid to help support the expenses of the club. The building could be duplicated at a cost of from $14,000 to $20,000.

Parsons (Pop. 12,463)

In 1917 Parsons voted $150,000 in bonds for a community building for meeting place and concerts.

Russell (Pop. 1,601)

A building called Community Hall has been built at Russell on ground belonging to the city which is loaned for this purpose. It is valued at about $3,000, the money having been raised by the sale of shares at $5.00 each. The building is used as a gymnasium and auditorium.

Topeka (Pop. 48,726)

The community building and the adjoining outdoor swimming pool at Ripley Park, Topeka, were built in the summer of 1917 at a cost of $23,000, of which the Santa Fe Railroad donated $15,000 through its president. The building is a two-story structure of burnt brick with gray and wine trimmings. The interior is divided into a large gymnasium, with a balcony, a reading and committee room, and shower-bath apartments for both boys and girls. The rooms are complete with hammered brass fixtures with invisible lights. The building will be a branch of the city library and a branch of the city Y. M. C. A. offices. The gymnasium room which is floored with maple will be used for both basket ball and dancing. The big play room equipped with gymnasium apparatus will make an ideal playhouse for the children of the community. The large balcony which completely encircles this room, will furnish ample seating capacity for on-lookers at games and dances. Near the community building are located the baseball diamond, tennis court, running track and the swimming pool.

MASSACHUSETTS

Brookline (Pop. 32,730)

Brookline has a municipal gymnasium connected with and administered in conjunction with the famous natatorium of the town, erected at a cost of about $150,000. The building, T-shape in construction, is of red brick with window trimmings, cornice and gable front of light terra cotta; it has a slate roof. The interior is of pointed brick with heavy plank floors. At the left of the entrance are the superintendent's office, the store-room, a lavatory and apparatus room, and the meeting room of the Brookline Gymnasium Athletic Association. At the right are the waiting room, the office of the director, the men's exam-ination room, and the dressing room of the instructors. Fac-ing the entrance is the large gymnasium. This is seventy-one feet four inches wide, one hundred feet eight inches long, twenty-five feet high on the side walls and forty-five feet in the middle. Twelve feet above the floor is a gallery, eight feet wide, on which has been laid out a modern running track, twenty laps to the mile. Raised platforms, with railings and chairs for visitors are situated in the corner. In the end corners are two fire exits. Light and ventilation are supplied by 12 large win-dows and skylights. A small gymnasium for women, 34 feet eight inches wide, 74 feet long and 21 feet high is located on the second floor. Adjoining it are a rest room, the office of the woman instructor, the women's examination room, dressing rooms, lockers, and baths, in all forty-nine dressing rooms, 350 lockers, and ten shower baths. In the basement are two large rooms. The east room is used for men's lockers and has dress-ing rooms and shower baths attached. The west room is given over to the track team of the High School and Brookline Gym-nasium Athletic Association.

COMMUNITY HOUSES

Framingham (Pop. 13,982)

The old city hall in Framingham has been made over into a community building.

Holden (Pop. 2,147)

Holden also has a Community House, bought by selling shares at $5.00 each. An old colonial house was remodeled for the House. A Town Club has been formed which leases half the second floor. The Daughters of the American Revolution and the Boy Scouts have permanent headquarters there; a tearoom and the renting of the assembly room furnish the revenue.

Worcester (Pop. 145,986)

Green Hill Mansion, the people's club house in Worcester, Mass., housed 287 parties attended by 9,441 persons from its opening October 12, 1914 to February 1, 1916. It contains a kitchen, piazzas and shower baths.

MICHIGAN

Grand Rapids (Pop. 128,291)

In Garfield Park, Grand Rapids, a two-story house of cement, plaster and frame construction has been erected at a cost of $2,500. The first floor contains a dancing hall with several small rest rooms equipped with all conveniences. The second floor is a model living apartment. The house is known as Garfield Lodge and is given over free for the use of any party not to exceed thirty persons on application to the secretary of the Board of Parks and Cemeteries. As light and heat are furnished by the city, it is quite possible for a group to give an enjoyable entertainment without a cent of expense. The caretaker who also acts as a special policeman lives on the third floor, thus reducing greatly his maintenance.

In the winter time the lodge is always in use. Dance parties are not the only functions given but they predominate. Sunday school affairs and musicals and mothers' clubs meetings are held there. In the summer time lawn fetes are given in groves surrounding the lodge. Its success is unquestioned; it is as much a part of the community as the park itself. The expense of light, heat, fuel and water is not great and the city

517

feels that the increased social activities and community interest more than compensate for the cost of the building.

Harbor Beach (Pop. 1,556)

In 1917 $25,000 was donated for a community building by two public-spirited citizens and $25,000 subscribed by citizens of Harbor Beach.

MINNESOTA

Eveleth (Pop. 7,036)

The Eveleth City Auditorium is used more extensively for recreational purposes than any other building in that part of the country. It is estimated that in six months nearly 30,000 persons have attended entertainments and parties in the auditorium. The building is also used for gymnasium purposes by the school children four times each week and by the militia on Thursday evenings. It is equipped with an excellent stage and scenery, has an exceptionally fine floor for dancing or gymnasium purposes, and a kitchen and dining room for serving luncheons and church suppers.

Wheaton (Pop. 1,300)

As the result of an election called to vote on bonds for the Wheaton recreation center building the bond issue carried by a vote of three to one. A bid of $22,000 was accepted and a location secured near the center of the town. The building has three floors; one floor houses the County Farm Bureau and to it throng the farmers of the whole county. It is supplied with all conveniences, magazines, easy chairs, boys' and men's lockers and shower rooms. On the second floor is the auditorium and also the girls' and women's lockers and shower rooms. The auditorium will accommodate 1,500 people. When not in use it can be turned into a gymnasium; on account of the height of the ceilings practically any game can be played here and there is a complete gymnasium equipment. On the third floor are the rest and recreation rooms for women. The agricultural department of the high school is housed in the building.

Willmar (Pop. 4,135)

The community house at Willmar, a community of less

than 5,000 people, has an interesting history. The City Council, the Commercial and Auto Clubs of Willmar feeling that there was special need for a rest and recreation room for the wives and children from the rural districts who came in frequently to do their shopping, formed a committee. The city council promised to give a certain amount towards the upkeep of such an undertaking and to furnish the water and light. The home of a widow near the center of the town was rented for $20 a month and the services of its owner secured for $13 a month. She has her quarters on the top floor. The house has become the center of the social activities of the town; during the first month 245 visitors were entertained and the attendance is constantly growing.

MISSOURI

Boonville (Pop. 4,252)

Boonville, Mo., has a community building.

NEBRASKA

Elgin (Pop. 606)

The Elgin opera house was purchased by the people of Elgin and an architect employed to remodel the building into a modern country club house. This building contains an auditorium, a women's rest room, a gymnasium, banquet hall and dance hall, a well-furnished kitchen, a game room which is located in the basement and contains two bowling alleys, two pool tables and a billiard table, a library and a business office. On all floors are wash rooms and toilet facilities and the gymnasium has shower baths.

NEW JERSEY

Oceanic (Pop. 600)

This community house was formerly an old Presbyterian church, remodeled and enlarged at a cost of $4,500. The building is now nearly twice the size of the original church. It has a vestibule, a coat room and a ticket office at the entrance. The main hall which will seat about 400 persons, has a very large stage with foot-lights and other electrical equipment. The

519

stage is so arranged as to be available as a parlor, reading and game room, sewing room, or dining room, according to the wish of the organization which uses it. In the rear of the stage is a well-equipped kitchen with a large gas range, china closet and an ample supply of china, silverware, kitchen and cooking utensils. There is also a women's retiring and dressing room nicely furnished. A gymnasium in the basement measures 24' x 36' with a 12 foot ceiling. A gallery, capable of seating about 100 persons is at the front of the building. It is equipped with a billiard and pool table. Back of the gallery is an electrical apparatus for a moving-picture machine. The whole building is heated with steam, and has a splendid system of lighting of which one member remarked, "No saloon or theatre has anything on Oceanic's Community House when it comes to lights." Two lots adjoining have been donated to the House and will be used for tennis and other recreation.

NEW YORK

Chatham (Pop. 2,389)

The Morris Memorial building at Chatham cost $50,000. It has a 40' x 60' gymnasium, shower baths, bowling alleys, pool and billiard rooms. Some of the activities carried on there are gymnasium classes for boys, men, women and girls, athletic meets, baseball, basket ball and bowling games, entertainments, lectures, meetings of Boy Scouts, village improvement association and various clubs.

Locust Valley (Pop. 450)

Locust Valley has a community club house erected by the Matinecock Neighborhood Association. The building provides space for bowling alleys, fire company headquarters, committee rooms, auditorium and social room, while an uncompleted part, to be finished when need is evident, will provide for a library and billiard rooms.

Newark (Pop. 6,000)

A gymnasium or community recreation center has been built at Newark, N. Y., by funds voted for this purpose by the people. It was formally dedicated by Dr. Finley, State Commissioner of Education.

520

COMMUNITY HOUSES

Salisbury (Pop. 7,153)

The old courthouse of Rowan County at Salisbury, N. C., was remodeled for the use of the people when the new courthouse was put in service. Through the efforts of the Industrial Club, Y. M. C. A., Civic League and various women's organizations, the old structure was renovated. It now provides rooms for various clubs and societies, the public library, rest-rooms for out-of-town visitors, an exhibition hall and an auditorium with a well-equipped stage which can be rented for a nominal sum.

OHIO

Columbus (Pop. 214,878)

Columbus, Ohio, has a building at Glenwood Park which was constructed at a cost of $25,000. It is a one-story building of composite construction with hard pine floors and finished in oak. The basement provides for a swimming pool 18 by 31 feet three inches, a girls' locker room 11 feet six inches by 24 feet, five inches, a boys' locker room a little larger, showers and toilets for boys and girls, restaurant and kitchen. A gymnasium built with a circular running track is constructed as an addition to the main floor which contains a social hall 30 feet three inches by 48 feet. The main floor contains a balcony, office, library, two club rooms (one for boys and one for girls) and two game rooms.

PENNSYLVANIA

Butler (Pop. 27,632)

The community building at Butler was opened on April 9, 1917. The Chamber of Commerce leased this building with two objects in view, the first being to advance the civic interests in the community by uniting all the forces, working to the same end. Six organizations covering somewhat the same field have been provided with suitable quarters in this building at a nominal rental, and through being under one roof, much duplication of effort is eliminated. On the first floor of the

521

building are the offices and committee rooms of the various organizations. On the second floor is an auditorium capable of seating 400 people, which is equipped with a stage and a balcony. Adjoining the auditorium are a dining-room and a kitchen.

The second object was to promote commercial activity by making it more convenient and pleasant for the people from the country to visit Butler. The gymnasium is furnished with substantial tables, comfortable chairs and benches and here the County Farm Bureau maintains an elaborate exhibition. Adjoining this club room is a check room. On this same floor is a toilet and wash room, comfortably furnished with couches and small beds for children. Buildings similar to this are being used in Washington and Huntingdon, Pa.

VERMONT

Randolph (Pop. 1,787)

In Randolph there is a music hall and parish house called the "Chandler Music Hall." It is the social and entertainment center not only of the large village, but of the surrounding country as well. The old village hall where all sorts of shows formerly took place has been abandoned for the church social center where not only boys', men's and girls' clubs have their home with the use of the gymnasium, bowling alley, bathroom, dining room, and large public hall, but where the pastor and his committees select best modern dramas and operas to be presented.

Rutland (Pop. 14,831)

The community house at Rutland, Vt., is a three-story brick building, originally occupied by the Bank of Rutland, later used as a residence by ex-governor John A. Mead and finally purchased by him in 1915 and presented as a Christmas gift to the Congregational church to be used as a recreation center. All persons, regardless of church affiliations are welcome. A gymnasium, also the gift of Governor Mead, is connected with the kitchen in the Community House so that meals may be served in the large hall. The seating capacity of the hall is 600. The walls of the house were re-papered, hardwood floors laid and a central heating plant installed in the basement of the community building for heating the house and the gymnasium. A large reception room in which there is a piano, men's club rooms, containing leather furniture and a pool table, a small office, dining room, spacious kitchen and pantries occupy the first floor. On the second floor there are four large front rooms to be used by the women's societies of the church and for girl's clubs. The third floor with five large rooms, one extending the length of the building is devoted to boys' club activities. Here are two pool tables and a table bowling alley.

The gymnasium is 84 by 52 feet. The main floor is given to a single room, two stories high, to be used for games, dancing, gymnastic exercises and entertainments. There is a large stage with footlights and dressing rooms at either side. The basement is divided into two sections to be used as locker rooms, one for women and girls, the other for men and boys. Each of these rooms is provided with steel lockers, three shower baths, a tub and toilets.

VIRGINIA

Powell Fort, Shenendoah County

Powell Fort has a modern community building, erected by the people themselves.

WISCONSIN

Green Bay (Pop. 29,353)

In 1912 Brown County erected a new court house. The County Board of Commissioners thereupon granted the use of the old building to the women of Brown County for a number of years. Five thousand dollars equipped and furnished the building; all sanitary conveniences were put in, with rest rooms for women and children and social gathering rooms; dances and other forms of entertainments can be given. On Sunday afternoons the house is kept open for the employed young women of the town, many of whom live in boarding houses. To the country people especially it is a great boon as it gives them a meeting place.

Racine (Pop. 46,486)

Racine, Wisconsin, has a one-story community house erected by the Park Commission at a cost of less than $7,500 which, it is felt, is adequately meeting community needs. The building contains a gymnasium 40 by 70 feet, 12 shower baths, toilets for both men and women, a reading room, recreation room and a kitchen. Economy of space has been effected by using the recreation room as a dressing room and at having a sectional movable platform instead of a permanent stage. The locker room contains a few steel lockers but for economy of space it is fitted with pigeon holes in which are slipped wire baskets. for the accommodation of the people using the gymnasium.

Sheboygan (Pop. 28,559)

The James H. Mead Club, with building and equipment valued at $50,000, was opened in September, 1916. The building includes a fine gymnasium and auditorium combined (capacity 1,000), an attractive general reception room furnished with leather furniture, a ladies' rest room, a well-equipped pool room with two pocket tables and one rail table, a reading room with thirty-two of the best magazines, a smoking room for men, four bowling alleys, six shower baths for men and three for women in addition to locker rooms and dressing rooms. There is a dressing room just off the stage and two small club rooms for Boy Scouts, Camp Fire Girls and similar organizations. The attendance in gymnasium classes for three weeks was over 1,300. Club membership dues ranging from $1.00 to $5.00 help defray expenses.

Spring Valley (Pop. 972)

The destruction by fire of the old village hall in Spring Valley heralded the awakening of a new civic pride and community spirit. A petition was signed for a bond issue to build a hall; $5,000 was voted; citizens vied with one another in donations of labor and material and a new building speedily arose from the ashes of the old. The lower floor of the hall which measures 50 by 100 feet, contains furnace rooms, kitchen, dining room, a suite of club rooms and the village library room. The upper floor is used as an auditorium. The cost of the building in cash was $7,388, and the many gifts of furniture, time, labor and material greatly increased its value. Ownership is with the village, the Village Board comprising the Board of Directors of the community house. The village clerk who is manager, books plays and entertainments and rents the dining room and auditorium to societies and individuals wishing to use them. The hall is used for plays, moving pictures, entertainments, class plays, banquets, suppers and dances. Janitor work is done by the village marshall without extra pay.

MUNICIPAL AUDITORIUMS

The following cities have municipal auditoriums:

CALIFORNIA

Oakland (Pop. 198,604)

This "civic auditorium and opera house" is a particularly successful building.

COLORADO

Denver (Pop. 260,800)

This municipal auditorium was built at a cost of $400,000 for the use of the Democratic National Convention of 1908; the hall which seats 12,000 can be transformed into a theatre seating 3,500.

Longmont (Pop. 4,256)

A combined auditorium, armory and exhibition hall comprises Longmont's municipal auditorium.

GEORGIA

Atlanta (Pop. 190,558)

The main amphitheatre of the Atlanta, Ga. auditorium armory seats 7,500; the small convention hall, 1,000.

IOWA

Clinton (Pop. 27,386)

The Clinton, Ia., Coliseum Building was built at a cost of $100,000 and is used as the home of the Clinton Commercial Club and Battery "A" of the Iowa National Guard. The entire building covers a space of about 100 x 200 feet. The coliseum portion occupies 100 x 150 feet of this space. The side walls are brick, the roof is a single arch from side to side of the building, supported on five massive steel arches. The height of this arch above the floor in the center is about 55 feet.

MINNESOTA

St. Paul (Pop. 247,232)

This auditorium was built by the municipality aided by private subscription, at a cost of $460,000; it seats 10,000 or may be changed into a theatre seating 3,200. The building measures 181 x 301 and is used for all kinds of meetings and entertainments.

OHIO

Akron (Pop. 85,625)

Akron has a combined auditorium, armory and exhibition hall.

PENNSYLVANIA

Pittsburgh (Pop. 579,090)

The Pittsburgh combined exposition hall and music hall was financed by private subscriptions on property leased by the city for 50 years without cost or taxes; it cost $858,253 and seats 12,000.

TEXAS

Houston (Pop. 112,307)

The municipal auditorium at Houston cost $300,000 without taxation or bonding for the purpose, out of money saved from the general revenues of the city. It seats about 7,000.

WISCONSIN

Eau Claire (Pop. 18,807)

A combined auditorium, armory and exhibition hall is the property of Eau Claire.

Milwaukee (Pop. 436,535)

The site of the Milwaukee auditorium valued at $500,000 is owned by the city; one-half of the funds for this building were raised by municipal bond issue and the remainder by private subscriptions.

WEST VIRGINIA

Wheeling (Pop. 43,377)

This building is designed to serve as a market as well as an auditorium. The enterprise cost $150,000.

Among the other cities having municipal auditoriums are Jacksonville, Fla., San Francisco, Calif., Dodge City and Wichita, Kansas, Portland, Maine, Springfield, Mass., Littleton, N. H., Akron and Cincinnati, Ohio, Portland, Oregon, Ft. Worth, and Houston, Texas, and Richland Center, Wisconsin.

In addition to the above, plans for the construction of auditoriums have been set on foot in Peoria, Ill., Roanoke, Va., Rochester, N. Y., Sioux Falls, S. D., and Spokane, Washington.

Community buildings range from simple one-story buildings to elaborate structures. The requirements of such a building should be governed by local conditions, the character of the population, the public facilities already existing and the purposes which it is desired the building shall serve. It ought to be centrally located where it is available for all the people. Above all, it should be a real community house, supported by the people, and in which every community member has a part.

Theodore Roosevelt

A Man Who Played

The play movement has never had a truer friend than Theodore Roosevelt. In his own life he demonstrated what a strong play spirit, what vigorous, happy, athletic effort can do to make a man's life efficient, to give a man abundant life. Throughout all his years, no man more than he embodied the spirit of the play and recreation movement.

When Jacob Riis, who was always so close to Colonel Roosevelt, united with others to form the Playground and Recreation Association of America in June, 1906, it was natural that Theodore Roosevelt should be chosen Honorary President and should

527

accept and should remain for twelve years, until his death, in this position. Jacob Riis several times during the last year of his life, as he sat in the office of the secretary of the Playground and Recreation Association of America in the Metropolitan Tower, said, "I never see the letterhead of the Association without pleasure that Theodore Roosevelt's name and my name are side by side—he as Honorary President and I as Honorary Vice-President."

Colonel Roosevelt, as president of the United States, threw his influence enthusiastically for the play movement and by his utterances helped greatly. In speaking of the Chicago recreation centers, he said, "Playgrounds are a necessary means for the development of wholesome citizenship in modern cities. The Chicago playgrounds are the greatest civic achievement the world has ever seen."

Because of the peculiar way in which Colonel Roosevelt belonged to the recreation movement, as well as because he has from the beginning been our Honorary President, may we not all arrange that a brief memorial service of song be held on each playground, in each recreation centre, and by each recreation commission and each recreation association? I believe we shall gain in thinking together on the play and recreation life of our great leader and rejoicing that he was given to us.

H. S. BRAUCHER

Roosevelt Memorial Park

To be Erected at Oyster Bay, L. I.

The memorial planned in honor of Colonel Theodore Roosevelt, who was Honorary President of War Camp Community Service, practically within sight of his old home, is rapidly taking form. The Committee, which has this matter in charge, has for its President, William Loeb, Jr., at one time private secretary to President Roosevelt. Associated with him are John F. Bermingham, Vice-President, and the following members:

Mortimer L. Schiff	William L. Peters
Colgate Hoyt	Howard C. Smith
Joseph H. Sears	William L. Swan
George Bullock	Rev. Father Canivan

Rev. Doctor George Talmadge

The site already obtained consists of eighteen acres near the railroad station at Oyster Bay, fronting the water. Colonel Roosevelt frequently referred to this site as an ideal spot for such a park as is now to be constructed there. Scores of landscape artists have offered their services to make this park one of the most attractive and practical in the United States. It will contain an athletic field, a stadium and a bathing beach. Bulkheads will be built at the water front, trees planted, walks laid out and benches provided for the people of Oyster Bay and the thousands who are expected to make a pilgrimage to this spot in the days to come.

The Committee decided to make this a national movement, as hundreds of letters were received from all sections of the country asking to be allowed to contribute. Many of these letters were accompanied by cash contributions, chiefly in small amounts, from persons who sent all they could afford, but who were earnestly desirous of having a part in the tribute to the man they so admired. In many states, the Republican organization will work for contributions, and a treasurer will be appointed in each state to take charge of these.

In Memoriam

Horace E. Andrews

Mr. Horace E. Andrews, whose death on December 1, 1918 last was so great a loss not only to the business world but to the entire community, was a director and a member of the Executive Committee of War Camp Community Service, had been for a short time a director of the Playground and Recreation Association of America, and took part in the important meetings of the two organizations on the occasion of the incorporation of the former.

Mr. Andrews by his espousal of the cause of War Camp Community Service made an essential contribution to its success. Personally he was a most delightful man to have dealings with. His kindliness and sympathetic understanding and his sense of humor made even budget meetings a joy when he was present.

The following resolutions were passed by the Executive Committee of War Camp Community Service at the meeting following his death:

Resolutions

War Camp Community Service desires to express its sense of irreparable loss in the death of Horace E. Andrews, in whom it has lost a most able, sympathetic and highly respected friend. Mr. Andrews accepted a position upon the Budget Committee of War Camp Community Service at a time when its work was little known or understood and has, through his faith in it, and his invaluable participation in the work of its most important Committee, been a principal cause of its success.

War Camp Community Service desires to express to Mrs. Andrews and the other members of Mr. Andrews' family, its sympathy with them in their loss and its sense of gratitude for its part in the great services which Mr. Andrews has rendered to the community.

JOSEPH LEE

Ira W. Jayne

With the beginning of 1919 Ira W. Jayne severs his connection, in a professional way, at least, with recreation. At that time he becomes Judge of the Circuit Court for Wayne County, Michigan.

Judge Jayne has had a very varied experience in social work. In the first place, he was attorney for the Society for the Prevention of Cruelty to Children and became largely responsible for the merger of that society with an institution known as the "Home of the Friendless," in which children with none, with one or with two parents were lodged, sometimes temporarily and sometimes permanently. In one fell swoop, under the guidance of Judge Jayne, the Childrens' Aid Society was formed as a central place for looking after the care of children having special needs and the names "Home of the

Friendless" and "Prevention of Cruelty to Children" were lost from general usage.

Judge Jayne served on the Detroit Board of Commerce Commission which superintended the survey for recreation made by the Playground and Recreation Association of America. This survey, conducted by Rowland Haynes, was a document of immense advertising value and became the basis of necessary charter legislation for instituting an effective recreation system.

Judge Jayne was the first director of recreation when the new recreation department of Detroit was formed. Instead of making a campaign for playgrounds and buildings he used his utmost efforts to build up the recreation elements in the public schools, the libraries, the settlements, the parks and various mutual societies for music, athletics and play. He sought an adequate budget for the direction of these efforts and assumed that when the principle of recreation was once accepted the appropriations for land and buildings would easily follow. At one time the Board of Estimates, since then abolished, as a part of the City government, practically wiped out the recreation budget. The following evening and day every newspaper in Detroit carried a cartoon on the front page and a leading editorial conveying to the Board of Estimates the sentiment of the people of Detroit about a government that did not recognize the value of recreation. It is needless to say that the budget item was speedily restored.

Judge Jayne, in his platform for the campaign to obtain his present office, has emphasized the necessity of humanizing the courts so that our divorce and domestic relations matters are approached not only from a legal but from a sociological standpoint. Although he won the election by a very creditable majority, it is generally believed that the bench and bar disapproved of the election of a Judge from the ranks of social workers rather than the leading lights at the bar. It is to be hoped that Judge Jayne will have the opportunity to organize the domestic relations business of Wayne County as he has organized the recreation of the City of Detroit. If he has the opportunity it can be safely assumed that he will bring to the task sanity, common sense, good will and the ability to build up a popular support which is so necessary in the working of government.

FRED M. BUTZEL

531

Keeping Service Men Happy in Winter

A moving picture which showed the winter activities of the War Camp Community Service would be of keen interest to every community in these more than ever United States, but it would take days for the showing. Rather let us do our ·own moving and flit mentally over the country as we view the succeeding pages, which help us to visualize the panorama of winter sports from Maine to Florida, across to San Diego, up the Western coast and back to the starting point.

Healthful recreation for men in service, one of the first ideals of War Camp Community Service (conducted by the Playground and Recreation Association of America for the War Department and Navy Department Commissions on Training Camp Activities) has been consistently provided in camp communities, and is continuing in the period of readjustment as our soldiers, sailors and marines return from that far-away, horizon-blue land of poilus. With the varied climates which the United States affords, it is not surprising to find everything in the list of outdoor winter sports from ice skating and tobogganing to bathing and beach picnics.

One of the most fascinating events in the northern realm was the Outdoor Sports Carnival in St. Paul, which emphasized sports of all kinds, ski-ing, tobogganing, skating and outdoor push-ball. In ante-bellum days the carnival was established and carnival clubs had been organized in all business houses, each club having a distinctive carnival costume with brilliant color schemes designed for snow backgrounds. The peace time program included contests and parades which seemed scarcely adequate for war days. Accordingly War Camp Community Service was requisitioned to "carry on" and under its guidance the carnival clubs, resplendent in gay costumes, went out to Fort Snelling for an afternoon of typical carnival play with the soldiers. About ten thousand people from St. Paul took part in the events and the soldiers entered the contests with much verve. Probably nothing in the life at Fort Snelling was more successful in bringing to the men in training the conviction that the civilian population is back of them and interested in them.

Winter sports at Camp Devens, in Ayer, Mass., under the direction of War Camp Community Service, have been a rather continuous carnival. The situation of the Robbins Pond Club House is admirable, located, as it is, a few feet from the pond with a frontage of 200 feet on the main thoroughfare of the camp. During the winter months the boats and canoes of the summer-time are stored away and the little sheet of ice, when not in use as a drill field, is utilized for tobogganing. The farther shore of the pond consists of a steep hill, and, Nature thus providing the slide, rare sport has resulted.

In Pensacola, Florida, vastly different sports have been provided by War Camp Community Service. There, on dates when up North the wind blew raw and cold, and only strenuous play on ice tempted men to stay long in the open, sport meets under balmy Florida skies were held with the Army and Navy competing against each other. At one of these there were 40 entries on both sides, the events including the mile, half mile, high jump, broad jump, 100-yard dash and 3-legged race. Football and pushball have each been promoted with much success by directors in many camps throughout the South, and in the war camp communities farthest below the Mason and Dixon line baseball has been popular, even in the dead of winter.

Completion of the list of strictly southern fetes would include street fairs in Charleston, "oyster roasts" in Washington, and outdoor community sings in Miami, Key West, Anniston, Alabama, Biloxi, Mobile, and a baker's dozen more southern camp towns.

In Florida and Southern California War Camp Community Service has promoted orange grove picnics, arranging in this way for many men to have their first experience in groves of the luscious fruit long viewed only when emerging from packing boxes.

At Christmas time many camp cities held open-air celebrations, some—as Oakland, for instance—staging Percy MacKaye's Christmas masque, *The Evergreen Tree,* out of doors. Whenever climate permitted, Christmas trees were erected out of doors and Christmas pageants and games took place in the fascinating, fitful glow of the tree lights. The *Patriotic Christmas Pageant* written by Constance D'Arcy Mackay, which was put on by the San Francisco W. C. C. S. in cooperation with the city, proved to be the largest community program ever attempted by that city.

Salt Lake City's sleighing parties combine outdoor and indoor sports in a delightful fashion. The combination of sleighing and home parties for various little groups afterward was a special inspiration of the local W. C. C. S. director, which brought from the soldier guests the comment, "Gee! every kind of a good time!"

An ice-skating pond in Seattle, which was made for War Camp Community Service, afforded not only great pleasure in skating, but provided some very exciting contests as well for men from Camp Lewis. The use of the rink was free to men in uniform, whose appreciation was shown by crowded attendance.

No survey of War Camp Community Service winter activities, however compactly summarized, is complete with an outline of outdoor festivities alone. With literally thousands of "Khaki and Blue" dances and indoor parties given in the Red Circle Clubs, and theatre parties a frequent event in Red Circle weekly programs, it cannot be said that winter affairs have been entirely sports, nor entirely out of doors.

In December in New York City, War Camp Community Service entertained many hundreds of convalescent soldiers at theatre parties. This did not mean that the usual flow of free tickets stopped for other uniformed men, who did not bear wound stripes, but that special theatre parties were arranged for the convalescent veterans.

Home hospitality, too, has been especially prized by men in service, and this feature, especially emphasized by W. C. C. S. from the beginning of the war, has brought the civilian element of communities into closer touch with the men in service than any other one activity on the entertainment list. In many ways besides hospitality in their own homes the townspeople in war camp communities have been brought into close and sympathetic relationship with the uniformed guests within their gates. Such understanding means that the communities through their respective Red Circle Clubs and through personal service can better serve the men in camps during the coming period of their greater need. With sports, with community singing, with home parties and club dances, War Camp Community Service, under its Red Circle emblem, is continuing true to its original motto, "Surround the camps with hospitality," and better still is bringing through the hospitality extended a close communion between military and civilian minds and a realization on the part of communities of the needs, present and future of the men in the service of the country.

Index to Volume XII

Volume XII

Number 2

MAY, 1918

The Playground

War Camp Community Service

Surround the Camps with Hospitality

Twenty-five Cents a Copy   Two Dollars a Year

The Playground

Published monthly at Cooperstown, New York

for the

Playground and Recreation Association of America

1 Madison Avenue, New York City

Membership

Any person contributing five dollars or more shall be a
member of the Association for the
ensuing year

WAR CAMP COMMUNITY SERVICE

"The Commission on Training Camp Activities asks the Playground and
Recreation Association of America to be responsible for the work of stimulating
and aiding communities in the neighborhood of training camps to develop and
organize their social and recreational resources in such a way as to be of the
greatest possible value to the officers and soldiers in the camps."

Voted by the Commission on Training Camp Activities,
May 5, 1917

"Resolved, that in addition the Playground and Recreation Association is
assigned the duty of supplementing these resources, where, after consultation
with local agencies it seems to be necessary or desirable."

Voted by the Commission on Training Camp Activities,
January 18, 1918

WAR DEPARTMENT

Commission on Training Camp Activities
Washington

RAYMOND B. FOSDICK, Chairman
LEE F. HANMER
THOMAS J. HOWELLS
JOSEPH LEE
MALCOLM L. McBRIDE

JOHN R. MOTT
CHARLES P. NEILL
MAJOR P. E. PIERCE, U. S. A.
JOSEPH E. RAYCROFT
MARC KLAW

NAVY DEPARTMENT

Commission on Training Camp Activities
Washington

RAYMOND B. FOSDICK, Chairman
LIEUT. RICHARD E. BYRD, Sec'y.
CLIFFORD W. BARNES
WALTER CAMP
SELAH CHAMBERLAIN
JOHN J. EAGAN
JOSEPH LEE

E. T. MEREDITH
BARTON MYERS
CHARLES P. NEILL
Mrs. HELEN RING ROBINSON
Mrs. FINLEY J. SHEPARD
Mrs. DAISY McLAURIN STEVENS
JOHN S. TICHENOR

Entered as second-class matter August 8, 1916, at the Post Office at
Cooperstown, New York, under the act of March 3, 1879

Help Win the War

Many among us are now tired. To those I would say that victory will belong to the side which holds out the longest. There is no other course open to us but to fight it out.

Every position must be held to the last man. The safety of our homes and the freedom of mankind depend alike upon the conduct of each one of us at this critical moment.

SIR DOUGLAS HAIG, Field Marshal
British Army

Volume XII

Number 3

JUNE, 1918

The Playground

The Kindergarten and First Grade
THE BALANCE BEAM

T   t -five Cents a Co

The Playground

Published monthly at Cooperstown, New York

for the

Playground and Recreation Association of America

1 Madison Avenue, New York City

Membership

Any person contributing five dollars or more shall be a
member of the Association for the
ensuing year

TABLE OF CONTENTS

Entered as second-class matter August 8, 1916, at the Post Office at
Cooperstown, New York, under the act of March 3, 1879

STATEMENT OF THE OWNERSHIP, MANAGEMENT, CIRCULA-
TION, ETC., REQUIRED BY THE ACT OF CONGRESS OF AU-
GUST 24, 1912

Of THE PLAYGROUND, published monthly at Cooperstown, N. Y.,
for April 1, 1918

State of New York, ⎰
County of Nw York. ⎱ ss.

Before me, a Notary Public in and for the state and county aforesaid, personally appeared H. S. Braucher, who, having been duly sworn according to
law, deposes and says that he is the editor of THE PLAYGROUND and that
the following is, to the best of his knowledge and belief, a true statement of
the ownership, management (and if a daily paper, the circulation), etc., of the
aforesaid publication for the date shown in the above caption required by the
Act of August 24, 1912, embodied in section 443, Postal Laws and Regulations,
printed on the reverse of this form, to wit:

1.   That the names and addresses of the publisher, editor, managing editor,
and business managers are:

Publisher, Playground and Recreation Association of America, 1 Madi-
son Ave., New York City; Editor, H. S. Braucher, 1 Madison Ave., New York
City; Managing Editor, H. S. Braucher, 1 Madison Ave., New York City;
Business Manager, H. S. Braucher, 1 Madison Ave., New York City.

2.   That the owners are: (Give names and addresses of individual owners, or, if a corporation, give its name and the names and addresses of stockholders owning or holding 1 per cent or more of the total amount of stock).

Playground and Recreation Association of America, 1 Madison Ave., New
York City which is composed of about four thousand members.   The following
comprise the Board of Directors:

Mrs. Edward W. Biddle, Carlisle, Pa.; Richard C. Cabot, Boston, Mass.;
Clarence M. Clark, Philadelphia, Pa.; Grenville Clark, New York City; B.
Preston Clark, Boston, Mass.; Everett Colby, Newark, N. J.; Mrs. E. P. Earle,
Montclair, N. J.; Mrs. Thomas A. Edison, West Orange, N. J.; John H. Finley,
Albany, N. Y.; Charles W. Garfield, Grand Rapids, Mich.; Robert Garrett, Balti-
more, Md.; C. M. Goethe, Sacramento, Cal.; Mrs. Charles A. Goodwin, Hart-
ford, Conn.; Austin E. Griffiths, Seattle, Wash.; J. M. Hankins, Birmingham,
Ala.; Mrs. Appleton R. Hillyer, Hartford, Conn.; Mrs. Francis DeLacy Hyde,
Plainfield, N. J.; Mrs. Howard Ives, Portland, Me.; William Kent, Washington,
D. C.; Gustavus T. Kirby, New York City; Walter B. Lasher, Bridgeport, Conn.;
G. M. Landers, New Britain, Conn.; H. McK. Landon, Indianapolis, Ind.; Joseph
Lee, Boston, Mass.; Eugene W. Lewis, Detroit, Mich.; Edward E. Loomis, New
York City; J. H. McCurdy, Springfield, Mass.; Otto T. Mallery, Philadelphia,
Pa.; Samuel Mather, Cleveland, O.; R. B. Maury, Memphis, Tenn.; Walter A.
May, Pittsburgh, Pa.; Carl E. Milliken, Augusta, Me.; F. Gordon Osler, Toronto,
Canada; James H. Perkins, New York City; John T. Pratt, New York City;
Ellen Scripps, La Jolla, Cal.; Clement Studebaker, Jr., South Bend, Ind.; F. S.
Titsworth, Denver, Colo.; Harold H. Swift, Chicago, Ill.; Theodore N. Vail,
New York City; Mrs. James W. Wadsworth, Jr., Washington, D. C.; J. C.
Walsh, New York City; R. D. Waugh, Winnipeg, Canada; Harris Whittemore,
Naugatuck, Conn.

3.   That the known bond holders, mortgagees, and other security holders
owning or holding 1 per cent or more of total amount of bonds, mortgages, or
other securities, are: See list of directors.

H. S. BRAUCHER,
Editor

Sworn to and subscribed before me this 9th day of April, 1918.
(Seal)   MABEL M. GLASSEY.
     Notary Public, Cert. filed in New York, Bronx and Kings Counties.   (My
commission expires March 30, 1919).

We must out-sing and out-play Germans, if we are to outfight them.

—*Major J. M. Wainwright*

Volume XII

Number 4

JULY, 1918

The Playground

Recreation Board, Philadelphia, Pa.

THE JOYS OF SAND AND WATER

Twent -five Cents a Co   Two Dollars

The Playground

Published monthly at Cooperstown, New York

for the

Playground and Recreation Association of America

1 Madison Avenue, New York City

Membership

Any person contributing five dollars or more shall be a
member of the Association for the
ensuing year

TABLE OF CONTENTS

Entered as second-class matter August 8, 1916, at the Post Office at
Cooperstown, New York, under the act of March 3, 1879

¶ "Do not let the needs of the hour, however heavily they may fall upon the men and women of the day, permit neglect of the defenses of tomorrow," was the advice given by school officials of France.

¶ "France has restricted the use of fuel; she has restricted travel, except for reasons of necessity. She has mobilized every able bodied man for present defense; but she has not for one moment forgotten her future defense. She has even opened schools in caves and provided teachers and pupils with gas masks; she has put women by thousands in place of men called to the front from teaching; she has received back into service with honor many who have been incapacitated."

Volume XII

Number 5

AUGUST, 1918

The Playground

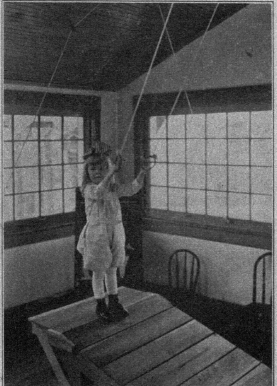

The Kindergarten and First Grade
HAPPY PLAY FOR THE CHILDREN KEEPS UP THE
MORALE OF THE ARMY AND OF AMERICA

Twenty-five Cents a Copy   Two Dollars a Year

The Playground

Published monthly at Cooperstown, New York

for the

Playground and Recreation Association of America

1 Madison Avenue, New York City

Membership

Any person contributing five dollars or more shall be a
member of the Association for the
ensuing year

TABLE OF CONTENTS

Entered as second-class matter August 8, 1916, at the Post Office at
Cooperstown, New York, under the act of March 3, 1879

Provide Rather Than Prohibit

Why not try to get a little more legislation along the lines of providing
things for the boys to do, rather than
constantly passing prohibitory laws?
Why not definitely declare that playgrounds and playground expenditures
are fundamental parts—not only of
the school system, but of the general
health laws of the state? Why not
require that for every thousand children under twenty-one in a community
there shall be maintained a certain
number of supervised entertainment
halls and playgrounds and provide for
the maintenance thereof? Why not
take part of the money now spent in
delinquent courts and give the boy out
of school something to occupy his time?

—JOHN H. GARNSEY,
In the Evening Herald News, Joliet, Ill.

Volume XII

Number 6

SEPTEMBER, 1918

The Playground

War Time Recreation Drive and Patriotic Play Week
September 1—8

Los Angeles, Cal.

BITE THE BUBBLE, BUT DON'T BITE THE BULB

Twenty-five Cents a Copy

Two Dollars a Year

The Playground

Published monthly at Cooperstown, New York

for the

Playground and Recreation Association of America

1 Madison Avenue, New York City

Membership

Any person contributing five dollars or more shall be a
member of the Association for the
ensuing year

TABLE OF CONTENTS

Entered as second-class matter August 8, 1916, at the Post Office at
Cooperstown, New York, under the act of March 3, 1879

"If anything should happen to me, let's have no mourning in spirit or in dress. Like a Liberty Bond, it is an investment not a loss when a man dies for his country."

(From a letter Lieutenant Dinsmore Ely wrote his parents shortly before he was killed in May, 1918.)

Vol. XII   No. 7

OCTOBER, 1918

The Playground

War Camp Community Service

Pennsylvania Station, New York City

Twenty-five Cents a Copy   Two Dollars a Year

The Playground

Published monthly at Cooperstown, New York

for the

Playground and Recreation Association of America

1 Madison Avenue, New York City

Membership

Any person contributing five dollars or more shall be a
member of the Association for the
ensuing year

TABLE OF CONTENTS

Entered as second-class matter August 8, 1916, at the Post Office
at Cooperstown, New York, under the act of March 3, 1879.

THE DAY

(A "day" of an exactly opposite sort from that toasted by Germans before the war is hailed in the following article by a member of The Vigilantes.)

IT will come some day—do you realize it? On some one glorious day the enemy will cry "Kamarad!' in good earnest, and there will be Peace.

Picture that day. The crowds in the streets are going about their business, the Red Cross rooms are humming with work, the thousand war activities are grinding at full speed, every mother and father is facing the morning with a heart braced for loss, every loyal citizen is at his post of service; and suddenly—the news!

The crowded avenues turn white; all up and down their length they have blossomed white with the open newspapers that have magically sprung into everyone's outstretched hands. Everybody in the long, stopped stream of humanity holds a newspaper or reads his neighbors; everybody knows everybody, shares with everybody; strange hands clasp, strange eyes, meeting, overflow; and there is just one first thought, not triumph, nor democracy, but—"Those boys—those good boys—they can come home!" And the second thought will be, "We've done it! We've put it through!"

And then, standing there, they begin to sing, the men with bared heads; they send up such a song as the skies have never heard since time was—"Glory, glory, hallelujah!"—"Praise God, from whom all blessings flow!" The melting-pot is a slow process—that song will melt all into blood brothers at the first chord. Oh, how they will sing, those standing men and women! And then with one impulse they will surge into the churches, into the cathedrals—for when man has been granted the supreme boon, he must fall on his knees, whether he knows God or not. And no one who rises up from that silence will ever lose its mighty vibration.

That day is not a vision; it is coming as surely as tomorrow. Then will you have it tomorrow? Or will you put it off for four more bleeding years? It is in your hands. Every effort, every dollar, you give to service shortens the waiting. If all gave all they could, the day could not hold back another hour. When you buy the thing you most want, you are not conscious of sacrifice in paying the sum demanded. Fix your eyes on the day—the day when the avenues will suddenly blossom white with the news of peace—and you will want that with so burning an urgency that you will come running with its price.

JULIET WILBUR TOMPKINS

Courtesy of *Current Opinion*

Vol. XII   No. 8

NOVEMBER, 1918

The Playground

War Camp Community Service

Copyright by M. Leon Bracker

KEEP 'EM SMILING

UNITED WAR WORK CAMPAIGN, NOV. 11—18

Twenty-five Cents a Copy   Two Dollars a Year

The Playground

Published monthly at Cooperstown, New York

for the

Playground and Recreation Association of America

1 Madison Avenue, New York City

Membership

Any person contributing five dollars or more shall be a
member of the Association for the
ensuing year

TABLE OF CONTENTS

Entered as second-class matter August 8, 1916, at the Post Office
at Cooperstown, New York, under the act of March 3, 1879.

WHEN I was at the front, General Edwards, who commands the 26th Division in France—a division that has made itself a terror to the Huns—gave me a copy of a letter which the Colonel of the 104th Infantry in his command had received from the mother of one of his men. The letter follows:

"We think of the 104th in its time of service without any thought of self or the things which may happen to our boys to mar them or to destroy them. We think only of the more than honor which has come to us to be the mothers of such men. We are asking ourselves, 'Are we worthy of the honor their work has already brought to us?' and 'How can we become more worthy mothers of such good sons?'

"When my son left this home he took a great big patch of each day's sunshine with him. He has been the tenderest son of an invalid mother. We have been chums for twenty-five years—reading, studying, thinking, and loving together. I never shed a tear over his being away. I know his great heart could not stand to see love, home, and women outraged and destroyed. I know he is only a type of every man in your command, and if he dies it is as one of an army of noblemen.

"Because you are his war chief and all we could be to him I wanted to speak to you. Daily reports of the 104th Inf. at the front show us how splendid you all are and how faithfully you have worked to be ready to do the work you are doing today. We send you our most reverent affectionate greeting."

It seems to me that this mother caught the spirit of the thing more clearly and accurately than anything I have ever heard or seen.

RAYMOND B. FOSDICK.

The Rotarian, September, 1918

Vol. XII   No. 9

DECEMBER, 1918

The Playground

War Camp Community Service

THE SOLDIER ASKS TO HAVE CHRISTMAS DINNER IN A HOME
WHERE THERE ARE CHILDREN

Twenty-five Cents a Copy   Two Dollars a Year

The Playground

Published monthly at Cooperstown, New York

for the

Playground and Recreation Association of America

1 Madison Avenue, New York City

Membership

Any person contributing five dollars or more shall be a
member of the Association for the
ensuing year

TABLE OF CONTENTS

Entered as second-class matter August 8, 1916, at the Post Office
at Cooperstown, New York, under the act of March 3, 1879

STATEMENT OF THE OWNERSHIP, MANAGEMENT, CIRCU-
LATION, ETC., REQUIRED BY THE ACT OF CONGRESS
OF AUGUST 24, 1912
OF THE PLAYGROUND, published monthly at Cooperstown,
N. Y., for October, 1, 1918

State of New York,
County of New York, ss.

Before me, a Notary Public in and for the state and county aforesaid, personally appeared H. S. Braucher, who, having been duly sworn
according to law, deposes and says that he is the editor of THE
PLAYGROUND and that the following is, to the best of his knowledge
and belief, a true statement of the ownership, management (and if a
daily paper, the circulation), etc., of the aforesaid publication for the
date shown in the above caption required by the Act of August 24, 1912,
embodied in section 443, Postal Laws and Regulations, printed on the
reverse of this form, to wit:

1.   That the names and addresses of the publisher, editor, managing
editor, and business managers are:
Publisher, Playground and Recreation Association of America, 1
Madison Ave., New York City; Editor, H. S. Braucher, 1 Madison
Ave., New York City; Managing Editor, H. S. Braucher, 1 Madison
Ave., New York City; Business Manager, H. S. Braucher, 1 Madison
Ave., New York City.

2.   That the owners are: (Give names and addresses of individual
owners, or, if a corporation, give its name and the names and addresses
of stockholders owning or holding 1 per cent or more of the total
amount of stock).
Playground and Recreation Association of America, 1 Madison
Ave., New York City which is composed of about four thousand
five hundred members. The following comprise the Board of Directors:
Mrs. Edward W. Biddle, Carlisle, Pa.; Dr. Richard C. Cabot,
Boston, Mass.; Clarence M. Clark, Philadelphia, Pa.; Grenville Clark.
New York City; Dr. B. Preston Clark, Boston, Mass; Everett Colby,
Newark, N. J.; Mrs. E. P. Earle, Montclair, N. J.; Henry W. DeForest,
New York City; Mrs. Thomas A. Edison, West Orange, N. J.; John H.
Finley, Albany, N. Y.; Charles W. Garfield, Grand Rapids, Mich.; C. M.
Goethe, Sacramento, Cal.; Mrs. Charles A. Goodwin, Hartford, Conn.;
Austin E. Griffiths, Seattle, Wash.; Dr. J. M. Hankins, Birmingham, Ala.;
Mrs. Appleton R. Hillyer, Hartford, Conn.; Mrs. Francis DeLacy Hyde,
Plainfield, N. J.; Mrs. Howard R. Ives, Portland, Me.; Gustavus T.
Kirby, New York City; Walter B. Lasher, Bridgeport, Conn.; G. M.
Landers, New Britian, Conn.; H. McK. Landon, Indianapolis, Ind.; Rob-
ert Lassiter, Charlotte, N. C.; Joseph Lee, Boston, Mass; Eugene W.
Lewis, Detroit, Mich.; Edward E. Loomis, New York City; J. H. Mc-
Curdy, Springfield, Mass.; Otto T. Mallery, Philadelphia, Pa.; Samuel
Mather, Cleveland, O.; Dr. R. B. Maury, Memphis, Tenn.; Walter A.
May, Pittsburgh, Pa.; Carl E. Milliken, Augusta, Me.; F. Gordon Osler,
Toronto, Canada; James H. Perkins, New York City; John T. Pratt,
New York City; Ellen Scripps, La Jolla, Cal.; Clement Studebaker, Jr.,
South Bend, Ind.; F. S. Titsworth, Denver, Colo.; Harold H. Swift,
Chicago, Ill.; Theodore N. Vail, New York City; Mrs. James W.
Wadsworth, Jr., Washington, D. C.; J. C. Walsh, New York City;
Harris Wittemore, Naugatuck, Conn.

3.   That the known bond holders, mortgagees, and other security
holders owning or holding 1 per cent or more of total amount of
bonds, mortgages, or other securities, are: See list of directors.

H. S. BRAUCHER,
Editor.

Sworn to and subscribed before me this 30th day of September, 1918.
(Seal)   MABEL M. GLASSEY.
Notary Public, Cert. filed in New York, Bronx and Kings Counties.
(My commission expires March 30, 1919.)

Who Will Sign This Check?

A Christmas Gift to the Children of Our Country

1.6

Notice to Reader: When you finish reading this magazine, place a one-cent stamp on this notice, mail the magazine, and it will be placed in the hands of our soldiers or sailors destined to proceed over seas. No wrapping. No address. *A. S. Burleson, Postmaster General*

Vol. XII   No. 10

JANUARY, 1919

The Playground

War Camp Community Service

New York War Camp Community Service

A STRATEGICAL RETREAT

Twenty-five Cents a Copy   Two Dollars a Year

The Playground

Published monthly at Cooperstown, New York

for the

Playground and Recreation Association of America

1 Madison Avenue, New York City

Membership

Any person contributing five dollars or more shall be a
member of the Association for the
ensuing year

TABLE OF CONTENTS

Entered as second-class matter August 8, 1916, at the Post Office
at Cooperstown, New York, under the act of March 3, 1879

What Memorial for Our Soldiers

What is going to be our form of memorial for the soldiers in this war? In the main it has got to be in the kind of lives we lead. They have given the flower of their life, looking to us for the fulfillment which will never come unless we embody it.

It seems that the best thing we can do in the way of a visible symbol of our consecration will be something that shall express the ideal of human service for which they died. The soldiers' monuments through which we strove to honor the soldiers of our last great war are better than nothing, unsuccessful as most of them are from an artistic point of view—monuments to the unknown god of beauty as well as to the spirit of the men who gave their lives for freedom—but cannot we find something more appropriate?

Would not a community building of some kind, which should serve as a center of community service and expression, be a fitting memorial of the soldiers in this present war? It is a war for democracy and, as the American City magazine has said, democracy should have a home.

The building in a small town might be the town hall itself or an adjunct to it. Of course we cannot all suddenly build new town halls, but we could, when the occasion comes for rebuilding or through supplementing what we already have, provide a place in each smaller community, and several places in the larger ones, where people can come together for all sorts of public purposes, community sings, dances, concerts, lectures, public service by groups of citizens each as we have seen in working for the Red Cross. In large cities like our own these buildings might be the larger of the new schoolhouses in each district.

Such a memorial would fitly commemorate our soldiers by serving as an instrument for the continuance of that enhanced spirit of public service which has been to us the one great compensating gift of the war.

JOSEPH LEE

*A letter to the Boston Transcript

℮
Playground

War Camp Community Service

Fᴇʙʀᴜᴀʀʏ 1919   *25 Cents*

MEMBERSHIP

Any person contributing five dollars or more shall be a member of the Association for the ensuing year.

During the demobilization period the need for War Camp Community Service is greater than it has ever been before.

—RAYMOND B. FOSDICK

ᴛhe
Playground

War Camp Community Service

Courtesy of Mann and MacNeille

A LIBERTY BUILDING

Mᴀʀᴄʜ 1919

25 Cents

The Playground

Published monthly at Cooperstown, New York

for the

Playground and Recreation Association of America

1 Madison Avenue, New York City

Membership

Any person contributing five dollars or more shall be a
member of the Association for the
ensuing year

TABLE OF CONTENTS

Entered as second-class matter August 8, 1916, at the Post Office
at Cooperstown, New York, under the act of March 3, 1879